The Faith of Scientists

The Faith of Scientists

IN THEIR OWN WORDS

EDITED, WITH COMMENTARY, BY

Nancy K. Frankenberry

PRINCETON UNIVERSITY PRESS
PRINCETON AND OXFORD

Published by Princeton University Press, 41 William Street, Princeton, New Jersey 08540
In the United Kingdom: Princeton University Press, 3 Market Place, Woodstock,
Oxfordshire OX20 1SY

Library of Congress Cataloging-in-Publication Data
The faith of scientists in their own words / edited, with commentary,
by Nancy K. Frankenberry.
  p. cm.
Includes bibliographical references and index.
ISBN 978-0-691-13487-1 (hardcover : alk. paper)
1. Religion and science. 2. Scientists—Religious life. I. Frankenberry, Nancy, 1947–
BL241.F358 2008
201'.65—dc22   2007048853

British Library Cataloging-in-Publication Data is available

This book has been composed in Sabon text with Helvetica Neue Display

Printed on acid–free paper. ∞

press.princeton.edu

Printed in the United States of America

10 9 8 7 6 5 4 3 2 1

Contents

Introduction vii
Acknowledgments xvii

Introduction

~

No simple formula suffices for understanding the shifting relationship between science and religion over the last five hundred years in the West. From 1600 to the twenty-first century, in different times and places, science and religion have been constructed as overlapping, complementary, separated, fused, or conflicted. Contemporary discussions about science and religion tend to focus either on mapping different models of how they *might* relate or on proposing one model of how they *should* relate. Both tendencies risk reifying the problematic terms "science" and "religion" into abstractions without human or historical grounding. I have found that a good way of engaging the human and historical questions is to ask what scientists themselves have to say about God, religion, or the sacred. We know a remarkable amount these days about the faith of ordinary people; our bookstores and airwaves are clogged with testimonies to the resurgent strength and global reach of traditional forms of religious faith. But what of the faith of scientists? What have the giants and geniuses believed in the past? What kind of religious or antireligious faith do contemporary scientists express in the twenty-first century?

In this book, I try to present and interpret what scientists themselves say about their faith, their view of God, or what today is often called their spirituality. In twenty-one chapters, the volume brings together primary source documents from books, essays, speeches, letters, or interviews by scientists from the beginning of the scientific revolution in the West until the present. Each chapter opens with a short commentary or profile in which I attempt to frame the distinctive voice of that scientist. I have sought to keep footnotes and academic jargon to a minimum and instead provide at the end of every chapter a list of sources that I think will interest the larger reading public. I hope that readers will be inspired to consult the primary sources from which the excerpts are taken, as well as to dip into the secondary literature.

Such a project could easily run to many volumes of primary source material, and I have found it daunting to compress so much fascinating material into only one volume, covering no more than twenty-one scientists. My criteria for selection were three. First, the individual had to be a working scientist of some eminence, whose primary credentials have been earned as a practitioner of one of the natural or mathematical sciences. This deliberately excludes the important work of social scientists, from E. B. Tylor and Émile Durkheim to Daniel Dennett and Mary Douglas, whose views about religion could easily fill another entire volume. Second, he or she had to be a major historical figure or public intellectual whose reflections on God or religious faith or the spiritual value of nature could be expected to hold wide interest for the readers I hope to reach, that is, nonspecialists and the general public, as well as students in the classroom or seekers of any sort. Third, any scientist included in this volume needed to have written in some fashion on these topics, leaving documented material. That last criterion may seem obvious, but it is interesting to discover how many famous scientists turn out not to have written anything about religion. Marie Curie, for example, Catholic-born to a pious Polish family, writes only the disappointingly brief statement that she and Pierre had no use for religion and never gave it any thought in their lives.

Inevitably, there are omissions, even among those with documented and vivid religious views. Robert Boyle and Joseph Priestley and Michael Faraday are not mentioned. Charles Darwin is included, but his contemporaries Albert Russel Wallace and Thomas H. Huxley are not. Einstein is featured, but not Eddington. In part 2, I have included physicist Sir John Polkinghorne, a prolific author with impeccable scientific credentials whose religious vision owes as much to Christian theology as to modern science. Regrettably, that has meant that I have not had space to include geneticist Francis Collins, eminent director of the National Human Genome Research Institute, whose faith manifesto, *The Language of God: A Scientist Presents Evidence of Belief*, explains how he moved from atheism to a Bible-based faith, reconciling science with Christian convictions.

Two overall impressions will strike even the casual reader. The first is how seamlessly the historical titans of the scientific revolution—Galileo, Kepler, Bacon, Pascal, and Newton—all devout believers to a man—could interrelate their Christian faith and their scientific discoveries. Nevertheless, pockets of perplexity, elements of eccentricity, and unconventional forms within conventional Christian faith stand out. The Catholic Galileo thought that in matters on which the Bible is silent, scientific observations and theories might step in and guide interpretations of biblical faith. The Protestant Kepler started out wanting to be a humble Lutheran pastor, but his view of the meaning of the body and blood of Christ in Communion fell through the widening cracks between Catholics and Lutherans and Calvinists, and satisfied no single orthodoxy. Neither could he accept the doctrine of predestination. He finally found religious ecstasy in the act of scientific discovery itself, seeing the Trinity revealed in the very structure of the heavens. No less obsessed with the doctrine of the Trinity, Isaac Newton considered it an abomination foisted on the Church in the fourth century by Athanasius and his followers. Copious writings that he labored over for decades and kept secret, now available to scholars but only in recent decades, show a new Newton who was no deist, no rationalist, and not much of a Newtonian mechanist either. With a profound sense of Providence at work in history, Newton never espoused the view of a remote and uninvolved Creator God that his scientific work sometimes inspired in others. Charles Darwin's faith as a young man was firmly anchored in William Paley's design argument, which he said he found "convincing," but by the time he was an old man his faith had, in a word, evolved. In a candid and humble credo written at the end of his life, the old agnostic wonders if in his "sense of the sublime" he might still deserve to be called a theist. The Christian doctrine of damnation, however, was nothing but "damnable" to Darwin.

When we come to Einstein, we see the unconventional spirit of a great genius meshing with the intellectual creativity of the Jewish tradition to produce an ardent faith. Einstein's pantheism, like that of Spinoza, whom he admired, was based on a belief in an underlying mathematical intelligence pervading a deterministic universe, a belief he could not relinquish even in the face of the indeterminism of the science of quantum mechanics he helped to establish. Einstein could not conceive of a personal God who would directly intervene in the world or influence the actions of individuals or sit in judgment on creatures of His own creation. His faith consisted in a profound admiration of the infinitely superior spirit that reveals itself in the little that we humans, with our weak and transitory understanding, can comprehend of reality. He said that morality is of the highest importance, but for us, not for God.

Mathematician Alfred North Whitehead also developed a theory of gravitation, one that differed from Einstein's in putting "creative passage" at its center and emphasizing indeterminism. Turning to philosophy late in his career, Whitehead is unique among the scientists in this volume in that his influence on philosophy and religion flourishes today in the form of a school, known as process theology and philosophy. In his own words, Whitehead's striking religious vision bursts the conventional confines of theism. "Love neither rules nor is it unmoved; also it is a little oblivious as to morals," he wrote, thus disqualifying the God modeled after Caesar as well as the Aristotelian unmoved mover. One could argue that both Einstein and Whitehead, still our contemporaries, belong as much in part 2 of this book as in part 1.

The second impression readers will have is that, in contrast to the historical titans, many of the contemporary scientists who appear in part 2 are moved by fresh visions and alternative forms of spirituality. Some, like Stephen Hawking, are pouring new scientific descriptions into old God-language in a way that is tantalizing to millions of readers. Others, like Jane Goodall, personally convinced of "a great spiritual power we call God, Allah, or Brahma," are embarked on a spiritual journey that enjoins activism around environmental damage, genocide, and animal abuse. Some of the scientists featured in part 2 share a dedication to a naturalistic worldview and ethics; their faith thus becomes a matter of this-worldly rather than other-worldly significance. Even those who are avowed critics of conventional religions, like Carl Sagan, Steven Weinberg, and Richard Dawkins, contribute powerful reflections on perennial religious questions such as the argument from design and the cause of the cosmos. They are imbued with a secular faith and a moral passion that is every bit as important in our time as religious faith was in previous eras. They speak forcefully for all those who believe that, in Sagan's words, "a religion, old or new, that stressed the magnificence of the universe as revealed by modern science, might be able to draw forth the reserves of reverence and awe tapped by the conventional faiths. Sooner or later, such a religion will emerge." In selections from his best-selling book *The God Delusion*, Richard Dawkins brings an astringent presence to these pages, reminding readers that "We are all atheists about most of the gods that societies have ever believed in. Some of us just go one god further." Yet in "Snake Oil and Holy Water" (included in chapter 12), Dawkins shows a fine, intuitive feel for the ordinary religious believer's use of language.

Entomologist Edward O. Wilson and astrobiologist Paul Davies articulate the diversity of forms that the faith of scientists takes today. Both stand free of any religious orthodoxy, yet each exemplifies the definition of faith found in the Pauline formula, "the substance of things hoped for, the evidence of things not seen" (Hebrews 11). Animated by the hope that religion and science will take up arms together to encourage environmental justice and ecological awareness, Wilson calls for a common respect for nature, which he deems "the Creation." For Davies, the substance of things hoped for is nothing less than a scientific understanding of the very origins of life itself.

One reason I prefer to discuss the "faith" of scientists rather than their "religion" is that faith is a far more flexible term that can stretch to cover the creative and sometimes heterodox views of original and searching minds. Another reason is that within the academic study of religion, where I mainly work, certain conventions and methodological constraints prevail. Religion, long a matter of contentious theoretical debate, is best defined as a communal system of propositional attitudes and practices that are related to superhuman agents.[1] Traffic with superhuman agents is foreign to most of the scientists selected in part 2. This makes their "faith" all the more interesting, I would argue, at the same time that it makes "religion" the wrong category for what we are studying when we read them.

For example, biologist Ursula Goodenough calls herself a "religious naturalist." She means that her spirituality is at home with the conviction that only the world of nature, the evolving universe, is real, and that "transcendence" is a function of "something more from nothing but." Part of a growing group of intellectuals and scientists and church members attracted to religious naturalism, Goodenough writes passionately about the sacred depths of nature. Her detailed view of life and living organisms helps to give reductionism back its good name. As she explains, "we reduce, and then we synthesize, and then we find another occasion to reduce. How did Mozart generate that modulation into B-flat? Ah, with that chord. How lovely." Goodenough's lucid, reductionist explanations even extend to a plausible scenario for the evolution of the modern bacterial cell's flagellum.

Rachel Carson never called herself a religious naturalist, but she wrote like one. Her evocative spiritual vision of a life lived in wonder and ecological awareness is presented here for the first time in her own words. With only a master's degree in zoology, little field experience, and no academic appointment, Rachel Carson may not

---

[1] For an explanation and illustrations of this methodological stricture, see Nancy K. Frankenberry, ed., *Radical Interpretation in Religion* (Cambridge: Cambridge University Press, 2002).

seem like a professional scientist by today's standards. However, the assiduous study that led to her important discovery of the effect of pesticides on the environment, with the subsequent publication of the best-selling *Silent Spring* in 1962, was as rigorous as that of any bench scientist. She also had a gift for exceptionally vivid writing: her nature books, essays, and lectures contributed to the contemporary ecospirituality movement and deserve to be better known today.

No less vivid are the writings, lectures, and interviews of Princeton physicist Freeman Dyson. Like Jane Goodall, Dyson is British-born and attends Christian services, but he can also describe himself intriguingly as "a practicing Christian but not a believing Christian." His reflections on making religion into a force for progress, on the mystifications of theology, and on Christianity as a religion for sinners are pungent, witty, and elegantly personal. Countering fellow physicist Steven Weinberg's claim that "Good people will do good things, and bad people will do bad things. But for good people to do bad things—that takes religion," Dyson says: "Weinberg's statement is true as far as it goes, but it is not the whole truth. To make it the whole truth, we must add an additional clause: 'And for bad people to do good things—that takes religion.'"

In the very distinct voices of the biologists Stuart Kauffmann and Stephen Jay Gould, we hear what John Dewey termed "natural piety," an immense awe and wonder in the face of the complexities and intricacies of life, of the natural world, and of the vast universe. These scientists write as eloquently as any religious believer of the awe and sense of mystery that attends the living of life in the midst of vastness and beauty. Is a sense of awe and mystery the heart of religion or even a fitting substitute for it? Without making a religion out of it, theoretical biologist Kauffman can write movingly of the need to follow the call of Native American novelist Scott Momaday to "reinvent the sacred." Kauffman's science goes a long way toward comprehending the way in which we humans are both "the children of ultimate law," born out of chemistry, and "the children of the filigrees of historical accident," the remnants of contingent adaptations and selections. That living systems might be ontologically emergent in the way that Kauffman describes in chapter 20 is a matter for the deepest awe.

From Stephen Jay Gould's perspective as an evolutionary biologist, nothing can match the natural wonders that science has discovered and explained. More extraordinary than anything claimed by religion is the discovery, for example, of DNA, a miraculous three-foot-long string curled up in its entirety in a cell no more than fifteen micrometers across. Compared to that, what are a few burning bushes or loaves and fishes? Gould believes we humans are glorious accidents of an unpredictable process with no drive to complexity, not the expected results of evolutionary principles yearning to produce a creature capable of comprehending the manner of its own necessary appearance. In chapter 11 he articulates a view of science and religion that has become almost the default position in the current cultural debates: scientific truth and religious faith do not belong to the same dimension of meaning, so science has no right or power to pronounce on faith, and faith no right to interfere with science.

Einstein described the emotional state that accompanies and inspires great scientific achievements as similar to that of the religious person or a person in love. He recognized the importance to science of the kind of very broad faith shared by the scientists in this book. "Science can only be created," Einstein said, "by those who are thoroughly imbued with the aspiration toward truth and understanding. This source of feeling, however, springs from the sphere of religion. To this there also belongs the faith in the possibility that the regulations valid for the world of existence are rational, that is, comprehensible to reason. I cannot conceive of a genuine scientist without that profound faith."

The voices that speak in these pages attest to the variety of ways in which Einstein's observation is still valid. The faith of scientists, I would say, is alive and well in the twenty-first century—albeit complex, changing, and always challenging. From Galileo to Goodenough, from the seventeenth century to the twenty-first, these scientists show how seriously misleading is the picture—still fostered in some religious quarters—of scientists as cold, hard, soulless individuals who try to reduce the splendor of nature to sterile mathematical formulas or the mystery of life to laboratory manipulations. Far from conforming to any caricature, the twenty-one scientists surveyed here offer vivid personal accounts of their intellectual commitments and struggles for meaning, honesty, and excellence. In meeting them in their own words, readers from any faith perspective—or none—can expect to be stimulated, inspired, and instructed.

Acknowledgments

This book originated in my classroom at Dartmouth College. I am indebted to the research of the following remarkable students, who helped me select and edit the material: Elana Bannerman, Vaughn Booker Jr., Donald Brooks, Joel Dahl, Parker Fagrelius, Clinton Hedges, S. Ali Husain, Varun Jain, Davida Kornreich, Andrew Kraebel, Brennan Mallone, Cameron Mitchell, Lindsey Pryor, Emma Sloan, John Stern, Earl Thompson IV, Emily Winkler, Marnie Wolfe, and James Young Jr.

I would also like to acknowledge the help of Baker-Berry Library's splendid librarians, chiefly Bill Fontaine, Debra Agnoli, and Jennifer Taxman. The expertise of Barbara Knauff and Susan Simon in Kiewit Computing and of Tom Garboletti and Otmar Foelsche in Humanities Computing was indispensable at key stages. The invaluable work of Gail Vernazza in the preparation of the manuscript and securing of permissions has made all the difference. In the final checking of sources and footnotes, I am grateful to Joel Dahl for both legwork and advice. Among colleagues whose conversation and counsel I have benefited from in the conception and editing of this book, I thank especially Marcelo Gleiser, Ehud Benor, Hans Penner, Tom West, Mary Kelley, and Nancy Howell. Two anonymous readers for Princeton University Press made important recommendations for which I am grateful. Fred Appel has been the acquisitions editor every one should have. I thank him and the editorial staff at Princeton University Press for their professional work on the book, especially Deborah Tegarden and Vicky Wilson-Schwartz.

Dartmouth College has provided generous financial support through the John Phillips Chair and the Dickinson Fund in the Department of Religion. In addition, I want to thank Barry Scherr, provost of Dartmouth, for his support of this project.

PART ONE

Founders of Modern Science

Science without religion is lame;
religion without science is blind.
—Albert Einstein

1 Galileo Galilei
(1564–1642)

Introduction

The playwright Bertolt Brecht labored for two decades over his anti–Third Reich play *Leben des Galilei*. The seventh scene is set on March 5, 1616, just as the Inquisition has censured the Copernican texts positing the heliocentric model of the universe. Galileo learns of this event during a conversation with several cardinals at a dinner party in Rome. Brecht dramatically captures the heart of Galileo's religious faith:

> BARBERINI: He's [i.e., Galileo is] really dreadful. In all innocence he accuses God of the juiciest boners in astronomy! I suppose God didn't work hard enough at His astronomy before He wrote Holy Scripture? My dear friend!
>
> BELLARMINE: Don't you think it likely that the Creator knows more about His creation than any of His creatures?
>
> GALILEO: But, gentlemen, after all we can misinterpret not only the movements of the heavenly bodies, but the Bible as well.

> BELLARMINE: But wouldn't you say that after all the interpreta-
> tion of the Bible is the business of the Holy Church?
> (Galileo is silent.)[1]

Galileo is silent because in fact he believes that the business of biblical interpretation, in the hands of fallible humans, can prove to be highly fallible. He is silent because he does not believe the Bible is meant to be read literally, and biblical literalism has been hardening into a new position within some circles of the Counter-reformation Catholic Church following the Council of Trent.

Far from being a biblical literalist, Galileo believed that the Bible was intentionally simplified by the Church so that lay people could access its meaning. In the letter excerpted to his student Benedetto Castelli, Galileo underscores the Brechtian point by clearly stating "though Holy Scripture cannot err, nevertheless some of its inter-preters and expositors can sometimes err in various ways."[2] As the other texts selected in this chapter show, however, Galileo's strong religious faith is rooted in a conviction that truth is always one and cannot be at odds with itself. Knowledge of the truth is available through two avenues, one scientific and one religious. Reason and mathematics produce the exciting and disturbing astronomical data that Galileo regarded as a true reflection of the craftsmanship of the divine *work*, and Holy Scripture presents a true reflection of the divine *word*. Fallible humans can misinterpret both of these, as Brecht's Galileo observes, but neither one can ever be fundamen-tally in conflict with the other. If truth cannot be at odds with it-self, then scientific truth and religious truth will never contradict each other, Galileo believed. When they appear to conflict, it is be-cause one or the other has been mistakenly interpreted.

Galileo makes it still clearer, in the second excerpt, which is taken from his unpublished writings, that he champions the autonomy

---

[1] Bertolt Brecht, *Collected Plays*, vol. 5, *Life of Galileo*, trans. W. Sauerlander and R. Mainheim, ed. R. Manheim and J. Willet (New York: Vintage Books, 1972), 51.

[2] Maurice A. Finocchiaro, ed., *The Galileo Affair: A Documentary History* (Berkeley: University of California Press, 1989), 49.

of science with respect to faith. Science—then called "natural philosophy"—does not proceed from theology, Galileo declares, and in disputes about natural phenomena one must begin not with the authority of scriptural passages but with sensory experience and necessary demonstrations. Here he advances the argument that two truths cannot contradict one another, so that in cases where a known scientific fact is available, the Bible, an inspired text, ought to be interpreted in such a way as to be compatible with the scientific truth. Augustine had argued along similar lines in the fourth century, and many contemporary theologians take much the same position today, but Galileo was warned a year later, in 1616, not to teach or to defend the Copernican view except as a possible hypothesis.

Had he been content only to differentiate two senses in which biblical texts could be interpreted, either as commonsense language or as scientific language, Galileo's position might have been as simple as that of Cardinal Cesare Baronio, the sixteenth-century Vatican librarian whose quip he quotes approvingly: the Bible is a book that tells us how one goes to heaven, not how the heavens go. If the sun were said to stand still during Joshua's surprisingly long day, this should be given an allegorical meaning, not a scientific sense that would present a challenge to Copernican astronomy. But Galileo went further and argued for the mutual relevance of science and religion. In his letter to the grand duchess Christina in 1615, Galileo argued that known scientific truths should help *guide* biblical exegesis. It was as though he expected the theologians to become astronomers first! Creatively theologizing himself, Galileo interpreted Joshua's command that the sun stand still in the middle of the heavens as referring to the sun's axial rotation. His conclusion was unmistakable: it is the Copernican framework that preserves and best understands the biblical record.

Recent scholarship on the so-called "Galilean affair" dispels two popular myths about Galileo and his conflict with the Catholic Church. Both have persisted despite the lack of historical evidence for them. We might call these the "Myth of Galileo the Religious Rebel" and the "Myth of the Catholic Church as Arch-Enemy of

Science." The more complex picture that now emerges in the work of contemporary historians of science depicts a Galileo who was generally committed to the Church and a Church that was traditionally committed to natural philosophy as a rational, independent route to truth. In other words, Galileo was far more inclined to a conservative religious position and the Church much better disposed to the new astronomical data than is commonly believed. Galileo was not eager to undermine the Church, especially not his once friendly ally Pope Urban VIII, and the Church, at least as represented by the Jesuits, was not especially eager to condemn the Copernican heliocentric cosmology adopted by Galileo, and also championed by Johannes Kepler as early as 1590. It is easy to see how Copernicus and Kepler escaped Galileo's fate of virtual house arrest. Copernicus died soon after his heliocentric theory became public, and the actual printing of his six-volume, generally unreadable book, *On the Revolutions of the Heavenly Spheres*, did not get underway until his death in 1543; it took more than seventy years for it to create much of a storm in Europe. Johannes Kepler, on the other hand, enjoyed not only a different status as a Protestant, outside the jurisdiction of Rome, but also royal patronage once he was settled in Prague as official imperial astronomer.

Why then was Galileo sentenced to house arrest in the year 1633 and forced to abjure his former beliefs for the remaining nine years of his life? Part of the answer is that this was simply a tragically unnecessary outcome: Copernican heliocentrism was gaining the day within the Catholic hierarchy and might very well have succeeded on its own merits had Galileo not brought matters to a head with his forceful *Dialogue Concerning the Two Chief World Systems* in 1632. More deeply, this was a highly complex and ambiguous story involving multiple levels of faith and reason, political machinations in the Italian Renaissance court system, the gathering storm of the counter-reformation, and a personal sense of betrayal between Galileo and Pope Urban VIII, who had, as Maffeo Barberini, earlier assured Galileo he could write about Copernicus's theory if he presented it as just that—a theoretical hypothesis, not a truth. One of the most fascinating parts of the story is Galileo's growing conviction that science should stipulate or help determine theology. The modernization of Catholic teaching, he thought, could succeed best by replacing Aristotelian astronomy with Copernican. The new seat of authority was to be science, and those who could claim expertise in astronomy and mathematics ought to be allowed to pronounce on theology as well. Above all, the old seats of authority—whether Aristotelian or biblical—were no longer the arbiters of scientific truth.

An intemperate zeal for hermeneutics was perhaps finally responsible for Galileo's troubles with the Church hierarchy, but his very insistence on the inescapable need for interpretation, rather than any simple acceptance of literal readings of scripture, produced the most important statements of Galileo's own faith. Had he not allowed himself to be drawn into an argument about the proper interpretation of scripture, we would not have the fascinating document *Dialogue Concerning the Two Chief World Systems* (1632). The dialogue, excerpted here, engages three characters: Simplicio, a geocentric Aristotelian; Salviati, an obvious alter ego for Galileo and spokesman for the Copernican view; and Sagredo, an interested and intelligent bystander to the debate. In a masterful polemic, the *Dialogue* teaches that astronomy and the science of motion go hand in glove. There is no need to fear, Galileo explains, that earth's rotation will cause it to fly to pieces. Salviati systematically destroys Simplicio's arguments, and with a final flourish Sagredo concludes that Salviati is right, Aristotle is wrong, and wine and cheese are waiting.

Though marked by Galileo's characteristic caustic wit, the document is also somewhat marred by arguments so convoluted that one marvels that heliocentrism ever prevailed. For all its notoriety, Galileo's *Dialogue* offered no proof that the earth truly moved. Yet in religious matters, he exhibits a sophisticated form of faith. In his own words, Galileo is by turns poetic, didactic, reverent, combative, and witty. Whatever serious doubts he might harbor about the institutional Church and the rectitude of some of its interpretations, he has no doubt about faith itself. He can artfully embrace all the elements of a typical Renaissance Roman Catholic piety with one remarkable exception, its Aristotelian cosmology.

In fact, Galileo was always much more an opponent of Aristotelian physics than of Church theology. And the Catholic Church, for its part, was committed to the role of reason in support of faith, and to philosophical thinking as an aid to reason. Far from opposing faith to reason, the Jesuits, if not the Dominicans, deliberated with, for, and against Galileo, all the while valuing natural philosophy and championing a reasonable faith. Perhaps the deepest difference between Galileo and those who opposed him was a very basic philosophical outlook. The longing for permanence over and against change defined the ancient and medieval worldview. Largely because of Plato and Aristotle, the assumption that perfection and permanence go hand in hand—as do imperfection and change—became axiomatic in Western thought. Galileo's challenge to that assumption was thorough, as seen in this emphatic passage from the *Dialogue*, where he states a philosophical belief every bit as fundamental to him as his religious beliefs: "I cannot without great wonder, nay, more, disbelief, hear it being attributed to natural bodies as a great honor and perfection that they are impassible, immutable, inalterable, etc.: as conversely, I hear it esteemed a great imperfection to be alterable, generable, and mutable. . . . These men who so extol incorruptibility, inalterability, and so on, speak, I believe, out of the great desire they have to live long and for fear of death. . . . These people deserve to meet with a Medusa's head that would transform them into statues of diamond and jade, so that they might become more perfect than they are."

Galileo was born in the same year that Michelangelo died, and he died in the same year that Isaac Newton was born. In that span, an entire cosmological worldview was overturned. Yet it was only in 1992 that the Roman Catholic Church formally admitted to having erred in dealing with Galileo. It is a remarkable irony that the very words used by Pope John Paul II come so close to those of Galileo himself, and that the two men seem to share an almost identical position on the relation between science and religion. "There exist two realms of knowledge," the pope explained, "one which has its source in revelation and one which reason can discover by its own power. To the latter belong especially the experimental sciences . . . the distinction . . . ought not to be understood as opposition. The two realms are not altogether foreign to each other; they have points of contact. The methodologies proper to each make it possible to bring out different aspects of reality. So there we have it. Science and religion do not conflict, but they describe two different aspects of reality."[3]

✌ Galileo's Contribution to Science

Galileo Galilei discovered new features on the moon's surface, four of the moons of Jupiter, the rays of Saturn, sunspots, and the fact that Venus undergoes a regular series of phases similar to the phases of Earth's moon. He determined the parabolic path of projectiles, calculated the law of free fall, invented a microscope, advocated the relativity of motion, and created a mathematical physics.

Galileo in His Own Words

Letter from Galileo to Benedetto Castelli, (December 21, 1613)[4]

Very Reverend Father and My Most Respectable Sir:
Yesterday Mr. Niccolò Arrighetti came to visit me and told me about you. Thus I took infinite pleasure in hearing about what I did not doubt at all, namely, about the great satisfaction you have been giving to the whole University. . . . However, the seal of my pleasure was to hear him relate the arguments which through the

---

[3] John Paul II, "Lessons of the Galileo Case," Address to the Pontifical Academy of Sciences, October 31, 1992, in *Origins* v. 22, no. 22 (November 12, 1992): 371.
[4] Finocchiaro, 49–54.

great kindness of their Most Serene Highness, you had the occasion of advancing at their table and then of continuing in the chambers of the Most Serene Ladyship, in the presence also of the Grand Duke and the Most Serene Archduchess, the Most Illustrious and Excellent Don Antonio and Don Paolo Giordano, and some of the very excellent philosophers there. What greater fortune can you wish than to see their Highnesses themselves enjoying discussing with you, putting forth doubts, listening to your solutions, and finally remaining satisfied with your answers?

After Mr. Arrighetti related the details you had mentioned, they gave me the occasion to go back to examine some general questions about the use of the Holy Scripture in disputes involving physical conclusions and some particular other ones about Joshua's passage, which was presented in opposition to the earth's motion and sun's stability by the Grand Duchess Dowager with some support by the Most Serene Archduchess.

In regard to the first general point of the Most Serene Ladyship, it seems to me very prudent of her to propose and of you to concede and to agree that the Holy Scripture can never lie or err, and that its declarations are absolutely and inviolably true. I should have added only that, though the Scripture cannot err, nevertheless some of its interpreters and expositors can sometimes err in various ways. One of these would be very serious and very frequent, namely, to want to limit oneself always to the literal meaning of the words; for there would thus emerge not only various contradictions but also serious heresies and blasphemies, and it would be necessary to attribute to God feet, hands and eyes, as well as bodily and human feelings like anger, regret, hate and sometimes even forgetfulness of things past and ignorance of future ones. Thus in the Scripture one finds many propositions which look different from the truth if one goes by the literal meaning of the words, but which are expressed in this manner to accommodate the incapacity of common people; likewise, for the few who deserve to be separated from the masses, it is necessary that wise interpreters produce their true meaning and indicate the particular reasons why they have been expressed by means of such words.

Thus, given that in many places the Scripture is not only capable but necessarily in need of interpretations different from the apparent meaning of the words, it seems to me that in disputes about natural phenomena it should be reserved to the last place. For the Holy Scripture and nature both equally derive from the divine Word, the former as the dictation of the Holy Spirit, the latter as the most obedient executrix of God's commands; moreover, in order to adapt itself to the understanding of all people, it was appropriate for the Scripture to say many things which are different from absolute truth, in appearance and in regard to the meaning of the words; on the other hand, nature is inexorable and immutable, and she does not care at all whether or not her recondite reasons and modes of operations are revealed to human understanding, and so she never transgresses the terms of the laws imposed on her; therefore, whatever sensory experience places before our eyes or necessary demonstrations prove to us concerning natural effects should not in any way be called into question on account of scriptural passages whose words appear to have a different meaning, since not every statement of the Scripture is bound to obligations as severely as each effect of nature. Indeed, because of the aim of adapting itself to the capacity of unrefined and undisciplined peoples, the Scripture has not abstained from somewhat concealing its most basic dogmas, thus attributing to God himself properties contrary to and very far from his essence; so who will categorically maintain that, in speaking even incidentally of the earth or the sun or other creatures, it abandoned this aim and chose to restrict itself rigorously within the limited and narrow meanings of the words? This would have been especially problematic when saying about these creatures things which are very far from the primary function of the Holy Writ, indeed, things which, if said and put forth in their naked and unadorned truth, would more likely harm its primary intention and make people more resistant to persuasion about the articles pertaining to salvation.

Given this, and moreover it being obvious that two truths can never contradict each other, the task of wise interpreters is to strive to find the true meanings of scriptural passages agreeing with those physical conclusions of which we are already certain and sure from clear sensory experience or from necessary demonstrations. Furthermore, as I already said, though the Scripture was inspired by the Holy Spirit, because of the mentioned reasons many passages admit of interpretations far removed from the literal meaning, and also we cannot assert with certainty that all interpreters speak by divine inspiration; hence I should think it would be prudent not to allow anyone to oblige scriptural passages to have to maintain the truth of any physical conclusions whose contrary could ever be proved to us by the senses and demonstrative and necessary reasons. Who wants to fix a limit for the human mind? Who wants to assert that everything which is knowable in the world is already known? Because of this, it would be most advisable not to add anything beyond necessity to the articles concerning salvation and the definition of the Faith, which are firm enough that there is no danger of any valid and effective doctrine ever rising against them. If this is so, what greater disorder would result from adding them upon request by persons of whom we do not know whether they speak with celestial inspiration, and of whom also we see clearly that they are completely lacking in the intelligence needed to understand, let alone to criticize, the demonstrations by means of which the most exact sciences proceed in the confirmation of some of their conclusions?

I should believe that the authority of the Holy Writ has merely the aim of persuading men of those articles and propositions which are necessary for their salvation and surpass all human reason, and so could not become credible through some other science or any other means except the mouth of the Holy Spirit itself. However, I do not think it necessary to believe that the same God who has furnished us with senses, language, and intellect would want to bypass their use and give us by other means the information we can obtain with them. This applies especially to those sciences about which one can read only very small phrases and scattered conclusions in the Scripture, as is particularly the case for astronomy, of which it contains such a small portion that one does not even find in it the names of all the planets; but if the first sacred writers had been thinking of persuading the people about the arrangement and the movements of the heavenly bodies, they would not have treated of them so sparsely, which is to say almost nothing in comparison to the infinity of very lofty and admirable conclusions contained in such a science.

So you see, if I am not mistaken, how disorderly is the procedure of those who in disputes about natural phenomena that do not directly involve the Faith give first place to scriptural passages, which they quite often misunderstand anyway. However, if these people really believe they have grasped the true meaning of a particular scriptural passage, and if they consequently feel sure of possessing the absolute truth on the question they intend to dispute about, then let them sincerely tell me whether they think that someone in a scientific dispute who happens to be right has a great advantage over another who happens to be wrong. I know they will answer Yes, and that the one who supports the true side will be able to provide a thousand experiments and a thousand necessary demonstrations for his side, whereas the other person can have nothing but sophisms, paralogisms, and fallacies. But if they know they have such an advantage over their opponents as long as the discussion is limited to physical questions and only philosophical weapons are used, why is it that when they come to the meeting they immediately introduce an irresistible and terrible weapon, the mere sight of which terrifies even the most skillful and expert champion? If I must tell the truth, I believe it is they who are the most terrified, and that they are trying to find a way of not letting the opponent approach because they feel unable to resist his assaults. However, consider that, as I just said, whoever has truth on his side has a great, indeed, the greatest, advantage over the opponent, and that it is impossible for two truths to contradict each other; it follows, therefore, that we must not fear any assaults launched against us by anyone, as long as we are allowed to speak and to be heard by competent persons who are not excessively upset by their own emotions and interests.

To confirm this I now come to examining the specific passage of Joshua, concerning which you put forth three theses for their

Most Serene Highnesses. I take the third one, which you advanced as mine (as indeed it is), but I add some other considerations that I do not believe I have ever told you.

Let us then assume and concede to the opponent that the words of the sacred text should be taken precisely in their literal meaning, namely, that in answer to Joshua's prayers God made the sun stop and lengthened the day, so that as a result he achieved victory; but I request that the same rule should apply to both, so that the opponent should not pretend to tie me and to leave himself free to change or modify the meanings of the words. Given this, I say that this passage shows clearly the falsity and impossibility of the Aristotelian and Ptolemaic world system, and on the other hand agrees very well with the Copernican one.

I first ask the opponent whether he knows with how many motions the sun moves. If he knows, he must answer that it moves with two motions, namely, with the annual motion from west to east and with the diurnal motion in the opposite direction from east to west.

Then, secondly, I ask him whether these two motions, so different and almost contrary to each other, belong to the sun and are its own to an equal extent. The answer must be No, but that only one is specifically its own, namely, the annual motion, whereas the other is not but belongs to the highest heaven, I mean the Prime Mobile; the latter carries along with it the sun as well as the other planets and the stellar sphere, forcing them to make a revolution around the earth in twenty-four hours, with a motion, as I said, almost contrary to their own natural motion.

Coming to the third question, I ask him with which of these two motions the sun produces night and day, that is, whether with its own motion or else with that of the Prime Mobile. The answer must be that night and day are effects of the motion of the Prime Mobile and that what depends on the sun's own motion is not night or day but the various seasons and the year itself.

Now, if the day derives not from the sun's motion but from that of the Prime Mobile, who does not see that to lengthen the day one must stop the Prime Mobile and not the sun? Indeed, is there anyone who understands these first elements of astronomy and does not know that, if God had stopped the sun's motion, He would have cut and shortened the day instead of lengthening it? For, the sun's motion being contrary to the diurnal turning, the more the sun moves toward the east the more its progression toward the west is slowed down, whereas by its motion being diminished or annihilated the sun would set that much sooner; this phenomenon is observed in the moon, whose diurnal revolutions are slower than those of the sun inasmuch as its own motion is faster than that of the sun. It follows that it is absolutely impossible to stop the sun and lengthen the day in the system of Ptolemy and Aristotle, and therefore either the motions must not be arranged as Ptolemy says or we must modify the meaning of the words of the Scripture; we would have to claim that, when it says that God stopped the sun, it meant to say that He stopped the Prime Mobile, and that it said the contrary of what it would have said if speaking to educated men in order to adapt itself to the capacity of those who are barely able to understand the rising and setting of the sun.

Add to this that it is not believable that God would stop only the sun, letting the other spheres proceed; for He would have unnecessarily altered and upset all the order, appearances, and arrangements of the other stars in relation to the sun, and would have greatly disturbed the whole system of nature. On the other hand, it is believable that He would stop the whole system of celestial spheres, which could then together return to their operations without any confusion or change after the period of intervening rest.

However, we have already agreed not to change the meaning of the words in the text; therefore it is necessary to resort to another arrangement of the parts of the world, and to see whether the literal meaning of the words flows directly and without obstacle from its point of view. This is in fact what we see happening.

For I have discovered and conclusively demonstrated that the solar globe turns on itself, completing an entire rotation in about one lunar month, in exactly the same direction as all the other heavenly revolutions; moreover, it is very probable and reasonable that, as the chief instrument and minister of nature and almost the heart of the world, the sun gives not only light (as it obviously does) but also motion to all the planets that revolve around it; hence, if in conformity with Copernicus's position the diurnal motion is attributed to the earth, anyone can see that it sufficed stopping the sun to stop the whole system, and thus to lengthen the period of the diurnal illumination without altering in any way the rest of the mutual relationships of the planets; and that is exactly how the words of the sacred text sound. Here then is the manner in which by stopping the sun one can lengthen the day on the earth, without introducing any confusion among the parts of the world and without altering the words of the Scripture.

I have written much more than is appropriate in the view of my slight illness. So I end by reminding you that I am at your service, and I kiss your hands and pray the Lord to give you happy holidays and all you desire.

Florence, 21 December 1613
To Your Very Reverend Paternity.
*   Your Most Affectionate Servant,*
*   Galileo Galilei.*

On Truth in Science and in Scripture (1615)[5]

The mobility of the earth and the stability of the sun could never be contrary to the faith or to Scripture, if this were ever actually proven to be true in nature by philosophers, astronomers, and mathematicians by means of sense experience, exact observations, and necessary demonstrations. In such a case, if any passages of Scripture seem to say the opposite, we should say that this is due to the weakness of our intellect, which has not been able to penetrate into the true meaning of Scripture on this point. For it is a

---

[5] From Galileo's unpublished notes, in Richard J. Blackwell, *Galileo, Bellarmine, and the Bible* (Notre Dame, IN: Notre Dame University Press, 1991), 273–76.

common and most correct teaching to say that one truth cannot be contrary to another truth. Therefore those who would juridically condemn something need first to prove that it is false in nature by challenging the arguments to the contrary.

Now as a protection against error, let us ask from what starting point should one begin; that is, from the authority of the Scriptures or from the refutation of the demonstrations and evidence of the philosophers and astronomers. I answer that we ought to begin from the place which is more secure and far removed from any occasion of scandal; and this is the starting point of natural and mathematical arguments. I claim that if the arguments to prove the mobility of the earth are found to be fallacious and demonstrative of the contrary, then we will have firmly established the falsity of that proposition and the truth of the contrary, which we now say is in agreement with the meaning of the Scriptures. Indeed, one could freely and without danger condemn that proposition as false.

On the other hand, if these arguments are found to be true and necessary, there will not be any occasion of prejudice against the authority of Scripture. For this will cause us to remain cautious that in our ignorance we have not penetrated into the true meaning of the Scripture, which we can then pursue aided by the newly discovered natural truth. Thus the starting point of reason is secure in every way. But on the contrary, if we stand solely on what seems to us to be the true and most certain sense of Scripture, and if we proceed to condemn such a proposition without examining the force of the demonstrations, then how great a scandal will follow when sense experience and arguments prove the contrary? And who will have plunged the Holy Church into confusion; those who have given the highest importance to demonstrations, or those who have neglected them? Thus we see which path is more secure.

We maintain that a natural proposition which is proven to be true by natural and mathematical demonstrations can never be contrary to the Scriptures; rather in such a case it is the weakness of our intellect which prevents us from penetrating into the true meaning of the Scriptures themselves. On the other hand, those who try to refute and falsify that same type of proposition by using the authority of the same passages of Scripture will commit the fallacy called "begging the question." For since the true sense of the Scripture will already have been put in doubt by the force of the argument, one cannot take it as clear and secure for the purpose of refuting that same proposition.

Rather, one needs to take the demonstrations apart and find their fallacies with the aid of other arguments, experiences, and more certain observations. And when the truth of fact and of nature has been found in this way, then, but not before, can we confirm the true sense of Scripture and securely use it for our purposes. Thus again the secure path is to begin with demonstrations, confirming the true and refuting the false.

If as a matter of fact the earth does move, then we cannot change nature so that it does not move. But we can easily eliminate inconsistency with Scripture simply by admitting that we have not penetrated into its true meaning. Thus the secure way to avoid error is to begin with astronomical and natural investigations, and not with Scripture.

I realize that in their explanation of the passages of Scripture pertaining to this issue, all the Fathers agree in interpreting them in the most simple sense and according to the direct meaning of the words; and that therefore it would not be proper, in response to a different point of view, to alter their common interpretation, because that would accuse the Fathers of inadvertence or negligence. I respond by admitting that this is a reasonable and proper concern, but add that we have a most ready excuse for the Fathers. It is that they never explained the Scriptures differently from the direct meaning of the words on this issue because the opinion of the mobility of the earth was totally buried in their day. It was not discussed or written about or defended. Hence no charge of negligence can fall on the Fathers for not reflecting on something which was hidden from all of them. That they did not reflect on this is clear from the fact that in their writings there is not found one word about such an opinion. To the contrary, if anyone says that they did consider it, that would make it much more dangerous to try to condemn it; for after considering it, they not only did not condemn it, but no one even raised a doubt about it.

The defense of the Fathers is, then, quite easy and quick. But on the other hand it would be most difficult, if not impossible, to excuse and defend from a similar charge of inadvertence, the popes, councils, and reformers of the *Index* who for eighty continuous years have failed to notice an opinion and a book which was originally written by order of a pope, which was later printed by order of a cardinal and a bishop, which was dedicated to another pope, which was so unique in regard to this doctrine that it cannot be said to have remain hidden, and which was accepted by the Holy Church, while supposedly its teaching was false and condemned. Thus if the notion of agreeing not to charge our ancestors with negligence should be defended and held in the highest regard, as indeed it should, then beware that in trying to flee from one absurdity, you do not fall into a greater one.

But if someone were still to think that it is improper to abandon the common interpretation of the Fathers, even in the case of natural propositions which they did not discuss and whose opposites have not come under their consideration, then I ask what one ought to do if necessary demonstrations were to conclude that the opposite is a fact in nature. Which of these two rules ought to be altered? That which says that no proposition can be both true and false? Or that which obliges us to take as a "matter of faith" natural propositions learned from the common interpretation of the Fathers? If I am not mistaken, it seems to me to be more secure to modify the second rule, i.e., the one which tries to oblige us to hold as a "matter of faith" a natural proposition which could by conclusive arguments be demonstrated to be false in fact and in nature. Furthermore it should be said that the common interpretation of the Fathers ought to have absolute authority for propositions which they examined and which do not have, and certainly never possibly could have, demonstrations to the contrary. Let me add that it seems to be abundantly clear that the council obliges agreement with the common explanation of the Fathers only "in matters of faith and morals, etc."

From Dialogue Concerning the Two Chief World Systems *(1632)*[6]

Præfatio

To the Discerning Reader:

Several years ago there was published in Rome a salutary edict which, in order to obviate the dangerous tendencies of our present age, imposed a seasonable silence upon the Pythagorean opinion that the earth moves. There were those who impudently asserted that this decree had its origin not in judicious inquiry, but in passion none too well informed. Complaints were to be heard that advisers who were totally unskilled at astronomical observations ought not to clip the wings of reflective intellects by means of rash prohibitions.

Upon hearing such carping insolence, my zeal could not be contained. Being thoroughly informed about that prudent determination, I decided to appear openly in the theater of the world as a witness of the sober truth. I was at that time in Rome; I was not only received by the most eminent prelates of that Court, but had their applause; indeed this decree was not published without some previous notice of it having been given to me. Therefore I propose in the present work to show to foreign nations that as much is understood of this matter in Italy, and particularly in Rome, as transalpine diligence can ever have imagined. Collecting all the reflections that properly concern the Copernican system, I shall make it known that everything was brought before the attention of the Roman censorship, and that there proceed from this clime not only dogmas for the welfare of the soul, but ingenious discoveries for the delight of the mind as well.

To this end I have taken the Copernican side in the discourse, proceeding as with a pure mathematical hypothesis and striving

[6] *Galileo Galilei, Dialogue Concerning the Two Chief World Systems: Ptolemaic and Copernican, trans. S. Drake (New York: Modern Library, 2001), 5–7, 425–28, 537–39.*

by every artifice to represent it as superior to supposing the earth motionless—not, indeed absolutely, but as against the arguments of some professed Peripatetics. These men indeed deserve not even that name, for they do not walk about; they are content to adore the shadows, philosophizing not with due circumspection but merely from having memorized a few ill-understood principles.

Three principal headings are treated. First, I shall try to show that all experiments practicable upon the earth are insufficient measures for proving its mobility, since they are indifferently adaptable to an earth in motion or at rest. I hope in so doing to reveal many observations unknown to the ancients. Secondly, the celestial phenomena will be examined strengthening the Copernican hypothesis until it might seem that this must triumph absolutely. Here new reflections are adjoined which might be used in order to simplify astronomy, though not because of any necessity imposed by nature. In the third place, I shall propose an ingenious speculation. It happens that long ago I said that the unsolved problem of the ocean tides might receive some light from assuming the motion of the earth. This assertion of mine, passing by word of mouth, found loving fathers who adopted it as a child of their own ingenuity. Now, so that no stranger may ever appear who, arming himself with our weapons, shall charge us with want of attention to such an important matter, I have thought it good to reveal those probabilities which might render this plausible, given that the earth moves.

I hope that from these considerations the world will come to know that if other nations have navigated more, we have not theorized less. It is not from failing to take count of what others have thought that we have yielded to asserting that the earth is motionless, and holding the contrary to be a mere mathematical caprice, but (if for nothing else) for those reasons that are supplied by piety, religion, the knowledge of Divine Omnipotence, and a consciousness of the limitations of the human mind I have thought it most appropriate to explain these concepts in the form of dialogues, which, not being restricted to the rigorous observance of mathematical laws, make room also for digressions which are sometimes no less interesting than the principal argument.

Many years ago I was often to be found in the marvelous city of Venice, in discussions with Signore Giovanni Francesco Sagredo, a man of noble extraction and trenchant wit. From Florence came Signore Filippo Salviati, the least of whose glories were the eminence of his blood and the magnificence of his fortune. His was a sublime intellect which fed no more hungrily upon any pleasure than it did upon fine meditations. I often talked with these two of such matters in the presence of a certain Peripatetic philosopher whose greatest obstacle in apprehending the truth seemed to be the reputation he had acquired by his interpretations of Aristotle.

Now, since bitter death has deprived Venice and Florence of those two great luminaries in the very meridian of their years, I have resolved to make their fame live on in these pages, so far as my poor abilities will permit, by introducing them as interlocutors in the present argument. (Nor shall the good Peripatetic lack a place; because of his excessive affection toward the *Commentaries* of Simplicius, I have thought fit to leave him under the name of the author he so much revered, without mentioning his own). May it please those two great souls, ever venerable to my heart, to accept this public monument of my undying love. And may the memory of their eloquence assist me in delivering to posterity the promised reflections.

It happened that several discussions had taken place casually at various times among these gentlemen, and had rather whetted than satisfied their thirst for learning. Hence very wisely they resolved to meet together on certain days during which, setting aside all other business, they might apply themselves more methodically to the contemplation of the wonders of God in the heavens and upon the earth. They met in the palace of the illustrious Sagredo; and, after the customary but brief exchange of compliments, Salviati commenced as follows.

The Third Day

SALVIATI: Simplicio, I wish you could for a moment put aside your affection for the followers of your doctrines and tell me frankly whether you believe that they comprehend in their own minds this magnitude which they subsequently decide cannot be ascribed to the universe because of its immensity. I myself believe that they do not. It seems to me that here the situation is just as it is with the grasp of numbers when one gets up into the thousands of millions, and the imagination becomes confused and can form no concept. The same thing happens in comprehending the magnitudes of immense distances; there comes into our reasoning an effect similar to that which occurs to the senses on a serene night, when I look at the stars and judge by sight that their distance is but a few miles, or that the fixed stars are not a bit farther off than Jupiter, Saturn, or even the moon.

But aside from all this, consider those previous disputes between the astronomers and the Peripatetic philosophers about the reasoning as to the distance of the new stars in Cassiopeia and Sagittarius, the astronomers placing these among the fixed stars and the philosophers believing them to be closer than the moon. How powerless are our senses to distinguish large distances from extremely large ones, even when the latter are in fact many thousands of times the larger!

And finally I ask you, O foolish man: Does your imagination first comprehend some magnitude for the universe, which you then judge to be too vast? If it does, do you like imagining that your comprehension extends beyond the Divine power? Would you like to imagine to yourself things greater than God can accomplish? And if it does not comprehend this, then why do you pass judgment upon things you do not understand?

SIMPLICIO: These arguments are very good, and no one denies that the size of the heavens may exceed our imaginings, since God could have created it even thousands of times larger than it is. But must we not admit that nothing has been created in vain, or is idle, in the universe? Now when we see this beautiful order among the planets, they being arranged around the earth at distances commensurate with their producing upon it their effects for our benefit, to what end would there then be interposed between the highest of their orbits (namely, Saturn's), and the stellar sphere, a vast space without anything in it, superfluous, and vain? For the use and convenience of whom?

SALVIATI: It seems to me that we take too much upon ourselves, Simplicio, when we will have it that merely taking care of us is the adequate work of Divine wisdom and power, and the limit beyond which it creates and disposes of nothing.

I should not like to have us tie its hand so. We should be quite content in the knowledge that God and Nature are so occupied with the government of human affairs that they could not apply themselves more to us even if they had no other cares to attend to than those of the human race alone. I believe that I can explain what I mean by a very appropriate and most noble example, derived from the action of the light of the sun. For when the sun draws up some vapors here, or warms a plant there, it draws these and warms this as if it had nothing else to do. Even in ripening a bunch of grapes, or perhaps just a single grape, it applies itself so effectively that it could not do more even if the goal of all its affairs were just the ripening of this one grape. Now if this grape receives from the sun everything it can receive, and is not deprived of the least thing by the sun simultaneously producing thousands and thousands of other results, then that grape would be guilty of pride or envy if it believed or demanded that the action of the sun's rays should be employed upon itself alone.

I am certain that Divine Providence omits none of the things which look to the government of human affairs, but I cannot bring myself to believe that there may not be other things in the universe dependent upon the infinity of its wisdom, at least so far as my reason informs me; yet if the facts were otherwise, I should not resist believing in reasoning which I had borrowed from a higher understanding. Meanwhile, when I am told that an immense space interposed between the planetary orbits and the starry sphere would be useless and vain, being idle and devoid of stars, and that any immensity going beyond our comprehension would be superfluous for holding the fixed stars, I say that it is brash for our feebleness to attempt to judge the reason for God's actions, and to call everything in the universe vain and superfluous which does not serve us.

SAGREDO: Say rather, and I think you will be speaking more accurately, "which we do not know to serve us." I believe that one of the greatest pieces of arrogance, or rather madness, that can be thought of is to say, "Since I do not know how Jupiter or Saturn is of service to me, they are superfluous, and even do not exist." Because, O deluded man, neither do I know how my arteries are of service to me, nor my cartilages, spleen, or gall, I should not even know that I had gall, or a spleen, or kidneys, if they had not been shown to me in many dissected corpses. Even then I could understand what my spleen does for me only if it were removed. In order to understand how some celestial body acted upon me (since you want all their actions to be directed at me), it would be necessary to remove that body for a while, and say that whatever effect I might then feel to be missing in me depended upon that star.

Besides, what does it mean to say that the space between Saturn and the fixed stars, which these men call too vast and useless, is empty of world bodies? That we do not see them, perhaps? Then did the four satellites of Jupiter and the companions of Saturn come into the heavens when we began seeing them, and not before? Were there not innumerable other fixed stars before men began to see them? The nebulae were once only little white patches; have we with our telescopes made them become clusters of many bright and beautiful stars? Oh, the presumptuous, rash ignorance of mankind!

The Fourth Day

SALVIATI: Now, since it is time to put an end to our discourses, it remains for me to beg you that if later, in going over the things that I have brought out, you should meet with any difficulty or any question not completely resolved, you will excuse my deficiency because of the novelty of the concept and the limitations of my abilities; then because of the magnitude of the subject; and finally because I do not claim and have not claimed from others that assent which I myself do not give to this invention, which may very easily turn out to be a most foolish hallucination and a majestic paradox.

To you, Sagredo, though during my arguments you have shown yourself satisfied with some of my ideas and have approved them highly, I say that I take this to have arisen partly from their novelty rather than from their certainty, and even more from your courteous wish to afford your assent that pleasure which one naturally feels from approbation and praise of what is one's own. And as you have obligated me to you by your urbanity, so Simplicio has pleased me by his ingenuity. Indeed, I have become very fond of him for his constancy in sustaining so forcibly and so undauntedly the doctrines of his master. And I thank you, Sagredo, for your most courteous motivation, just as I ask pardon of Simplicio if I have offended him sometimes with my too heated and opinionated speech. Be sure that in this I have not been moved by any ulterior purpose, but only by that of giving you every opportunity to introduce lofty thoughts, that I might be the better informed.

SIMPLICIO: You need not make any excuses; they are superfluous, and especially so to me, who, being accustomed to public debates, have heard disputants countless times not merely grow angry and get excited at each other, but even break out into insulting speech and sometimes come very close to blows.

As to the discourses we have held, and especially this last one concerning the reasons for the ebbing and flowing of the ocean, I am really not entirely convinced; but from such feeble ideas of the matter as I have formed, I admit that your thoughts seem to me more ingenious than many others I have heard. I do not therefore consider them true and conclusive; indeed, keeping always before my mind's eye a most solid doctrine that I once heard from a most eminent and learned person, and before which one must fall silent, I know that if asked whether God in His infinite power and wisdom could have conferred upon the watery element its observed reciprocating motion using some other means than moving its containing vessels, both of you would reply that He could have, and that He would have known how to do this in many ways which are unthinkable to our minds. From this I forthwith conclude that, this being so, it would be excessive boldness for anyone to limit and restrict the Divine power and wisdom to some particular fancy of his own.

SALVIATI: An admirable and angelic doctrine, and well in accord with another one, also Divine, which, while it grants to us the right to argue about the constitution of the universe (perhaps in order that the working of the human mind shall not be curtailed or made lazy) adds that we cannot discover the work of His hands. Let us, then, exercise these activities permitted to us and ordained by God, that we may recognize and thereby so much the more admire His greatness, however much less fit we may find ourselves to penetrate the profound depths of His infinite wisdom.

SAGREDO: And let this be the final conclusion of our four days' arguments, after which if Salviati should desire to take some interval of rest, our continuing curiosity must grant that much to him. But this is on condition that when it is more convenient for him, he will return and satisfy our desires—mine in particular—regarding the problems set aside and noted down by me to submit to him at one or two further sessions, in accordance with our agreement. Above all, I shall be waiting impatiently to hear the elements of our Academician's new science of natural and constrained local motions.

Meanwhile, according to our custom, let us go and enjoy an hour of refreshment in the gondola that awaits us.

End of the Fourth and Final Day

Letter from Galileo to Elia Diodati (January 15, 1633)[7]

Very Illustrious Sire and Most Honorable Patron:
I owe answers to two letters, one from you and the other from Mr. Pierre Gassendi, written 1 November of last year but received

---

[7] Finocchiaro, 223–26.

by me only ten days ago. Because I am extremely preoccupied and burdened, I should like this to serve as an answer to both of you, who are very good friends and whose letters deal with the same subject; that is, your having received my *Dialogue*, sent to both, and your having quickly looked at it with praise and approval. I thank you for that and feel obliged, though I shall be waiting for a more frank and critical judgment after you have reread it more calmly, for I fear you will find in it many things to contest.

I am sorry I did not get Morin's and Froidmont's book until six months after the publication of my *Dialogue*, since I would have had the occasion to say many things in praise of both and also to make some observations on certain details, primarily one in Morin and another in Froidmont. As regards Morin, I am surprised by the truly great respect he shows toward judicial astrology and that he should pretend to establish its certainty by his conjectures (which seem to me very uncertain, not to say most uncertain). It will really be astonishing if he has the cleverness to place astrology in the highest seat of the human sciences, as he promises; I shall be waiting with great curiosity to see such a stunning novelty. As for Froidmont, though he appears to be a man of great intellect, I wish he had not committed what I think is a truly serious error, albeit extremely common; that is, to confute Copernicus's opinion, he first begins with sneering and scornful barbs against those who hold it to be true, then (more inappropriately) he wants to establish it primarily with the authority of Scripture, and finally he goes so far as to label it in that regard little less than heretical.

It seems to me one can prove very clearly that this manner of proceeding is far from laudable. For if I ask Froidmont whose works are the sun, the moon, the earth, the stars, their arrangement, and their motions, I think he will answer they are works of God; and if I ask from whose inspiration Holy Scripture derives, I know he will answer that it comes from the Holy Spirit, namely, again God. Thus, the world is the works, and the Scripture is the words, of the same God. Then let me ask him whether the Holy Spirit has ever used, spoken, or pronounced words which, in appearance, are very contrary to the truth, and whether this was done to accommodate the capacity of the people, who are for the most part very uncouth and incompetent. I am very sure he will answer, together with all sacred writers, that such is the habit of the Scripture; in hundreds of passages the latter puts forth (for the said reason) propositions which, taken in the literal meaning of the words, would not be mere heresies, but very serious blasphemies, by making God himself subject to anger, regret, forgetfulness, etc. However, suppose I ask him whether, to accommodate the capacity and belief of the same people, God has ever changed his works; or whether nature is God's inexorable minister, is deaf to human opinions and desires, and has always conserved and continues to conserve her ways regarding the motions, shapes, and locations of the parts of the universe. I am certain he will answer that the moon has always been spherical, although for a long time common people thought it was flat; in short, he will say that nothing is ever changed by nature to accommodate her works to the wishes and opinions of men. If this is so, why should we, in order to learn about the parts of the world, begin our investigations from the words rather than from the works of God? Is it perhaps less noble and lofty to work than to speak? If Froidmont or someone else had established that it is heretical to say the earth moves, and that demonstrations, observations, and necessary correspondences show it to move, in what sort of plot would he have gotten himself and the Holy Church? On the contrary, were we to give second place to Scripture, if the works were shown to be necessarily different from the literal meaning of the words, then this would in no way be prejudicial to Scripture; and if to accommodate popular abilities the latter has many times attributed the most false characteristics to God himself, why should it be required to limit itself to a very strict law when speaking of the sun and the earth, thus disregarding popular incapacity and refraining from attributing to these bodies properties contrary to those that exist in reality? If it were true that motion belongs to the earth and rest to the sun, no harm is done to Scripture, which speaks in accordance with what appears to the popular masses.

Many years ago, at the beginning of the uproar against Copernicus, I wrote a very long essay showing, largely by means of the authority of the Fathers, how great an abuse it is to want to use Holy Scripture so much when dealing with questions about natural phenomena, and how it would be most advisable to prohibit the involvement of Scripture in such disputes; when I am less troubled, I shall send you a copy. I say less troubled because at the moment I am about to go to Rome, summoned by the Holy Office, which has already suspended my *Dialogue*. From reliable sources I hear the Jesuit Fathers have managed to convince some very important persons that my book is execrable and more harmful to the Holy Church than the writings of Luther and Calvin. Thus I am sure it will be prohibited, despite the fact that to obtain the license I went personally to Rome and delivered it into the hands of the Master of the Sacred Palace; he examined it very minutely (changing, adding, and removing as much as he wanted), and after licensing it he also ordered it to be reviewed again here. This reviewer did not find anything to modify, and so, as a sign of having read and examined it most diligently, he resorted to changing some words; for example, in many places he said *universe* instead of *nature, title* instead of *attribute, sublime* mind in place of *divine*; and he asked to be excused by saying that he predicted I would be dealing with very bitter enemies and very angry persecutors, as indeed it followed. The publisher essays that so far this suspension has made him lose a profit of 2000 scudi, since not only could he have sold the thousand volumes he had already printed, but he could have reprinted twice as many. As for me, to my other troubles is added the following very serious one—namely, to be unable to pursue the completion of my other works (especially the one on motion), so as to publish them before I die.

I read with special pleasure Mr. Pierre Gassendi's Disquisition against Fludd's philosophy, as well as the Appendix on celestial observations. I was unable to observe Mercury or Venus in front of the sun because of rain; but in regard to their smallness, I have been certain of it for a long time, and I am glad that Mr. Gassendi has found this to be a fact. Please share this information with the said gentleman, to whom I send warm greetings, as I also do to the Reverend Father Mersenne. Finally, I kiss your hands with all my heart and pray for your happiness.

Florence, 15 January 1633
To You Very Illustrious Sir.
    Your Most Devout and Most Obliged Servant,
    Galileo Galilei.

Reports from the Fourth Deposition (June 21, 1633)[8]

Called personally to the hall of Congregations in the palace of the Holy Office in Rome, fully in the presence of the Reverend Father Commissary General of the Holy Office, assisted by the Reverend Father Prosecutor, etc.

Galileo Galilei, Florentine, mentioned previously, having sworn an oath to tell the truth, was asked by the Fathers the following:

Q: Whether he had anything to say.

A: I have nothing to say.

Q: Whether he holds or has held, and for how long, that the sun is the center of the world and the earth is not the center of the world but moves also with diurnal motion.

A: A long time ago, that is, before the decision of the Holy Congregation of the Index, and before I was issued that injunction, I was undecided and regarded the two opinions, those of Ptolemy and Copernicus, as disputable, because either the one or the other could be true in nature. But after the above-mentioned decision, assured by the prudence of the authorities, all my uncertainty stopped, and I held, as I still hold, as very true and undoubted Ptolemy's opinion, namely, the stability of the earth and the motion of the sun.

[8] Finocchiaro, 286–87.

Having been told that he is presumed to have held the said opinion after that time, from the manner and procedure in which the said opinion is discussed and defended in the book he published after that time, indeed from the very fact that he wrote and published the said book, therefore he was asked to freely tell the truth whether he holds or has held that opinion.

> A: In regard to my writing of the *Dialogue* already published, I did not do so because I held Copernicus's opinion to be true. Instead, deeming only to be doing a beneficial service, I explained the physical and astronomical reasons that can be advanced for one side and for the other; I tried to show that none of these, neither those in favor of this opinion or that, had the strength of a conclusive proof and that therefore to proceed with certainty one had to resort to the determination of more subtle doctrines, as one can see in many places in the *Dialogue*. So for my part I conclude that I do not hold and, after the determination of the authorities, I have not held the condemned opinion.

Having been told that from the book itself and the reasons advanced for the affirmative side, namely, that the earth moves and the sun is motionless, he is presumed, as it was stated, that he holds Copernicus's opinion, or at least that he held it at the time, therefore he was told that unless he decided to proffer the truth, one would have recourse to the remedies of the law and to appropriate steps against him.

> A: I do not hold this opinion of Copernicus, and I have not held it after being ordered by injunction to abandon it. For the rest, here I am in your hands; do as you please.

And he was told to tell the truth; otherwise one would have recourse to torture.

> A: I am here to obey, but I have not held this opinion after the determination was made, as I said.

And since nothing else could be done for the execution of the decision, after he signed he was sent to his place.

I, Galileo Galilei, have testified as above.

Further Reading

The primary sources consist of the twenty volumes of *Le Opere di Galileo Galilei, Edizione Nazionale*, edited by Antonio Favaro (Florence: Barbera, 1890–1909; reprinted 1929–39 and 1964–66). The following English translations are available: *On Motion*, translated by I. E. Drabkin (Madison: University of Wisconsin Press, 1960); *On Mechanics*, translated by Stillman Drake (Madison: University of Wisconsin Press, 1960); *Sidereus Nuncias, or The Sidereal Messenger*, translated by Albert van Helden (Chicago: University of Chicago Press, 1989); *Discoveries and Opinions of Galileo: Including the Starry Messenger (1610), Letter to the Grand Duchess Christina (1615), and Excerpts from Letters on Sunspots (1613), the Assayer (1623),* translated with an introduction and notes by Stillman Drake (Garden City, NY, Doubleday, 1957); *Dialogue Concerning the Two Chief World Systems: Ptolemaic and Copernican,* 2d ed., translated by Stillman Drake (Berkeley: University of California Press, 1967); *Galileo's Logical Treatises: A Translation, with Notes and Commentary, of His Appropriated Latin Questions on Aristotle's Posterior Analytics,* by William A. Wallace (Boston: Kluwer Academic Publishers, 1992). The best translation of Galileo's 1638 *Dialogues Concerning Two New Sciences* is considered to be Stillman Drake's: *Discourses on the Two New Sciences* (Madison: University of Wisconsin, 1974). An important documentary history with an authoritative introduction is *The Galileo Affair: A Documentary History,* edited by Maurice A. Finocchiaro (Berkeley: University of California Press, 1989). Other works of interest are Richard J. Blackwell, *Galileo, Bellarmine, and the Bible* (Notre Dame, IN: University of Notre Dame Press, 1991); Stillman Drake, *Galileo* (Oxford: Oxford University Press, 1980); Rivka Feldhay, *Galileo and the Church: Political Inquisition or Critical Dialogue?* (Cambridge: Cambridge University Press, 1995); James Reston, *Galileo: A Life* (New York: HarperCollins, 1994); and David B. Wilson, "Galileo's Religion *Versus* the Church's Science? Rethinking the History of Science and Religion," *Physics in Perspective* 1 (1999): 65–84.

2 Johannes Kepler
(1571–1630)

Introduction

Johannes Kepler, according to astrophysicist Marcelo Gleiser, is the most fascinating figure in the whole of science. Many colorful and tragic stories surround the life and career of this intellectual giant who, late in life, was called upon to defend his own mother, a woman as stubborn as she was naïve, against the charge of witchcraft. But it is in his religious fervor that Kepler is the most fascinating. A poor boy without position or patronage, a prodigy who aspired to be but a humble prelate, a Protestant assigned to teach in the Catholic city of Graz, Kepler was turned by his teachers to the study of mathematics and brought to astronomy by his "longing for the harmonies," so unlike the discords of earth. Plato first spoke of the "music of the spheres" in *The Republic*, but the idea of a natural affinity between astronomy and music is even older. Pythagoras, the 6th century BCE Greek mathematician, believed that the cosmic order obeys the same mathematical rules and proportions as the tones on a musical scale. Kepler, an ardent Platonist and Pythagorean both, returns repeatedly in his book *The Harmony of the World* (1619) to the sweet music of the spheres "that imitates God." He may have regarded himself as a Christian priest of God in the temple of nature, but his deepest passion, like the Greeks', was for elegantly simple mathematical laws that form the basis of all natural phenomena. He thought he would find such mathematical relations in the motions of the different planets, and was convinced that in some sense they were all moving to a single cosmic harmony. Inspired by the Copernican revolution, which he accepted immediately, excited by the discoveries of Galileo, and eventually coming into possession of the Danish astronomer Tycho Brahe's copious observations and lifelong research, Kepler did succeed in discovering three famous laws of the solar system.

In Kepler we see a clear case of scientific data directly shaped by religious beliefs. The Trinity was the dominant doctrine in Kepler's version of Christianity and Trinitarian formulas and triangles abound in his writings. In his first book, *The Secret of the Universe* (1596), the Trinitarian formula produced a marked mathematical mysticism. Kepler recounts how on July 19, 1595, as he was showing his class the way the great conjunctions of Saturn and Jupiter occur successively eight zodiacal signs apart, and gradually pass from one trine to another, he inscribed within a circle many triangles, or quasi-triangles, such that the end of one was the beginning of the next. "In this manner," he pronounced, "a smaller circle was outlined by the points where the lines of the triangle crossed each other." Comparing these two circles, he saw the inner one as Jupiter and the outer circle as Saturn.

As it developed, Kepler's singular—some would say obsessive—preoccupation with the Trinity of Father, Son, and Holy Spirit, was played out in the language, the symbols, and the concepts of his science, suffusing it with a religious glow. The harmony of the heavens and the music of the spheres were no mere metaphors for Kepler. Each planet had its own melody and their perfect harmony gave to the ellipses he studied a splendid music. In *The Harmony of the World* Kepler assigned specific musical notes to the spheres and derived the heliocentric distances of the planets and their periods from considerations of musical harmony. In this work we find his third law, relating the periods of the planets to their mean orbital radii.

Replete with religious incantations, hymns, and prayers, the most intriguing part of *The Harmony of the World* is Kepler's idiosyncratic theology of the Trinity. He physicalizes all three Persons: God the Father is symbolized by the central sun, God the Son by the surface of the spherical universe, and God the Holy Spirit by the intermediate space. The sun, he said, is the most resplendent body in the universe, the very center, and itself an image of the living God, the Father. Earth, like the Son, is unique, the planet with the central orbit. The Spirit is the force from the sun in intervening space. Therefore, he explained, "the sphere possesses a threefold quality; surface, central point, intervening space. The same is also true of the motionless universe: the fixed stars, the sun, and the aura of intermediate aether; and it is also true of the Trinity: the Father, Son, and Holy Ghost." With this as its sacred foundation, Kepler's theory of forces in the universe was born.

Kepler's cosmos is an extremely organic, ordered whole, where the laws of nature are not yet the impersonal abstractions they would become by the end of the seventeenth century. Beginning with the seemingly gratuitous assumption that the universe resembles the Trinity, and throwing in a lot of math, Kepler attempted to calculate the density of the sun, the sphere of the fixed stars, and the intermediate ether. His religious faith inspired a scientific theory that entailed an equal division of matter between these three principal parts. Furthermore, there was no strict division between religious writing and scientific writing for Kepler. Possessed by a Pythagorean concern with geometrical principles and a Christian conviction that the universe was the Lord's own creation, Kepler made the audacious claim that in his astronomical calculations he was thinking God's own thoughts after him. Christianity was not merely a personal psychological influence on Kepler; it prescribed the very way in which science was to be written and conceptualized, and it proposed research questions and ways to solve them. Nearly a hundred years later, Newton would prove Kepler's laws from his own theories of mechanics and gravitation.

Since geometry had a mystical meaning for Kepler, it is no wonder that he sought to find how the five Platonic solids could nest one within another to determine the spacings of the six known planets in the solar system. It gave him undisguised religious ecstasy to think that the five known equal-faced geometrical shapes could be selected in such an order that they would fit tightly between the crystalline spheres of the six planets known at that time. The relative spacings of the spheres according to the cube (six faces), pyramid (four), dodecahedron (twelve), icosahedron (twenty), and octahedron (eight) were deeply indicative of the way in which "God, like a master builder, has laid the foundation of the world according to law and order," as Kepler wrote in his *Conversation with Galileo's Starry Messenger.* "Geometry, which before the origin of things was coeternal with the divine mind and is God himself," he added in *The Harmony of the World,* "supplied God with patterns for the creation of the world, and passed over to Man along with the image of God."[1]

Kepler was almost driven mad, he reported, trying to calculate the orbit of Mars according to circular motion. For centuries the circle had been a symbol of heavenly perfection. When he finally broke with the perfect circle and realized that the orbit of Mars was an ellipse—leading to a whole new model of planetary orbits—it was a discovery propelled as much by faith as by empirical evidence. For if an ellipse could be thought of as a combination of a circle that symbolizes spiritual perfection and a straight line that represents the material realm, Kepler reasoned, he could regard the elliptical orbit as only slightly veering from the ideal circularity—a necessary concession to the material dimension of the planets. Emanating from the sun was a real physical force, he insisted, that swayed the planetary motions. Even though Newton would later find this idea remarkably stimulating for his work on gravitation, Kepler worried at the time that he had laid a "monstrous egg." He never quite abandoned the neat, nested cosmos whose secret harmony, his faith insisted, was somehow locked within the shapes and periods of planetary motions.

---

[1] Johannes Kepler, *The Harmony of the World,* trans. E. J. Aiton, A. M. Duncan, and J. V. Field (Philadelphia: American Philosophical Society, 1997), 304.

Like Galileo, Kepler believed that the "book of Scripture" and the "book of Nature" were both so important that no conflict could be allowed between them. The critique of naïve literalism was part and parcel of the Reformation, no matter how much Protestants (and Catholics, too) wanted to stress the authority of Scripture. Kepler was only echoing Calvin's own sentiment when he claimed that Scripture was addressed to both "scientific and ignorant men," so that no scientific facts were literally imperiled by scriptural stories. The ignorance of men had to be taken into account, and that was why some biblical stories, like Joshua's commanding the sun to remain still, should be accepted as metaphor.

Theologically, Kepler was suspected of heresy. Devoutly religious in a time of social and political turbulence, he was no more conventional in his theology than in his scientific investigations. A Lutheran, Kepler disagreed with Lutheran orthodoxy and made concessions to both Catholics and Calvinists. On the matter of Communion, Catholics believed that "transubstantiation" physically transformed the wafer and wine into the body and blood of Christ. Lutherans explained that "consubstantiation" occurred: Christ's real body and blood were present even though the bread and wine looked unchanged, because, as divine, Christ's body and blood become "ubiquitous" and are everywhere present. Calvinists held that the bread and wine remained mere bread and wine but provided true communion with Christ, who is in heaven with the Father. Kepler got into trouble for not embracing the "ubiquity" doctrine of his fellow Lutherans. But even as he leaned toward the Calvinist account, he repudiated the Calvinist doctrine of predestination. He could not accept, for example, that pagans who had never heard of Christ and therefore could not possibly believe in him would be damned by a loving God.

In the end, it was in the pursuit of astronomy that Kepler found his own genuine pathway toward spiritual fulfillment. As a young man in 1595, recalling his disappointment at not becoming a theologian, he had written to his former teacher Mästlin in Tubingen that "I had the intention of being a theologian. For a long time I was restless: but now see how God is, by my endeavors, also glorified in astronomy."[2] For the next thirty-five years, until his death, Kepler's scientific endeavors only strengthened his conviction that "Our piety is the deeper, the greater is our awareness of creation and its grandeur."[3]

✎ Kepler's Contribution to Science

Johannes Kepler discovered three laws of planetary motion: Each planet moves in an elliptical orbit with the sun at a focus of the ellipse; the line between the sun and any planet marks out equal areas in equal times; the square of the time for a planet to travel one orbit is proportional to the cube of its mean distance from the sun. He also coined the word "satellite."

Kepler in His Own Words

From The Secret of the Universe *(1596)*[4]

It was matter which God created in the beginning; and if we know the definition of matter, I think it will be fairly clear why God created matter and not any other thing in the beginning. I say that what God intended was quantity. To achieve it he needed everything which pertains to the essence of matter; and quantity is a form of matter, in virtue of its being matter, and the source of its definition. Now God decided that quantity should exist before all other things so that there should be a means of comparing a curved with a straight line. For in this one respect Nicholas of Cusa and others seem to me divine, that they attached so much importance

---

[2] Carola Baumgardt, *Johannes Kepler: Life and Letters* (New York: Philosophical Library, 1951), 31.

[3] My translation from the dedication of Kepler's first book, *Mysterium Cosmographicum* (Tübingen, 1596).

[4] Johannes Kepler, *Mysterium Cosmographicum: The Secret of the Universe*, trans. A. M. Duncan, intro. by E. J. Aiton (New York: Abaris, 1981), 93–95.

to the relationship between a straight and a curved line and dared to liken a curve to God, a straight line to his creatures; and those who tried to compare the Creator to his creatures, God to Man, and divine judgments to human judgments did not perform much more valuable a service than those who tried to compare a curve with a straight line, a circle with a square.

And although under the power of God this alone would have been enough to constitute the appropriateness of quantities, and the nobility of a curve, yet to this was also added something else which is far greater: the image of God the Three in One in a spherical surface, that is of the Father in the center, the Son in the surface, and the Spirit in the regularity of the relationship between the point and the circumference. For what Nicholas of Cusa attributed to the circle, others as it happens have attributed to the globe; but I reserve it solely for a spherical surface. Nor can I be persuaded that any kind of curve is more noble than a spherical surface, or more perfect. For a globe is more than a spherical surface, and mingled with straightness, but which alone its interior is filled. Furthermore a circle exists only on a flat plane; that is, only if a spherical surface or a globe is cut by a flat plane, can a circle exist. Hence it may be seen that many properties are imparted both to the globe by the cube, and to the circle by the square, that is from an inferior source, on account of the straightness of the diameter.

But after all why were the distinctions between curved and straight, and the nobility of a curve, among God's intentions when he displayed the universe? Why indeed? Unless because by a most perfect Creator it was absolutely necessary that a most beautiful work should be produced. "For it neither is nor was right" (as Cicero in his book on the universe quotes from Plato's *Timaeus*) "that he who is the best should make anything except the most beautiful." Since, then, the Creator conceived the Idea of the universe in his mind (we speak in human fashion, so that being men we may understand), and it is the Idea of that which is prior, indeed, as has just been said, of that which is best, so that the Form of the future creation may itself be the best: it is evident that by those laws which God himself in his goodness prescribes for himself, the only thing of which he could adopt the idea for establishing the universe is his own essence, which can be considered as twofold, inasmuch as it is excellent and divine: first in itself, being one in essence but three in person, and secondly by comparison with created things.

This pattern, this Idea, he wished to imprint on the universe, so that it should become as good and as fine as possible; and so that it might become capable of accepting this Idea, he created quantity; and the wisest of Creators devised quantities so that their whole essence, so to speak, depended on these two characteristics, straightness and curvedness, of which curvedness was to represent God for us in the two aspects which have just been stated. For it must not be supposed that these characteristics which are so appropriate for the portrayal of God came into existence randomly, or that God did not have precisely that in mind but created quantity in matter for different reasons and with a different intention, and that the contrast between straight and curved, and the resemblance to God, came into existence subsequently of their own accord, as if by accident.

It is more probable that at the beginning of all things it was with a definite intention that the straight and the curved were chosen by God to delineate the divinity of the Creator in the universe; and that it was in order that those should come into being that quantities existed, and that it was in order that quantity should have its place that first of all matter was created.

Now let us see in what way the best of Creators used these quantities in the structure of the universe; and what is likely, by our reckoning, to have been made by the Creator; so that thereafter we may search for it, both in the ancient and in the new hypotheses, and award the palm to the one within which it is found.

That the whole universe is enclosed by a spherical shape has been thoroughly well argued by Aristotle, drawing arguments among others from the nobility of a spherical surface; and by these arguments even now Copernicus's outermost sphere, that of the fixed stars, although it is without motion, preserves the same shape, and takes the Sun, as its center, into its innermost recess. On the other hand the circular motion of the stars is evidence that the other orbits are round. Yet there is no lack of further proof that curvature was used in the pattern of the universe. Although we see three kinds of quantity in the universe, the shape, number, and extension of objects, so far we find the curved only in shape. For there is no measure of extension, from the fact that like is inscribed within like (sphere within sphere, circle within circle) about the same center, or touches it at all points, or at none; and the spherical itself, since it is alone and unique in its own kind of quantity, cannot be subject to any other number but three. But yet if at the Creation God had taken cognizance only of the curved, except for the Sun in the center, which was the image of the Father, the Sphere of the Fixed Stars, or the Mosaic waters, at the circumference, which was the image of the Son, and the heavenly air which fills all parts, or the space and firmament, which was the image of the Spirit— then, except for these, I say, nothing would exist in this cosmic structure. But in fact as there are innumerable fixed stars, and the well established tally of planets, and the irregular sizes of the heavens, we must of necessity seek the causes of them all in straightness, unless perhaps we suppose that God has made anything in the universe at random, even though excellent reasons were available. Of that nobody will persuade me; and that is my opinion even on the fixed stars, although their position is the most disordered of all, and looks to us like seed scattered indiscriminately.

Letter to the Baron von Herberstein (May 15, 1596)[5]

What I promised seven months ago, a work which, according to the testimony of the scholars, is beautiful and appealing and by far superior to the yearly calendar—this I at last bring before the high circle, illustrious gentlemen; a work which, though small in size and accomplished with not too much trouble, yet deals with a

---

[5] Baumgardt, 32–35.

most wonderful object . . . two thousand years ago Pythagoras[6] had already tried his hand at it. Does one desire something new? For the first time I make this subject generally known to mankind. Does one desire something of importance? Nothing is greater and larger than the universe. Does one desire something of dignity? Nothing is more precious, nothing more beautiful than our bright Temple of God. Does one want to gain mystical insight? Nothing in nature is or was more mysterious and more deeply hidden. There is only one reason why my subject will not interest all and everybody: its value will not appeal to the thoughtless. Here is treated the Book of Nature which is so highly praised by the Holy Scriptures. Paul presents it to the heathens so that they may see God in it just as the sun can be observed in water or a mirror. Why should we Christians take less pleasure in contemplating this since it is our task to honor God in the right way, to worship and admire Him? Our worship is all the more deep, the more clearly we recognize the creation and its greatness. Indeed how many songs did David sing, the true servant to the true God! He received the idea for his songs from the admiring observation of the skies. "The heavens declare the glory of God," he says. . . .

I do not want to stress that I present important evidence of the creation of the universe—an evidence which has been denied by the philosophers. Nevertheless here we see how God, like a human architect, approached the founding of the world according to order and rule and measured everything in such a manner, that one might think not art took nature for an example but God Himself, in the course of His creation took the art of man as an example, though man was to appear only later on.[7]

---

[6] According to Simplicius's commentary on Aristotle's *De caelo* (book II, 9, 290b, 291a), ed. Simon Karsten (1865), 208b f, the Greek philosopher Pythagoras of Samos (about 500 B.C.) spoke of a harmony of heavenly spheres. He and even more his followers about 400 B.C. put special emphasis on the use of mathematics in the exploration of nature. —CB.

[7] It is an old religious idea expressed especially graphically in a famous Jewish Sabbath song that man was the last object of God's creation but he was first in his plan of the creation. —CB.

Must one measure the value of the heavenly object with dimes as one does food? But, pray, one will ask, what is the good of the knowledge of nature, of all astronomy, to a hungry stomach? . . . Painters are allowed to go on with their work because they give joy to the eyes, musicians because they bring joy to the ears, though they are of no other use to us. . . . What insensibility, what stupidity, to deny the spirit an honest pleasure but permit it to the eyes and ears! He who fights against this joy fights against nature. . . . Should . . . the kind Creator who brought forth nature out of nothing . . . deprive the spirit of man, the master of creation and the Lord's own image, of every heavenly delight? Do we ask what profit the little bird hopes for in singing? We know that singing in itself is a joy to him because he was created for singing. We must not ask therefore why the human spirit takes such trouble to find out the secrets of the skies. Our creator has given us a spirit in addition to the senses, for another reason than merely to provide a living for ourselves. Many types of living creatures, in despite of the unreasonableness of their souls, are capable of providing for themselves more ably than we. But our Creator wishes us to push ahead from the appearance of the things which we see with our eyes to the first causes of their being in growth, although this may be of no immediate practical avail to us. The other creatures and the body of man are kept alive by taking food and drink. But man's soul is something quite different from the other part of man, and the soul is kept alive, enriched and grows by that food called knowledge. The man who does not long for these things is therefore more of a corpse than a living being. Now nature sees to it that there is no shortage of food for the living beings. We are therefore well justified in saying that the variety of the phenomena of nature is so great, the hidden treasures in the dome of the universe so rich, that nature should never run short in material for the human spirit, that the human spirit . . . ought never come to rest, but that there should be always in this world a workshop open for the training of man's spirit.

Letter from Graz (April 9 and 10, 1599)[8]

... To God there are, in the whole material world, material laws, figures and relations of special excellency and of the most appropriate order. ... Let us therefore not try to discover more of the heavenly and immaterial world than God has revealed to us. Those laws are within the grasp of the human mind; God wanted us to recognize them by creating us after his own image so that we could share in his own thoughts. For what is there in the human mind besides figures and magnitudes? It is only these which we can apprehend in the right way, and if piety allows us to say so, our understanding is in this respect of the same kind as the divine, at least as far as we are able to grasp something of it in our mortal life. Only fools fear that we make man godlike in doing so; for the divine counsels are impenetrable, but not his material creation.

From New Astronomy (1609)[9]

Introduction

There are, however, many more people who are moved by piety to withhold assent from Copernicus, fearing that falsehood might be charged against the Holy Spirit speaking in the scriptures if we say that the earth is moved and the sun stands still.[10]

But let them consider that since we acquire most of our information, both in quality and quantity, through the sense of sight, it

---

[8] Baumgardt, 50.

[9] Johannes Kepler, *New Astronomy*, trans. William H. Donahue (Cambridge: Cambridge University Press, 1992), 59–66, 385–386.

[10] The following arguments on the interpretation of scripture were to become the most widely read of Kepler's writings. They were often reprinted from the seventeenth century on, and translated into modern languages. Indeed, this part of the Introduction was the only work of Kepler's to appear in English before 1700. —*WHD*

is impossible for us to abstract our speech from this ocular sense. Thus, many times each day we speak in accordance with the sense of sight, although we are quite certain that the truth of the matter is otherwise. This verse of Virgil furnishes an example:

> We are carried from the port, and the land and cities recede.[11]

Thus, when we emerge from the narrow part of some valley, we say that a great plain is opening itself out before us.

Thus Christ said to Peter, "Lead forth on high,"[12] as if the sea were higher than the shores. It does seem so to the eyes, but optics shows the cause of this fallacy. Christ was only making use of the common idiom, which nonetheless arose from this visual deception.

Thus, we call the rising and setting of the stars "ascent" and "descent," though at the same time that we say the sun ascends, others say it descends. See the *Astronomiae pars optica* Ch. 10, 327.[13]

Thus, the Ptolemaic astronomers even now say that the planets are stationary when they are seen to stay near the same fixed stars for several days, even though they think the planets are then really moving downwards in a straight line, or upwards away from the earth.

Thus writers of all nations use the word "solstice," even though they in fact deny that the sun stands still.

Thus there has not yet been anyone so doggedly Copernican as to avoid saying that the sun is entering Cancer or Leo, even though he wishes to signify that the earth is entering Capricorn or Aquarius. And there are other like examples.

Now the holy scriptures, too, when treating common things (concerning which it is not their purpose to instruct humanity), speak with humans in the human manner, in order to be understood by

---

[11] *Aeneid* III.72. This line was also quoted by Copernicus, *De revolutionibus* I.8. —*Trans.*

[12] Luke 5:4. The Latin *altum* can mean either "high" or "deep." However, Kepler cannot have been unaware that the original Greek verse unambiguously has the latter meaning, and hence must be charged with making a rather silly distortion in order to prove a point. —*Trans.*

[13] In *K[epler] G[esammelte] W[erke]* 2, 281. —WHD.

them. They make use of what is generally acknowledged, in order to weave in other things more lofty and divine.

No wonder, then, if scripture also speaks in accordance with human perception when the truth of things is at odds with the senses, whether or not humans are aware of this. Who is unaware that the allusion in Psalm 19 is poetical? Here, under the image of the sun, are sung the spreading of the Gospel and even the sojourn of Christ the Lord in this world on our behalf, and in the singing the sun is said to emerge from the tabernacle of the horizon like a bridegroom from his marriage bed, exuberant as a strong man for the race. Which Virgil imitates thus:

Aurora leaving Tithonus's saffron-coloured bed[14]

(The Hebrew poetry was, of course, earlier.)

The psalmodist was aware that the sun does not go forth from the horizon as from a tabernacle (even though it may appear so to the eyes). On the other hand, he considered the sun to move for the precise reason that it appears so to the eyes. In either case, he expressed it so because in either case it appeared so to the eyes. He should not be judged to have spoken falsely in either case, for the perception of the eyes also has its truth, well suited to the psalmodist's more hidden aim, the adumbration of the Gospel and also of the Son of God. Likewise, Joshua makes mention of the valleys against which the sun and moon moved,[15] because when he was at the Jordan it appeared so to him. Yet each writer was in perfect control of his meaning. David was describing the magnificence of God made manifest (and Syracides with him), which he expressed so as to exhibit them to the eyes, and possibly also for the sake of a mystical sense spelled out through these visible things. Joshua meant that the sun should be held back in its place in the middle of the sky for an entire day with respect to the sense of his eyes, since for other people during the same interval of time it would remain beneath the earth.

[14] *Aeneid* IV.585. —WHD.
[15] Joshua 10:12ff. —WHD.

But thoughtless persons pay attention only to the verbal contradiction, "the sun stood still" versus "the earth stood still," not considering that this contradiction can only arise in an optical and astronomical context, and does not carry over into common usage. Nor are these thoughtless ones willing to see that Joshua was simply praying that the mountains not remove the sunlight from him, which prayer he expressed in words conforming to the sense of sight, as it would be quite inappropriate to think, at that moment, of astronomy and of visual errors. For if someone had admonished him that the sun doesn't really move against the valley of Ajalon, but only appears to do so, wouldn't Joshua have exclaimed that he only asked for the day to be lengthened, however that might be done? He would therefore have replied in the same way if anyone had begun to present him with arguments for the sun's perpetual rest and the earth's motion.

Now God easily understood from Joshua's words what he meant, and responded by stopping the motion of the earth, so that the sun might appear to him to stop. For the gist of Joshua's petition comes to this, that it might appear so to him, whatever the reality might meanwhile be. Indeed, that this appearance should come about was not vain and purposeless, but quite conjoined with the desired effect.

But see Chapter 10 of the *Astronomiae pars optica*, where you will find reasons why, to absolutely all men, the sun appears to move and not the earth: it is because the sun appears small and the earth large, and also because, owing to its apparent slowness, the sun's motion is perceived, not by sight, but by reasoning alone, through its change of distance from the mountains over a period of time. It is therefore impossible for a previously uninformed reason to imagine anything but that the earth, along with the arch of heaven set over it, is like a great house, immobile, in which the sun, so small in stature, travels from one side to the other like a bird flying in the air.

What absolutely all men imagine, the first line of holy scripture presents. "In the beginning," says Moses, "God created the heaven and the earth," because it is these two parts that chiefly present themselves to the sense of sight. It is as though Moses were to say to man, "This whole worldly edifice that you see, light above dark and widely spread out below, upon which you are standing and by which you are roofed over, has been created by God."

In another passage, Man is asked whether he has learned how to seek out the height of heaven above, or the depths of the earth below,[16] because to the ordinary man both appear to extend through equally infinite spaces. Nevertheless, there is no one in his right mind who, upon hearing these words, would use them to limit astronomers' diligence either in showing the contemptible smallness of the earth in comparison with the heavens, or in investigating astronomical distances. For these words do not concern measurements arrived at by reasoning. Rather, they concern real exploration, which is utterly impossible for the human body, fixed upon the land and drawing upon the free air. Read all of Chapter 38 of Job, and compare it with matters discussed in astronomy and in physics.

Suppose someone were to assert, from Psalm 24, that the earth is founded upon rivers, in order to support the novel and absurd philosophical conclusion that the earth floats upon rivers. Would it not be correct to say to him that he should regard the Holy Spirit as a divine messenger, and refrain from wantonly dragging Him into physics class? For in that passage the psalmodist intends nothing but what men already know and experience daily, namely, that the land, raised on high after the separation of the waters, has great rivers flowing through it and seas surrounding it. Not surprisingly, the same figure of speech is adopted in another passage, where the Israelites sing that they were seated upon the waters of Babylon,[17] that is, by the riverside, or on the banks of the Euphrates and Tigris.

If this is easily accepted, why can it not also be accepted that in other passages usually cited in opposition to the earth's motion we should likewise turn our eyes from physics to the aims of scripture?

[16] Jeremiah 31:37. —*WHD*.
[17] Psalm 137. —*WHD*.

A generation passes away (says Ecclesiastes),[18] and a generation comes, but the earth stands forever. Does it seem here as if Solomon wanted to argue with the astronomers? No; rather, he wanted to warn men of their own mutability, while the earth, home of the human race, remains always the same, the motion of the sun perpetually returns to the same place, the wind blows in a circle and returns to its starting point, rivers flow from their sources into the sea, and from the sea return to the sources, and finally, as these men perish, others are born. Life's tale is ever the same; there is nothing new under the sun.

You do not hear any physical dogma here. The message is a moral one, concerning something self-evident and seen by all eyes but seldom pondered. Solomon therefore urges us to ponder. Who is unaware that the earth is always the same? Who does not see the sun return daily to its place of rising, rivers perennially flowing towards the sea, the winds returning in regular alternation, and men succeeding one another? But who really considers that the same drama of life is always being played, only with different characters, and that not a single thing in human affairs is new? So Solomon, by mentioning what is evident to all, warns of that which almost everyone wrongly neglects.

It is said, however, that Psalm 104, in its entirety, is a physical discussion, since the whole of it is concerned with physical matters, and in it, God is said to have "founded the earth upon its stability, that it not be laid low unto the ages of ages."[19] But in fact, nothing could be farther from the psalmodist's intention than speculation about physical causes. For the whole thing is an exultation upon the greatness of God, who made all these things: the author has composed a hymn to God the Creator, in which he treats the world in order, as it appears to the eyes.

If you consider carefully, you will see that it is a commentary upon the six days of creation in Genesis. For in the latter, the first

---

[18] Ecclesiastes 1:4. —*WHD.*

[19] The Latin of the Vulgate, quoted by Kepler, differs markedly from the Greek (and hence from most English translations) here. —*WHD.*

three days are given to the separation of the regions: first, the region of light from the exterior darkness; second, the waters from the waters by the interposition of an extended region; and third, the land from the seas, where the earth is clothed with plants and shrubs. The last three days, on the other hand, are devoted to the filling of the regions so distinguished; the fourth, of the heavens; the fifth, of the seas and the air; and the sixth, of the land. And in this psalm there are likewise the same number of distinct parts, analogous to the works of the six days.

In the second verse, he enfolds the Creator with the vestment of light, first of created things, and the work of the first day.

The second part begins with the third verse, and concerns the water above the heavens, the extended region of the heavens, and atmospheric phenomena that the psalmodist ascribes to the waters above the heavens, namely, clouds, winds, tornadoes, and lightening.

The third part begins with the sixth verse, and celebrates the earth as the foundation of the things being considered. The psalmodist relates everything to the earth and to the things that live on it, because, in the judgment of six, the chief parts of the world are two: heaven and earth. He therefore considers that for so many ages now the earth has neither sunk nor cracked apart nor tumbled down, yet no one has certain knowledge of what it is founded upon.

He does not wish to teach things of which men are ignorant, but to recall to mind something they neglect, namely, God's greatness and potency in a creation of such magnitude,[20] so solid and stable. If an astronomer teaches that the earth is carried through the heavens, he is not spurning what the psalmodist says here, nor does he contradict human experience. For it is still true that the land, the work of God the architect, has not toppled as our buildings usually do, consumed by age and rot; that it has not slumped to one side; that the dwelling places of living things have not been set in disarray; that the mountains and coasts have stood firm, unmoved against the blast of wind and wave, as they were

---

[20] Cf. Virgil, *Aeneid*, 1.33. —*WHD*.

from the beginning. And then the psalmodist adds a beautiful sketch of the separation of the waters by the continents, and adorns his account by adding springs and the amenities that springs and crags provide for bird and beast. He also does not fail to mention the adorning of the earth's surface, included by Moses among the works of the third day, although the psalmodist derives it from its prior cause, namely, a humidification arising in the heavens, and embellishes his account by bringing to mind the benefits accruing from that adornment for the nurture and pleasure of humans and for the lairs of the beasts.

The fourth part begins with verse 20, and celebrates the work of the fourth day, the sun and the moon, but chiefly the benefit that the division of times brings to humans and other living things. It is this benefit that is his subject matter: it is clear that he is not writing as an astronomer here.

If he were, he would not fail to mention the five planets, than whose motion nothing is more admirable, nothing more beautiful, and nothing a better witness to the Creator's wisdom, for those who take note of it.

The fifth part, in verse 26, concerns the work of the fifth day, where He fills the sea with fish and ornaments it with sea voyages.

The sixth is added, though obscurely, in verse 28, and concerns the animals living on land, created on the sixth day. At the end in conclusion, he declares the general goodness of God in sustaining all things and creating new things. So everything the psalmodist said of the world relates to living things. He tells nothing that is not generally acknowledged, because his purpose was to praise things that are known, not to seek out the unknown. It was his wish to invite men to consider the benefits accruing to them from each of these works of the six days.

I, too, implore my reader, when he departs from the temple and enters astronomical studies, not to forget the divine goodness conferred upon men, to the consideration of which the psalmodist chiefly invites. I hope that, with me, he will praise and celebrate the Creator's wisdom and greatness, which I unfold for him in the more perspicacious explanation of the world's form, the investigation of causes, and the detection of errors of vision. Let him not only extol the Creator's divine beneficence in His concern for the well-being of all living things, expressed in the firmness and stability of the earth, but also acknowledge His wisdom expressed in its motion, at once so well hidden and so admirable.

But whoever is too stupid to understand astronomical science, or too weak to believe Copernicus without affecting his faith, I would advise him that, having dismissed astronomical studies and having damned whatever philosophical opinions he pleases, he mind his own business and betake himself home to scratch in his own dirt patch, abandoning this wandering about the world. He should raise his eyes (his only means of vision) to this visible heaven and with his whole heart burst forth in giving thanks and praising God the Creator. He can be sure that he worships God no less than the astronomer, to whom God has granted the more penetrating vision of the mind's eye, and an ability and desire to celebrate his God above those things he has discovered.

So much for the authority of holy scripture. As for the opinions of the pious on these matters of nature, I have just one thing to say: while in theology it is authority that carries the most weight, in philosophy it is reason. Therefore, Lactantius is pious, who denied that the earth is round, Augustine is pious, who, though admitting the roundness, denied the antipodes, and the Inquisition nowadays is pious, which, though allowing the earth's smallness, denies its motion. To me, however, the truth is more pious still, and (with all due respect for the Doctors of the Church) I prove philosophically not only that the earth is round, not only that it is inhabited all the way around at the antipodes, not only that it is contemptibly small, but also that it is carried along among the stars.

❧

The sun is a magnetic body, and rotates in its space

Concerning that power that is closely attached to, and draws, the bodies of the planets, we have already said how it is formed, how it is akin to light, and what it is in its metaphysical being. Next, we shall contemplate the deeper nature of its source, shown by the outflowing *species* (or archetype). For it may appear that there lies hidden in the body of the sun a sort of divinity, which may be compared to our soul, from which flows that *species* driving the planets around, just as from the soul of someone throwing pebbles a *species* of motion comes to inhere in the pebbles thrown by him, even when he who threw them removes his hand from them. And to those who proceed soberly, other reflections will soon be provided.

The power that is extended from the sun to the planets moves them in a circular course around the immovable body of the sun. This cannot happen, or be conceived in thought, in any other way than this, that the power traverses the same path along which it carries the other planets. This has been observed to some extent in catapults and other violent motions. Thus, Fracastoro[21] and others, relying on a story told by the most ancient Egyptians, spoke with little probability when they said that some of the planets perchance would have their orbits deflected gradually beyond the poles of the world, and thus afterwards would move in a path opposite to the rest and to their modern course. For it is much more likely that the bodies of the planets are always borne in that direction in which the power emanating from the sun tends.

But this *species* is immaterial, proceeding from its body out to this distance without the passing of any time, and is in all other respects like light. Therefore, it is not only required by the nature of the *species*, but likely in itself owing to this kinship with light, that along with the particles of its body or source it too is divided up, and when any particle of the solar body moves towards some part of the world, the particle of the immaterial *species* that from the beginning of creation corresponded to that particle of the

---

[21] Hieronymus Fracastorius, *Homocentrica,* Venice 1538, Sect. 3 Cap. 8. In this chapter, which bears the title, "Cur solis declinatio minuatur" (why the sun's declination changes), Fracastoro refers, in support of his remarkable opinion, to information received from the Egyptians by Herodotus and Pomponius Mela. — *JK.* (Citation from *K[epler] G[esammelte] W[erke]* 3, 468. —*WHD*).

body also always moves towards the same part. If this were not so, it would not be a *species*, and would come down from the body in curved rather than straight lines.

Since the *species* is moved in a circular course, in order thereby to confer motion upon the planets, the body of the sun, or source, must move with it, not, of course, from space to space in the world—for I have said, with Copernicus, that the body of the sun remains in the centre of the world—but upon its centre or axis, both immobile, its parts moving from place to place, while the whole body remains in the same place.

From Conversation with Galileo's Sidereal Messenger *(1610)*[22]

Geometry is unique and eternal, and it shines in the mind of God. The share of it which has been granted to man is one of the reasons why he is the image of God. Now in geometry the most perfect class of figures, after the sphere, consists of the five Euclidean solids. They constitute the very pattern and model according to which this planetary world of ours was apportioned. Suppose then that there is an unlimited number of other worlds. They will be either unlike ours or like it. You would not say, "like it." For what is the use of an unlimited number of worlds, if every single one of them contains all of perfection within itself? . . . Briefly, it is better to avoid the march to the infinite permitted by the philosophers. . . . Now let us tackle the other horn of the dilemma. Suppose those infinite worlds are unlike ours. They then will be supplied with something different from the five perfect solids. Hence they will be less noble than our world. There it follows that this world of ours is the most excellent of them all, if there should be a plurality of worlds.

[22] *Kepler's Conversation with Galileo's Sidereal Messenger*, 1st complete translation, with an introduction and notes, by Edward Rosen (New York: Johnson Reprint Corp., 1965), 33–34.

From The Harmony of the World, *Book III (1619)*[23]

Then contemplation of these axioms, especially of the first five, is lofty, Platonic, and analogous to the Christian faith, looking towards metaphysics and the theory of the soul. For geometry, the part of which that looks in this direction was embraced in the two previous books, is coeternal with God, and by shining forth in the divine mind supplied patterns to God, as was said in the preamble to this book, for the furnishing of the world, so that it should become best and most beautiful and above all most like to the Creator. Indeed all spirits, souls, and minds are images of God the Creator if they have been put in command each of their own bodies, to govern, move, increase, preserve, and also particularly to propagate them.

Then since they have embraced a certain pattern of the creation in their functions, they also observe the same laws along with the Creator in their operations, having derived them from geometry. Also they rejoice in the same proportions which God used, wherever they have found them, whether by bare contemplation, whether by the interposition of the senses, in things which are subject to sensation, whether even without reflection by the mind, by an instinct which is concealed and was created with them, or whether God Himself has expressed these proportions in bodies and in motions invariably, or whether by some geometrical necessity of infinitely divisible material, and of motions through a quantity of material, among an infinity of proportions which are not harmonic, those harmonic proportions also occur at their own time, and thus subsist not in BEING but in BECOMING. Nor do minds, the images of God, merely rejoice in these proportions; but they also use the very same as laws for performing their functions and for expressing the same proportions in the motions of their bodies, where they may. The following Books will offer two splendid examples. One is that of God the Creator Himself, who assigned

---

[23] *The Harmony of the World*, 146–47.

the motions of the heavens in harmonic proportions. The second is that of the soul which we generally call Sublunary Nature, which actuates objects in the atmosphere in accordance with the rules of the proportions which occur in the radiations of stars. So let the third example, and the one which is proper to this Book, be that of the human soul, and indeed also that of animals to a certain extent. For they take joy in the harmonic proportions in musical notes which they perceive, and grieve at those which are not harmonic. From these feelings of the soul the former (the harmonic) are entitled consonances, and the latter (those which are not harmonic) discords. But if we also take into account another harmonic proportion, that of notes and sounds which are long or short, in respect of time, then they move their bodies in dancing, their tongues in speaking, in accordance with the same laws. Workmen adjust the blows of their hammers to it, soldiers their pace. Everything is lively while the harmonies persist, and drowsy when they are disrupted.

Further Reading

The standard biography is Max Caspar's *Kepler*, translated by C. Doris Hellman (New York: Abelard Schuman, 1959; reprinted with a new introduction and notes by Owen Gingerich, New York: Dover Publications, 1993). A complete list of Kepler's works can be found in *Bibliographia Kepleriana*, 2d ed., edited by Martha List (Munich: Beck, 1968). There are two editions of his works: *Joannis Kepleri Astronomi Opera Omnia*, edited by C. Frisch (Frankfurt and Erlangen: Heyder and Zimmer, 1858–1871), and *Johannes Kepler Gesammelte Werke* (Munich: Beck, 1937–). Translations of single works in English include: *Mysterium Cosmographicum—The Secret of the Universe*, translated by A. M. Duncan (New York: Abaris Books, 1981); *New Astronomy*, translated by William H. Donahue (Cambridge: Cambridge University Press, 1992); *Kepler's Conversation with Galileo's Sidereal Messenger*, translated by Edward Rosen (New York: Johnson Reprint, 1965); *The Harmony of the World*, translated by E. J. Aiton et al. (Philadelphia: American Philosophical Society, 1997); *The Six-Cornered Snowflake*, translated by Colin Hardie (Oxford: Clarendon Press, 1966); *Somnium: The Dream, or Posthumous Work on Lunar Astronomy*, translated by

Edward Rosen (Madison: University of Wisconsin Press, 1967). Parts of the *Epitome* and *Harmonice Mundi* can be found in volume 16 of the Great Books of the Western World series (Chicago: Encyclopedia Britannica, 1952, 1955). A translation of Kepler's defense of Tycho Brahe against the astronomer Ursus can be found in Nicholas Jardine, *The Birth of History and Philosophy of Science: Kepler's A Defence of Tycho against Ursus* (Cambridge: Cambridge University Press, 1984). Interesting works that include discussion of Kepler's religious views are Marcelo Gleiser, *The Prophet and the Astronomer: A Scientific Journey to the End of Time* (New York: W. W. Norton, 2002); J. V. Field, *Kepler's Geometrical Cosmology* (Chicago: University of Chicago Press, 1988); Fernand Hallyn, *The Poetic Structure of the World: Copernicus and Kepler*, translated by Donald M. Leslie (New York: Zone Books, 1990); and Edward Rosen, *Three Imperial Mathematicians: Kepler Trapped between Tycho Brahe and Ursus* (New York: Abaris Books, 1986). See also science writer Kitty Ferguson's lively account *Tycho and Kepler, The Unlikely Partnership That Forever Changed Our Understanding of the Heavens* (New York: Walker and Co., 2002).

3 Francis Bacon
(1561–1626)

Introduction

While Kepler was at work in Prague and Germany, and Galileo in Italy, Francis Bacon was rising to eminence in Anglican England. A philosopher and statesman more than an experimental scientist, Bacon gave classic expression to empiricism as science's own philosophy and method. The one and only scientific experiment Bacon himself seems to have performed, although there is some debate about it, led to his death. In March 1626 he caught cold when stuffing a hen with snow in order to observe the effect of freezing on the preservation of flesh. He died a month later. Bacon belongs in this book not because of his scientific discoveries but because of his overwhelming importance in articulating the method by which science discovers anything, although there is growing debate about that as well.

Bacon's devotion to the great effort of articulating a new philosophy of science ran parallel with his career as a statesman. Just sixteen years old at the time he became a member of the embassy to France, Bacon was entrusted with secret letters to carry to Elizabeth's court and was able to hand them over in the presence of the queen. Having begun so precociously, however, his career ended in disgrace in 1621 when he was accused of taking bribes from criminals seeking acquittal.

Remembered by most people for pithy one-liners such as "knowledge is power," or "a little philosophy makes a man an atheist: a great deal reconciles him to religion," Bacon's own literary ambitions were far more sweeping. His single-minded and explicit ambition was to replace Aristotle's *Organum* based on logical syllogisms with his own complete philosophy based on natural science and the method of induction, a veritable *Novum Organum*. Science was to be not only inductive but also free of illusions, practical, and separate from religion. For true science to proceed, Bacon urged that four categories of "Idols" or "false notions" be smashed. Idols of the Tribe, he wrote, comprise ineradicable limitations of human intelligence and perceptual capacity that lead us to misinterpret the world or commit common fallacies, such as wishful thinking. Idols of the Cave refer to individual defects of education and prejudice that further "refract and discolor the light of nature." Idols of the Marketplace stem from the limitations and ambiguities of language whose power can "overrule the understanding" and give rise to "empty controversies and idle fancies." Finally, Aristotelianism and other philosophical systems lead to the prejudices Bacon called Idols of the Theater. All the world's a stage, said another Englishman, to which Bacon added the admonition that the philosophical stage should not create fictional worlds that float free of experimental checks or experiential tests. All these idols should be abjured and renounced, he concluded, "and the understanding [must be] thoroughly freed and cleansed."

Chief among Bacon's targets is any form of "superstitious" philosophy that illicitly mixes theology and science. Using Genesis or the Book of Job to found a system of natural philosophy, he makes clear, is no substitute for making systematic observations and experiments. Natural knowledge was to be acquired not from authority, however venerable, nor by syllogistic exercises, however subtle, but by paying attention to the evidence of the senses, evidence from which, according to Bacon, all deception and illusion could be stripped away.

The next step was for induction to become the lynchpin of the new science. Empirical data emerges not from first principles but from the systematic collection of all observations pertaining to a given phenomenon, along with a rigorous process of rejecting hypotheses in conflict with those observations. In this way Bacon thought that scientists will eventually come to understand all the underlying laws and relevant principles of nature. Data derived from the mechanical arts would help to guarantee the solidity of the sciences and to build the idea of progress into them. Technology, Bacon held, was the very engine of history.

One might suppose that Baconian induction, insistence on evidence, and rejection of superstition and illusion would pit science against religion, but Bacon so sharply distinguished the two spheres that no conflict could possibly occur. It was the same strategy that Galileo adopted and that Stephen Jay Gould would later recommend. A devout churchman, Bacon believed that faith takes over when science and philosophy can find no evidence. Empirical evidence and mechanistic explanations rule in science, whereas religion appeals to revelation and final causes. It is not wise, Bacon warns, to confound the Book of Nature with the Book of God, for the latter deals with God's inscrutable will and the former with God's work. Science explains God's work and can therefore be seen as a form of Christian service. Ever conscious of human sinfulness, Bacon believed that God's nature and majesty could not be discerned through inquiry into nature. Kepler's attempt to read the very face of God in the heavens would have struck Bacon as impious. The only proper attitude toward God was one of wonder, not of inquisitiveness.

And yet, at the same time, the defining characteristic of Bacon's new program of learning is nothing less than the restoration of our dominion over nature, lost in the fall from paradise. So he could call his most ambitious work the *Great Instauration*—a restitution of wisdom. A religious spirit spurs his recognition both of the plight of fallen and sinful humans and of the necessity of science as a means for undoing the effects of the Fall and the ejection from Eden. He never doubted the effectiveness of the argument from design as a basis for faith, and he could not in any form accept the arguments of atheists. Although not a confirmed atomist, Bacon argued that the prevalent assumption that all things were made from countless rapidly moving, invisibly small atoms seemed in itself to demand the supervision of a God, who alone could enable the atoms to produce such stable and complex forms.

Bacon's faith was in empirical method as much as in the Christian God. To express his faith in the vast potential of science, he used the Latin term *plus ultra*, "more beyond" or "further still," which became the motto of the New Baconians. The frontispiece of his *Great Instauration* shows a ship sailing through the Pillars of Hercules, which tradition had placed as the limits of possible human exploration. But instead of the traditional "ne plus ultra," Bacon's title page declares "plus ultra." The Latin quotation at the foot of the waves, taken from the Book of Daniel, reads: "Many will pass through and knowledge will be increased."

Bacon's insistence on the separation of the science of Divinity and natural science, or the book of God's word and the book of God's work, took a surprising twist in his call for equally energetic inquiries into Scripture and Nature. Commentators have often wondered if Bacon merely makes the conventional argument that Christianity regards reason as an aid to faith or rather hints more daringly at a bold mixing and matching of divinity and natural philosophy within the new sciences. The answer may best be approached by considering the difference between *The Advancement of Learning* (1605) and *Novum Organum* (1620). In the earlier work, the mixing of science and religion is unwise, according to Bacon, because it could leave science open to magical belief in hidden powers when instead it should search for physical causes. But over time Bacon seems to have arrived at the view that the new sciences could help to adapt or even renovate the religion to which they were handmaids.

Nevertheless, on certain crucial questions scientific conclusions were to be limited by religious belief. For example, the eternity of the universe, something that the pagan Aristotle affirmed, could not be admitted within a Christian cosmology because it was incompatible with a created universe. For a different reason, Bacon rejected Aristotle's notion of final causes, which he called "barren virgins." Only by concentrating exclusively on physical, efficient causes would science itself be possible.

Francis Bacon's name is often linked with that of René Descartes as complementary figures in seventeenth-century science, Descartes emphasizing the discovery of scientific knowledge by deductive thought from general principles, with experiment playing an auxiliary role, and Bacon emphasizing the crucial enterprise of collecting materials, carrying out experiments, and inductively discovering general features and principles. The one advocated a method of seeking certainty from self-evident metaphysical principles, the other from unmediated individual access to facts. Both the Baconian and the Cartesian philosophies have suffered an irreparable loss of cogency in our time; they are charged with being oblivious to the relevance of paradigms of inquiry, the influence of unconscious motivations, and the restrictions of the social conditions of knowledge.

But present critical concerns ought not obscure Bacon's stature as a chief architect present at the very creation of the modern scientific worldview. As Paolo Rossi reminds us, "around 1600 the English intellectual was more than half medieval and around 1660 he was more than half modern."[1] Francis Bacon is the best exemplar of this turning point in intellectual history.

✾ Bacon's Contribution to Science

Francis Bacon helped to shape the scientific enterprise as the collection of materials, the performance of experiments, and the inductive discovery of general features and principles. His writings form one of the roots of the English tradition of empiricism, of which the most important representative was John Locke. The

---

[1] Paolo Rossi, *Francis Bacon: From Magic to Science*, trans. Sacha Rabinovitch (London: Routledge & Kegan Paul, 1968), x.

word "experiment" as it was used until the nineteenth century stood for the concept of stretched or enlarged sensory experience, on the assumption that nature could be made to perform according to a scenario of human choosing, instead of merely watching nature's own artless improvisations. Bacon's championship of the idea of experimentation was closer to this older meaning than to the professional one we attach to the word today.

Bacon in His Own Words

From The Advancement of Learning *(1605)*[2]

And as for the conceit that too much knowledge should incline a man to atheism, and that the ignorance of second causes should make a more devout dependence upon God, which is the first cause; first, it is good to ask the question which Job asked of his friends: "Will you lie for God, as one man will lie for another, to gratify him?" For certain it is that God worketh nothing in Nature but by second causes; and if they would have it otherwise believed, it is mere imposture, as it were in favour towards God, and nothing else but to offer to the Author of truth the unclean sacrifice of a lie. But further, it is an assured truth, and a conclusion of experience, that a little or superficial knowledge of philosophy may incline the mind of men to atheism, but a further proceeding therein doth bring the mind back again to religion.

For it is an excellent observation which hath been made upon the answers of our Saviour Christ to many of the questions which were propounded to Him, how that they are impertinent to the state of the question demanded: the reason whereof is, because

---

[2] Sir Francis Bacon, *The Advancement of Learning*, ed. David Price (London: Cassell and Co., 1893), 6, 112–13.

not being like man, which knows man's thoughts by his words, but knowing man's thoughts immediately, He never answered their words, but their thoughts. Much in the like manner it is with the Scriptures, which being written to the thoughts of men, and to the succession of all ages, with a foresight of all heresies, contradictions, differing estates of the Church, yea, and particularly of the elect, are not to be interpreted only according to the latitude of the proper sense of the place, and respectively towards that present occasion whereupon the words were uttered, or in precise congruity or contexture with the words before or after, or in contemplation of the principal scope of the place; but have in themselves, not only totally or collectively, but distributively in clauses and words, infinite springs and streams of doctrine to water the Church in every part. And therefore as the literal sense is, as it were, the main stream or river, so the moral sense chiefly, and sometimes the allegorical or typical, are they whereof the Church hath most use; not that I wish men to be bold in allegories, or indulgent or light in allusions: but that I do much condemn that interpretation of the Scripture which is only after the manner as men use to interpret a profane book.

In this part touching the exposition of the Scriptures, I can report no deficiency; but by way of remembrance this I will add. In perusing books of divinity I find many books of controversies, and many of commonplaces and treatises, a mass of positive divinity, as it is made an art: a number of sermons and lectures, and many prolix commentaries upon the Scriptures, with harmonies and concordances.

The matter informed by divinity is of two kinds: matter of belief and truth of opinion, and matter of service and adoration; which is also judged and directed by the former—the one being as the internal soul of religion, and the other as the external body thereof. And, therefore, the heathen religion was not only a worship of idols, but the whole religion was an idol in itself; for it had no soul; that is, no certainty of belief or confession: as a man may well think, considering the chief doctors of their church were the poets; and the reason was because the heathen gods were no jealous gods, but were glad to be admitted into part, as they had reason. Neither did they respect the pureness of heart, so they might have external honour and rites.

But out of these two do result and issue four main branches of divinity: faith, manners, liturgy, and government. Faith containeth the doctrine of the nature of God, of the attributes of God, and of the works of God. The nature of God consisteth of three persons in unity of Godhead. The attributes of God are either common to the Deity, or respective to the persons. The works of God summary are two, that of the creation and that of the redemption; and both these works, as in total they appertain to the unity of the Godhead, so in their parts they refer to the three persons: that of the creation, in the mass of the matter, to the Father; in the disposition of the form, to the Son; and in the continuance and conservation of the being, to the Holy Spirit. So that of the redemption, in the election and counsel, to the Father; in the whole act and consummation, to the Son; and in the application, to the Holy Spirit; for by the Holy Ghost was Christ conceived in flesh, and by the Holy Ghost are the elect regenerate in spirit. This work likewise we consider either effectually, in the elect; or privately, in the reprobate; or according to appearance, in the visible Church.

For manners, the doctrine thereof is contained in the law, which discloseth sin. The law itself is divided, according to the edition thereof, into the law of nature, the law moral, and the law positive; and according to the style, into negative and affirmative, prohibitions and commandments. Sin, in the matter and subject thereof, is divided according to the commandments; in the form thereof it referreth to the three persons in Deity: sins of infirmity against the Father, whose more special attribute is power; sins of ignorance against the Son, whose attribute is wisdom; and sins of malice against the Holy Ghost, whose attribute is grace or love. In the motions of it, it either moveth to the right hand or to the left; either to blind devotion or to profane and libertine transgression; either in imposing restraint where God granteth liberty, or in taking liberty where God imposeth restraint. In the degrees and progress of it, it divideth itself into thought, word, or act. And in this part I commend much the deducing of the law of God to cases of conscience; for that I take indeed to be a breaking, and not exhibiting whole of the bread of life.

From **The New Organon** *(1620)*[3]

Our prayers done, we turn to men and offer some salutary advice and make some reasonable requests. First we advise (as we have prayed) that men may restrain their sense within their duty, so far as the things of God are concerned. For sense (like the sun) opens up the face of the terrestrial globe and closes and obscures the globe of heaven. And then we warn men not to err in the opposite direction as they avoid this evil; which will certainly happen if they believe that any part of the inquiry into nature is forbidden by an interdict. The pure and immaculate natural knowledge by which Adam assigned appropriate names to things did not give opportunity or occasion for the Fall. The method and mode of temptation in fact was the ambitious and demanding desire for moral knowledge, by which to discriminate good from evil, to the end that Man might turn away from God and give laws to himself. About the sciences which observe nature the sacred philosopher declares that "the Glory of God is to conceal a thing, but the glory of a king is to find out a thing," just as if the divine nature delighted in the innocent and amusing children's game in which they hide themselves purposely in order to be found; and has coopted the human mind to join this game in his kindness and goodness towards men. Finally, we want all and everyone to be advised to reflect on the true ends of knowledge: not to seek it for amusement or for dispute, or to look down on others, or for profit or for fame or for power or any such inferior ends, but for the uses and benefits of life, and to improve and conduct it in charity. For the angels fell because of an appetite for power; and

---

[3] Francis Bacon, *The New Organon*, ed. Lisa Jardine and Michael Silverthorne (Cambridge: Cambridge University Press, 2000), 12–13, 24, 79, 96, 126–27, 231.

men fell because of an appetite for knowledge; but charity knows no bounds; and has never brought angel or man into danger.

≫

The whole secret is never to let the mind's eyes stray from things themselves, and to take in images exactly as they are. May God never allow us to publish a dream of our imagination as a model of the world, but rather graciously grant us the power to describe the true appearance and revelation of the prints and traces of the Creator in his creatures.

And therefore, Father, you who have given visible light as the first fruits of creation and, at the summit of your works, have breathed intellectual light into the face of man, protect and govern this work, which began in your goodness and returns to your glory. After you had turned to view the works which your hands had made, you saw that all things were very good, and you rested. But man, turning to the works which his hands have made, saw that all things were vanity and vexation of spirit, and has had no rest. Wherefore if we labour in your works, you will make us to share in your vision and in your sabbath. We humbly beseech that this mind may remain in us; and that you may be pleased to bless the human family with new mercies, through our hands and the hands of those others to whom you will give the same mind.

≫

Empiricists, like ants, simply accumulate and use; Rationalists, like spiders, spin webs from themselves; the way of the bee is in between: it takes material from the flowers of the garden and the field; but it has the ability to convert and digest them. This is not unlike the true working of philosophy; which does not rely solely or mainly on mental power, and does not store the material provided by natural history and mechanical experiments in its memory untouched, but altered and adapted in the intellect. Therefore, much is to be hoped from a closer and more binding alliance (which has never yet been made) between these faculties (i.e. the experimental and the rational).

🦅

Here is another objection that will certainly come up: that (despite our criticisms of others) we ourselves have not first declared the true and best goal or purpose of the sciences. For the contemplation of truth is worthier and higher than any utility or power in effects; but the long and anxious time spent in experience and matter and in the ebb and flow of particular things keeps the mind fixed on the ground, or rather sinks it in a Tartarus of confusion and turmoil, and bars and obstructs its way to the serenity and tranquility of detached wisdom (a much more godlike condition). We willingly assent to this argument; it is precisely this thing which they hint and find preferable which we are chiefly and above all engaged on. For we are laying the foundations in the human understanding of a true model of the world, as it is and not as any man's own reason tells him it is. But this can be done only by performing a most careful dissection and anatomy of the world. We declare that the inept models of the world (like imitations by apes), which men's fancies have constructed in philosophies, have to be smashed. And so men should be aware (as we said above) how great is the distance between the *illusions* of men's minds and the ideas of God's mind. The former are simply fanciful abstractions; the latter are the true marks of the Creator on his creatures as they are impressed and printed on matter in true and meticulous lines. Therefore truth and usefulness are (in this kind) the very same things, and the works themselves are of greater value as pledges of truth than for the benefits they bring to human life.

🦅

The work and office of these three tables I call the Presentation of Instances to the Understanding. Which presentation having been made, induction itself must be set at work; for the problem is, upon a review of the instances, all and each, to find such a nature as is always present or absent with the given nature, and always increases and decreases with it; and which is, as I have said, a particular case of a more general nature. Now if the mind attempt this affirmatively from the first, as when left to itself it is always wont to do, the result will be fancies and guesses and notions ill defined, and axioms that must be mended every day, unless like the schoolmen we have a mind to fight for what is false; though doubtless these will be better or worse according to the faculties and strength of the understanding which is at work. To God, truly, the Giver and Architect of Forms, and it may be to the angels and higher intelligences, it belongs to have an affirmative knowledge of forms immediately, and from the first contemplation. But this assuredly is more than man can do, to whom it is granted only to proceed at first by negatives, and at last to end in affirmatives after exclusion has been exhausted.

❧

There are some useful additions to a natural history which may make it more fit and helpful to the subsequent work of an interpreter. They are five. First, questions (not of causes but of fact) should be added, to encourage and provoke further investigation; for example, in the history of land and sea, whether the Caspian sea has tides, and at what intervals; whether there is a Southern continent, or only islands; and so on.

Secondly, in any new experiment of any subtlety, we should append the actual method used in the experiment, so that men may have the opportunity to judge whether the information it produced is reliable or deceptive, and also to encourage men to apply themselves to look for more accurate methods (if there are any).

Thirdly, if there is anything doubtful or questionable in any account, we are wholly against suppression or silence about it; a full and clear note should be attached as a remark or warning. We want the first history to be composed with utter scrupulousness, as if an oath had been taken about the truth of every detail; for it is the volume of the works of God, and (so far as one may compare the majesty of the divine with the humble things of the earth) like a second Scripture.

Fourth, it would not be out of place to insert occasional observations. . . . Also it is a good thing to add canons (which are simply general and universal observations); for example, in the history of heavenly bodies, that Venus is never more than 46 degrees from the sun, Mercury, 23; and that the planets which lie above the sun move very slowly, since they are furthest from earth and the planets below the sun very fast. Another kind of observation to make, which has never yet been used, despite its importance, is this: to append to an account of what is a mention of what is not. For example, in the history of heavenly things, that no star is found to be oblong or triangular, but that every star is globular at the centre, like the other stars. . . .

Fifthly, something which quite depresses and destroys a believer will perhaps help an investigator: namely to survey in a brief and summary form of words the currently accepted opinions in all the variety of the different schools; enough to wake up the intellect and no more.

From The Great Instauration (1620)[4]

For my own part at least, in obedience to the everlasting love of truth, I have committed myself to the uncertainties and difficulties and solitudes of the ways and, relying on the divine assistance, have upheld my mind both against the shocks and embattled ranks of opinion, and against my own private and inward hesitations and scruples, and against the fogs and clouds of nature, and the phantoms flitting about on every side, in the hope of providing at last for the present and future generations guidance more faithful

[4] Francis Bacon, *New Atlantis* and *The Great Instauration*, ed. J. Weinberger (Arlington Heights, IL: H. Davidson, 1989), 14–16, 31–32.

and secure. Wherein if I have made any progress, the way has been opened to me by no other means than the true and legitimate humiliation of the human spirit. For all those who before me have applied themselves to the invention of arts have but cast a glance or two upon facts and examples and experience, and straightway proceeded, as if invention were nothing more than an exercise of thought, to invoke their own spirits to give them oracles. I, on the contrary, dwelling purely and constantly among the facts of nature, withdraw my intellect from them no further than may suffice to let the images and rays of natural objects meet in a point, as they do in the sense of vision; whence it follows that the strength and excellence of the wit has but little to do in the matter. And the same humility which I use in inventing I employ likewise in teaching. For I do not endeavor either by triumphs of confutation, or pleadings of antiquity, or assumption of authority, or even by the veil of obscurity, to invest these inventions of mine with any majesty; which might easily be done by one who sought to give luster to his own name rather than light to other men's minds. I have not sought (I say) nor do I seek either to force or ensnare men's judgments, but I lead them to things themselves and the concordances of things, that they may see for themselves what they have, what they can dispute, what they can add and contribute to the common stock. And for myself, if in anything I have been either too credulous or too little awake and attentive, or if I have fallen off by the way and left the inquiry incomplete, nevertheless I so present these things naked and open, that my errors can be marked and set aside before the mass of knowledge be further infected by them; and it will be easy also for others to continue and carry on my labors. And by these means I suppose that I have established forever a true and lawful marriage between the empirical and the rational faculty, the unkind and ill-starred divorce and separation of which has thrown into confusion all the affairs of the human family.

Wherefore, seeing that these things do not depend upon myself, at the outset of the work I most humbly and fervently pray to God the Father, God the Son, and God the Holy Ghost, that remembering the sorrows of mankind and the pilgrimage of this our life wherein we wear out days few and evil, they will vouchsafe through my hands to endow the human family with new mercies. This likewise I humbly pray, that things human may not interfere with things divine, and that from the opening of the ways of sense and the increase of natural light there may arise in our minds no incredulity or darkness with regard to the divine mysteries, but rather that the understanding being thereby purified and purged of fancies and vanity, and yet not the less subject and entirely submissive to the divine oracles, may give to faith that which is faith's. Lastly, that knowledge being now discharged of that venom which the serpent infused into it, and which makes the mind of man to swell, we may not be wise above measure and sobriety, but cultivate truth in charity.

And now, having said my prayers, I turn to men, to whom I have certain salutary admonitions to offer and certain fair requests to make. My first admonition (which was also my prayer) is that men confine the sense within the limits of duty in respect of things divine: for the sense is like the sun, which reveals the face of earth, but seals and shuts up the face of heaven. My next, that in flying from this evil they fall not into the opposite error, which they will surely do if they think that the inquisition of nature is in any part interdicted or forbidden.

For the matter in hand is no mere felicity of speculation, but the real business and fortunes of the human race, and all power of operation. For man is but the servant and interpreter of nature: what he does and what he knows is only what he has observed of nature's order in fact or in thought; beyond this he knows nothing and can do nothing. For the chain of causes cannot by any force be loosed or broken, nor can nature be commanded except by being obeyed. And so those twin objects, human knowledge and human power, do really meet in one; and it is from ignorance of causes that operation fails.

Of Atheism[5]

I had rather believe all the fables in the Legend,[6] and the Talmud, and the Alcoran, than that this universal frame is without a mind. And therefore, God never wrought miracle, to convince atheism, because his ordinary works convince it. It is true, that a little philosophy inclineth man's mind to atheism; but depth in philosophy bringeth men's minds about to religion. For while the mind of man looketh upon second causes scattered, it may sometimes rest in them, and go no further; but when it beholdeth the chain of them, confederate and linked together, it must needs fly to Providence and Deity. Nay, even that school which is most accused of atheism doth most demonstrate religion; that is, the school of Leucippus and Democritus and Epicurus. For it is a thousand times more credible, that four mutable elements, and one immutable fifth essence, duly and eternally placed, need no God, than that an army of infinite small portions, or seeds unplaced, should have produced this order and beauty, without a divine marshal. The Scripture saith, *The fool hath said in his heart, there is no God:* it is not said, *The fool hath thought in his heart;* so as he rather saith it, by rote to himself, as that he would have, than that he can thoroughly believe it, or be persuaded of it. For none deny, there is a God, but those, for whom it maketh that there were no God. It appeareth in nothing more, that atheism is rather in the lip, than in the heart of man, than by this; that atheists will ever be talking of that their opinion, as if they fainted in it, within themselves, and would be glad to be strengthened, by the consent of others. Nay more, you shall have atheists strive to get disciples, as it fareth with other sects. And, which is most of all, you shall have of them, that will suffer for atheism, and not recant; whereas if they did truly think, that there were no such thing as God, why

---

[5] Francis Bacon, *The Essayes or Counsels, Civill and Morall* (London: J. M. Dent and Co., 1909), 48–51. I have modernized the spelling and punctuation in this selection.

[6] Presumably Bacon is referring to the Golden Legend of Jacobus de Voraigne.

should they trouble themselves? Epicurus is charged, that he did but dissemble for his credit's sake, when he affirmed there were blessed natures, but such as enjoyed themselves, without having respect to the government of the world. Wherein they say he did temporize; though in secret, he thought there was no God. But certainly he is traduced; for his words are noble and divine: *Non deos vulgi negare profanum; sed vulgi opiniones diis applicare profanum.* Plato could have said no more. And although he had the confidence, to deny the administration, he had not the power, to deny the nature. The Indians of the West, have names for their particular gods, though they have no name for God: as if the heathens should have had the names Jupiter, Apollo, Mars, etc., but not the word Deus; which shows that even those barbarous people have the notion, though they have not the latitude and extent of it. So that against atheists, the very savages take part, with the very subtlest philosophers. The contemplative atheist is rare: a Diagoras, a Bion, a Lucian perhaps, and some others; and yet they seem to be more than they are; for that all that impugn a received religion, or superstition, are by the adverse part branded with the name of atheists. But the great atheists, indeed are hypocrites; which are ever handling holy things, but without feeling; so as they must needs be cauterized in the end. The causes of atheism are: divisions in religion, if they be many; for any one main division, addeth zeal to both sides; but many divisions introduce atheism. Another is, scandal of priests; when it is come to that which St. Bernard saith: *Non est jam dicere, ut populus sic sacerdos; quia nec sic populus ut sacerdos.* A third is, custom of profane scoffing in holy matters; which doth, by little and little, deface the reverence of religion. And lastly, learned times, specially with peace and prosperity; for troubles and adversities do more bow men's minds to religion. They that deny a God, destroy man's nobility; for certainly man is of kin to the beasts, by his body; and, if he be not of kin to God, by his spirit, he is a base and ignoble creature. It destroys likewise magnanimity, and the raising of human nature; for take an example of a dog, and mark what a generosity and courage he will put on, when he finds himself maintained by a man; who to him is instead of a God, or *melior natura;* which courage is manifestly such, as that creature, without that confidence of a better nature than his own, could never attain. So man, when he resteth and assureth himself, upon divine protection and favor, gathered a force and faith, which human nature in itself could not obtain. Therefore, as atheism is in all respects hateful, so in this, that it depriveth human nature of the means to exalt itself, above human frailty. . . .

Of the Interpretation of Nature[7]

In the divine nature both religion and philosophy hath acknowledged goodness in perfection, science or providence comprehending all things, and absolute sovereignty or kingdom. In aspiring to the throne of power the angels transgressed and fell, in presuming to come within the oracle of knowledge man transgressed and fell; but in pursuit towards the similitude of God's goodness or love (which is one thing, for love is nothing else but goodness put in motion or applied) neither man or spirit ever hath transgressed, or shall transgress.

The angel of light that was, when he presumed before his fall, said within himself, *I will ascend and be like unto the Highest;* not God, but the highest. To be like to God in goodness, was no part of his emulation; knowledge, being in creation an angel of light, was not the want which did most solicit him; only because he was a minister he aimed at a supremacy; therefore his climbing or ascension was turned into a throwing down or precipitation.

Man on the other side, when he was tempted before he fell, had offered unto him this suggestion, *that he should be like unto God.* But how? Not simply, but in this part, *knowing good and evil.* For being in his creation invested with sovereignty of all inferior creatures, he was not needy of power or dominion; but again, being a

---

[7] In *The Works of Francis Bacon,* ed. James Spedding et al. (London: Longmans & Co., 1887), 3:217–18.

spirit newly inclosed in a body of earth, he was fittest to be allured with appetite of light and liberty of knowledge; therefore this approaching and intruding into God's secrets and mysteries was rewarded with a further removing and estranging from God's presence. But as to the goodness of God, there is no danger in contending or advancing towards a similitude thereof, as that which is open and propounded to our imitation. For that voice (whereof the heathen and all other errors of religion have ever confessed that it sounds not like man), *Love your enemies; be you like unto your heavenly Father, that suffereth his rain to fall both upon the just and the unjust,* doth well declare, that we can in that point commit no excess; so again we find it often repeated in the old law, *Be you holy as I am holy;* and what is holiness else but goodness, as we consider it separate and guarded from all mixture and all access of evil?

Wherefore seeing that knowledge is of the number of those things which are to be accepted of with caution and distinction; being now to open a fountain, such as it is not easy to discern where the issues and streams thereof will take and fall; I thought it good and necessary in the first place to make a strong and sound head or bank to rule and guide the course of the waters; by setting down this position or firmament, namely, *That all knowledge is to be limited by religion, and to be referred to use and action.*

For if any man shall think by view and inquiry into these sensible and material things, to attain to any light for the revealing of the nature or will of God, he shall dangerously abuse himself. It is true that the contemplation of the creatures of God hath for end (as to the natures of the creatures themselves) knowledge, but as to the nature of God, no knowledge, but wonder; which is nothing else but contemplation broken off, or losing itself. Nay further, as it was aptly said by one of Plato's school *the sense of man resembles the sun, which openeth and revealeth the terrestrial globe, but obscureth and concealeth the celestial;* so doth the sense discover natural things, but darken and shut up divine. And this appeareth sufficiently in that there is no proceeding in invention of knowledge but by similitude; and God is only self-like, having nothing in common with any creature, otherwise than as in shadow and trope. Therefore attend his will as himself openeth it, and give unto faith that which unto faith belongeth; for more worthy it is to believe than to think or know, considering that in knowledge (as we now are capable of it) the mind suffereth from inferior natures; but in all belief it suffereth from a spirit which it holdeth superior and more authorised than itself.

Further Reading

The standard edition of Bacon's Works is that of James Spedding, R. L. Ellis, and D. D. Heath (London: Longmans and Co., 1857–74). Volumes 1–7 contain the works, together with translations of all the major Latin ones into English; volumes 8–14 contain Bacon's life, letters, and miscellanea. All important works appear in English in *Philosophical Works of Francis Bacon*, edited by J. M. Robertson (London: George Routledge and Sons, 1905). Noteworthy among editions of individual works is *The Advancement of Learning and New Atlantis*, 3d ed., edited by Arthur Johnston (Oxford: Clarendon Press, 1974), which is scrupulously annotated. Three interesting and previously untranslated minor works appear in Benjamin Farrington's *The Philosophy of Francis Bacon* (Liverpool: Liverpool University Press, 1964), together with a valuable monograph on Bacon's thought. A useful, although thoroughly adulatory, account of Bacon's philosophy is Fulton H. Anderson's *The Philosophy of Francis Bacon* (Chicago: University of Chicago Press, 1948, 1971); more critical is Anthony Quinton's *Francis Bacon* (Oxford: Oxford University Press. 1980). Paulo Rossi's *Francis Bacon: From Magic to Science* (Chicago: University of Chicago Press, 1968) offers an intriguing study linking Bacon's thought with the hermetic tradition. Other aspects of Bacon scholarship are covered in *Essential Articles for the Study of Francis Bacon*, edited by Brian Vickers (Hamden, CT: Archon, 1968). A recent and reliable volume of scholarly essays on Bacon's thought is *The Cambridge Companion to Bacon,* edited by Mark Peltonen (Cambridge: Cambridge University Press, 1996).

4 Blaise Pascal
(1623–1662)

Introduction

In many ways, Blaise Pascal belongs as much to our contemporary epoch, with its acute awareness of human contingency, the immensity of the universe, and the mysteries of the microscopic, as to his own seventeenth-century French milieu. In the celebrated Fragment 230 of his *Pensées*, Pascal expressed with particular poignancy the feeling of existential isolation: "When I consider the brief span of my life, absorbed into the eternity before and after, the small space I occupy and which I see swallowed up in the infinite immensity of spaces of which I know nothing and which know nothing of me, I take fright and am amazed to see myself here rather than there: there is no reason for me to be here rather than there, now rather than then. Who put me here? By whose command and act were this time and place allotted to me? . . . The eternal silence of these infinite spaces terrifies me."

Terrifying, too, was the random world of the atoms. "I want to make us see within it a new abyss," Pascal wrote. "Let us see in it an infinity of universes, of which each has its own firmament, planets, and earth in the same proportion as in the visible world." Suspended between this "double infinity" of greatness and smallness, the human mind can plumb neither the world of the infinitely large nor that of the infinitely small. The heights and the depths elude reason's grasp. Neither ground nor closure can be had, for "nothing can fix the finite between the two infinites which both enclose and escape it."

Other polarities structure Pascal's thoughts as they appear in stunning fragments: light and darkness, certainty and doubt, anxiety and "divertissement," the greatness and misery of the human condition. No one would deny the profound influence his own historical context had on Pascal, particularly Jansenism[1] and the theological quarrels it occasioned, yet the religious themes he plumbs remain very modern: human wretchedness and despair, the paradoxes of freedom and determinism, the powerlessness of the human will to deliver itself from evil, to escape ignorance, or to cure death. Stylistically, his writing is fragmentary, paradoxical, and digressive. We can even read him as a postmodern author, celebrating undecidability, aporia, and circularity.

Although Galileo, Kepler, and Bacon believed in the Bible as the Word of God, they could also find in the Book of Nature an equally inspiring source of faith. Pascal is their opposite. Mystical insight overwhelmed him, not in a rational grasp of the perfect beauty of mathematics, but in an encounter with the God of revelation, the burning bush, the sacred fire, the vital passion that breaks down reason and punctures its pretensions altogether. Pascal's faith, more than the expressions we find in Galileo or Kepler or Bacon, is articulated around Jesus Christ as Savior and rooted in what he experienced as profound religious exaltation.

Extraordinarily gifted as a scientist and mathematician, Pascal was feeling empty and unfulfilled spiritually in his Roman Catholicism around the age of thirty. For some time he had been seeking

---

[1] The Jansenists emphasized original sin, human depravity, the necessity of divine grace, and predestination. The Molinists answered that God wills all human beings to be saved and gives them the grace that is the indispensable means. Pascal withdrew from the controversy after writing the *Provincial Letters*, was never charged with any heresy, and died a Catholic.

spiritual counsel at the Jansenist retreat in Port-Royal. Then, on the evening of November 23, 1654, he underwent a powerful "second conversion," in which he felt the presence of God. Pascal preserved the recollection of this "Night of Fire" in "The Memorial," the first entry included here. We know of this fragment only because it was discovered upon his death at the age of thirty-nine, sewn into the clothing he wore.

In the second fragment (680) included here, "Discourse Concerning the Machine," we find Pascal's famous wager, where modern probability theory was born. Pascal has already rejected both radical skepticism and Descartes's method of doubt as too rigid. He has also ruled out the use of authority in attempting to persuade others of the truth in important matters. He wants a middle way between the Cartesian quest for certainty and the skepticism that grows out of the failure of that quest. He finds this in a new notion of probability. Following Ian Hacking's classic article, it has been customary to distinguish three versions of Pascal's wager within the compressed paragraphs of Fragment 680: the argument from dominance, the argument from expectation, and the argument from dominating expectation.[2] Tracing these out briefly should help readers see the bearing of Pascal's mathematical work on his religious faith.

Starting from the agnostic assumption that if there is a God we are incapable of knowing what God is, or whether God is, and that reason can settle nothing here, Pascal proceeds to invoke reason to say that a prudent person, in his cosmic ignorance, should bet his life on God's existence. If one does, then the two possible outcomes that may occur have the following consequences:

1. God exists: one enjoys an eternity of bliss (infinite gain).
2. God does not exist: one's belief is unjustified ("loss of nought"), or, at worst, one is chagrined for being fooled (finite loss).

Since outcome 1 promises an infinite gain, whereas outcome 2 leads to only a finite loss, the choice seems clear to Pascal: one

[2] See Ian Hacking, "The Logic of Pascal's Wager," *American Philosophical Quarterly* 9, no. 2 (1972): 186–92.

should believe in God's existence. The first version is an example of a decision under uncertainty. Whenever one deliberates with knowledge of the outcomes but no knowledge of the probabilities associated with those outcomes, one faces a decision under uncertainty. By contrast, deliberating both with knowledge of the outcomes and the probabilities associated with those outcomes, one faces a decision under risk.

The interlocutor imagined in the text objects that the wagerer might indeed be worse off if he bets on God's existence and turns out to be wrong. In response, Pascal introduces probability assignments and the idea of an infinite utility to the second version of the wager. This is an argument from expectation, built upon the concept of maximizing expected utility. It assumes that the probability that God exists is one-half, and that if God exists, the outcome of right belief is of infinite utility. With these assumptions, belief easily trumps nonbelief, no matter what finite value or disvalue is found in the other 0.5 probabilities. The most useful thing about infinite utility is that infinity multiplied by any finite value is still infinite!

In the third version of the wager, the argument from dominating expectation takes over. "God exists" represents a positive probability, with a range greater than zero and less than one-half. No matter how unlikely it is that God exists, as long as there is some positive non-zero probability that God exists, believing is the best bet, according to Pascal.

The fact that Pascal did not complete this projected apologetic for the Christian religion, and that posthumously published editions of it have been chaotic until Lafuma (1952) and Levi (1995), makes it difficult to answer many of the questions raised by his *Pensées*. One thing, however, is sure. Pascal wanted to accord the heart "reasons of its own, which reason does not know." The heart for him is an intuitive organ, not merely a faculty of emotion. It is the seat of both religious belief and our common cognitive framework. It gives rise to faith, but faith is belief, not knowledge. It would be irrational, Pascal thought, to accept as true nothing but what one knows or can prove. Demonstrable rational knowledge itself is founded on a set of beliefs that cannot be proved, such as the reality of space, time, movement, and certain other unchallengeable concepts that undergird perception. Pascal calls all these beliefs "sentiments." They are the result of custom. Religious beliefs, too, can be transformed by custom into sentiment. Custom, according to Pascal, inclines the body and carries the mind along with it, unreflectingly. This is so in the case of true beliefs, as well as of irrational beliefs. The "machine" is Pascal's image for summing up custom, esteem, and self-interest, whose power can only be broken by humility.

The best way to express Pascal's complex account of the relationship between reason and custom and divine inspiration is to say that reason is to faith as moral effort is to salvation—necessary, but not sufficient without God's grace. Finally, Pascal understands his own faith as a gift of God, and divine revelation as the most significant source of knowledge, without which he would have no certain knowledge of his origin, his nature, or his destiny—those things that science cannot tell him. While revelation's claims cannot be empirically tested, they can nevertheless be trusted as valid on the basis of what has come to be called "inference to the best explanation." Science employs the same method of reasoning, as Pascal was among the first to point out, championing an abductive mode of reasoning.

Sometimes mistakenly labeled a fideist, Pascal was not in any way an irrationalist; he was too good a scientist and mathematician for that. He held that the intricate relationship between faith and reason meant that "Faith certainly tells us what the senses do not, but not the contrary of what they see; it is above, not against them." The principles of logic and scientific experimentation take us far and should never be abandoned, but finally they are insufficient. For justification and salvation, human beings are absolutely dependent on God's grace.

Insoluble paradoxes lurk here and may help to explain why Pascal abandoned his jumble of jottings short of completion. If salvation depends entirely on grace, and grace depends entirely on the arbitrary will of God, then no amount of human capacity or rational voluntarism can make a difference. If any degree of human merit or will were allowed to matter, then God's grace would not be freely given but coerced. But because God's grace is not coerced, it is arbitrary. Those on whom God does not choose to bestow grace are eternally damned, through no personal choice of their own. Such were the bleak premises of Blaise Pascal's own theology, somewhat at odds with any hopes he had of writing an apologetic to persuade others freely to accept Christianity.

✌ Pascal's Contributions to Science

Blaise Pascal's first major work, Essay on Conic Sections *(1640), treated conics as plane sections through a circular cone. He invented a proof for the binomial theorem and worked on the properties of the cycloid. He formulated the idea for a calculating machine in 1642 and had one built two years later. His barometric experiments were published in 1647 as* New Experiments Concerning the Vacuum. *He made original contributions to the science of mathematics as the creator of the mathematical theory of probability and combinatorial analysis in his* Treatise on the Arithmetical Triangle. *He provided the essential link between the mechanics of fluids and the mechanics of rigid bodies. He was one of the first to provide experimental proof of the possibility of vacuums, and he invented the barometer and the syringe.*

Pascal in His Own Words

The Memorial[3]

The year of grace 1654
Monday 23 November, feast of Saint Clement

[3] Blaise Pascal, *Pensées and other Writings*, trans. H. Levi (Oxford: Oxford University Press, 1995), 178–81. The formatting of "The Memorial" attempts to reflect Pascal's own layout in the scrap of paper sewn into his coat.

Pope and martyr, and others of the Roman Martyrology.
Eve of Saint Chrysogonus, martyr, and others.
From about half past ten in the evening until about
half past midnight.

Fire.
God of Abraham, God of Isaac, God of Jacob.
not of philosophers and scholars.
Certainty, joy, certainty, emotion, sight, joy
God of Jesus Christ.
Deum meum et Deum vestrum.
Your God will be my God. Ruth.
Oblivious to the world and to everything except GOD.
He can only be found in the ways taught
in the Gospel. Greatness of the human soul.

Righteous Father, the world did not know you,
but I knew you. John.
Joy, Joy, Joy and tears of joy.
I have cut myself off from him.
Dereliquerunt me fontem.
My God, will you forsake me?
Let me not be cut off from him for ever.

This is life eternal, that they might know you,
the only true God, and him whom you sent,
Jesus Christ
Jesus Christ
I have cut myself off from him, I have fled from him, denied
him, crucified him.
Let me never be cut off from him.
He can only be kept by the ways taught in the Gospel.
Total submission to Jesus Christ and my director.
Everlasting joy for one day's tribulation on earth.
Non obliviscar sermons tuos. Amen.

Discourse Concerning the Machine[4]

Infinity nothingness. Our soul is thrust into the body, where it finds number, time, dimension. It ponders them and calls them nature, necessity, and can believe nothing else.

❧

A unit added to infinity does not increase it at all, any more than a foot added to an infinite length. The finite dissolves in the presence of the infinite and becomes pure nothingness. So it is with our mind before God, with our justice before divine justice. There is not so great a disproportion between our justice and God's justice as there is between unity and infinity.

❧

God's justice must be as vast as his mercy. But justice towards the damned is not so vast, and ought to shock less than mercy towards the elect.

❧

We know that there is an infinite, but we do not know its nature; as we know that it is false that numbers are finite, so therefore it is true that there is an infinite number, but we do not know what it is: it is false that it is even and false that it is odd, for by adding a unit it does not change its nature; however it is a number, and all numbers are even or odd (it is true that this applies to all finite numbers).

So we can clearly understand that there is a God without knowing what he is.

[4] *Pensées*, 152–58.

Is there no substantial truth, seeing that there are so many true things which are not truth itself?

❧

We therefore know the existence and nature of the finite, because we too are finite and have no extension.

We know the existence of the infinite, and do not know its nature, because it has extent like us, but not the same limits as us.

But we know neither the existence nor the nature of God, because he has neither extent nor limits.

❧

But we know of his existence through faith. In glory we will know his nature.

Now I have already shown that we can certainly know the existence of something without knowing its nature.

Let us now speak according to natural lights.

If there is a God, he is infinitely beyond our comprehension, since, having neither parts nor limits, he bears no relation to ourselves. We are therefore incapable of knowing either what he is, or if he is. That being so, who will dare to undertake a resolution of this question? It cannot be us, who bear no relationship to him.

Who will then blame the Christians for being unable to provide a rational basis for their belief, they who profess a religion for which they cannot provide a rational basis? They declare that it is a folly, *stultitiam* (1 Cor. 1:18) in laying it before the world: and then you complain that they do not prove it! If they did prove it, they would not be keeping their word. It is by the lack of proof that they do not lack sense. "Yes, but although that excuses those who offer their religion as it is, and that takes away the blame from them of producing it without a rational basis, it does not excuse those who accept it."

Let us therefore examine this point, and say: God is, or is not. But towards which side will we lean? Reason cannot decide anything.

There is an infinite chaos separating us. At the far end of this infinite distance a game is being played and the coin will come down heads or tails. How will you wager? Reason cannot make you choose one way or the other, reason cannot make you defend either of the two choices.

So do not accuse those who have made a choice of being wrong, for you know nothing about it! "No, but I will blame them not for having made this choice, but for having made any choice. For, though the one who chooses heads and the other one are equally wrong, they are both wrong. The right thing is not to wager at all."

Yes, but you have to wager. It is not up to you, you are already committed. Which then will you choose? Let us see. Since you have to choose, let us see which interests you the least. You have two things to lose: the truth and the good, and two things to stake: your reason and will, your knowledge and beatitude; and your nature has two things to avoid: error and wretchedness. Your reason is not hurt more by choosing one rather than the other, since you do have to make the choice. That is one point disposed of. But your beatitude? Let us weigh up the gain and the loss by calling heads that God exists. Let us assess the two cases: if you win, you win everything; if you lose, you lose nothing. Wager that he exists then, without hesitating! "This is wonderful. Yes, I must wager. But perhaps I am betting too much." Let us see. Since there is an equal chance of gain and loss, if you won only two lives instead of one, you could still put on a bet. But if there were three lives to win, you would have to play (since you must necessarily play), and you would be unwise, once forced to play, not to chance your life to win three in a game where there is an equal chance of losing and winning. But there is an eternity of life and happiness. And that being so, even though there were an infinite number of chances of which only one were in your favour, you would still be right to wager one in order to win two, and you would be acting wrongly, since you are obliged to play, by refusing to stake one life against three in a game where out of an infinite number of chances there is one in your favour, if there were an infinitely happy infinity of life to be won. But here there is an infinitely happy infinity of life to be won, one chance of winning against a finite number of chances of losing, and what you are staking is finite. That removes all choice: wherever there is infinity and where there is no infinity of chances of losing against one of winning, there is no scope for wavering, you have to chance everything. And thus, as you are forced to gamble, you have to have discarded reason if you cling on to your life, rather than risk it for the infinite prize which is just as likely to happen as the loss of nothingness.

For it is no good saying that it is uncertain if you will win, that it is certain you are taking a risk, and that the infinite distance between the CERTAINTY of what you are risking and the UNCERTAINTY of whether you win makes the finite good of what you are certainly risking equal to the uncertainty of the infinite. It does not work like that. Every gambler takes a certain risk for an uncertain gain; nevertheless he certainly risks the finite uncertainty in order to win a finite gain, without sinning against reason. There is no infinite distance between this certainty of what is being risked and the uncertainty of what might be gained: that is untrue. There is, indeed, an infinite distance between the certainty of winning and the certainty of losing. But the uncertainty of winning is proportional to the certainty of the risk, according to the chances of winning or losing. And hence, if there are as many chances on one side as on the other, the odds are even, and then the certainty of what you risk is equal to the uncertainty of winning. It is very far from being infinitely distant from it. So our argument is infinitely strong, when the finite is at stake in a game where there are equal chances of winning and losing, and the infinite is to be won.

That is conclusive, and, if human beings are capable of understanding any truth at all, this is the one.

"I confess it, I admit it, but even so . . . Is there no way of seeing underneath the cards?" "Yes, Scripture and the rest, etc." "Yes, but my hands are tied and I cannot speak a word. I am being forced to wager and I am not free, they will not let me go. And I am made in such away that I cannot believe. So what do you want me to do?" "That is true. But at least realize that your inability to believe, since reason urges you to do so and yet you cannot, arises from your passions: So concentrate not on convincing yourself by increasing the number of proofs of God but on diminishing your passions. You want to find faith and you do not know the way? You want to cure yourself of unbelief and you ask for the remedies? Learn from those who have been bound like you, and who now wager all they have. They are people who know the road you want to follow and have been cured of the affliction of which you want to be cured. Follow the way by which they began: by behaving just as if they believed, taking holy water, having masses said, etc. That will make you believe quite naturally, and according to your animal reactions." "But that is what I am afraid of." "Why? What do you have to lose? In order to show you that this is where it leads, it is because it diminishes the passions, which are your great stumbling-blocks, etc."

"How these words carry me away, send me into raptures," etc. If these words please you and seem worthwhile, you should know that they are spoken by a man who knelt both before and afterwards to beg this infinite and indivisible Being, to whom he submits the whole of himself, that you should also submit yourself, for your own good and for his glory, and that strength might thereby be reconciled with this lowliness.

End of this discourse.

But what harm will come to you from taking this course? You will be faithful, honest, humble, grateful, doing good, a sincere and true friend. It is, of course, true; you will not take part in corrupt pleasure, in glory, in the pleasures of high living. But will you not have others?

I tell you that you will win thereby in this life, and that at every step you take along this path, you will see so much certainty of winning and so negligible a risk, that you will realize in the end that you have wagered on something certain and infinite, for which you have paid nothing.

❧

We owe a great deal to those who warn us of our faults, for they mortify us; they teach us that we have been held in contempt, but they do not prevent it from happening to us in the future, for we have many other faults to merit it. They prepare us for the exercise of correction, and the removal of a fault.

❧

Custom is natural to us. Anyone who becomes accustomed to faith believes it, and can no longer not fear hell, and believes in nothing else. Anyone who becomes accustomed to believing that the king is to be feared, etc. Who can then doubt that our soul, being accustomed to seeing number, space, movement, believes in this and nothing else?

❧

Do you believe that it is impossible that God should be infinite and indivisible? "Yes." I want to show you, then (*an image of God in his boundlessness*), an infinite and indivisible thing: it is a point moving everywhere at infinite speed.

For it is a single entity everywhere, and complete in every place.

Let this fact of nature, which previously seemed to you impossible, make you understand that there may be others which you do not yet know. Do not draw the conclusion from your apprenticeship that there is nothing left for you to learn, but that you have an infinite amount to learn.

It is not true that we are worthy of being loved by others. It is unfair that we should want to be loved. If we were born reasonable and impartial, knowing ourselves and others, we would not incline our will in that direction. However, we are born with it.

We are therefore born unfair. For everything is biased towards it-self: this is contrary to all order. The tendency should be towards the generality, and the leaning towards the self is the beginning of all disorder: war, public administration, the economy, the individ-ual body.

The will is therefore depraved. If the members of the natural and civil communities tend towards the good of the body, the communities themselves should tend towards another, more gen-eral body, of which they are the members. We should therefore tend towards the general. We are born, then, unjust and depraved.

No religion apart from our own has taught that man is born sinful. No philosophical sect has said so. So none has told the truth.

No sect or religion has always existed on earth, apart from the Christian religion.

Only the Christian religion makes men together both LOVABLE AND HAPPY. We cannot be both capable of being loved and happy in formal society.

It is the heart that feels God, not reason: that is what faith is, God felt by the heart, not by reason.

The heart has its reasons which reason itself does not know: we know that through countless things.

I say that the heart loves the universal being naturally, and itself naturally, according to its own choice. And it hardens itself against one or the other, as it chooses. You have rejected one and kept the other: is it reason that makes you love yourself?

The only knowledge which is contrary to both common sense and human nature is the only one which has always existed among men.

Various Fragments from the Pensées

743 The nature of self-love and of this human self is to love only self and consider only self. But what is it to do? It cannot prevent this object it loves from being full of shortcomings and

wretchedness; it wants to be great and sees that it is small; it wants to be happy and sees that it is wretched; it wants to be perfect and sees that it is full of imperfections; it wants to be the object of people's love and esteem and sees that its shortcomings merit only their dislike and their contempt. This predicament in which it finds itself arouses in it the most unjust and criminal passion that it is possible to imagine; for it conceives a deadly hatred for that truth which rebukes it, and which convinces it of its shortcomings. It would like to crush it, and, being unable to destroy it as such, it destroys it, as best it can, in its consciousness and in that of others; that is to say that it takes every care to hide its shortcomings both from others and from itself, and cannot bear to have them pointed out or observed.

It is no doubt an evil to be full of shortcomings; but it is an even greater evil to be full of them and unwilling to recognize them, since this entails the further evil of deliberate self-delusion. We do not want others to deceive us; and we do not think it right that they should want to be esteemed by us more than they merit: neither, therefore, is it just that we should deceive them and want them to esteem us more than we deserve.

And so, when they reveal only the imperfections and vices which we actually have, it is obvious that they do us no wrong, since it is not they who are under scrutiny; and that they are doing us good, since they are helping us to escape from an evil, which is the ignorance of these imperfections. We ought not to be angry that they know them and despise us, it being just that they know us for what we are, and despise us if we are despicable.

These are the feelings which would spring from a heart full of equity and justice. What should we then say of ours, seeing in it a quite different disposition? For is it not true that we hate both the truth and those who tell it to us, and that we like them to be deceived to our advantage, and want to be esteemed by them as other than we really are?

And here is a proof which horrifies me. The Catholic religion does not oblige us to reveal our sins indiscriminately to everyone. It allows us to remain hidden from all others; but it makes a single exception, to whom we are enjoined to reveal our innermost heart, and show ourselves for what we are. There is only this one person in the world whom we are enjoined to disillusion, and it lays on this person the obligation of inviolable secrecy, which means that this knowledge is known, but might as well not be. Can you imagine anything more charitable or more gentle? And yet people's corruption is such that they find even this law harsh; and this is one of the main reasons why a large part of Europe has rebelled against the Church.

How unjust and unreasonable the heart of mankind is, to resent the obligation to behave towards one person in a fashion that, in some ways, would be right to behave towards everyone! For is it right that we should deceive them?

There are different degrees in this aversion for the truth; but we can say that it is in everyone to some degree, because it is inseparable from self-love. It is false delicacy which makes those who have to rebuke others choose so many devious ways and qualifications to avoid offending them. They must minimize our shortcomings, pretend to excuse them, combine them with praise and expressions of affection and esteem. Even then, this medicine still tastes bitter to self-love. It takes as little of it as possible, always with distaste, and often even with hidden resentment for those who offer it.

It follows from this that, if anyone has an interest in being loved by us, they shy away from rendering us a service they know we would find disagreeable. We are treated as we want to be treated: we hate the truth and it is kept from us; we want to be flattered and we are flattered; we like to be deceived and we are deceived.

This is why each degree of good fortune which takes us up in the world distances us further from the truth, because people are more afraid of offending those whose affection is more useful and whose dislike more dangerous. A prince can be the laughing-stock of all Europe and only he will not know it. I am not surprised: telling the truth is useful to the hearer but harmful to the teller, because they incur hatred. Now those who live with princes prefer their own interests to that of the prince they serve; and so they are careful not to procure an advantage for him by harming themselves.

This misfortune is no doubt greater and more common among those with large fortunes; but those less well-off are not exempt, because we always have some interest in being popular. And so human life is nothing but a perpetual illusion; there is nothing but mutual deception and flattery. No one talks about us in our presence as they do in our absence. Human relationships are founded only on this mutual deception; and few friendships would survive if everyone knew what their friend said about them when they were not there. Even though the friend spoke sincerely and without passion.

Mankind is therefore nothing but disguise, lies, and hypocrisy, both as individuals and with regard to others. They therefore do not want to be told the truth. They avoid telling it to others. And all these tendencies, so remote from justice and reason, are naturally rooted in their heart.

501 *Church, Pope. Unity/multiplicity.* Considering the Church as a unity, the Pope, who is its head, represents the whole. Considering it as a multiplicity, then the Pope is only a part. The Fathers considered it sometimes one way and sometimes the other, and so spoke of the Pope in different ways.

St. Cyprian, SACERDOS DEI [the priest of God].

But in establishing one of these two truths, they have not excluded the other. Multiplicity which is not reduced to unity is confusion. Unity which does not depend on multiplicity is tyranny.

556 The Pope hates and fears scholars who have not taken vows to obey him.

584 *Binding and loosing.* God did not want to allow absolution without the Church: as it is involved in the offence, he wants it to be involved in the pardon. He associates it with this power, as do kings their parliaments. But if it absolves or binds without God, it is no longer the Church. The same with parliament: for while the king may have pardoned someone, it must be registered; but if parliament registers without the king or if it refuses to register on

the king's orders, it is no longer the king's parliament, but a rebellious body.

585 They cannot have perpetuity, yet they seek universality. For that they make the whole Church corrupt, so that they can be saints.

586 *Popes.* Kings control their empire, but popes cannot control theirs.

The Due Subordination and Use of Reason[5]

The highest attainment of reason, is to know that there is an infinity of knowledge beyond its limits. It must be sadly weak if it has not discovered this. We ought to know where we should doubt, where we should be confident, and where we should submit. He who knows not this does not comprehend the true power of reasoning. There are men who fail severally on each of these points. Some from ignorance of what is demonstration, assume every thing to be demonstrable; others not knowing where it becomes them to submit silently, doubt of every thing; and others again, unconscious of the right field for the exercise of judgment, submit blindly to all.

2. If we subject every thing to reason, our religion would have nothing in it mysterious and supernatural. If we violate the principles of reason, our religion would be absurd and contemptible. . . .

3. Piety differs from superstition. Superstition is the death of piety. The heretics reproach us with this superstitious submission of the understanding. We should deserve their reproach, if we required this surrender in things which do not require it rightly. Nothing is more consistent with reason, than the repression of reasoning in matters of faith. Nothing more contrary to reason than the repression of reasoning in matters which are not of faith.

[5] Blaise Pascal, *Thoughts on Religion and Other Subjects*, trans. Rev. Edward Craig (Edinburgh: H. S. Baynes, 1825), 84–87.

To exclude reasoning altogether, or to take no other guide, are equally dangerous extremes.

4. Faith affirms many things, respecting which the senses are silent; but nothing that they deny. It is always superior, but never opposed to their testimony.

5. Some men say, If I had seen a miracle, I should have been converted. But they would not so speak if they really understood conversion. They imagine that conversion consists in the recognition of a God; and that to adore him, is but to offer him certain addresses, much resembling those which the pagans made to their idols. True conversion, is to feel our nothingness before that Sovereign Being whom we have so often offended; and who might, at any moment, justly destroy us. It is to acknowledge, that without Him we can do nothing, and that we have deserved nothing but his wrath. It consists in the conviction, that between God and us, there is an invincible enmity; and that, without a Mediator, there can be no communion between us.

6. Do not wonder to see some unsophisticated people believe without reasoning. God gives them the love of his righteousness, and the abhorrence of themselves. He inclines their heart to believe. We should never believe with a living and influential faith, if God did not incline the heart; but we do so as soon as he inclines it. This David felt, when he said, *Incline my heart, O Lord, unto thy testimonies.*

7. If any believe truly, without having examined the evidence of religion, it is, that they have received within, a holy disposition, and that they find the averments of our religion conformed to it. They feel that God has made them. They wish but to love him, and to hate only themselves. They feel that they are without strength; that they are unable to go to God, and that unless he comes to them, they can have no communication with him. And then they learn from our religion, that they should love only God, and hate only themselves, but that being utterly corrupt, and alienated from God, God became man, that he might unite himself to us. Nothing more is wanting to convince men, who have

this principle of piety in their hearts, and who know also both their duty and their weakness.

8. Those whom we see to be Christians, without the inspection of the prophecies and other evidences, are found equally good judges of the religion itself, as others who have this knowledge. They judge by the heart, as others do by the understanding. God himself has inclined their hearts to believe, and hence they are effectively persuaded.

I grant that a Christian who thus believes without examining evidence, would probably not have the means of convincing an infidel, who could put his own case strongly. But those who know well the evidence for Christianity, can prove, without difficulty, that this belief is truly inspired of God, though the man is not able to prove it in himself.

To Further the Search for God[6]

In this way those who only affect these feelings would be miserable indeed if they were to coerce their nature in order to become the most insolent of men. If they are angry in their innermost heart at their lack of understanding, let them not hide it. Such an admission would not be shameful. The only shame is to have none. Nothing more surely underlines an extreme weakness of mind than the failure to recognize the unhappiness of someone without God. Nothing more surely betrays an evil mind than the failure to desire the truth of eternal promises. Nothing is more cowardly than to pit oneself against God. Let them then leave such impieties to those who are ill-bred enough to be genuinely capable of them: let them at least be honourable, even if they cannot be Christians! And let them realize, finally, that there are only two sorts of people who can be called reasonable: those who serve God with all their heart because they know him, and those who seek him with all their heart because they do not know him.

---

[6] *Pensées*, 163–64.

But as for those who live without knowing him and without seeking him, they consider themselves so unworthy of their own consideration that they are unworthy of the consideration of others, and we need all the charity of that religion they despise not to despise them to the extent of abandoning them to their foolishness. But because this religion obliges us always to look on them, as long as they live, as being capable of the grace which can enlighten them, and to believe that in a short while they can be filled with more faith than ourselves, and that we on the other hand can fall into the blindness where they are now, we must do for them what we would want others to do for us if we were in their place, and appeal to them to have pity on themselves and take at least a few steps to see whether they cannot find enlightenment. Let them apply to this reading a few of the hours they so uselessly employ on other things: with whatever reluctance they approach it, they will perhaps find something, and at least they will not lose a great deal. But for those who bring absolute sincerity to it and a real desire to find the truth, I hope they will be satisfied, and will be convinced by the proofs of so divine a religion which I have collected here, and in which I have followed more or less this order. . . .

Discourse Concerning Corruption[7]

690 It is therefore true that everything teaches man about his condition, but it must be properly understood: for it is not true that everything reveals God, but it is true that at the same time he hides himself from those who tempt him, and reveals himself to those who seek him, because humanity is at the same time unworthy of God and capable of God; unworthy through its corruption, capable through its first nature.

What shall we conclude from all our obscurities then but our unworthiness?

---

[7] *Pensées*, 169–72.

If there were no obscurity, we would not feel our corruption. If there were no light we could not hope for a remedy. And so it is not only just, but useful for us, that God should be hidden in part and revealed in part, since it is equally dangerous for man to know God without knowing his wretchedness, and to know his wretchedness without knowing God.

❦

So it teaches men both these truths: that there is a God of whom we are capable, and that there is a corruption in nature which makes us unworthy of him. It is equally important for us to know both these points, and it is equally dangerous for man to know God without knowing his own wretchedness, and to know his wretchedness without knowing the Redeemer who can cure him of it. Knowledge of only one of these points leads either to the arrogance of the philosophers, who have known God and not their own wretchedness, or to the despair of the atheists, who know their wretchedness without knowing the Redeemer.

And so, as it is equally necessary for us to know both these points, it is also equally due to God's mercy that he made us aware of them. The Christian religion does this, and it is indeed in this that it consists.

❦

The God of Christians does not consist of a God who is simply the author of mathematical truths and the order of the elements: that is the job of the pagans and Epicureans. He does not consist simply of a God who exerts his providence over the lives and property of people in order to grant a happy span of years to those who worship him: that is the allocation of the Jews. But the God of Abraham, the God of Isaac, the God of Jacob, the God of the Christians is a God of love and consolation; he is a God who fills the souls and hearts of those he possesses; he is a God who makes them inwardly aware of their wretchedness and his infinite mercy, who unites with them in the depths of their soul, who makes them incapable of any other end but himself.

The Vanity of Science[8]

Knowledge of physical science will not console me for ignorance of morality [in] time of affliction, but knowledge of morality will always console me for ignorance [of] physical science.

Further Reading

The eighteen *Provincial Letters*, considered Pascal's literary best, resulted from his collaboration with the Jansenists in their pamphlet war with the Molinists in 1656. Filled with scorching irony, they were written against what Pascal thought were the moral teachings of the Jesuits. His unfinished *Writings on Grace* date from 1655. Around the same time Pascal also wrote *The Mathematical Mind*, which included *The Art of Persuasion*. The document translated as *Discussion with Monsieur de Sacy* is based on notes supplied by Pascal and contains his reflections on Epictetus and Montaigne and more apologetics based on Christian revelation. In English, Pascal's most important writings on religion can be found in three collections: his *Pensées and Other Writings*, translated by Honor Levi (Oxford: Oxford University Press, 1995); his *Thoughts on Religion*, translated by Rev. Edward Craig, (Amherst: J. S. and C. Adams, 1829); and *The Thoughts on Religion and Evidences of Christianity of Pascal*, translated by George Pearce (London: Longman, Brown, Green and Longmans, 1850). In French, the standard critical edition is *Oeuvres complètes*, edited by Jean Mesnard (Paris: Bibliothèque Europénne, Desclée De Brouwer, 1942). For background on the theological controversy between the Jansenists and the Molinists, see the brilliantly cynical study by Leszek Kolakowski, *God Owes Us Nothing: A Brief Remark on Pascal's Religion and on the Spirit of Jansenism* (Chicago: University of Chicago Press, 1995).

---

[8] *Pensées*, 57.

5 Isaac Newton
(1643–1727)

Introduction

Not until after the famous 1936 sale of Isaac Newton's papers in auction at Sotheby's did the full extent of Newton's heterodox theology begin to be revealed. Scattered as far as Jerusalem, some manuscripts only became generally accessible at the end of the 1960s. Finally, with the release in 1991 of the majority of Newton's unpublished writings on microfilm, the availability of his unpublished theological papers has revolutionized Newton scholarship. The 1998 foundation of the Newton Project has so far managed to put online an astonishing number of transcriptions, but more astonishing still is Newton's own vast outpouring of alchemical, theological, prophetic, and historical writings, estimated to run at least several million words. From these we are able to see today a new Newton: an intensely driven genius (and a bit of a quirky megalomaniac) who for over fifty years dabbled in alchemy, collated New Testament manuscripts, pored over the records of the primitive church, railed against the Trinity, looked into the secrets of the prophetic future, and insisted over and over that all these enterprises were not inconsistent with his work in physics, optics, and mathematics.

Newton's religious views were as idiosyncratic as his science was brilliant. If Kepler was obsessed with the Trinity and able to find it everywhere, Newton was supremely suspicious of its biblical basis and able to find it nowhere. A fiercely pious Anglican Christian, he was scarcely orthodox. In his rejection of the doctrine of the Trinity, Newton could best be described as an Arian, after the heretic Arius (250–336), who held that Jesus was the son of God, but not divine. As a created intermediary between God and man, Jesus was subordinate to God, chosen to be a prophet and messenger, and then exalted to the right hand of the omnipotent Pantocrator. The notion that Christ is an eternal person in a triune God was the work of "idolators, blasphemers, and spiritual fornicators," Newton fumed, and he would not even use the initials for Anno Domini in designating dates. For the most part, he kept these views private, finessed a chair at Cambridge University that dispensed with the usual requirement of ordination that his unorthodoxy would have prohibited, and enjoyed a career that afforded prolonged immersion in theology and alchemy as much as in scientific and mathematical work.

Two fascinating features of Newton's faith are evident in his secret theological writings: an abiding interest in biblical prophecy, particularly the books of Daniel and Revelation, and a devotion to chronology and the history of the early Church. Possessed of a powerful millenarian outlook, he believed that the complex prophecies of the Bible were not ways of foretelling the future but rather of seeing, after the fact, the providence of God. The second obsession, for chronological precision, drove Newton into another discipline, astronomy, in which he had no peer. He determined the dates of ancient events, such as Christ's birth and Artaxerxes' decree to rebuild Jerusalem, by measuring the precession of equinoxes and locating eclipses, comets, and natural disasters that were often mentioned in ancient chronicles. In his *Chronology of Ancient Kingdoms Amended,* published by relatives in the year after his death, Newton managed, using characteristic erudition and astronomic and mathematical precision, to encompass universal history within Archbishop James Ussher's chronology, beginning with creation in 4004 BCE and proceeding down to Solomon's Temple in 1012. Rescuing history from myth is always a dubious undertaking, today dubbed "euhemerism," but Newton devoted decades to reading ancient history in an effort to establish historical benchmarks for the prophecies in the Book of Daniel. He treated the visions narrated in the Apocalypse realistically and translated their symbols into political actors and events.

In this chapter, all the excerpts are devoted to Newton's core faith. Evident in the first selection, one of Newton's famous four letters to Richard Bentley, is the version of the teleological argument that Newton found most compelling, consisting in a particular aspect of celestial structure: the fact that "planets move all one and the same way in orbs concentric, while comets move all manner of ways in orbs very eccentric." Even if the waywardness in the motions of the comets could be ascribed to some natural cause, planetary motions, on the other hand, "must have been the effect of counsel." No *natural* cause could have given the planets and moons the precise velocity that each needed to maintain an almost circular orbit, rather than a hyberbolic, parabolic, or eccentric elliptical orbit. The cause of it all must be "not blind or fortuitous but very well skilled in mechanics and geometry," he noted to Bentley.

The second selection consists in the entirety of the short but densely packed General Scholium that Newton appended to the second edition of his masterwork, *The Mathematical Principles of Natural Philosophy*, known as the *Principia*, first published in Latin in 1687. To this day it is one of the most influential and important scientific books ever published. In the General Scholium to the 1713 edition, Newton makes clear that he was not a deist, and for that matter not much of a "Newtonian" either. His God had "a propensity toward action" in the universe. What is striking about this document is its layered litany of theological themes, ranging from the exoteric to the esoteric. In a very short space, Newton covers a cascade of topics—comets, gravity, planetary motion, space, tides, active powers, electricity—and manages to embed in his natural philosophy a potent theology built on the argument from design. Along the way he takes swipes at Descartes and Leibniz and, obliquely, the Trinity.

The issue between Newton and René Descartes concerned the image of God as watchmaker, creating a universe that ran by itself. Newton emphatically rejected such a view and championed instead the God of prophecy and presence, actively involved in the mechanical world. Indeed, his version of mechanism was shaped expressly in the service of his religious views. The only way a mechanistic universe could possibly run, he thought, was by continual divine providence. Material bodies, being passive, do not move of their own accord; they therefore must have some source of motion other than their own nature. Newton reasoned in this way to such "active principles" as gravity, magnetism, fermentation, and other nonmechanical forces. One of his most conclusive arguments for the universality of the laws of motion, in fact, seems based on his understanding of divine omnipresence, for "If there be an universal life and all space be the sensorium of a thinking being who by immediate presence perceives all things in it . . . the laws of motion arising from life or will may be of universal extent."[1]

Could the universe have arisen by blind chance through the mere action of passive laws of nature? Never! Furthermore, Newton believed that without continual divine supervision, the universe would run down. The planetary orbits, he calculated, were unstable enough to eventually break down if God did not sustain them. Comets were perhaps the means by which God realigned the cosmos when needed. This proposal alienated not only Descartes but also Gottfried Leibniz, the other formidable continental rationalist of Newton's time. Was God such a poor craftsman to begin with that he had to fiddle and tinker and learn on the job? Wouldn't an all-wise and all-perfect Creator get it right at the outset and

[1] Quoted in Richard Westfall, *Force in Newton's Physics* (London: Macdonald, 1971), 340.

make it run forever, Leibniz wondered? Newton's retort was that such a God would seem finally unnecessary, superfluous to the smooth running of the universe, and no different than no God at all.

It was God who placed the planets at different distances from the sun so that according to their degrees of density they might enjoy a greater or less proportion of the sun's heat. Convinced of the reality of intelligent purpose in the cosmic order, Newton believed that underlying the phenomena of nature there is a being, incorporeal, living, intelligent, omnipresent, who, in infinite space—as it were in his sensory—sees the phenomena of nature intimately. The main purpose of natural philosophy, he explained, was to find this First Cause and thence to resolve questions such as the following: How does the force of gravity work? What stops the stars from falling toward each other? What is the significance of comets, and why is their behavior so different from that of the planets? How is it that organic life is so excellently functional? What is the source of all the order, economy, and beauty in the world?

On the most challenging question of all, whether natural processes are governed by their own innate active principles or by God, Newton was ambivalent. He refers at some stages to natural processes being governed by active principles, which he invokes as agents of God; through their ministrations, the total amount of motion in the universe is conserved rather than steadily dissipated. At other stages he implies that God, as the mathematical mechanic par excellence, is directly active in the cosmos—for example, enabling the forces of gravity (the "puppet strings of God") both to maintain the orbits of the planets and to nudge them back on course whenever their accumulation of interactions with other celestial bodies leads them toward instability. One can see here why Leibniz, his great rival, accused Newton of making God an inept creator, who had to keep tinkering with the universe. Subsequently, with the dramatic success of Newtonian physics, others were to draw the conclusion that gravity is an innate property of material bodies, but Newton himself vehemently rejected the idea, writing that it was "so great an absurdity that I believe no man who has in philosophical matters a competent faculty of thinking can ever fall into it."[2]

The final selection, "Queries about the word Homoousios," is a piece of rhetorical writing that reveals two of Newton's most vehement convictions: that the Greek word for "same substance" is an unscriptural metaphysical innovation, and that those who defended the word were Papists in thrall to Rome. In the *General Scholium*, Newton's antitrinitarian reasoning, though evident, is submerged. In his theological manuscripts, he clearly situates Jesus Christ as a man who mediates between God and humans but who should not be worshiped in place of the Father.

Samuel Johnson reportedly said "if Newton had flourished in ancient Greece, he would have been worshipped as a Divinity."[3] When one considers his invention of the calculus and discovery of universal gravitation and other laws of physics, one is inclined to agree. But Newton himself would have considered it a blasphemous compliment; his own self-assessment near the end of his life, measured against the most exacting of standards, was less exalted: "I do not know what I may appear to the world, but to myself I seem to have been only like a boy playing on the seashore, and diverting myself in now and then finding a smoother pebble or a prettier shell than ordinary, whilst the great ocean of truth lay all undiscovered before me."[4]

✺ Newton's Contribution to Science

Isaac Newton's monumental work, Mathematical Principles of Natural Philosophy *(1687) has been described as the greatest feat in all*

---

[2] Quoted in Morris Kline, *Mathematics and the Search for Knowledge* (New York: Oxford University Press, 1985), 121.

[3] James Boswell, *The Life of Samuel Johnson* (London: H.G. Bohn, 1857), 2:144, n. 1.

[4] David Brewster, *The Life of Sir Isaac Newton* (New York: Harper, 1831), 300–301.

of science. Its three sections cover the general principles governing the motion of bodies (dynamics); the application of these principles to the motion of celestial bodies, especially the planets and their satellites, under the force of gravity; and fluid mechanics, the theory of waves, and certain other aspects of physics. He developed the powerful tool of differential calculus from the work of Fermat and Descartes (though Leibniz challenged him for priority). Building upon Galileo's mathematical relations, he formulated the laws of motion: (1) any body will continue to move with constant velocity unless compelled to change its velocity by an applied force (the law of inertia); (2) the change of velocity is proportional to the force applied and is parallel to it (or "force equals mass times acceleration"); and (3) to every action (force) there is an equal and opposite reaction (force). By combining his second law of motion with Kepler's laws of planetary motion, Newton formulated the law of universal gravitation for the force F between two masses, M_1 and M_2, separated by a distance R: so that, F is proportional to the product $M_1 M_2$ and inversely proportional to R squared. It took genius to see that all of heaven and earth are united by a single set of laws.

Newton in His Own Words

Letter from Newton to Richard Bentley[5] (December 10, 1692)

Sir

When I wrote my treatise about our system, I had an eye upon such principles as might work with considering men for the belief of a Deity; and nothing can rejoice me more than to find it useful for that purpose. But if I have done the public any service this way, it is due to nothing but industry and patient thought.

---

[5] Richard Bentley, Alexander Dyce, and Isaac Newton, *The Works of Richard Bentley*, collected and ed. A. Dyce (London: F. Macpherson, 1838), 203–7.

As to your first query, it seems to me that if the matter of our sun and planets, and all the matter of the universe were evenly scattered throughout all the heavens, and every particle had an innate gravity towards all the rest, and the whole space throughout which this matter was scattered was but finite; the matter on the outside of this space would, by its gravity, tend towards all the matter on the inside, and, by consequence, fall down into the middle of the whole space, and there compose one great spherical mass. But if the matter was evenly disposed throughout an infinite space, it could never convene into one mass; but some of it would convene into one mass, and some into another, so as to make an infinite number of great masses, scattered at great distances from one to another throughout all that infinite space. And thus might the sun and fixed stars be formed, supposing the matter were of a lucid nature. But how the matter should divide itself into two sorts, and that part of it which is fit to compose a shining body should fall down into one mass and make a sun, and the rest which is fit to compose an opaque body should coalesce, not into one great body, like the shining matter, but into many little ones; or if the sun at first were an opaque body like the planets, or the planets lucid bodies like the sun, how he alone should be changed into a shining body, whilst all they continue opaque, or all they be changed into opaque ones, whilst he remains unchanged; I do not think explicable by mere natural causes, but am forced to ascribe it to the counsel and contrivance of a voluntary Agent. The same Power, whether natural or supernatural, which placed the sun in the centre of the six primary planets, placed Saturn in the centre of the orbs of his five secondary planets, and Jupiter in the centre of his four secondary planets, and the earth in the centre of the moon's orb; and therefore, had this cause been a blind one, without contrivance or design, the sun would have been a body of the same kind with Saturn, Jupiter, and the earth, that is, without light and heat. Why there is one body in our system qualified to give light and heat to all the rest, I know no reason, but because the Author of the system thought it convenient; and why there is but one body of this kind, I know no reason, but because one was sufficient to warm and enlighten all the rest. For the Cartesian hypothesis of suns losing their light, and then turning into comets, and comets into planets, can have no place in my system, and is plainly erroneous; because it is certain, that as often as they appear to us, they descend into the system of our planets, lower than the orb of Jupiter, and sometimes lower than the orbs of Venus and Mercury, and yet never stay here, but always return from the sun with the same degrees of motion by which they approached him.

To your second query, I answer, that the motions which the planets now have could not spring from any natural cause alone, but were impressed by an intelligent Agent. For since comets descend into the region of our planets, and here move all manner of ways, going sometimes the same way with the planets, sometimes the contrary way, and sometimes in cross ways, in planes inclined to the plane of the ecliptic, and at all kinds of angles, 'tis plain that there is no natural cause which could determine all the planets, both primary and secondary, to move the same way and in the same plane, without any considerable variation: this must have been the effect of counsel. Nor is there any natural cause which could give the planets those just degrees of velocity, in proportion to their distances from the sun and other central bodies, which were requisite to make them move in such concentric orbs about those bodies. Had the planets been as swift as comets, in proportion to their distances from the sun, (as they would have been, had their motion been caused by their gravity, whereby the matter, at the first formation of the planets, might fall from the remotest regions towards the sun,) they would not move in concentric orbs, but in such eccentric ones as the comets move in. Were all the planets as swift as Mercury, or as slow as Saturn or his satellites; or were their several velocities otherwise much greater or less than they are, as they might have been, had they arose from any other cause than their gravities; or had the distances from the centres about which they move been greater or less than they are, with the same velocities; or had the quantity of matter in the sun, or in Saturn, Jupiter, and the earth, and, by consequence, their gravitating power, been greater or less than it is; the primary planets could not have revolved about the sun, nor the secondary ones about Saturn, Jupiter, and the earth, in concentric circles, as they do, but would have moved in hyperbolas, or parabolas, or in ellipses very eccentric. To make this system, therefore, with all its motions, required a cause which understood and compared together the quantities of matter in the several bodies of the sun and planets, and the gravitating powers resulting from thence; the several distances of the primary planets from the sun, and of the secondary ones from Saturn, Jupiter, and the earth; and the velocities with which these planets could revolve about those quantities of matter in the central bodies; and to compare and adjust all these things together, in so great a variety of bodies, argues that cause to be, not blind and fortuitous, but very well skilled in mechanics and geometry.

To your third query, I answer, that it may be represented that the sun may, by heating those planets most which are nearest to him, cause them to be better concocted, and more condensed by that concoction. But, when I consider that our earth is much more heated in its bowels below the upper crust by subterraneous fermentations of mineral bodies than by the sun, I see not why the interior parts of Jupiter and Saturn might not be as much heated, concocted, and coagulated by those fermentations as our earth is; and therefore this various density should have some other cause than the various distances of the planets from the sun. And I am confirmed in this opinion by considering, that the planets of Jupiter and Saturn, as they are rarer than the rest, so they are vastly greater, and contain a far greater quantity of matter, and have many satellites about them; which qualifications surely arose not from their being placed at so great a distance from the sun, but were rather the cause why the Creator placed them at great distance. For, by their gravitating powers they disturb one another's motions very sensibly, as I find by some late observations of Mr. Flamsteed; and had they been placed much nearer to the sun and to one another, they would, by the same powers, have caused a considerable disturbance in the whole system.

To your fourth query, I answer, that, in the hypothesis of vortices, the inclination of the axis of the earth might, in my opinion, be ascribed to the situation of the earth's vortex before it was absorbed by the neighbouring vortices, and the earth turned from a sun to a comet; but this inclination ought to decrease constantly in compliance with the motion of the earth's vortex, whose axis is much less inclined to the ecliptic, as appears by the motion of the moon carried about therein. If the sun by his rays could carry about the planets, yet I do not see how he could thereby effect their diurnal motions.

Lastly, I see nothing extraordinary in the inclination of the earth's axis for proving a Deity, unless you will urge it as a contrivance for winter and summer, and for making the earth habitable towards the poles; and that the diurnal rotations of the sun and planets, as they could hardly arise from any cause purely mechanical, so by being determined all the same way with the annual and menstrual motions, they seem to make up that harmony in the system, which, as I explained above, was the effect of choice rather than chance. There is yet another argument for a Deity, which I take to be a very strong one; but till the principles on which it is grounded are better received, I think it more advisable to let it sleep. I am

Your most humble Servant to command
        Is. NEWTON.

The General Scholium to Principia Mathematica[6]

The hypotheses of Vortices is press'd with many difficulties. That every Planet by a radius drawn to the Sun may describe areas proportional to the times of description, the periodic times of the several parts of the Vortices should observe the duplicate proportion of their distances from the Sun. But that the periodic times of the Planets may obtain the sesquiplicate proportion of their distances from the Sun, the periodic times of the parts of the Vortex ought to

---

[6] Isaac Newton, *The Mathematical Principles of Natural Philosophy*, trans. Andrew Motte (London, 1729), 387–93.

be in sesquiplicate proportion of their distances. That the smaller Vortices may maintain their lesser revolutions about Saturn, Jupiter, and other Planets, and swim quietly and undisturb'd in the greater Vortex of the Sun, the periodic times of the parts of the Sun's Vortex should be equal. But the rotation of the Sun and Planets about their axes, which ought to correspond with the motions of their Vortices, recede far from all these proportions. The motions of the Comets are exceedingly regular, are govern'd by the same laws with the motions of the Planets, and can by no means be accounted for by the hypotheses of Vortices. For Comets are carry'd with very eccentric motions through all parts of the heavens indifferently, with a freedom that is incompatible with the notion of a Vortex.

Bodies, projected in our air, suffer no resistance but from the air. Withdraw the air, as is done in Mr. Boyle's vacuum, and the resistance ceases. For in this void a bit of fine down and a piece of solid gold descend with equal velocity. And the parity of reason must take place in the celestial spaces above the Earth's atmosphere; in which spaces, where there is no air to resist their motions, all bodies will move with the greatest freedom; and the Planets and Comets will constantly pursue their revolutions in orbits given in kind and position, according to the laws above explain'd. But though these bodies may indeed persevere in their orbits by the mere laws of gravity, yet they could by no means have at first deriv'd the regular position of the orbits themselves from those laws.

The six primary Planets are revolv'd about the Sun, in circles concentric with the Sun, and with motions directed towards the same parts and almost in the same plan. Ten Moons are revolv'd about the Earth, Jupiter and Saturn, in circles concentric with them, with the same direction of motion, and nearly in the planes of the orbits of those Planets. But it is not to be conceived that mere mechanical causes could give birth to so many regular motions: since the Comets range over all parts of the heavens, in very eccentric orbits. For by that kind of motion they pass easily through the orbits of the Planets, and with great rapidity; and in their aphelions, where they move the slowest, and are detain'd the longest, they recede to the greatest distances from each other, and thence suffer the least disturbance from their mutual attractions. This most beautiful System of the Sun, Planets, and Comets, could only proceed from the counsel and dominion of an intelligent and powerful being. And if the fixed Stars are the centers of other like systems, these, being form'd by the like wise counsel, must be all subject to the dominion of One; especially since the light of the fixed Stars is of the same nature with the light of the Sun, and from every system light passes into all the other systems. And lest the systems of the fixed Stars should, by their gravity, fall on each other mutually, he hath placed those Systems at immense distances from one another.

This Being governs all things, not as the soul of the world, but as Lord over all: And on account of his dominion he is wont to be called Lord God Pantokrator,[7] or Universal Ruler. For God is a relative word, and has a respect to servants; and Deity is the dominion of God, not over his own body, as those imagine who fancy God to be the soul of the world, but over servants. The supreme God is a Being eternal, infinite, absolutely perfect; but a being, however perfect, without dominion, cannot be said to be Lord God; for we say, my God, your God, the God of Israel, the God of Gods, and Lord of Lords; but we do not say, my Eternal, your Eternal, the Eternal of Israel, the Eternal of Gods; we do not say, my Infinite, or my Perfect: These are titles which have no respect to servants. The word God usually[8] signifies Lord; but every lord is not a God. It is the dominion of a spiritual being which constitutes a God; a true, supreme, or imaginary dominion makes a true, supreme, or imaginary God. And from his true dominion it follows that the true God is a Living, Intelligent, and Powerful

---

[7] *Pantokrator* in Greek in Newton's text.

[8] Dr. Pocock derives the Latin word Deus from the Arabic du (in the oblique case di,) which signifies Lord. And in this sense Princes are called Gods, Psal. lxxxii. ver. 6; and John x. ver. 35. And Moses is called a God to his brother Aaron, and a God to Pharaoh (Exod. iv. ver. 16; and vii. ver. 1 [correction for the 1729 edition, which reads: 8]). And in the same sense the souls of dead princes were formerly, by the Heathens, called gods, but falsely, because of their want of dominion. —*IN* (3d ed., 1726).

Being; and, from his other perfections, that he is Supreme or most Perfect. He is Eternal and Infinite, Omnipotent and Omniscient; that is, his duration reaches from Eternity to Eternity; his presence from Infinity to Infinity; he governs all things, and knows all things that are or can be done. He is not Eternity and Infinity, but Eternal and Infinite; he is not Duration and Space, but he endures and is present. He endures forever, and is every where present; and, by existing always and every where, he constitutes Duration and Space. Since every particle of Space is always, and every indivisible moment of Duration is every where, certainly the Maker and Lord of all things cannot be never and no where. Every soul that has perception is, though in different times and in different organs of sense and motion, still the same indivisible person. There are given successive parts in duration, co-existent parts in space, but neither the one nor the other in the person of a man, or his thinking principle; and much less can they be found in the thinking substance of God. Every man, so far as he is a thing that has perception, is one and the same man during his whole life, in all and each of his organs of sense. God is the same God, always and everywhere. He is omnipresent, not virtually only, but also substantially; for virtue cannot subsist without substance. In him[9] are all things contained and moved; yet neither affects the other: God suffers nothing from the motion of bodies; bodies find no resistance from the omnipresence of God. 'Tis allowed by all that the supreme God exists necessarily; and by the same necessity he exists always and every where. Whence also he is all similar, all eye, all ear, all brain, all arm, all power to perceive, to understand,

---

[9] This was the opinion of the Ancients. So Pythagoras in Cicer. de Nat. Deor. lib. i. Thales, Anaxagoras, Virgil, Georg. lib. iv. ver. 220. and Aeneid. lib. vi. ver. 721. Philo Allegor. at the beginning of lib. i. Aratus in his Phænom. at the beginning. So also the sacred Writers, as St. Paul, Acts xvii. ver. 27, 28. St. John's Gosp. chap. xiv. ver. 2. Moses in Deut. iv. ver. 39; and x. ver. 14. David, Psal. cxxxix. ver. 7, 8, 9. Solomon, 1 Kings viii. ver. 27. Job xxii. ver. 12, 13, 14. Jeremiah xxiii. ver. 23, 24. The Idolaters supposed the Sun, Moon, and Stars, the Souls of Men, and other parts of the world, to be parts of the supreme God, and therefore to be worshiped; but erroneously. —IN.

and to act; but in a manner not at all human, in a manner not at all corporeal, in a manner utterly unknown to us. As a blind man has no idea of colours, so have we no idea of the manner by which the all-wise God perceives and understands all things. He is utterly void of all body and bodily figure, and can therefore neither be seen, nor heard, nor touched; nor ought he to be worshipped under the representation of any corporeal thing. We have ideas of his attributes, but what the real substance of anything is we know not. In bodies, we see only their figures and colours, we hear only the sounds, we touch only their outward surfaces, we smell only the smells, and taste the savours; but their inward substances are not to be known, either by our senses, or by any reflex act of our minds; much less then have we any idea of the substance of God. We know him only by his most wise and excellent contrivances of things, and final causes; we admire him for his perfections; but we reverence and adore him on account of his dominion. For we adore him as his servants; and a God without dominion, providence, and final causes, is nothing else but Fate and Nature. Blind metaphysical necessity, which is certainly the same always and every where, could produce no variety of things. All that diversity of natural things which we find, suited to different times and places, could arise from nothing but the ideas and will of a Being necessarily existing. But, by way of allegory, God is said to see, to speak, to laugh, to love, to hate, to desire, to give, to receive, to rejoice, to be angry, to fight, to frame, to work, to build. For all our notions of God are taken from the ways of mankind, by a certain similitude which, though not perfect, has some likeness, however. And thus much concerning God; to discourse of whom from the appearances of things, does certainly belong to Natural Philosophy.[10]

Hitherto we have explain'd the phænomena of the heavens and of our sea, by the power of Gravity, but have not yet assign'd the cause of this power. This is certain, that it must proceed from a cause that penetrates to the very centers of the Sun and Planets, without suffering the least diminution of its force; that operates,

---

[10] 1713 edition: Experimental Philosophy. —AM.

not according to the quantity of surfaces of the particles upon which it acts, (as mechanical causes use to do,) but according to the quantity of the solid matter which they contain, and propagates its virtue on all sides, to immense distances, decreasing always in the duplicate proportion of the distances. Gravitation towards the Sun, is made up out of the gravitations towards the several particles of which the body of the Sun is compos'd; and in receding from the Sun, decreases accurately in the duplicate proportion of the distances, as far as the orb of Saturn, as evidently appears from the quiescence of the aphelions of the Planets; nay, and even to the remotest aphelions of the Comets, if those aphelions are also quiescent. But hitherto I have not been able to discover the cause of those properties of gravity from phænomena, and I frame no hypotheses. For whatever is not deduc'd from the phænomena, is to be called an hypothesis; and hypotheses, whether metaphysical or physical, whether of occult qualities or mechanical, have no place in experimental philosophy. In this philosophy particular propositions are inferr'd from the phænomena, and afterwards render'd general by induction. Thus it was that the impenetrability, the mobility, and the impulsive force of bodies, and the laws of motion and of gravitation, were discovered. And to us it is enough, that gravity does really exist, and act according to the laws which we have explained, and abundantly serves to account for all the motions of the celestial bodies, and of our sea.

And now we might add something concerning a certain most subtle Spirit, which pervades and lies hid in all gross bodies; by the force and action of which Spirit, the particles of bodies mutually attract one another at near distances, and cohere, if contiguous; and electric bodies operate to greater distances, as well repelling as attracting the neighbouring corpuscles; and light is emitted, reflected, refracted, inflected, and heats bodies; and all sensation is excited, and the members of animal bodies move at the command of the will, namely, by the vibrations of this Spirit, mutually propagated along the solid filaments of the nerves, from the outward organs of sense to the brain, and from the brain into the muscles. But these are things that cannot be explain'd in few words, nor are we furnish'd with that sufficiency of experiments which is required to an accurate determination and demonstration of the laws by which this electric and elastic spirit operates.

From Newton's Theological Manuscripts[11]

Queries about the Word *Homoousios*

Quære 1. Whether Christ sent his Apostles to preach Metaphysicks to the unlearned common people & to their wives & children.

Quære 2. Whether the word ομοουσιος ever was in any Creed before the Nicene; or any Creed was produced by any one Bishop at the Council of Nice for authorizing the use of that word.

Quære 3. Whether the introducing the use of that word is not contrary to the Apostles rule of holding fast the form of sound words.

Quære 4. Whether the use of that word was not pressed upon the Council of Nice against the inclination of the major part of the Council.

Quære 5. Whether it was not pressed upon them by the Emperor Constantine the great a Chatechumen not yet baptized & no member of the Council.

Quære 6. Whether it was not agreed by the Council that that word when applied to the Son of God should signify nothing more then that Christ was the express image of the father, & whether many of the Bishops in pursuance of that interpretation of the word allowed by the Council, did not in their subscriptions by way of caution add τουτ εστιν ομοιουσιος?

Quære 7. Whether Hosius (or whoever translated that Creed into Latin) did not impose upon the western Churches by translating ομοουσιος by the words *unius substantiæ* instead of

---

[11] Sir Isaac Newton, *Theological Manuscripts,* selected and ed. H. McLachlan (Liverpool: University Press, 1950), 44ff. None of Newton's primarily theological writings were published in his lifetime.

consubstantialis & whether by that translation the Latin Churches were not drawn into an opinion that the father & son had one common substance called in the Greek Hypostasis & whether they did not thereby give occasion to the eastern Churches to cry out (presently after the Council of Serdica) that the western Churches were become Sabellian.

Quære 8. Whether the Greeks in opposition to this notion & language did not use the language of three hypostases, & whether in those days the word hyposta did not signify a substance.

Quære 9. Whether the Latins did not at that time accuse all those of Arianism who used the language of three hypostases & thereby charge Arianism upon the Council of Nice without knowing the true meaning of the Nicene Creed.

Quære 10. Whether the Latines were not convinced in the Council of Ariminum that the Council of Nice by the word ομοουσιος understood nothing more than that the son was the express image of the father. The Acts of the Council of Nice were not produced for convincing them. And whether upon producing the Acts of that Council for proving this, the Macedonians & some others did not accuse the Bishops of hypocrisy who in subscribing those Acts had interpreted them by the word ομοιουσιος in their subscriptions.

Quære 11. Whether Athanasius, Hilary & in general the Greeks & Latines did not from the time of the reign of Iulian the Apostate acknowledge the father Son & holy Ghost to be three substances & continue to do so till the Schoolmen changed the signification of the word hypostasis & brought in the notion of three persons in one single substance.

Quære 12. Whether the opinion of the equality of the three substances was not first set on foot in the reign of Iulian the Apostate by Athanasius Hilary &c.

Quære 13. Whether the worship of the Holy Ghost was not first set on foot presently after the Council of Serdica.

Quære 14. Whether the Council of Serdica was not the first Council which declared for the doctrine of the consubstantial Trinity & whether the same Council did not affirm that there was but one hypostasis of the father son & H. Ghost.

Quære 15. Whether the Bishop of Rome five years after the death of Constantine the great A.C. 341 did not receive appeals from the Greek Councils & thereby begin to usurp the universal Bishopric.

Quære 16. Whether the Bishop of Rome in absolving the Appellants from excommunication & communicating with them & did not excommunicate himself & begin a quarrel with the Greek Church.

Quære 17. Whether the Bishop of Rome in summoning all the Bishops of the Greek Church to appear at the next Council of Rome A.C. 342 did not challenge dominion over them & begin to make war upon them for obteining it.

Quære 18. Whether that Council of Rome in receiving the Appellants into Communion did not excommunicate themselves & support the Bishop of Rome in claiming appeals from all the world.

Quære 19. Whether the Council of Serdica in receiving the Appellants into Communion & decreeing Appeals from all the Churches to the Bishop of Rome did not excommunicate themselves & become guilty of the schism which followed thereupon, & set up Popery in all the west.

Quære 20. Whether the Emperor Constantius did not by calling the Council of Millain & Aquileia A.C. 365, abolish Popery, & whether Hilary, Lucifer, were not banished for adhering to the authority of the Pope to receive appeals from the Greek Councils.

Quære 21. Whether the Emperor Gratian A.C. 379 did not by his Edict restore the Universal Bishopric of Rome over all the west? And whether this authority of the Bishop of Rome hath not continued ever since.

Quære 22. Whether Hosius Saint Athanasius, Saint Hilary, Saint Ambrose, Saint Hierome, Saint Austin were not Papists.

Further Reading

For transcriptions of Newton's original manuscripts, the reader is best referred to the extraordinary "Newton Project" at http://www.newtonproject .ic.ac.uk. This is a dynamic site, as more and more of the theological tracts and alchemical texts come online each month. The best short and up-to-date biography of Newton is James Gleick, *Isaac Newton* (New York: Vintage Books, 2004), complete with a treasure trove of footnote references to the Newton manuscripts known as "Keynes" and "Yahuda." Robert S. Westfall's *Never at Rest: A Biography of Isaac Newton* (Cambridge: Cambridge University Press, 1980) remains authoritative in the main but downplays the influence of Newton's theology on his natural philosophy. Frank Manuel's *The Religion of Isaac Newton* (Oxford: Clarendon Press, 1974) is notable for a Freudian reading of Newton and for the appendix containing Newton's "Fragments from a Treatise on Revelation" and "Of the Day of Judgment and World to Come." Newton the alchemist is the subject of Betty Jo Dobbs, *The Foundation of Newton's Alchemy* (Cambridge: Cambridge University Press, 1975). For a variety of recent scholarly views of Newton's theology, see *Essays on the Context, Nature and Influence of Isaac Newton's Theology*, edited by James E. Force and Richard H. Popkin (Dordrecht and Boston: Kluwer Academic Publishers, 1990), and *Newton and Religion: Context, Nature, and Influence*, edited by James E. Force and Richard H. Popkin (Dordrecht and Boston: Kluwer, 1999). Important background can be found in *Leibniz-Clarke Correspondence*, edited by. H. G. Alexander (New York: Philosophical Library, 1956).

6 Charles Darwin
(1809–1882)

Introduction

Look up "creationist" in the *Oxford English Dictionary* and you will find an early 1859 use of the word credited to Charles Darwin. As might be expected, Darwin argued against the creationists, but in his time they were rival scientists, mostly geologists like Adam Sedgwick, who believed in a special creation for each species.

Nowhere is it more important to differentiate periods of a scientist's life and outlook than in the case of Charles Darwin's complex religious views. The young Darwin received an orthodox Anglican education and had a conventional Christian faith. He firmly believed the Bible to be the inspired word of God. His freethinking father wanted him to become a clergyman, as it would provide a comfortable lifestyle, and Darwin did spend three years at Cambridge preparing for ordination. Throughout the voyage of the HMS *Beagle* (1831–36), Darwin largely accepted the argument from design given classic expression in William Paley's *Natural Theology* (1802). But by the time he returned to England, Darwin was having doubts about the reliability of the Bible. Back in England he began to realize the importance of geographic variation within the islands and set about using his own notes and specimens and those of other researchers to piece together what, in fact, he did not see in the Galapagos. During this time he also realized the impossibility of miracles as a support for Christianity, the discrepancies among the Gospels, and the difficulty he was having trying imaginatively "to invent evidence which would suffice to convince me" of the truth of Christianity. By 1840 Darwin had become an evolutionist and sometime in the 1840s he abandoned traditional Christianity. His position in the next period might be described as a form of deism in which God, the unmoved mover, was thought to work through unbroken natural laws. But by the end of his life even Darwin's deism had faded. "Disbelief crept over me at a very slow rate," he reported, causing "no distress." The mystery of the beginning of all things, he declared, is insoluble by us. He was content to remain an "Agnostic." Agnosticism, a term coined by Thomas Huxley, whose support of the theory of evolution was so tenacious he was nicknamed "Darwin's Bulldog," meant a strict denial of judgment. In Darwin's case, it meant that he was unable to believe in God and unwilling to admit to atheism.

Two factors seemed to have played a major role in Darwin's shift: the problem of pain and suffering and the excesses of evangelical Christianity, with its doctrine of damnation. Interestingly, neither one had to do with the theory of evolution. Darwin's disenchantment with Christianity stemmed more from moral concerns and personal devastation over the death of his father in 1848 and then of his beloved ten-year-old daughter Anne in 1851. A second child would later die also, and Darwin's own illnesses were debilitating. His question, therefore, was Job's question. How can one believe in a just and merciful Omnipotence who allows the suffering of the innocent? How could an omnipotent and benevolent God damn to hell his freethinking father? Questions like these only widened the religious rift between Darwin and his wife.

Darwin had married his cousin Emma Wedgwood, who bore him ten children. They loved each other deeply, but throughout their otherwise happy marriage each agonized over their irreconcilable religious differences. Janet Browne, in her splendid biography *Charles Darwin* (1995), reprints one of Emma's letters to Charles, written before they married, in which she implores him to give up his habit of "believing nothing until it is proved." Darwin called it a "beautiful letter" and wrote on its envelope, "When I am dead, know how many times I have kissed and cried over this."

A writer of beautiful letters himself, Darwin carried on an extensive correspondence that left an unmistakable record of his religious doubt and ambivalence, mixed with great intellectual honesty and modesty. Several of those letters are reprinted or excerpted below.

In the letter to geologist Charles Lyell in 1861, Darwin rejects outright the hypothesis that the variation inherent in natural selection is the result of some form of divine design. In the first of two letters to the Harvard botanist Asa Gray, his great American advocate, Darwin doubts whether every action of every animal, even a specific swallow eating a particular gnat at a certain moment, can reasonably fall into God's pattern of design. And if these minute actions are not designed, then why should one believe the origins of man or other species are designed? Asa Gray's side of the correspondence deserves its own chapter in this volume, if only space permitted. Maintaining that natural selection was compatible with Christian belief in a Creator God, since "the physical cause of variation is utterly unknown and mysterious," Gray even detected a theological advantage to using Darwin's theory to account for the imperfections and failures, as well as the successes, of nature. It permitted a more convincing theodicy: the seeming waste is part and parcel of a great economical process that serves God's ultimate purposes. A God who left the details to chance was somehow nobler. Darwin thought that this theodicy was most improbable. In the second letter to Gray, he responded that the real source of his objection was not that Gray's designed variation would make natural selection superfluous but rather that Darwin's studies of domestic variations had shown him what an enormous field of undesigned variability there was for natural selection to appropriate for any purpose useful to a particular creature. Species are mutable, continuously evolving entities whose explanation is non-teleological. The world does indeed *seem* designed; but that is due entirely to the workings of natural selection. Moreover, the biblical Creator God, unlike the distant God of eighteenth-century deism, could be expected to be less indifferent to the ongoing needs of creatures. The variation on which the process of natural selection depended had to be spontaneous rather than designed. This much Darwin's science established. His faith consisted in seeing that there is "grandeur in this view of life."

The next two excerpts are the concluding paragraphs of *On the Origin of Species* (1859) and *The Descent of Man* (1871). Consider the difference between the denouement of the first edition of the *Origin of Species* and the modified final lines of later editions as represented here. The first edition read as follows: "There is grandeur in this view of life, with its several powers, having been originally breathed into a few forms or into one; and that, whilst this planet has gone cycling on according to the fixed law of gravity, from so simple a beginning endless forms most beautiful and most wonderful have been, and are being, evolved."[1] In later editions, Darwin added the words "by the Creator" after "breathed." Many have speculated on his motive, especially since it is known that he became less religious as he got older. One suggestion is that it was done for diplomatic reasons, to balance the other seven times the word "Creator" appeared in the book, always with skepticism and to illustrate the superiority of evolutionary explanations. In any case, Darwin, who abhorred conflict, later wrote to a friend in 1863 that he regretted the use of creationist terminology and that he had "truckled to public opinion." No such equivocation can be discerned in the concluding paragraphs of *The Descent of Man.*

---

[1] As Stephen Jay Gould has noted, the word "evolved" appears only in this one instance in *Origin of Species* and "evolution" never. Darwin did not want his theory of natural selection to be confused with any postulate of "progress" as a necessary feature of organic history. Victorian England had made progress the centerpiece of its credo.

In another excerpt from *The Descent of Man*, Darwin devotes a few pages to developing a history of belief in God as a natural progression from belief in spiritual agencies, a theory akin to that of E. B. Tylor, an early anthropologist of religion.

The best source for understanding Darwin's loss of faith is the *Autobiography* he wrote between 1876 and 1881 (not for publication but only to be read by his wife and children), an entire section of which concerns his religious beliefs. It is a remarkably honest and humble statement, running to eleven pages and given in its entirety in the last selection below. The edition used here is the unexpurgated one, republished by Darwin's granddaughter Nora Barlow in 1958. The original published version of Darwin's *Autobiography* appeared in 1887 in *The Life and Letters of Charles Darwin*, edited by his botanist son Francis Darwin. Darwin's family had heavily censored it, omitting almost six thousand words. Readers curious to see what omissions were considered necessary in 1887 should compare the two editions.

Self-portraits often conceal as much as they reveal. But there is every reason to trust that in this autobiographical statement written in his sixty seventh year Darwin expressed his religious doubts as freely as his scientific convictions. Agnosticism, gentle and hesitant, was the only position he could espouse at the end of his religious journey. In the words of his granddaughter, "No one can read his own words and fail to recognize a character of rare simplicity and complete integrity."

☙ Darwin's Contribution to Science

Charles Darwin's lasting contribution is the concept of natural selection as the mechanism that explains adaptation within local environments. He showed that natural selection follows from just three assumptions: all species produce more offspring than can survive; there is variation within a species; and there is at least some principle of inheritance.

Darwin in His Own Words

Letters from Darwin[2]

To Geologist Charles Lyell in Response to His Questions Concerning the *Origin of Species* (1861)

I declare that you read the reviews on the *Origin* more carefully than I do. I agree with all your remarks. The point of correlation struck me as well put, and on varieties growing together; but I have already begun to put things in train for information on this latter head, on which Bronn also enlarges. With respect to sexuality, I have often speculated on it, and have always concluded that we are too ignorant to speculate: no physiologist can conjecture why the two elements go to form a new being, and, more than that, why nature strives at uniting the two elements from two individuals. What I am now working at in my orchids is an admirable illustration of the law. I should certainly conclude that all sexuality had descended from one prototype. Do you not underrate the degree of lowness of organisation in which sexuality occurs—viz., in *Hydra*, and still lower in some of the one-celled free conferva: which "conjugate," which good judges (Thwaites) believe is the simplest form of true sexual generation? But the whole case is a mystery.

There is another point on which I have occasionally wished to say a few words. I believe you think with Asa Gray that I have not allowed enough for the stream of variation having been guided by a higher power. I have had lately a good deal of correspondence on this head. Herschel, in his *Physical Geography*, has a sentence with respect to the *Origin*, something to the effect that the

---

[2] The letters to Lyell and Gray appear in *More Letters of Charles Darwin*, vol. 1, ed. Francis Darwin and A. C. Seward (London: Hazell, Watson and Viney, 1903), 190–92. The last two letters are quoted by Francis Darwin in his edition of *The Autobiography of Charles Darwin* (London: John Murray, 1887), 306–07.

higher law of Providential Arrangement should always be stated. But astronomers do not state that God directs the course of each comet and planet. The view that each variation has been providentially arranged seems to me to make Natural Selection entirely superfluous, and indeed takes the whole case of the appearance of new species out of the range of science. But what makes me most object to Asa Gray's view is the study of the extreme variability of domestic animals. He who does not suppose that each variation in the pigeon was providentially caused, by accumulating which variations, man made a Fantail, cannot, I think, logically argue that the tail of the woodpecker was formed by variations providentially ordained. It seems to me that variations in the domestic and wild conditions are due to unknown causes, and are without purpose, and in so far accidental; and that they become purposeful only when they are selected by man for his pleasure, or by what we call Natural Selection in the struggle for life, and under changing conditions. I do not wish to say that God did not foresee everything which would ensue; but here comes very nearly the same sort of wretched imbroglio as between freewill and preordained necessity. I doubt whether I have made what I think clear; but certainly A. Gray's notion of the courses of variation having been led like a stream of water by gravity, seems to me to smash the whole affair. It reminds me of a Spaniard whom I told I was trying to make out how the Cordillera was formed; and he answered me that it was useless, for "God made them." It may be said that God foresaw how they would be made. I wonder whether Herschel would say that you ought always to give the higher providential law, and declare that God had ordered all certain changes of level, that certain mountains should arise. I must think that such views of Asa Gray and Herschel merely show that the subject in their minds is in Comte's theological stage of science. . . .

Of course I do not want any answer to my quasi-theological discussion, but only for you to think of my notions, if you understand them.

I hope to Heaven your long and great labours on your new edition are drawing to a close.

To Botanist Asa Gray, Questioning God's Design in Nature (1860)

One word more on "designed laws" and "undesigned results." I see a bird which I want for food, take my gun, and kill it, I do this *designedly*. An innocent and good man stands under a tree and is killed by a flash of lightning. Do you believe (and I really should like to hear) that God *designedly* killed this man? Many or most persons do believe this; I can't and don't. If you believe so, do you believe that when a swallow snaps up a gnat that God designed that that particular swallow should snap up that particular gnat at that particular instant? I believe that the man and the gnat are in the same predicament. If the death of neither man nor gnat are designed, I see no good reason to believe that their *first* birth or production should be necessarily designed.

To Asa Gray, on Design and Chance (1860)

With respect to the theological view of the question. This is always painful to me. I am bewildered. I had no intention to write atheistically. But I own that I cannot see as plainly as others do, and as I should wish to do, evidence of design and beneficence on all sides of us. There seems to me too much misery in the world. I cannot persuade myself that a beneficent and omnipotent God would have designedly created the Ichneumonidae with the express intention of their feeding within the living bodies of Caterpillars, or that a cat should play with mice. Not believing this, I see no necessity in the belief that the eye was expressly designed. On the other hand, I cannot anyhow be contented to view this wonderful universe, and especially the nature of man, and to conclude that everything is the result of brute force. I am inclined to look at everything as resulting from designed laws, with the details, whether good or bad, left to the working out of what we may call chance. Not that this notion at all satisfies me. I feel most deeply that the whole subject is too profound for the human intellect. A dog might as well speculate on the mind of Newton. Let each man hope and believe what he can. Certainly I agree with you that my views are not at all necessarily atheistical. The lightning kills a man, whether a good one or bad one, owing to the excessively complex action of natural laws. A child (who may turn out an idiot) is born by the action of even more complex laws, and I can see no reason why a man, or other animal, may not have been aboriginally produced by other laws, and that all these laws may have been expressly designed by an omniscient Creator, who foresaw every future event and consequence. But the more I think the more bewildered I become; as indeed I probably have shown by this letter.

To an Unnamed Correspondent, Espousing Agnosticism, not Atheism (1873)

What my own views may be is a question of no consequence to any one but myself. But, as you ask, I may state that my judgment often fluctuates. . . . In my most extreme fluctuations I have never been an Atheist in the sense of denying the existence of a God. I think that generally (and more and more as I grow older), but not always, that an Agnostic would be the more correct description of my state of mind.

To a Dutch Student, Expressing Ambivalence about a First Cause (1873)

It is impossible to answer your question briefly; and I am not sure that I could do so, even if I wrote at some length. But I may say that the impossibility of conceiving that this grand and wondrous universe, with our conscious selves, arose through chance, seems to me the chief argument for the existence of God; but whether this is an argument of real value, I have never been able to decide. I am aware that if we admit a First Cause, the mind still craves to know whence it came, and how it arose. Nor can I overlook the difficulty from the immense amount of suffering through the world. I am, also, induced to defer to a certain extent to the judgment of the many able men who have fully believed in God; but here again I see how poor an argument this is. The safest conclusion seems to me that the whole subject is beyond the scope of man's intellect, but man can do his duty.

Concluding Statement, On the Origin of Species (Sixth Edition, 1872)

It is interesting to contemplate a tangled bank, clothed with many plants of many kinds, with birds singing on the bushes, with various insects flitting about, and with worms crawling through the damp earth, and to reflect that these elaborately constructed forms, so different from each other, and dependent upon each other in so complex a manner, have all been produced by laws acting around us. These laws, taken in the largest sense, being Growth with Reproduction; Inheritance which is almost implied by reproduction; Variability from the indirect and direct action of the conditions of life and from use and disuse: a Ratio of Increase so high as to lead to a Struggle for Life, and as a consequence to Natural Selection, entailing Divergence of Character and the Extinction of less-improved forms. Thus, from the war of nature, from famine and death, the most exalted object which we are capable of conceiving, namely, the production of the higher animals, directly follows. There is grandeur in this view of life, with its several powers, having been originally breathed by the Creator into a few forms or into one; and that, whilst this planet has gone cycling on according to the fixed law of gravity, from so simple a beginning endless forms most beautiful and most wonderful have been and are being evolved.

Concluding Statement, The Descent of Man (First Edition, 1871)

The main conclusion arrived at in this work, namely, that man is descended from some lowly organised form, will, I regret to think, be highly distasteful to many. But there can hardly be a doubt that we are descended from barbarians. The astonishment which I felt on first seeing a party of Fuegians on a wild and broken shore will never be forgotten by me, for the reflection at once rushed into my mind—such were our ancestors. These men were absolutely naked and bedaubed with paint, their long hair was tangled, their mouths frothed with excitement, and their expression was wild, startled, and distrustful. They possessed hardly any arts, and like wild animals lived on what they could catch; they had no government, and were merciless to every one not of their own small tribe. He who has seen a savage in his native land will not feel much shame, if forced to acknowledge that the blood of some more humble creature flows in his veins. For my own part I would as soon be descended from that heroic little monkey, who braved his dreaded enemy in order to save the life of his keeper, or from that old baboon, who descending from the mountains, carried away in triumph his young comrade from a crowd of astonished dogs—as from a savage who delights to torture his enemies, offers up bloody sacrifices, practices infanticide without remorse, treats his wives like slaves, knows no decency, and is haunted by the grossest superstitions.

Man may be excused for feeling some pride at having risen, though not through his own exertions, to the very summit of the organic scale; and the fact of his having thus risen, instead of having been aboriginally placed there, may give him hope for a still higher destiny in the distant future. But we are not here concerned with hopes or fears, only with the truth as far as our reason permits us to discover it; and I have given the evidence to the best of my ability. We must, however, acknowledge, as it seems to me, that man with all his noble qualities, with sympathy which feels for the most debased, with benevolence which extends not only to other men but to the humblest living creature, with his god-like intellect which has penetrated into the movements and constitution of the solar system—with all these exalted powers—Man still bears in his bodily frame the indelible stamp of his lowly origin.

Comments on Religion as a Mental Faculty from The Descent of Man[3]

Belief in God, religion. There is no evidence that man was aboriginally endowed with the ennobling belief in the existence of an Omnipotent God. On the contrary there is ample evidence, derived not from hasty travelers, but from men who have long resided with savages, that numerous races have existed, and still exist, who have no idea of one or more gods, and who have no words in their languages to express such an idea. The question is of course wholly distinct from that higher one, whether there exists a Creator and Ruler of the universe; and this has been answered in the affirmative by some of the highest intellects that have ever existed.

If, however, we include under the term "religion" the belief in unseen or spiritual agencies, the case is wholly different; for this belief seems to be universal with the less civilized races. Nor is it difficult to comprehend how it arose. As soon as the important faculties of the imagination, wonder, and curiosity, together with some power of reasoning, had become partially developed, man would naturally crave to understand what was passing around him, and would have vaguely speculated on his own existence. As Mr. M'Lennan has remarked, "Some explanation of the phenomena of life, a man must feign for himself; and to judge from the universality of it, the simplest hypothesis and the first to occur to men, seems to have been that natural phenomena are ascribable to the presence in animals, plants, and things, and in the forces of nature, of such spirits prompting to action as men are conscious they themselves possess." It is also probable, as Mr Tylor has shewn, that dreams may have first given rise to the notion of spirits; for savages do not readily distinguish between subjective and objective impressions. When a savage dreams, the figures which appear before him are believed to have come from a distance, and

[3] Charles Darwin, *The Descent of Man and Selection in Relation to Sex*, (New York: D. Appleton and Co., 1871), 62–64, 65–66.

to stand over him; or "the soul of the dreamer goes out on its travels, and comes home with a remembrance of what it has seen." But until the faculties of imagination, curiosity, reason, etc., had been fairly well developed in the mind of man, his dreams would not have led him to believe in spirits, any more than in the case of a dog.

The feeling of religious devotion is a highly complex one, consisting of love, complete submission to an exalted and mysterious superior, a strong sense of dependence, fear, reverence, gratitude, hope for the future, and perhaps other elements. No being could experience so complex an emotion until advanced in his intellectual and moral faculties to at least a moderately high level. Nevertheless, we see some distant approach to this state of mind in the deep love of a dog for his master, associated with complete submission, some fear, and perhaps other feelings. The behaviour of a dog when returning to his master after an absence, and, as I may add, of a monkey to his beloved keeper, is widely different from that towards their fellows. In the latter case the transports of joy appear to be somewhat less, and the sense of equality is shown in every action. Professor Braubach goes so far as to maintain that a dog looks on his master as on a god.

The same high mental faculties which first led man to believe in unseen spiritual agencies, then in fetishism, polytheism, and ultimately in monotheism, would infallibly lead him, as long as his reasoning powers remained poorly developed, to various strange superstitions and customs. Many of these are terrible to think of—such as the sacrifice of human beings to a blood-loving god; the trial of innocent persons by the ordeal of poison or fire; witchcraft, etc.—yet it is well occasionally to reflect on these superstitions, for they show us what an infinite debt of gratitude we owe to the improvement of our reason, to science, and to our accumulated knowledge. As Sir J. Lubbock has well observed, "it is not too much to say that the horrible dread of unknown evil hangs like a thick cloud over savage life, and embitters every pleasure." These miserable and indirect consequences of our highest faculties may be compared with the incidental and occasional mistakes of the instincts of the lower animals.

Chapter on Religious Belief, Darwin's Autobiography [4]

During these two years I was led to think much about religion. Whilst on board the *Beagle* I was quite orthodox, and I remember being heartily laughed at by several of the officers (though themselves orthodox) for quoting the Bible as an unanswerable authority on some point of morality. I suppose it was the novelty of the argument that amused them. But I had gradually come, by this time, to see that the Old Testament from its manifestly false history of the world, with the Tower of Babel, the rainbow as a sign, etc., etc., and from its attributing to God the feelings of a revengeful tyrant, was no more to be trusted than the sacred books of the Hindoos, or the beliefs of any barbarian. The question then continually rose before my mind and would not be banished,—is it credible that if God were now to make a revelation to the Hindoos, would he permit it to be connected with the belief in Vishnu, Siva, &c., as Christianity is connected with the Old Testament. This appeared to me utterly incredible.

By further reflecting that the clearest evidence would be requisite to make any sane man believe in the miracles by which Christianity is supported,—that the more we know of the fixed laws of nature the more incredible do miracles become,—that the men at that time were ignorant and credulous to a degree almost incomprehensible by us,—that the Gospels cannot be proved to have been written simultaneously with the events,—that they differ in many important details, far too important as it seemed to me to be admitted as the usual inaccuracies of eyewitnesses;—by such

[4] Charles Darwin, *The Autobiography of Charles Darwin 1809–1882, with Original Omissions Restored*, ed. Nora Barlow (London: Collins, 1958), 85–96.

reflections as these, which I give not as having the least novelty or value, but as they influenced me, I gradually came to disbelieve in Christianity as a divine revelation. The fact that many false religions have spread over large portions of the earth like wild-fire had some weight with me. Beautiful as is the morality of the New Testament, it can hardly be denied that its perfection depends in part on the interpretation which we now put on metaphors and allegories.

But I was very unwilling to give up my belief;—I feel sure of this for I can well remember often and often inventing day-dreams of old letters between distinguished Romans and manuscripts being discovered at Pompeii or elsewhere which confirmed in the most striking manner all that was written in the Gospels. But I found it more and more difficult, with free scope given to my imagination, to invent evidence which would suffice to convince me. Thus disbelief crept over me at a very slow rate, but was at last complete. The rate was so slow that I felt no distress, and have never since doubted even for a single second that my conclusion was correct. I can indeed hardly see how anyone ought to wish Christianity to be true; for if so the plain language of the text seems to show that the men who do not believe, and this would include my Father, Brother and almost all my friends, will be everlastingly punished.

And this is a damnable doctrine.

Although I did not think much about the existence of a personal God until a considerably later period of my life, I will here give the vague conclusions to which I have been driven. The old argument of design in nature, as given by Paley, which formerly seemed to me so conclusive, fails, now that the law of natural selection has been discovered. We can no longer argue that, for instance, the beautiful hinge of a bivalve shell must have been made by an intelligent being, like the hinge of a door by man. There seems to be no more design in the variability of organic beings and in the action of natural selection, than in the course which the wind blows. Everything in nature is the result of fixed laws. But I have discussed this subject at the end of my book on the *Variation of Domestic Animals and Plants*, and the argument there given has never, as far as I can see, been answered.

But passing over the endless beautiful adaptations which we everywhere meet with, it may be asked how can the generally beneficent arrangement of the world be accounted for? Some writers indeed are so much impressed with the amount of suffering in the world, that they doubt if we look to all sentient beings, whether there is more of misery or of happiness;—whether the world as a whole is a good or a bad one. According to my judgment happiness decidedly prevails, though this would be very difficult to prove. If the truth of this conclusion be granted, it harmonises well with the effects which we might expect from natural selection. If all the individuals of any species were habitually to suffer to an extreme degree they would neglect to propagate their kind; but we have no reason to believe that this has ever or at least often occurred. Some other considerations, moreover, lead to the belief that all sentient beings have been formed so as to enjoy, as a general rule, happiness.

Every one who believes, as I do, that all the corporeal and mental organs (excepting those which are neither advantageous or disadvantageous to the possessor) of all beings have been developed through natural selection, or the survival of the fittest, together with use or habit, will admit that these organs have been formed so that their possessors may compete successfully with other beings, and thus increase in number. Now an animal may be led to pursue that course of action which is the most beneficial to the species by suffering, such as pain, hunger, thirst, and fear,—or by pleasure, as in eating and drinking and in the propagation of the species, &c. or by both means combined, as in the search for food. But pain or suffering of any kind, if long continued, causes depression and lessens the power of action; yet is well adapted to make a creature guard itself against any great or sudden evil. Pleasurable sensations, on the other hand, may be long continued without any depressing effect; on the contrary they stimulate the whole system to increased action. Hence it has come to pass that most or all sentient beings have been developed in such a manner through natural selection, that pleasurable sensations serve as their habitual guides. We see this in the pleasure from exertion, even occasionally from great exertion of the body or mind,—in the pleasure of our daily meals, and especially in the pleasure derived from sociability and from loving our families. The sum of such pleasures as these, which are habitual or frequently recurrent, give, as I can hardly doubt, to most sentient beings an excess of happiness over misery, although many occasionally suffer much. Such suffering, is quite compatible with the belief in Natural Selection, which is not perfect in its action, but tends only to render each species as successful as possible in the battle for life with other species, in wonderfully complex and changing circumstances.

That there is much suffering in the world no one disputes. Some have attempted to explain this in reference to man by imagining that it serves for his moral improvement. But the number of men in the world is as nothing compared with that of all other sentient beings, and these often suffer greatly without any moral improvement. A being so powerful and so full of knowledge as a God who could create the universe, is to our finite minds omnipotent and omniscient, and it revolts our understanding to suppose that his benevolence is not unbounded, for what advantage can there be in the sufferings of millions of the lower animals throughout almost endless time? This very old argument from the existence of suffering against the existence of an intelligent first cause seems to me a strong one; whereas, as just remarked, the presence of much suffering agrees well with the view that all organic beings have been developed through variation and natural selection.

At the present day the most usual argument for the existence of an intelligent God is drawn from the deep inward conviction and feelings which are experienced by most persons. But it cannot be doubted that Hindoos, Mahomadans and others might argue in the same manner and with equal force in favour of the existence of one God, or of many Gods, or as with the Buddists of no God. There are also many barbarian tribes who cannot be said with any truth to believe in what we call God: they believe indeed in spirits or ghosts, and it can be explained, as Tyler and Herbert Spencer have shown, how such a belief would be likely to arise.

Formerly I was led by feelings such as those just referred to, (although I do not think that the religious sentiment was ever strongly developed in me), to the firm conviction of the existence of God, and of the immortality of the soul. In my Journal I wrote that whilst standing in the midst of the grandeur of a Brazilian forest, "it is not possible to give an adequate idea of the higher feelings of wonder, admiration, and devotion which fill and elevate the mind." I well remember my conviction that there is more in man than the mere breath of his body. But now the grandest scenes would not cause any such convictions and feelings to rise in my mind. It may be truly said that I am like a man who has become colour-blind, and the universal belief by men of the existence of redness makes my present loss of perception of not the least value as evidence. This argument would be a valid one if all men of all races had the same inward conviction of the existence of one God; but we know that this is very far from being the case. Therefore I cannot see that such inward convictions and feelings are of any weight as evidence of what really exists. The state of mind which grand scenes formerly excited in me, and which was intimately connected with a belief in God, did not essentially differ from that which is often called the sense of sublimity; and however difficult it may be to explain the genesis of this sense, it can hardly be advanced as an argument for the existence of God, any more than the powerful though vague and similar feelings excited by music.

With respect to immortality, nothing shows me how strong and almost instinctive a belief it is, as the consideration of the view now held by most physicists, namely that the sun with all the planets will in time grow too cold for life, unless indeed some great body dashes into the sun and thus gives it fresh life.—Believing as I do that man in the distant future will be a far more perfect creature than he now is, it is an intolerable thought that he and all other sentient beings are doomed to complete annihilation after such long-continued slow progress. To those who fully admit the immortality of the human soul, the destruction of our world will not appear so dreadful.

Another source of conviction in the existence of God, connected with the reason and not with the feelings, impresses me as having much more weight. This follows from the extreme difficulty or rather impossibility of conceiving this immense and wonderful universe, including man with his capacity of looking far backwards and far into futurity, as the result of blind chance or necessity. When thus reflecting I feel compelled to look to a First Cause having an intelligent mind in some degree analogous to that of man; and I deserve to be called a Theist.

This conclusion was strong in my mind about the time, as far as I can remember, when I wrote the *Origin of Species*; and it is since that time that it has very gradually with many fluctuations become weaker. But then arises the doubt—can the mind of man, which has, as I fully believe, been developed from a mind as low as that possessed by the lowest animal, be trusted when it draws such grand conclusions? May not these be the result of the connection between cause and effect which strikes us as a necessary one, but probably depends merely on inherited experience? Nor must we overlook the probability of the constant inculcation in a belief in God on the minds of children producing so strong and perhaps an inherited effect on their brains not yet fully developed, that it would be as difficult for them to throw off their belief in God, as for a monkey to throw off its instinctive fear and hatred of a snake.

I cannot pretend to throw the least light on such abstruse problems. The mystery of the beginning of all things is insoluble by us; and I for one must be content to remain an Agnostic.

A man who has no assured and ever present belief in the existence of a personal God or of a future existence with retribution and reward, can have for his rule of life, as far as I can see, only to follow those impulses and instincts which are the strongest or which seem to him the best ones. A dog acts in this manner, but he does so blindly. A man, on the other hand, looks forwards and backwards, and compares his various feelings, desires and recollections. He then finds, in accordance with the verdict of all the wisest men that the highest satisfaction is derived from following certain impulses, namely the social instincts. If he acts for the good of others, he will receive the approbation of his fellow men and gain the love of those with whom he lives; and this latter gain undoubtedly is the highest pleasure on this earth. By degrees it will become intolerable to him to obey his sensuous passions rather than his higher impulses, which when rendered habitual may be almost called instincts. His reason may occasionally tell him to act in opposition to the opinion of others, whose approbation he will then not receive; but he will still have the solid satisfaction of knowing that he has followed his inner-most guide or conscience.—As for myself I believe that I have acted rightly in steadily following and devoting my life to science. I feel no remorse from having committed any great sin, but have often and often regretted that I have not done more direct good to my fellow creatures. My sole and poor excuse is much ill-health and my mental constitution, which makes it extremely difficult for me to turn from one subject or occupation to another. I can imagine with high satisfaction giving up my whole time to philanthropy, but not a portion of it; though this would have been a far better line of conduct.

Nothing is more remarkable than the spread of scepticism or rationalism during the latter half of my life. Before I was engaged to be married, my father advised me to conceal carefully my doubts, for he said that he had known extreme misery thus caused with married persons. Things went on pretty well until the wife or husband became out of health, and then some women suffered miserably by doubting about the salvation of their husbands, thus making them likewise to suffer. My father added that he had known during his whole long life only three women who were sceptics; and it should be remembered that he knew well a multitude of persons and possessed extraordinary power of winning confidence. When I asked him who the three women were, he had to own with respect to one of them, his sister-in-law Kitty Wedgwood, that he had no good evidence, only the vaguest hints, aided by the conviction, that so clear-sighted a woman could not be a believer. At the present time, with my small acquaintance, I know (or have known) several married ladies, who believe very little more than their husbands. My father used to quote an unanswerable argument, by which an old lady, a Mrs. Barlow, who suspected him of unorthodoxy, hoped to convert him:—"Doctor, I know that sugar is sweet in my mouth, and I know that my Redeemer liveth."

Further Reading

Charles Darwin's four great books are *The Voyage of the Beagle* (perhaps the most important travel book of all time), *On the Origin of Species* (written, Darwin said, "as one long argument"), *The Descent of Man, and Selection in Relation to Sex* (making explicit his faith that evolution is universal), and *The Expression of the Emotions in Man and Animals* (a book of keenly observed descriptions that anticipates much of modern psychology). The two-volume *Collected Papers of Charles Darwin* is edited by P. H. Barrett (Chicago: University of Chicago Press, 1977). *The Correspondence of Charles Darwin*, edited by F. Burkhardt and S. Smith (Cambridge: Cambridge University Press, 1985–), now runs to fifteen volumes with more to come. The unexpurgated *Autobiography of Charles Darwin, 1809–1882* is edited by Nora Barlow (London: Collins, 1958). The first two volumes of Janet Browne's projected three-volume biography are magisterial: *Charles Darwin: A Biography,* vol. 1, *Voyaging* (Princeton: Princeton University Press, 1995) and *Charles Darwin: A Biography,* vol. 2, *The Power of Place* (Princeton: Princeton University Press, 2000). A thoughtful analysis of Darwin's religious views is found in Frank Burch Brown, *The Evolution of Darwin's Religious Views* (Macon, GA: Mercer University Press, 1986). See also John Hedley Brooke, "Darwin's Science and His Religion," in *Darwinism and Divinity: Essays on Evolution and Religious Belief,* edited by John Durant (Oxford: Blackwell, 1985), 40–75. For a nuanced illumination of the nineteenth-century use of the term "creationist," see Neal C. Gillespie, *Darwin and the Problem of Creation* (Chicago: University of Chicago Press, 1979).

7 Albert Einstein
(1879–1955)

Introduction

The Swiss novelist and playwright Friedrich Dürrenmatt commented that "Einstein used to speak so often of God that I tend to believe he has been a disguised theologian."[1] Like many undisguised modern theologians, Einstein drew a crucial distinction between naïve, anthropomorphic belief in a personal God of miracles, rewards, and punishments and a faith that is more reflective and intellectual. He would have agreed with the theologian Paul Tillich, who redefined the concept of God on the grounds that "you have to save concepts before you can save souls." The concept of God was an important part of Einstein's religious faith. But what did he mean by the term? Answering that question brings to light three important elements of Einstein's faith: first, his preference for an impersonal cosmic order rather than a personal Being, epitomized in his saying "I believe in Spinoza's God, Who reveals Himself in the lawful harmony of the world, not in a God Who concerns Himself with the fate and the doings of mankind"; second,

---

[1] Quoted in Max Jammer, *Einstein and Religion: Physics and Theology* (Princeton: Princeton University Press 1999), 7.

his outright espousal of determinism, epitomized in his epigrammatic remark "God does not play at dice [with the universe]"; and third, his conviction that the universe is trustworthy and intelligible, not malevolent or capricious.[2] These elements converged for Einstein in what he called a powerful "cosmic religious feeling." His life-long compulsion to unify—reflected in his science, his politics, and his social ideals—was especially apparent in his religious sense of the universe.

The key to Einstein's conception of God is contained in the writings of the seventeenth-century Dutch philosopher Baruch Spinoza, particularly his *Ethics*, which Einstein read in Bern in his early twenties. Einstein never quotes directly from Spinoza and does not offer an extended exegesis of any texts. It seems likely that the real influence Spinoza had on him was in confirming ideas he was already entertaining. What, then, did Spinoza believe? Primarily, he believed that motion is intrinsic to matter, a claim that seemed counterintuitive to many of his contemporaries, for it would imply that God didn't have to give matter a nudge to make it move. But Spinoza did not shrink from the conclusion that "God's decrees and commandments, and consequently God's Providence are, in truth, nothing but Nature's order." *Deus sive Natura*: whether one called it God or Nature, one was speaking of the same reality, a causally concatenated totality. In Proposition 15 of his *Ethics*, Spinoza wrote, "Whatever is, is in God, and without God nothing can be, or be conceived."

Spinoza's conception of God represented two things that Einstein believed in deeply: the unity of nature and its utterly deterministic character. Perhaps no two people have believed more religiously in the ultimate rational nature of reality than Spinoza and Einstein. As Einstein wrote in a letter to his friend Maurice Solovine, "I can understand your aversion to the use of the term

---

[2] "Spinoza's God," in *The Expanded Quotable Einstein*, ed., Alice Calaprice (Princeton: Princeton University Press, 2000), 204, originally from a telegram to a Jewish newspaper, 1929 (Einstein Archive 33–272). "Dice" remark quoted in Jammer, 58; though its origin is now the stuff of myth, it was apparently a verbal observation never written down by Einstein himself but quoted often by others.

'religion' to describe an emotional and psychological attitude which shows itself most clearly in Spinoza. I have not found a better expression than 'religious' for the trust in the rational nature of reality that is, at least to a certain extent, accessible to human reason."[3]

Einstein saw in Spinoza, someone who, like himself, accepted determinism and a view of the universe as a fully rational system and lawful. "God does not play at dice" was simply Einstein's catchy way of making the point Spinoza argued in Proposition 29 of his *Ethics*: "In the nature of things nothing accidental is granted, but all things are determined by the necessity of the divine nature for existing and working in a certain way. In short, there is nothing accidental in nature." In "What I Believe," excerpted below, Einstein freely declares, "I do not believe in free will." Although he cites Schopenhauer here rather than Spinoza, when he explains that this awareness keeps him from taking himself and others too seriously and from losing his temper, he seems to be echoing another passage of Spinoza's: "The mind is determined to this or that choice by a cause which is also determined by another cause, and this again by another, and so on ad infinitum. This doctrine teaches us to hate no one, to despise no one, to mock no one, to be angry with no one, and to envy no one." Einstein's belief that every event that occurs is caused by other events and that causes determine, that is, bring about their effects, meshed well with his general theory of relativity, for there are no probabilities in this theory. All of the quantities that appear in the theory have definite values at all times, and the equations dictate how those quantities evolve in time. Immutable laws govern reality, and no will, human or divine, violates this cosmic causality, he believed.

However, physicists learned in the first quarter of the twentieth century that the real world is not quite like that. So there is a certain irony in the fact that from 1916 on, Einstein distanced himself from quantum mechanics, the very branch of physics he had helped give birth to during his "miracle year" of 1905. Max

[3] Albert Einstein, *Lettres à Maurice Solovine* (Paris: Gauthier-Villars, 1956), 102.

Planck's discovery that energy comes in little units called "quanta" led to the birth of a new model for investigating subatomic particles. It turned out that at the level of quantum mechanics it is impossible to measure both position and momentum at once. If the observer's measurement of an electron's position is precise, the measurement of its momentum will be imprecise, and vice versa. Called the Heisenberg "uncertainty principle," this discovery made indeterminism convincing for the first time in the history of modern physics. The behavior of the fundamental constituents of matter could suddenly be seen as unpredictable, contingent, and free. But if events at the quantum level occur randomly, by pure chance, undetermined by any causes whatever, Einstein's belief in causal determinism was wrong. Physicists like Werner Heisenberg and Niels Bohr were forced to renounce the ideal of causality, at least in quantum mechanics. Einstein could not. Fully aware of the philosophical challenges quantum mechanics posed to his own deeply held beliefs, Einstein fought hard against a view of the universe in terms of probability. As fellow physicist Heisenberg would recall, "Einstein would not admit that it was impossible, even in principle, to discover all the partial facts needed for a complete description of a physical process."[4]

Having glimpsed so much of the very face of God revealed in the workings of a majestically rational and deterministic universe, Einstein could not bring himself to abandon the sublime vision of a certain God for one of probability and uncertainty. But an abyss of chance and probability had emerged in modern physics and was soon gaping at the heart of Einstein's harmonious and rational unity. Its full mapping still eludes physicists. The dream of unification—a Theory of Everything—is less urgent among younger physicists today, but for Einstein, whose genius was driven by a need to generalize, the hope of finding a unified field theory for the four forces of nature (the strong and weak nuclear forces, electromagnetism, and gravity) persisted to the end of his

---

[4] Werner Heisenberg, *Physics and Beyond* (New York: Harper and Row, 1971), 80.

life. Perhaps it was akin to a religious hope. Einstein himself acknowledged this:

> our actual knowledge of these laws is only imperfect and fragmentary, so that, actually the belief in the existence of basic all-embracing laws in nature also rests on a sort of faith. All the same this faith has been largely justified so far by the success of scientific research. But, on the other hand, everyone who is seriously involved in the pursuit of science becomes convinced that a spirit is manifest in the laws of the Universe—a spirit vastly superior to that of man, and one in the face of which we with our modest powers must feel humble. In this way the pursuit of science leads to a religious feeling of a special sort, which is indeed different from the religiosity of someone more naïve.[5]

The ease with which Einstein could declare that free will does not exist except as an illusion may surprise many people accustomed to associating freedom with moral responsibility. The idea that the universe is governed by a mechanical or immutable mathematical order has as its corollary that people do not act freely but are governed by inexorable laws. How was Einstein's determinism compatible with his well-known devotion to justice, humanitarian ideals, and social responsibility, all of which presume at least some degree of free will and indeterminism in the universe? It is far from clear how Einstein reconciled his espousal of determinism with his social and ethical principles. Max Jammer suggests that Einstein believed that "the theoretical endorsement of determinism in no way affects the demands of practical ethics," and that we must conduct our moral lives "as if" we are free, even though causal constraints rule.[6]

Just as disturbing as the idea that free will is an illusion is the thought that time is an illusion. And yet that is the central consequence of Einstein's special theory of relativity. Relativity does not mean "relativism" in the sense of "anything goes," but rather

---

[5] *Albert Einstein, The Human Side*, ed. Helen Dukas and Banesh Hoffmann (Princeton: Princeton University Press, 1979), 32f.

[6] Jammer, 86–87.

stands for the utmost in objectivity and rationality, both hallmarks of Einstein's faith. The fact that no coordinate system or reference frame is privileged is an objective feature of space-time. But Einstein's description of time is disorientingly different from our personal experience of time as lived, as flow, since there is by his account no possible meaning to an absolute "now" moment flowing along on the stream of temporality. The concept of time as irreversible and as divided into past, present, and future disappears. The humanly felt passage of time, our sense of flow and unidirectional passage from the settled past to an open future, cannot be accommodated in relativity theory. In this respect, Einstein's theory resembles classical Western theism, whose eternal God sees the history of the world all laid out before him, as it were, all events taking place simultaneously in a tenseless four-dimensional space-time manifold. The doctrine of predestination associated with classical theism led to a paradox of determinism and free will not unlike what we find in Einstein. Characteristically, Einstein himself seemed to find comfort rather than discomfort in knowing that for his physics the distinction between past, present, and future is as much an illusion as free will.

The material excerpted here is of two kinds. Some of it expresses Einstein's personal faith; in it he explains what he means in describing himself as a "deeply religious nonbeliever." Other excerpts contain his philosophical reflections on the relation of religion and science, mostly found in a series of remarkable essays he wrote in the 1930s and 1940s.

Two weeks before he died, Einstein received a visit from I. Bernard Cohen, a historian of science. The two men sat in Einstein's study and discussed some of his illustrious predecessors in the evolution of physics. Einstein had surprising things to say about Isaac Newton, his only competitor for the title of "most influential scientist in history." The words below are Cohen's.

> The conversation then turned to Newton's life and his private speculations: his investigations of theology. I mentioned to Einstein

that Newton had essayed a linguistic analysis of theology, in an attempt to find the corruptions that had been introduced into Christianity. Newton was not an orthodox Trinitarian. He believed his own views were hidden away in Scripture, but that the revealed documents had been corrupted by later writers who had introduced new concepts and even new words. So Newton sought by linguistic analysis to find the truth. Einstein remarked that for him this was a "weakness" in Newton. He did not see why Newton, finding his own ideas and the orthodox ones at variance, did not simply reject the established views and assert his own. For instance, if Newton could not agree with the accepted interpretations of Scripture, why did he believe that Scripture must nevertheless be true? Was it only because the common point of view was that fundamental truths are contained in the Bible? It did not seem to Einstein that in theology Newton showed the same great quality of mind as in physics. Einstein apparently had little feeling for the way in which a man's mind is imprisoned by his culture and the character of his thoughts are molded by his intellectual environment. I did not press the point, but I was struck by the fact that in physics Einstein could see Newton as a man of the seventeenth century, but that in the other realms of thought and action he viewed each man as a timeless, freely acting individual to be judged as if he were a contemporary of ours.

Einstein seemed particularly impressed by the fact that Newton had not been entirely satisfied with his theological writings, and had sealed them all up in a box. This seemed to indicate to Einstein that Newton was aware of the imperfect quality of his theological conclusions and would not present to public view any writings that did not measure up to his own high standards. Since Newton obviously did not wish to publish his speculations on theology, Einstein asserted with some passion that he personally hoped no one else would publish them. Einstein said a man has a right to privacy, even after his death. He praised the Royal Society for having resisted all pressure to edit and print writings of Newton which their author had not wanted to publish. He believed that Newton's correspondence could justly be published, because a letter written and sent was intended to be read, but he added that even in correspondence there might be some personal things which should not be published.[7]

Commendable as Einstein's respect for privacy was, it is impossible to agree with him. Scholars were already piecing together Newton's theological and alchemical papers as Einstein spoke, and their discoveries have illuminated the details of Newton's profoundly held and complicated spirituality. Evoking Newton's name against the theory of indeterminacy in matter as Einstein continued to do until the end of his life proved equally futile. The Newtonian union of physical reality and strict causality would not be restored in the twentieth century, and the religious sensibility that suited a new age of uncertainty, relativity, and incompleteness resembled neither Newton's nor Einstein's religious outlook. Alfred North Whitehead, to be considered in chapter 8, posed a greater challenge to classical physics and deterministic philosophy than Einstein dreamt of, and also ushered in a novel from of theism that departed radically from traditional theologies of Judaism, Christianity, and Islam.

✑ Einstein's Contribution to Science

In 1905 Albert Einstein published three seminal papers. The first paper addressed certain problems concerning electromagnetic energy, the second concerned an aspect of electron theory, which came to be known as Einstein's special theory of relativity, and the third addressed features related to statistical mechanics. In 1915 Einstein combined his insights into gravity space, time, matter, and energy to produce a general theory of relativity.

[7] Excerpted from I. Bernard Cohen, "An Interview with Einstein," *Scientific American*, 193, no. 1 (July 1955): 68–73.

Einstein in His Own Words

Short Statements on God, Religion, and His Faith, 1930–40[8]

My comprehension of God comes from the deeply felt conviction of a superior intelligence that reveals itself in the knowable world. In common terms, one can describe it as "pantheistic."

In every true searcher of Nature there is a kind of religious reverence, for he finds it impossible to imagine that he is the first to have thought out the exceedingly delicate threads that connect his perceptions.

I believe in Spinoza's God who reveals himself in the harmony of all that exists, but not in a God who concerns himself with the fate and actions of human beings.

I am of the opinion that all the finer speculations in the realm of science spring from a deep religious feeling . . . I also believe that this kind of religiousness . . . is the only creative religious activity of our time.

In view of such harmony in the cosmos, which I, with my limited human mind, am able to recognize, there are yet people who say there is no God. But what makes me really angry is that they quote me for support of such views.

My position concerning God is that of an agnostic. I am convinced that a vivid consciousness of the primary importance of moral principles for the betterment and ennoblement of life does not need the idea of a lawgiver, especially a lawgiver who works on the basis of reward and punishment.

If something is in me that can be called religious, then it is the unbounded admiration for the structure of the world so far as science can reveal it.

[8] Selected from Calaprice, 202–18.

I am a deeply religious nonbeliever. . . . This is a somewhat new kind of religion.

I want to know how God created this world. I am not interested in this or that phenomenon, in the spectrum of this or that element. I want to know his thoughts. The rest are details.

I see a pattern, but my imagination cannot picture the maker of that pattern. I see a clock, but I cannot envision the clockmaker. The human mind is unable to conceive of the four dimensions, so how can it conceive of a God, before whom a thousand years and a thousand dimensions are as one?

Whatever there is of God and goodness in the universe, it must work itself out and express itself through us. We cannot stand aside and let God do it.

I have found no better expression than "religious" for confidence in the rational nature of reality, insofar as it is accessible to human reason. Whenever this feeling is absent, science degenerates into uninspired empiricism.

My views are near those of Spinoza: admiration for the beauty and belief in the logical simplicity of the order and harmony that we can grasp humbly and only imperfectly. I believe that we have to content ourselves with our imperfect knowledge and understanding and treat values and moral obligations as purely human problems.

From a Letter to Queen Elizabeth of Belgium, Who Was Suffering a Great Grief (1956)[9]

And yet, as always, the springtime sun brings forth new life, and we may rejoice because of this new life and contribute to its unfolding. And Mozart remains as beautiful and tender as he always was and always will be. There is, after all, something eternal that

[9] Dukas and Hoffmann, 51–52.

lies beyond the hand of fate and of all human delusions. And such eternals lie closer to an older person than to a younger one, oscillating between fear and hope. For us there remains the privilege of experiencing beauty and truth in their purest forms.

Neither an Atheist nor a Pantheist[10]

I'm not an atheist, and I don't think I can call myself a pantheist. We are in the position of a little child entering a huge library filled with books in many languages. The child knows someone must have written those books. It does not know how. It does not understand the languages in which they are written. The child dimly suspects a mysterious order in the arrangement of the books but doesn't know what it is. That, it seems to me, is the attitude of even the most intelligent human being toward God. We see the universe marvelously arranged and obeying certain laws but only dimly understand those laws. Our limited minds grasp the mysterious force that moves the constellations. I am fascinated by Spinoza's pantheism, but admire even more his contributions to modern thought because he is the first philosopher to deal with the soul and body as one, not two separate things.

His Belief in Determinism, the Mysterious, and a Nonpersonal God[11]

I do not believe we can have any freedom at all in the philosophical sense, for we act not only under external compulsion but also by inner necessity. Schopenhauer's saying—"A man can surely do what he wills to do, but he cannot determine what he wills"— impressed itself upon me in youth and has always consoled me

---

[10] From an interview with Einstein published in G. S. Viereck, *Glimpses of the Great* (New York: Macauley, 1930), quoted in Jammer, 48.

[11] Albert Einstein, "What I Believe," *Forum and Century (1930–1940).* 84, no. 4 (October 1930): 192–93.

when I have witnessed or suffered life's hardships. This conviction is a perpetual breeder of tolerance, for it does not allow us to take ourselves or others too seriously; it makes rather for a sense of humor.

. . . The most beautiful thing we can experience is the mysterious. It is the source of all true art and science. He to whom this emotion is a stranger, who can no longer pause to wonder and stand rapt in awe, is as good as dead: his eyes are closed. This insight into the mystery of life, coupled though it be with fear, has also given rise to religion. To know that what is impenetrable to us really exists, manifesting itself as the highest wisdom and the most radiant beauty which our dull faculties can comprehend only in their most primitive forms—this knowledge, this feeling, is at the center of true religiousness. In this sense, and in this sense only, I belong in the ranks of devoutly religious men.

I cannot imagine a God who rewards and punishes the objects of his creation, whose purposes are modeled after our own—a God, in short, who is but a reflection of human frailty. Neither can I believe that the individual survives the death of his body, although feeble souls harbor such thoughts through fear or ridiculous egotism. It is enough for me to contemplate the mystery of conscious life perpetuating itself through all eternity, to reflect upon the marvelous structure of the universe which we can dimly perceive, and to try humbly to comprehend even an infinitesimal part of the intelligence manifested in nature.

On Religion and Science[12]

Everything that the human race has done and thought is concerned with the satisfaction of deeply felt needs and the assuagement of pain. One has to keep this constantly in mind if one wishes to

---

[12] Albert Einstein, *Ideas and Opinions* (New York: Crown, 1982 [1954]), 36–40; originally appeared in the *New York Times Magazine*, November 9, 1930, 1–4.

understand spiritual movements and their development. Feeling and longing are the motive force behind all human endeavor and human creation, in however exalted a guise the latter may present themselves to us. Now what are the feelings and needs that have led men to religious thought and belief in the widest sense of the words? A little consideration will suffice to show us that the most varying emotions preside over the birth of religious thought and experience. With primitive man it is above all fear that evokes religious notions—fear of hunger, wild beasts, sickness, death.

༕

The social impulses are another source of the crystallization of religion. . . . This is the God of Providence, who protects, disposes, rewards, and punishes; the God who, according to the limits of the believer's outlook, loves and cherishes the life of the tribe or of the human race, or even of life itself; the comforter in sorrow and unsatisfied longing; he who preserves the souls of the dead. This is the social or moral conception of God.

༕

Common to all these types is the anthropomorphic character of their conception of God. In general, only individuals of exceptional endowments, and exceptionally high-minded communities, rise to any considerable extent above this level. But there is a third stage of religious experience which belongs to all of them, even though it is rarely found in a pure form: I shall call it cosmic religious feeling. It is very difficult to elucidate this feeling to anyone who is entirely without it, especially as there is no anthropomorphic conception of God corresponding to it.

The individual feels the futility of human desires and aims and the sublimity and marvelous order which reveal themselves both in nature and in the world of thought. Individual existence impresses him as a sort of prison and he wants to experience the universe as a single significant whole. The beginnings of cosmic religious feeling already appear at an early stage of development, e.g., in many of the Psalms of David and in some of the Prophets. Buddhism, as we have learned especially from the wonderful writings of Schopenhauer, contains a much stronger element of this.

The religious geniuses of all ages have been distinguished by this kind of religious feeling, which knows no dogma and no God conceived in man's image; so that there can be no church whose central teachings are based on it. Hence it is precisely among the heretics of every age that we find men who were filled with this highest kind of religious feeling and were in many cases regarded by their contemporaries as atheists, sometimes also as saints. Looked at in this light, men like Democritus, Francis of Assisi, and Spinoza are closely akin to one another.

How can cosmic religious feeling be communicated from one person to another, if it can give rise to no definite notion of a God and no theology? In my view, it is the most important function of art and science to awaken this feeling and keep it alive in those who are receptive to it.

We thus arrive at a conception of the relation of science to religion very different from the usual one. When one views the matter historically, one is inclined to look upon science and religion as irreconcilable antagonists, and for a very obvious reason. The man who is thoroughly convinced of the universal operation of the law of causation cannot for a moment entertain the idea of a being who interferes in the course of events—provided, of course, that he takes the hypothesis of causality really seriously. He has no use for the religion of fear and equally little for social or moral religion. A God who rewards and punishes is inconceivable to him for the simple reason that a man's actions are determined by necessity, external and internal, so that in God's eyes he cannot be responsible, any more than an inanimate object is responsible for the motions it undergoes. Science has therefore been charged with undermining morality, but the charge is unjust. A man's ethical behavior should be based effectually on sympathy, education, and social ties and needs; no religious basis is necessary. Man would indeed be in a poor way if he had to be restrained by fear of punishment and hopes of reward after death.

It is therefore easy to see why the churches have always fought science and persecuted its devotees. On the other hand, I maintain that the cosmic religious feeling is the strongest and noblest motive for scientific research. Only those who realize the immense efforts and, above all, the devotion without which pioneer work in theoretical science cannot be achieved are able to grasp the strength of the emotion out of which alone such work, remote as it is from the immediate realities of life, can issue. What a deep conviction of the rationality of the universe and what a yearning to understand, were it but a feeble reflection of the mind revealed in this world, Kepler and Newton must have had to enable them to spend years of solitary labor in disentangling the principles of celestial mechanics! Those whose acquaintance with scientific research is derived chiefly from its practical results easily develop a completely false notion of the mentality of the men who, surrounded by a skeptical world, have shown the way to kindred spirits scattered wide through the world and through the centuries. Only one who has devoted his life to similar ends can have a vivid realization of what has inspired these men and given them the strength to remain true to their purpose in spite of countless failures. It is cosmic religious feeling that gives a man such strength. A contemporary has said, not unjustly, that in this materialistic age of ours the serious scientific workers are the only profoundly religious people.

Science and Religion Are Reconcilable[13]

During the last century, and part of the one before, it was widely held that there was an unreconcilable conflict between knowledge and belief. The opinion prevailed among advanced minds that it

[13] *Ideas and Opinions*, 41–49.

was time that belief should be replaced increasingly by knowledge; belief that did not itself rest on knowledge was superstition, and as such had to be opposed. According to this conception, the sole function of education was to open the way to thinking and knowing, and the school, as the outstanding organ for the people's education, must serve that end exclusively.

One will probably find but rarely, if at all, the rationalistic standpoint expressed in such crass form; for any sensible man would see at once how one-sided is such a statement of the position. But it is just as well to state a thesis starkly and nakedly, if one wants to clear up one's mind as to its nature.

It is true that convictions can best be supported with experience and clear thinking. On this point one must agree unreservedly with the extreme rationalist. The weak point of his conception is, however, this, that those convictions which are necessary and determinant for our conduct and judgments cannot be found solely along this solid scientific way.

For the scientific method can teach us nothing else beyond how facts are related to, and conditioned by, each other. The aspiration toward such objective knowledge belongs to the highest of which man is capable, and you will certainly not suspect me of wishing to belittle the achievements and the heroic efforts of man in this sphere. Yet it is equally clear that knowledge of what is does not open the door directly to what should be. One can have the clearest and most complete knowledge of what is, and yet not be able to deduct from that what should be the goal of our human aspirations. Objective knowledge provides us with powerful instruments for the achievements of certain ends, but the ultimate goal itself and the longing to reach it must come from another source. And it is hardly necessary to argue for the view that our existence and our activity acquire meaning only by the setting up of such a goal and of corresponding values. The knowledge of truth as such is wonderful, but it is so little capable of acting as a guide that it cannot prove even the justification and the value of the aspiration toward that very knowledge of truth. Here we face, therefore, the limits of the purely rational conception of our existence.

But it must not be assumed that intelligent thinking can play no part in the formation of the goal and of ethical judgments. When someone realizes that for the achievement of an end certain means would be useful, the means itself becomes thereby an end. Intelligence makes clear to us the interrelation of means and ends. But mere thinking cannot give us a sense of the ultimate and fundamental ends. To make clear these fundamental ends and valuations, and to set them fast in the emotional life of the individual, seems to me precisely the most important function which religion has to perform in the social life of man. And if one asks whence derives the authority of such fundamental ends, since they cannot be stated and justified merely by reason, one can only answer: they exist in a healthy society as powerful traditions, which act upon the conduct and aspirations and judgments of the individuals; they are there, that is, as something living, without its being necessary to find justification for their existence. They come into being not through demonstration but through revelation, through the medium of powerful personalities. One must not attempt to justify them, but rather to sense their nature simply and clearly.

The highest principles for our aspirations and judgments are given to us in the Jewish-Christian religious tradition. It is a very high goal which, with our weak powers, we can reach only very inadequately, but which gives a sure foundation to our aspirations and valuations. If one were to take that goal out of its religious form and look merely at its purely human side, one might state it perhaps thus: free and responsible development of the individual, so that he may place his powers freely and gladly in the service of all mankind.

&

It would not be difficult to come to an agreement as to what we understand by science. Science is the century-old endeavor to bring together by means of systematic thought the perceptible phenomena of this world into as thoroughgoing an association as possible. To put it boldly, it is the attempt at the posterior reconstruction of existence by the process of conceptualization. But when asking myself what religion is I cannot think of the answer so easily. And even after finding an answer which may satisfy me at this particular moment, I still remain convinced that I can never under any circumstances bring together, even to a slight extent, the thoughts of all those who have given this question serious consideration.

At first, then, instead of asking what religion is I should prefer to ask what characterizes the aspirations of a person who gives me the impression of being religious: a person who is religiously enlightened appears to me to be one who has, to the best of his ability, liberated himself from the fetters of his selfish desires and is preoccupied with thoughts, feelings, and aspirations to which he clings because of their superpersonal value. It seems to me that what is important is the force of this superpersonal content and the depth of the conviction concerning its overpowering meaningfulness, regardless of whether any attempt is made to unite this content with a divine Being, for otherwise it would not be possible to count Buddha and Spinoza as religious personalities. Accordingly, a religious person is devout in the sense that he has no doubt of the significance and loftiness of those superpersonal objects and goals which neither require nor are capable of rational foundation. They exist with the same necessity and matter-of-factness as he himself. In this sense religion is the age-old endeavor of mankind to become clearly and completely conscious of these values and goals and constantly to strengthen and extend their effect. If one conceives of religion and science according to these definitions then a conflict between them appears impossible. For science can only ascertain what is, but not what should be, and outside of its domain value judgments of all kinds remain necessary. Religion, on the other hand, deals only with evaluations of human thought and action: it cannot justifiably speak of facts and relationships between facts. According to this interpretation the well-known conflicts between religion and science in the past must all be ascribed to a misapprehension of the situation which has been described.

For example, a conflict arises when a religious community insists on the absolute truthfulness of all statements recorded in the

Bible. This means an intervention on the part of religion into the sphere of science; this is where the struggle of the Church against the doctrines of Galileo and Darwin belongs. On the other hand, representatives of science have often made an attempt to arrive at fundamental judgments with respect to values and ends on the basis of scientific method, and in this way have set themselves in opposition to religion. These conflicts have all sprung from fatal errors.

Now, even though the realms of religion and science in themselves are clearly marked off from each other, nevertheless there exist between the two strong reciprocal relationships and dependencies. Though religion may be that which determines the goal, it has, nevertheless, learned from science, in the broadest sense, what means will contribute to the attainment of the goals it has set up. But science can only be created by those who are thoroughly imbued with the aspiration toward truth and understanding. This source of feeling, however, springs from the sphere of religion. To this there also belongs the faith in the possibility that the regulations valid for the world of existence are rational, that is, comprehensible to reason. I cannot conceive of a genuine scientist without that profound faith. The situation may be expressed by an image: science without religion is lame, religion without science is blind.

Nobody, certainly, will deny that the idea of the existence of an omnipotent, just, and omnibeneficent personal God is able to accord man solace, help, and guidance; also, by virtue of its simplicity it is accessible to the most undeveloped mind. But, on the other hand, there are decisive weaknesses attached to this idea in itself, which have been painfully felt since the beginning of history. That is, if this being is omnipotent, then every occurrence, including every human action, every human thought, and every human feeling and aspiration is also His work; how is it possible to think of holding men responsible for their deeds and thoughts before such an almighty Being? In giving out punishment and rewards He would to a certain extent be passing judgment on Himself. How can this be combined with the goodness and righteousness ascribed to Him?

The main source of the present-day conflicts between the spheres of religion and of science lies in this concept of a personal God. It is the aim of science to establish general rules which determine the reciprocal connection of objects and events in time and space. For these rules, or laws of nature, absolutely general validity is required—not proven. It is mainly a program, and faith in the possibility of its accomplishment in principle is only founded on partial successes. But hardly anyone could be found who would deny these partial successes and ascribe them to human self-deception. The fact that on the basis of such laws we are able to predict the temporal behavior of phenomena in certain domains with great precision and certainty is deeply embedded in the consciousness of the modern man, even though he may have grasped very little of the contents of those laws. He need only consider that planetary courses within the solar system may be calculated in advance with great exactitude on the basis of a limited number of simple laws . . .

To be sure, when the number of factors coming into play in a phenomenological complex is too large, scientific method in most cases fails us. One need only think of the weather, in which case prediction even for a few days ahead is impossible. Nevertheless no one doubts that we are confronted with a causal connection whose causal components are in the main known to us. Occurrences in this domain are beyond the reach of exact prediction because of the variety of factors in operation, not because of any lack of order in nature.

We have penetrated far less deeply into the regularities obtaining within the realm of living things, but deeply enough nevertheless to sense at least the rule of fixed necessity. One need only think of the systematic order in heredity, and in the effect of poisons, as for instance alcohol, on the behavior of organic beings. What is still lacking here is a grasp of connections of profound generality, but not a knowledge of order in itself.

The more a man is imbued with the ordered regularity of all events the firmer becomes his conviction that there is no room left by the side of this ordered regularity for causes of a different nature. For him neither the rule of human nor the rule of divine will exists as an independent cause of natural events. To be sure, the doctrine of a personal God interfering with natural events could never be refuted, in the real sense, by science, for this doctrine can always take refuge in those domains in which scientific knowledge has not yet been able to set foot.

But I am persuaded that such behavior on the part of the representatives of religion would not only be unworthy but also fatal. For a doctrine which is able to maintain itself not in clear light but only in the dark, will of necessity lose its effect on mankind, with incalculable harm to human progress. In their struggle for the ethical good, teachers of religion must have the stature to give up the doctrine of a personal God, that is, give up that source of fear and hope which in the past placed such vast power in the hands of priests. In their labors they will have to avail themselves of those forces which are capable of cultivating the Good, the True, and the Beautiful in humanity itself. This is, to be sure, a more difficult but an incomparably more worthy task. (This thought is convincingly presented in Herbert Samuel's book, *Belief and Action*.) After religious teachers accomplish the refining process indicated they will surely recognize with joy that true religion has been ennobled and made more profound by scientific knowledge.

If it is one of the goals of religion to liberate mankind as far as possible from the bondage of egocentric cravings, desires, and fears, scientific reasoning can aid religion in yet another sense. Although it is true that it is the goal of science to discover rules which permit the association and foretelling of facts, this is not its only aim. It also seeks to reduce the connections discovered to the smallest possible number of mutually independent conceptual elements. It is in this striving after the rational unification of the manifold that it encounters its greatest successes, even though it is precisely this attempt which causes it to run the greatest risk of falling a prey to illusions. But whoever has undergone the intense experience of successful advances made in this domain is moved by profound reverence for the rationality made manifest in existence. By way of the understanding he achieves a far-reaching emancipation from the shackles of personal hopes and desires, and thereby attains that humble attitude of mind toward the grandeur of reason incarnate in existence, and which, in its profoundest depths, is inaccessible to man. This attitude, however, appears to me to be religious, in the highest sense of the word. And so it seems to me that science not only purifies the religious impulse of the dross of its anthropomorphism but also contributes to a religious spiritualization of our understanding of life.

The further the spiritual evolution of mankind advances, the more certain it seems to me that the path to genuine religiosity does not lie through the fear of life, and the fear of death, and blind faith, but through striving after rational knowledge. In this sense I believe that the priest must become a teacher if he wishes to do justice to his lofty educational mission.

Why Religion Will Not Be Superseded by Science[14]

Does there truly exist an insuperable contradiction between religion and science? Can religion be superseded by science? The answers to these questions have, for centuries, given rise to considerable dispute and, indeed, bitter fighting. Yet, in my own mind there can be no doubt that in both cases a dispassionate consideration can only lead to a negative answer. What complicates the solution, however, is the fact that while most people readily agree on what is meant by "science," they are likely to differ on the meaning of "religion."

As to science, we may well define it for our purpose as "methodical thinking directed toward finding regulative connections between our sensual experiences." Science, in the immediate, produces knowledge and, indirectly, means of action. It leads to methodical action if definite goals are set up in advance. For the

---

[14] *Ideas and Opinions*, 49–52.

function of setting up goals and passing statements of value transcends its domain. While it is true that science, to the extent of its grasp of causative connections, may reach important conclusions as to the compatibility and incompatibility of goals and evaluations, the independent and fundamental definitions regarding goals and values remain beyond science's reach.

As regards religion, on the other hand, one is generally agreed that it deals with goals and evaluations and, in general, with the emotional foundation of human thinking and acting, as far as these are not predetermined by the inalterable hereditary disposition of the human species. Religion is concerned with man's attitude toward nature at large, with the establishing of ideals for the individual and communal life, and with mutual human relationship. These ideals religion attempts to attain by exerting an educational influence on tradition and through the development and promulgation of certain easily accessible thoughts and narratives (epics and myths) which are apt to influence evaluation and action along the lines of the accepted ideals.

It is this mythical, or rather this symbolic, content of the religious traditions which is likely to come into conflict with science. This occurs whenever this religious stock of ideas contains dogmatically fixed statements on subjects which belong in the domain of science. Thus, it is of vital importance for the preservation of true religion that such conflicts be avoided when they arise from subjects which, in fact, are not really essential for the pursuance of the religious aims.

When we consider the various existing religions as to their essential substance, that is, divested of their myths, they do not seem to me to differ as basically from each other as the proponents of the "relativistic" or conventional theory wish us to believe. And this is by no means surprising. For the moral attitudes of a people that is supported by religion need always aim at preserving and promoting the sanity and vitality of the community and its individuals, since otherwise this community is bound to perish. A people that were to honor falsehood, defamation, fraud, and murder would be unable, indeed, to subsist for very long.

When confronted with a specific case, however, it is no easy task to determine clearly what is desirable and what should be eschewed, just as we find it difficult to decide what exactly it is that makes good painting or good music. It is something that may be felt intuitively more easily than rationally comprehended. Likewise, the great moral teachers of humanity were, in a way, artistic geniuses in the art of living. In addition to the most elementary precepts directly motivated by the preservation of life and the sparing of unnecessary suffering, there are others to which, although they are apparently not quite commensurable to the basic precepts, we nevertheless attach considerable importance. Should truth, for instance, be sought unconditionally even where its attainment and its accessibility to all would entail heavy sacrifices in toil and happiness? There are many such questions which, from a rational vantage point, cannot easily be answered or cannot be answered at all. Yet, I do not think that the so-called "relativistic" viewpoint is correct, not even when dealing with the more subtle moral decisions.

When considering the actual living conditions of present day civilized humanity from the standpoint of even the most elementary religious commands, one is bound to experience a feeling of deep and painful disappointment at what one sees. For while religion prescribes brotherly love in the relations among the individuals and groups, the actual spectacle more resembles a battlefield than an orchestra. Everywhere, in economic as well as in political life, the guiding principle is one of ruthless striving for success at the expense of one's fellow men. This competitive spirit prevails even in school and, destroying all feelings of human fraternity and cooperation, conceives of achievement not as derived from the love for productive and thoughtful work, but as springing from personal ambition and fear of rejection.

There are pessimists who hold that such a state of affairs is necessarily inherent in human nature; it is those who propound such views that are the enemies of true religion, for they imply thereby that religious teachings are utopian ideals and unsuited to afford guidance in human affairs. The study of the social patterns in certain so-called primitive cultures, however, seems to have made it sufficiently evident that such a defeatist view is wholly unwarranted. Whoever is concerned with this problem, a crucial one in the study of religion as such, is advised to read the description of the Pueblo Indians in Ruth Benedict's book, *Patterns of Culture*. Under the hardest living conditions, this tribe has apparently accomplished the difficult task of delivering its people from the scourge of competitive spirit and of fostering in it a temperate, cooperative conduct of life, free of external pressure and without any curtailment of happiness.

The interpretation of religion, as here advanced, implies a dependence of science on the religious attitude, a relation which, in our predominantly materialistic age, is only too easily overlooked. While it is true that scientific results are entirely independent from religious or moral considerations, those individuals to whom we owe the great creative achievements of science were all of them imbued with the truly religious conviction that this universe of ours is something perfect and susceptible to the rational striving for knowledge. If this conviction had not been a strongly emotional one and if those searching for knowledge had not been inspired by Spinoza's *Amor Dei Intellectualis*, they would hardly have been capable of that untiring devotion which alone enables man to attain his greatest achievements.

The Scientist's Own Religious Sense[15]

You will hardly find one among the profounder sort of scientific minds without a religious feeling of his own. But it is different from the religiosity of the naïve man. For the latter, God is a being from whose care one hopes to benefit and whose punishment one fears; a sublimation of a feeling similar to that of a child for its father, a being to whom one stands, so to speak, in a personal relation, however deeply it may be tinged with awe.

[15] *Ideas and Opinions*, 40.

But the scientist is possessed by the sense of universal causation. The future, to him, is every whit as necessary and determined as the past. There is nothing divine about morality; it is a purely human affair. His religious feeling takes the form of a rapturous amazement at the harmony of natural law, which reveals an intelligence of such superiority that, compared with it, all the systematic thinking and acting of human beings is an utterly insignificant reflection. This feeling is the guiding principle of his life and work, insofar as he succeeds in keeping himself from the shackles of selfish desire. It is beyond question closely akin to that which has possessed the religious geniuses of all ages.

On the Meaning of Life[16]

What is the meaning of human life, or, for that matter, of the life of any creature? To know an answer to this question means to be religious. You ask: Does it make any sense, then, to pose this question? I answer, the man who regards his own life and that of his fellow creatures as meaningless is not merely unhappy but hardly fit for life.

On Jewish and Christian Teachings[17]

If one purges the Judaism of the Prophets and Christianity as Jesus Christ taught it of all subsequent additions, especially those of the priests, one is left with a teaching which is capable of curing all the social ills of humanity.

It is the duty of every man of good will to strive steadfastly in his own little world to make this teaching of pure humanity a living force, so far as he can. If he makes an honest attempt in this direction without being crushed and trampled underfoot by his

---

[16] *Ideas and Opinions*, 11.
[17] *Ideas and Opinions*, 186.

contemporaries, he may consider himself and the community to which he belongs lucky.

☙

Judaism is not a creed: the Jewish God is simply a negation of superstition, an imaginary result of its elimination. It is also an attempt to base the moral law on fear, a regrettable and discreditable attempt. Yet it seems to me that the strong moral tradition of the Jewish nation has to a large extent shaken itself free from this fear. It is clear also that "serving God" was equated with "serving the living." . . . Judaism is thus no transcendental religion; it is concerned with life as we live it and as we can, to a certain extent, grasp it, and nothing else. It seems to me, therefore, doubtful whether it can be called a religion in the accepted sense of the word particularly as no "faith" but the sanctification of life in a supra-personal sense is demanded of the Jew.

But the Jewish tradition also contains something else, something which finds splendid expression in many of the Psalms, namely, a sort of intoxicated joy and amazement at the beauty and grandeur of this world, of which man can form just a faint notion. This joy is the feeling from which true scientific research draws its spiritual sustenance, but which also seems to find expression in the song of birds. To tack this feeling to the idea of God seems mere childish absurdity.

On Moral Decay[18]

All religions, arts and sciences are branches of the same tree. All these aspirations are directed toward ennobling man's life, lifting it from the sphere of mere physical existence and leading the individual toward freedom. It is no mere chance that our older

[18] Albert Einstein, *Out of my Later Years* (New York: Philosophical Library, 1950), 9–10.

universities have developed from clerical schools. Both churches and universities—insofar as they live up to their true function—serve the ennoblement of the individual. They seek to fulfill this great task by spreading moral and cultural understanding, renouncing the use of brute force.

The essential unity of ecclesiastical and secular cultural institutions was lost during the 19th century, to the point of senseless hostility. Yet there never was any doubt as to the striving for culture. No one doubted the sacredness of the goal. It was the approach that was disputed. The political and economic conflicts and complexities of the last few decades have brought before our eyes dangers which even the darkest pessimists of the last century did not dream of. The injunctions of the Bible concerning human conduct were then accepted by believer and infidel alike as self-evident demands for individuals and society. No one would have been taken seriously who failed to acknowledge the quest for objective truth and knowledge as man's highest and eternal aim.

Yet today we must recognize with horror that these pillars of civilized human existence have lost their firmness. Nations that once ranked high bow down before tyrants who dare openly to assert: Right is that which serves us! The quest for truth for its own sake has no justification and is not to be tolerated. Arbitrary rule, oppression, persecution of individuals, faiths and communities are openly practiced in those countries and accepted as justifiable or inevitable.

And the rest of the world has slowly grown accustomed to these symptoms of moral decay. One misses the elementary reaction against injustice and for justice—that reaction which in the long run represents man's only protection against a relapse into barbarism. I am firmly convinced that the passionate will for justice and truth has done more to improve man's condition than calculating political shrewdness which in the long run only breeds general distrust. Who can doubt that Moses was a better leader of humanity than Machiavelli?

During the War someone tried to convince a great Dutch scientist that might went before right in the history of man. "I cannot disprove the accuracy of your assertion," he replied, "but 1 do know that I should not care to live in such a world."

Let us think, feel and act like this man, refusing to accept fateful compromise. Let us not even shun the fight when it is unavoidable to preserve right and the dignity of man. If we do this we shall soon return to conditions that will allow us to rejoice in humanity.

On Morality and Emotions[19]

We all know, from what we experience with and within ourselves, that our conscious acts spring from our desires and our fears. Intuition tells us that that is true also of our fellows and of the higher animals. We all try to escape pain and death, while we seek what is pleasant. We all are ruled in what we do by impulses; and these impulses are so organized that our actions in general serve for our self-preservation and that of the race. Hunger, love, pain, fear are some of those inner forces which rule the individual's instinct for self-preservation. At the same time, as social beings, we are moved in the relations with our fellow beings by such feelings as sympathy, pride, hate, need for power, pity, and so on. All these primary impulses, not easily described in words, are the springs of man's actions. All such action would cease if those powerful elemental forces were to cease stirring within us.

Though our conduct seems so very different from that of the higher animals, the primary instincts are much alike in them and in us. The most evident difference springs from the important part which is played in man by a relatively strong power of imagination and by the capacity to think, aided as it is by language and other symbolical devices. Thought is the organizing factor in man, intersected between the causal primary instincts and the resulting actions. In that way imagination and intelligence enter into our existence in the part of servants of the primary instincts. But their

---

[19] *Out of my Later Years*, 15–20.

intervention makes our acts to serve ever less merely the immediate claims of our instincts. Through them the primary instinct attaches itself to ends which become ever more distant. The instincts bring thought into action, and thought provokes intermediary actions inspired by emotions which are likewise related to the ultimate end. Through repeated performance, this process brings it about that ideas and beliefs acquire and retain a strong effective power even after the ends which gave them that power are long forgotten. In abnormal cases of such intensive borrowed emotions, which cling to objects emptied of their erstwhile effective meaning, we speak of fetishism.

Yet the process which I have indicated plays a very important part also in ordinary life. Indeed there is no doubt that to this process—which one may describe as a spiritualizing of the emotions and of thought—that to it man owes the most subtle and refined pleasures of which he is capable: the pleasure in the beauty of artistic creation and of logical trains of thought.

As far as I can see, there is one consideration which stands at the threshold of all moral teaching. If men as individuals surrender to the call of their elementary instincts, avoiding pain and seeking satisfaction only for their own selves, the result for them all taken together must be a state of insecurity, of fear, and of promiscuous misery. If, besides that, they use their intelligence from an individualist, i.e., a selfish standpoint, building up their life on the illusion of a happy unattached existence, things will be hardly better. In comparison with the other elementary instincts and impulses, the emotions of love, of pity and of friendship are too weak and too cramped to lead to a tolerable state of human society.

The solution of this problem, when freely considered, is simple enough, and it seems also to echo from the teachings of the wise men of the past always in the same strain: All men should let their conduct be guided by the same principles; and those principles should be such, that by following them there should accrue to all as great a measure as possible of security and satisfaction, and as small a measure as possible of suffering.

Of course, this general requirement is much too vague that we should be able to draw from it with confidence specific rules to guide the individuals in their actions. And indeed, these specific rules will have to change in keeping with changing circumstances. If this were the main difficulty that stands in the way of that keen conception, the millenary fate of man would have been incomparably happier than it actually was, or still is. Man would not have killed man, tortured each other, exploited each other by force and by guile. The real difficulty, the difficulty which has baffled the sages of all times, is rather this: how can we make our teaching so potent in the emotional life of man, that its influence should withstand the pressure of the elemental psychic forces in the individual? We do not know, of course, if the sages of the past have really asked themselves this question, consciously and in this form; but we do know how they have tried to solve the problem.

Long before men were ripe, namely, to be faced with such a universal moral attitude, fear of the dangers of life had led them to attribute to various imaginary personal beings, not physically tangible, power to release those natural forces which men feared or perhaps welcomed. And they believed that those beings, which everywhere dominated their imagination, were psychically made in their own image, but were endowed with superhuman powers. These were the primitive precursors of the idea of God. Sprung in the first place from the fears which filled man's daily life, the belief in the existence of such beings, and in their extraordinary powers, has had so strong an influence on men and their conduct, that it is difficult for us to imagine. Hence it is not surprising that those who set out to establish the moral idea, as embracing all men equally, did so by linking it closely with religion. And the fact that those moral claims were the same for all men, may have had much to do with the development of mankind's religious culture from polytheism to monotheism.

The universal moral idea thus owed its original psychological potency to that link with religion. Yet in another sense that close association was fatal for the moral idea. Monotheistic religion acquired different forms with various peoples and groups. Although those differences were by no means fundamental, yet they soon were felt more strongly than the essentials that were common. And in that way religion often caused enmity and conflict, instead of binding mankind together with the universal moral idea.

Then came the growth of the natural sciences, with their great influence on thought and practical life, weakening still more in modern times the religious sentiment of the peoples. The causal and objective mode of thinking—though not necessarily in contradiction with the religious sphere—leaves in most people little room for a deepening religious sense. And because of the traditional close link between religion and morals, that has brought with it, in the last hundred years or so, a serious weakening of moral thought and sentiment. That, to my mind, is a main cause for the barbarization of political ways in our time. Taken together with the terrifying efficiency of the new technical means, the barbarization already forms a fearful threat for the civilized world.

Needless to say, one is glad that religion strives to work for the realization of the moral principle. Yet the moral imperative is not a matter for church and religion alone, but the most precious traditional possession of all mankind. Consider from this standpoint the position of the Press, or of the schools with their competitive method! Everything is dominated by the cult of efficiency and of success and not by the value of things and men in relation to the moral ends of human society. To that must be added the moral deterioration resulting from a ruthless economic struggle. The deliberate nurturing of the moral sense also outside the religious sphere, however, should help also in this, to lead men to look upon social problems as so many opportunities for joyous service towards a better life. For looked at from a simple human point of view, moral conduct does not mean merely a stern demand to renounce some of the desired joys of life, but rather a sociable interest in a happier lot for all men.

This conception implies one requirement above all—that every individual should have the opportunity to develop the gifts which may be latent in him. Alone in that way can the individual obtain the satisfaction to which he is justly entitled; and alone in that way can the community achieve its richest flowering. For everything that is really great and inspiring is created by the individual who can labour in freedom. Restriction is justified only in so far as it may be needed for the security of existence.

There is one other thing which follows from that conception—that we must not only tolerate differences between individuals and between groups, but we should indeed welcome them and look upon them as an enriching of our existence. That is the essence of all true tolerance; without tolerance in this widest sense there can be no question of true morality. Morality in the sense here briefly indicated is not a fixed and stark system. It is rather a standpoint from which all questions which arise in life could and should be judged. It is a task never finished, something always present to guide our judgment and to inspire our conduct. Can you imagine that any man truly filled with this ideal could be content—

Were he to receive from his fellow men a much greater return in goods and services than most other men ever receive?

Were his country, because it feels itself for the time being militarily secure, to stand aloof from the aspiration to create a supra-national system of security and justice?

Could he look on passively, or perhaps even with indifference, when elsewhere in the world innocent people are being brutally persecuted, deprived of their rights or even massacred?

To ask these questions is to answer them!

On His Seventieth Birthday, an Expression of His Life-Long Belief in an Extra-Personal World[20]

It is quite clear to me that the religious paradise of youth, which was thus lost, was a first attempt to free myself from the chains of the "merely personal," from an existence which is dominated by wishes, hopes, and primitive feelings. Out yonder there was this

---

[20] Albert Einstein, "Autobiographical Notes," in *Albert Einstein: Philosopher-Scientist*, ed. Paul Schilpp (Evanston, IL: Library of Living philosophers, 1949), 5.

huge world, which exists independently of us human beings and which stands before us like a great, eternal riddle, at least partially accessible to our inspection and thinking. The contemplation of this world beckoned like a liberation. . . . The mental grasp of this extra-personal world within the frame of the given possibilities swam as highest aim half consciously and half unconsciously before my mind's eye. . . . The road to this paradise was not as comfortable and alluring as the road to the religious paradise; but it has proved itself as trustworthy, and I have never regretted having chosen it.

Further Reading

The essays in which Einstein recorded his views about ultimate questions, the meaning of God, and the relation between science and religion can be found in three books: Albert Einstein, *Ideas and Opinions* (based on *Mein Weltbild*, edited by Carl Seelig, and other sources), new translations and revisions by Sonja Bergmann (New York: Crown Publishers, 1954); Albert Einstein, *Out of My Later Years* (New York: Philosophical Library, 1950); and Albert Einstein, *The World As I See It* (New York: Covici, Friede, 1934). Important short statements can be found in Einstein's essay "What I Believe," *Forum and Century (1930–1940)* 84, no. 4 (October 1930); and in his contribution to *Science, Philosophy, and Religion: A Symposium* (New York: Conference on Science, Philosophy and Religion in Their Relation to the Democratic Way of Life, 1941). Alice Calaprice has edited an excellent volume, *The Expanded Quotable Einstein* (Princeton: Princeton University Press, 2000), with a chapter entitled "On Religion, God, and Philosophy." The best book-length study of Einstein's faith is Max Jammer, *Einstein and Religion* (Princeton: Princeton University Press, 1999); the final chapter, "Physics and Theology," relates Einstein's thought to other cosmological theories based on general relativity and to various twentieth-century theological proposals, including those influenced by Alfred North Whitehead. See also Gerald Holton, *Victory and Vexation in Science: Einstein, Bohr, Heisenberg and Others* (Cambridge, MA: Harvard University Press, 2005), especially chapter 8, "Paul Tillich, Albert Einstein, and the Quest for the Ultimate." The most comprehensive biography of Einstein, one that makes use of newly opened archives, is Walter Isaacson, *Einstein: His Life and Universe* (New York: Simon and Schuster, 2007).

8 Alfred North Whitehead
(1861–1947)

Introduction

It is fascinating to imagine a conversation between Einstein and Whitehead on any subject, but especially on the subject of the theory of relativity. Two of the most powerful and original minds of the twentieth century, they went in two different directions. Although he regarded Einstein's discovery of the convertibility of mass and energy as brilliant, Whitehead was inspired to formulate his own theory of gravitation in his 1922 book *The Principle of Relativity*, and in his famous 1925 lecture series, published as *Science and the Modern World*, he offered audiences an early exposure to quantum mechanics. In brief, Whitehead proposed events as the primary category, not things or objects or matter. In both quantum mechanics and relativity theory, he wanted to replace the concept of an "object" with the concept of an event that is both determined (by other past events) and self-determining. Although he shows no direct indication of being influenced by early developments in quantum mechanics, Whitehead's mature philosophy expresses significant compatibilities with modern quantum theories of various types. Not surprisingly, in view of his objections to the uncertainty principle, the idea that each particle in some sense determines its own destiny was deeply distasteful to Einstein.

Too technical to trace in any detail here, the differences between Whitehead and Einstein boil down chiefly to three. First, Whitehead's world is a world of events, while Einstein's is a world of matter. For Whitehead matter is contingent, and for Einstein matter is necessary. Both wrestle with how and why space, time, and matter are related, but their starting points are quite different. Leaving matter behind, Whitehead views space, time, matter as constructs of something yet more general. What is deeper and more fundamental than space-time-matter? Whitehead's answer is Creative Passage—the passage of time. Neither "time" nor "space" is fundamental, but rather *passage*. It is the processive-relational creative passage of nature that gives rise to the concept of "time" itself and to the delineation of "before" from "after" and ultimately from "during." Second, Whitehead challenges the central feature of Einstein's theory of relativity, which does not support the view of the world as an evolving process and does not allow the definition of a global past, present, and future. Third, and crucially, Whitehead differs from Einstein in showing how and why indeterminism is just as much a feature of the universe as determinism.

Whitehead's genius was to connect. And then to generalize. He was lucky to become indelibly disillusioned early in his career. Lucien Price reports Whitehead as saying: "By 1900 the Newtonian physics were demolished, done for! Still, speaking personally, it had a profound effect on me; I have been fooled once, and I'll be damned if I'll be fooled again! Einstein is supposed to have made an epochal discovery. I am respectful and interested, but also skeptical. There is no more reason to suppose that Einstein's relativity is anything final, than Newton's *Principia*. The danger is dogmatic thought; it plays the devil with religion, and science is not immune from it."[1]

---

[1] Lucien Price, *Dialogues of Alfred North Whitehead* (Boston: Little, Brown, 1954), 345–46.

In a similar vein, reflecting much later on his Cambridge University years, he said: "Who ever dreamed that the ideas and institutions which then looked so stable would be so impermanent? Yet, since the turn of the century I have lived to see every one of the basic assumptions of science and mathematics set aside. Why, some of the assumptions which we have seen upset had endured for more than twenty centuries. This experience has profoundly affected my thinking. To have supposed you had certitude once, and then to have it blow up in your hands into inconceivable infinities has affected everything else in the universe for me."[2]

Experiencing the revolution in physics firsthand, Whitehead became convinced that its conceptual foundations needed to be transformed. For the classical ideas of space, time, and matter, he substituted events and relations. The least bits of matter-energy are not bits at all for Whitehead, and the building blocks of the universe are not blocks. As events, the basic units of reality can be described as processive and relational, a far cry from the category of "substance" or "being" that philosophers talk about. Science has exhausted the mechanistic metaphor, Whitehead said, and needs now an organismic one. Like a complex and growing organism, the universe, including the universe of human experience, is a flow of interrelated processive events. To emphasize process is to emphasize the space between two points. What is important is neither the starting point nor the end, but the traveling between. Whitehead saw the traveling as what makes up reality.

For a long period of his adult life Whitehead was an agnostic or an atheist. As a young man, he was all but converted to Roman Catholicism by the influence of Cardinal Newman. Then, with his wife Evelyn, he undertook a careful reading of the Fathers of the Church, the history of the councils, Thomas Aquinas, Thomas Hooker, and other theologians. At the end of six or seven years, Whitehead renounced Christianity, sold all his theology books,

---

[2] Victor Lowe, *Alfred North Whitehead: The Man and His Work*, vol. 1 (Baltimore: Johns Hopkins University Press, 1985), 188.

and signed on with the freethinkers. He remained agnostic or atheist for at least the next twenty-five years.

The main reason that Whitehead rejected both Canterbury and Rome was his opposition to the doctrine of God's omnipotence. Whitehead came to believe that "the presentation of God under the aspect of power awakens every modern instinct of critical reaction."[3] Alternately, he claimed, "The worship of glory arising from power is not only dangerous: it arises from a barbaric conception of God. I suppose that even the world itself could not contain the bones of those slaughtered because of men intoxicated by its attraction."[4] In the selection below, he dismisses as idolatry the idea of fashioning God in the image of imperial rulers: "The Church gave unto God the attributes which belonged exclusively to Caesar." The carnage of the First World War, in which his son Eric died, weighed on Whitehead heavily. He began to abandon agnosticism, looking for something that would give meaning to what had happened. An age of secular progress and hope had decisively ended. Not religion as it was customarily understood, but *as it could be*, now concerned Whitehead. From here on, his faith took a thoroughly philosophical form, emphatically rejecting supernaturalism; he subscribed to no creed and he joined no church.

Whitehead's vision of God is most systematically presented in the closing pages of his masterpiece, *Process and Reality*, excerpted here. If creative passage is the ultimate category descriptive of all reality, Whitehead reasoned, it is also suitable for describing the reality of God. This may have been his most revolutionary proposal of all, expressed in the maxim that "God is not to be treated as an exception to all metaphysical principles, invoked to save their collapse. He is their chief exemplification."[5] Beginning with reality as we know it (contingent, relational, finite, and changing)

[3] Alfred North Whitehead, *Science and the Modern World* (New York: Macmillan, 1925), 274.

[4] Alfred North Whitehead, *Religion in the Making* (New York: Macmillan, 1926), 55.

[5] Alfred North Whitehead, *Process and Reality*, corrected edition, ed. David Ray Griffin and Donald W. Sherburne (New York: Free Press, 1978 [1929]), 343.

and only then, in light of these categories, considering the nature of God, Whitehead reversed the lingering idealist metaphysics that had dominated nineteenth-century theology. God, he explained, has a twofold nature as primordial and consequent, just as actual occasions have mental and physical poles. Emerging within the natural world and giving it creative possibilities, God, as primordial, is the conceptual valuation of the wealth of potentials. As the "lure" for their realization, God is the beginning of feelings in the world, immanent in each occasion, as an urge to life. The consequent nature of God is physical and temporal, able to receive the experiences of all other actualities, regardless of whether those actualities freely accept or reject the divine ideal for them. What is preserved is not the actual occasion's subjectivity, which perishes, but God's cosmic memory of each actuality, woven into a great aesthetic harmony in which "the many become one" in God's everlastingness. Neither God nor the world ever reaches a state of static completion in Whitehead's vision—both are moving through a great evolutionary adventure without end.

It is a religious vision that provides no postmortem guarantees or emotional emollients. Whitehead's faith can speak of risk and adventure, of becoming and perishing, of a peace that emerges from suffering and keeps vivid a sensitiveness to tragedy. "God" and "World" are contrasts rather than antitheses as Whitehead's vision reaches its apotheosis in the closing pages of *Process and Reality* that appear below.

✋ Whitehead's Contribution to Science

With Bertrand Russell, Alfred North Whitehead spent ten years working on the three-volume Principia Mathematica *(1910–13), an attempt to derive all mathematical truths from logic. Whitehead also published the following science studies:* A Treatise on Universal Algebra *(1898);* On Mathematical Concepts of the Material World *(1906);* The Axioms of Projective Geometry *(1906);* The Axioms of Descriptive Geometry *(1907);* An Introduction to

Mathematics *(1911)*; An Enquiry Concerning the Principles of Natural Knowledge *(1919)*; The Concept of Nature *(1920)*; The Principle of Relativity with Applications to Physical Science *(1922)*.

Whitehead in His Own Words

God and the World[6]

Section I

... The notion of God as the "unmoved mover" is derived from Aristotle, at least so far as Western thought is concerned. The notion of God as "eminently real" is a favorite doctrine of Christian theology. The combination of the two into the doctrine of an aboriginal, eminently real, transcendent creator, at whose fiat the world came into being, and whose imposed will it obeys, is the fallacy which has infused tragedy into the histories of Christianity and of Mahometanism.

When the Western world accepted Christianity, Caesar conquered; and the received text of western theology was edited by his lawyers. The code of Justinian and the theology of Justinian are two volumes expressing one movement of the human spirit. The brief Galilean vision of humility flickered throughout the ages, uncertainly. In the official formulation of the religion it has assumed the trivial form of the mere attribution to the Jews that they cherished a misconception about their Messiah. But the deeper idolatry, of the fashioning of God in the image of the Egyptian, Persian, and Roman imperial rulers, was retained. The Church gave unto God the attributes which belonged exclusively to Caesar.

In the great formative period of theistic philosophy, which ended with the rise of Mahometanism, after a continuance coeval with civilization, three strains of thought emerge which, amid many variations in detail, respectively fashion God in the image of

[6] *Process and Reality*, 342–51.

an imperial ruler, God in the image of a personification of moral energy, God in the image of an ultimate philosophical principle. Hume's *Dialogues* criticize unanswerably these modes of explaining the system of the world.

The three schools of thought can be associated respectively with the divine Caesars, the Hebrew prophets, and Aristotle. But Aristotle was antedated by Indian, and Buddhistic, thought; the Hebrew prophets can be paralleled in traces of earlier thought; Mahometanism and the divine Caesars merely represent the most natural, obvious, idolatrous theistic symbolism, at all epochs and places.

The history of theistic philosophy exhibits various stages of combination of these three diverse ways of entertaining the problem. There is, however, in the Galilean origin of Christianity yet another suggestion which does not fit very well with any of the three main strands of thought. It does not emphasize the ruling Caesar, or the ruthless moralist, or the unmoved mover. It dwells upon the tender elements in the world, which slowly and in quietness operate by love; and it finds purpose in the present immediacy of a kingdom not of this world. Love neither rules, nor is it unmoved; also, it is a little oblivious as to morals. It does not look to the future; for it finds its own reward in the immediate present.

Section II

Apart from any reference to existing religions as they are, or as they ought to be, we must investigate dispassionately what the metaphysical principles, here developed, require on these points, as to the nature of God. There is nothing here in the nature of proof. There is merely the confrontation of the theoretic system with a certain rendering of the facts. But the unsystematized report upon the facts is itself highly controversial, and the system is confessedly inadequate. The deductions from it in this particular sphere of thought cannot be looked upon as more than suggestions as to how the problem is transformed in the light of that system. What follows is merely an attempt to add another speaker to that masterpiece, Hume's *Dialogues Concerning Natural Religion*. Any cogency of argument entirely depends upon elucidation of somewhat exceptional elements in our conscious experience—those elements which may roughly be classed together as religious and moral intuitions.

In the first place, God is not to be treated as an exception to all metaphysical principles, invoked to save their collapse. He is their chief exemplification.

Viewed as primordial, he is the unlimited conceptual realization of the absolute wealth of potentiality. In this aspect, he is not *before* all creation, but *with* all creation. But, as primordial, so far is he from "eminent reality," that in this abstraction he is "deficiently actual"—and this in two ways. His feelings are only conceptual and so lack the fullness of actuality. Secondly, conceptual feelings, apart from complex integration with physical feelings, are devoid of consciousness in their subjective forms.

Thus, when we make a distinction of reason, and consider God in the abstraction of a primordial actuality, we must ascribe to him neither fullness of feeling, nor consciousness. He is the unconditioned actuality of conceptual feeling at the base of things; so that, by reason of this primordial actuality, there is an order in the relevance of eternal objects to the process of creation. His unity of conceptual operations is a free creative act, untrammeled by reference to any particular course of things. It is deflected neither by love, nor by hatred, for what in fact comes to pass. The *particularities* of the actual world presuppose *it*; while *it* merely presupposes the *general* metaphysical character of creative advance, of which it is the primordial exemplification. The primordial nature of God is the acquirement by creativity of a primordial character. . . .

He is the lure for feeling, the eternal urge of desire. . . .

Section III

There is another side to the nature of God which cannot be omitted. Throughout this exposition of the philosophy of organism we have been considering the primary action of God on the world.

From this point of view, he is the principle of concretion—the principle whereby there is initiated a definite outcome from a situation otherwise riddled with ambiguity. Thus, so far, the primordial side of the nature of God has alone been relevant.

But God, as well as being primordial, is also consequent. He is the beginning and the end. He is not the beginning in the sense of being in the past of all members. He is the presupposed actuality of conceptual operation, in unison of becoming with every other creative act. Thus, by reason of the relativity of all things, there is a reaction of the world on God. The completion of God's nature into a fullness of physical feeling is derived from the objectification of the world in God. He shares with every new creation its actual world; and the concrescent creature is objectified in God as a novel element in God's objectification of that actual world. This prehension into God of each creature is directed with the subjective aim, and clothed with the subjective form, wholly derivative from his all-inclusive primordial valuation. God's conceptual nature is unchanged, by reason of its final completeness. But his derivative nature is consequent upon the creative advance of the world.

Thus, analogously to all actual entities, the nature of God is dipolar. He has a primordial nature and a consequent nature. The consequent nature of God is conscious; and it is the realization of the actual world in the unity of his nature, and through the transformation of his wisdom. The primordial nature is conceptual, the consequent nature is the weaving of God's physical feelings upon his primordial concepts.

One side of God's nature is constituted by his conceptual experience. This experience is the primordial fact in the world, limited by no actuality which it presupposes. It is therefore infinite, devoid of all negative prehensions. This side of his nature is free, complete, primordial, eternal, actually deficient, and unconscious. The other side originates with physical experience derived from the temporal world, and then acquires integration with the primordial side. It is determined, incomplete, consequent, "everlasting," fully actual, and conscious. His necessary goodness expresses the determination of his consequent nature.

Conceptual experience can be infinite, but it belongs to the nature of physical experience that it is finite. An actual entity in the temporal world is to be conceived as originated by physical experience with its process of completion motivated by consequent, conceptual experience initially derived from God. God is to be conceived as originated by conceptual experience with his process of completion motivated by consequent, physical experience, initially derived from the temporal world.

Section IV

The perfection of God's subjective aim, derived from the completeness of his primordial nature, issues into the character of his consequent nature. In it there is no loss, no obstruction. The world is felt in a unison of immediacy. The property of combining creative advance with the retention of mutual immediacy is what in the previous section is meant by the term "everlasting."

The wisdom of subjective aim prehends every actuality for what it can be in such a perfected system—its sufferings, its sorrows, its failures, its triumphs, its immediacies of joy—woven by rightness of feeling into the harmony of the universal feeling, which is always immediate, always many, always one, always with novel advance, moving onward and never perishing. The revolts of destructive evil, purely self-regarding, are dismissed into their triviality of merely individual facts; and yet the good they did achieve in individual joy, in individual sorrow, in the introduction of needed contrast, is yet saved by its relation to the completed whole. The image—and it is but an image—the image under which this operative growth of God's nature is best conceived, is that of a tender care that nothing be lost.

The consequent nature of God is his judgment on the world. He saves the world as it passes into the immediacy of his own life. It is the judgment of a tenderness which loses nothing that can be saved. It is also the judgment of a wisdom which uses what in the temporal world is mere wreckage.

Another image which is also required to understand his consequent nature is that of his infinite patience. The universe includes a threefold creative act composed of (i) the one infinite conceptual realization, (ii) the multiple solidarity of free physical realizations in the temporal world, (iii) the ultimate unity of the multiplicity of actual fact with the primordial conceptual fact. If we conceive the first term and the last term in their unity over against the intermediate multiple freedom of physical realizations in the temporal world, we conceive of the patience of God, tenderly saving the turmoil of the intermediate world by the completion of his own nature. The sheer force of things lies in the intermediate physical process: this is the energy of physical production. God's role is not the combat of productive force with productive force, of destructive force with destructive force; it lies in the patient operation of the overpowering rationality of his conceptual harmonization. He does not create the world, he saves it: or, more accurately, he is the poet of the world, with tender patience leading it by his vision of truth, beauty, and goodness.

Section V

The vicious separation of the flux from the permanence leads to the concept of an entirely static God, with eminent reality, in relation to an entirely fluent world, with deficient reality. But if the opposites, static and fluent, have once been so explained as separately to characterize diverse actualities, the interplay between the thing which is static and the things which are fluent involves contradiction at every step in its explanation. Such philosophies must include the notion of "illusion" as a fundamental principle—the notion of "*mere* appearance." This is the final Platonic problem.

Undoubtedly, the intuitions of Greek, Hebrew, and Christian thought have alike embodied the notions of a static God condescending to the world, and of a world *either* thoroughly fluent, *or* accidentally static, but finally fluent—"heaven and earth shall pass away." In some schools of thought, the fluency of the world is mitigated by the assumption that selected components in the world are exempt from this final fluency, and achieve a static survival. Such components are not separated by any decisive line from analogous components for which the assumption is not made. Further, the survival is construed in terms of a final pair of opposites, happiness for some, torture for others. . . .

But civilized intuition has always, although obscurely, grasped the problem as double and not as single. There is not the mere problem of fluency *and* permanence. There is the double problem: actuality with permanence, requiring fluency as its completion; and actuality with fluency, requiring permanence as its completion. The first half of the problem concerns the completion of God's primordial nature by the derivation of his consequent nature from the temporal world. The second half of the problem concerns the completion of each fluent actual occasion by its function of objective immortality, devoid of "perpetual perishing," that is to say, "everlasting."

This double problem cannot be separated into two distinct problems. Either side can only be explained in terms of the other. The consequent nature of God is the fluent world become "everlasting" by its objective immortality in God. Also the objective immortality of actual occasions requires the primordial permanence of God, whereby the creative advance ever re-establishes itself endowed with initial subjective aim derived from the relevance of God to the evolving world.

But objective immortality within the temporal world does not solve the problem set by the penetration of the finer religious intuition. "Everlastingness" has been lost; and "everlastingness" is the content of that vision upon which the finer religions are built—the "many" absorbed everlastingly in the final unity. The problems of the fluency of God and of the everlastingness of passing experience are solved by the same factor in the universe. This factor is the temporal world perfected by its reception and its reformation, as a fulfillment of the primordial appetition which is the basis of all order. In this way God is completed by the individual, fluent satisfactions of finite fact, and the temporal occasions are completed by their everlasting union with their transformed selves, purged into conformation with the eternal order which is the final absolute "wisdom." The final summary can only be expressed in terms of a group of antitheses, whose apparent self-contradictions depend on neglect of the diverse categories of existence. In each antithesis there is a shift of meaning which converts the opposition into a contrast.

It is as true to say that God is permanent and the World fluent, as that the World is permanent and God is fluent.

It is as true to say that God is one and the World many, as that the World is one and God many.

It is as true to say that, in comparison with the World, God is actual eminently, as that, in comparison with God, the World is actual eminently.

It is as true to say that the World is immanent in God, as that God is immanent in the World.

It is as true to say that God transcends the World, as that the World transcends God.

It is as true to say that God creates the World, as that the World creates God.

God and the World are the contrasted opposites in terms of which creativity achieves its supreme task of transforming disjoined multiplicity, with its diversities in opposition, into concrescent unity, with its diversities in contrast. In each actuality there are two concrescent poles of realization—"enjoyment" and "appetition," that is, the "physical" and the "conceptual." For God the conceptual is prior to the physical, for the world the physical poles are prior to the conceptual poles. . . .

God and the World stand over against each other, expressing the final metaphysical truth that appetitive vision and physical enjoyment have equal claim to priority in creation. But no two actualities can be torn apart: each is all in all. Thus each temporal occasion embodies God, and is embodied in God. In God's nature, permanence is primordial and flux is derivative from the World: in the World's nature, flux is primordial and permanence is derivative from God. Also the World's nature is a primordial datum for God; and God's nature is a primordial datum for the World. Creation achieves the reconciliation of permanence and flux when it has reached its final term which is everlastingness— the Apotheosis of the World.

Opposed elements stand to each other in mutual requirement. In their unity, they inhibit or contrast. God and the World stand to each other in this opposed requirement. God is the infinite ground of all mentality, the unity of vision seeking physical multiplicity. The World is the multiplicity of finites, actualities seeking a perfected unity. Neither God, nor the World, reaches static completion. Both are in the grip of the ultimate metaphysical ground, the creative advance into novelty. Either of them, God and the World, is the instrument of novelty for the other.

In every respect God and the World move conversely to each other in respect to their process. God is primordially one, namely, he is the primordial unity of relevance of the many potential forms; in the process he acquires a consequent multiplicity, which the primordial character absorbs into its own unity. The World is primordially many, namely, the many actual occasions with their physical finitude; in the process it acquires a consequent unity, which is a novel occasion and is absorbed into the multiplicity of the primordial character. Thus God is to be conceived as one and as many in the converse sense in which the World is to be conceived as many and as one. The theme of Cosmology, which is the basis of all religions, is the story of the dynamic effort of the world passing into everlasting unity, and of the static majesty of God's vision, accomplishing its purpose of completion by absorption of the world's multiplicity of effort.

Section VI

The consequent nature of God is the fulfillment of his experience by his reception of the multiple freedom of actuality into the harmony of his own actualization. It is God as really actual, completing the deficiency of his mere conceptual actuality. . . .

But God's conceptual realization is nonsense if thought of under the guise of a barren, eternal hypothesis. It is God's conceptual realization performing an efficacious role in multiple unifications of the universe, which are free creations of actualities arising out of decided situations. Again this discordant multiplicity of actual things, requiring each other and neglecting each other, utilizing and discarding, perishing and yet claiming life as obstinate matter of fact, requires an enlargement of the understanding to the comprehension of another phase in the nature of things. In this later phase, the many actualities are one actuality, and the one actuality is many actualities. Each actuality has its present life and its immediate passage into novelty; but its passage is not its death. This final phase of passage in God's nature is ever enlarging itself. In it the complete adjustment of the immediacy of joy and suffering reaches the final end of creation. This end is existence in the perfect unity of adjustment as means, and in the perfect multiplicity of the attainment of individual types of self-existence. The function of being a means is not disjoined from the function of being an end. The sense of worth beyond itself is immediately enjoyed as an overpowering element in the individual self-attainment. It is in this way that the immediacy of sorrow and pain is transformed into an element of triumph. This is the notion of redemption through suffering which haunts the world. It is the generalization of its very minor exemplification as the aesthetic value of discords in art.

Thus the universe is to be conceived as attaining the active self-expression of its own variety of opposites—of its own freedom and its own necessity, of its own multiplicity and its own unity, of its own imperfection and its own perfection. All the "opposites" are elements in the nature of things, and are incorrigibly there. The concept of "God" is the way in which we understand this incredible fact that what cannot be, yet is.

Section VII

Thus the consequent nature of God is composed of a multiplicity of elements with individual self-realization. It is just as much a multiplicity as it is a unity; it is just as much one immediate fact as it is an unresting advance beyond itself. Thus the actuality of God must also be understood as a multiplicity of actual components in process of creation. This is God in his function of the kingdom of heaven.

Each actuality in the temporal world has its reception into God's nature. The corresponding element in God's nature is not temporal actuality, but is the transmutation of that temporal actuality into a living, ever-present fact. An enduring personality in the temporal world is a route of occasions in which the successors with some peculiar completeness sum up their predecessors. The correlate fact in God's nature is an even more complete unity of life in a chain of elements for which succession does not mean loss of immediate unison. This element in God's nature inherits from the temporal counterpart according to the same principle as in the temporal world the future inherits from the past. Thus in the sense in which the present occasion is the person *now*, and yet with his own past, so the counterpart in God is that person in God.

But the principle of universal relativity is not to be stopped at the consequent nature of God. This nature itself passes into the temporal world according to its gradation of relevance to the various concrescent occasions. There are thus four creative phases in which the universe accomplishes its actuality. There is first the phase of conceptual origination, deficient in actuality, but infinite in its adjustment of valuation. Secondly, there is the temporal phase of physical origination, with its multiplicity of actualities. In this phase full actuality is attained; but there is deficiency in the solidarity of individuals with each other. This phase derives its determinate conditions from the first phase. Thirdly, there is the phase of perfected actuality, in which the many are one everlastingly, without the qualification of any loss either of individual identity or of completeness of unity. In everlastingness, immediacy is reconciled with objective immortality. This phase derives the conditions of its being from the two antecedent phases. In the fourth phase, the creative action completes itself. For the perfected actuality passes back into the temporal world, and qualifies this world so that each temporal actuality includes it as an immediate fact of relevant experience. For the kingdom of heaven is with us today. The action of the fourth phase is the love of God for the world. It is the particular providence for particular occasions. What is done in the world is transformed into a reality in heaven, and the reality in heaven passes back into the world. By reason of this reciprocal relation, the love in the world passes into the love in heaven, and floods back again into the world. In this sense, God is the great companion—the fellow-sufferer who understands.

We find here the final application of the doctrine of objective immortality. Throughout the perishing occasions in the life of each temporal Creature, the inward source of distaste or of refreshment, the judge arising out of the very nature of things, redeemer or goddess of mischief, is the transformation of Itself, everlasting in the Being of God. In this way, the insistent craving is justified—the insistent craving that zest for existence be refreshed by the ever-present, unfading importance of our immediate actions, which perish and yet live for evermore.

Further Reading

For Whitehead's contribution to thinking about relativity theory and quantum mechanics, two helpful books are Shimon Malin's *Nature Loves to Hide: Quantum Physics and the Nature of Reality, A Western Perspective* (Oxford and New York: Oxford University Press, 2001) and *Physics and Whitehead: Quantum, Process, and Experience* edited by Timothy E. Eastman and Hank Keeton (Albany, NY: SUNY Press, 2004), a collection of essays by contemporary physicists and process philosophers. An online complement to the latter book can be found at a valuable resource for studies in Whitehead and modern science. http://www.ctr4process.org/publications/PSS/. The work of Australian physicist Reginald T. Cahill is currently at the cutting edge of the new approach known as "process physics"; see his *Process Physics: From Information Theory to Quantum Space and Matter* (New York: Nova Science Publishers, 2005). The Japanese scholar Yutaka Tanaka forges brilliant bridges in "Einstein and Whitehead: the Principle of Relativity

Reconsidered," *Historia Scientiarum* 32 (1987): 45–61; and "Bell's The-orem and the Theory of Relativity: An Interpretation of Quantum Cor-relation at a Distance Based on the Philosophy of Organism," *Annals of Japan Association for Philosophy of Science* 8 (1992): 49–67. Michael Epperson explores in detail the compatibility of Whitehead's meta-physics with various quantum theories in *Quantum Mechanics and the Philosophy of Alfred North Whitehead* (New York: Fordham University Press, 2004). With the 2002 publication of Isabelle Stengers's pathbreak-ing volume *Penser avec Whitehead* (Paris: Seuil), Whitehead has been resurrected for science studies. A special issue in volume 13 of *Configura-tions*—the journal of the Society for Literature, Science, and the Arts—is devoted to Whitehead. The best source for biographical information on Whitehead is Victor Lowe, *Alfred North Whitehead: The Man and His Work*, 2 vols. (Baltimore: Johns Hopkins University Press, 1985, 1990). Academic theologians and philosophers of religion early appropriated Whitehead's metaphysics, as well as the work of Charles Hartshorne. "Process theology" is not a single or unified position but has always given special attention to the relationship between science and religion. Ian Barbour's early presentation of process thought in *Issues in Science and Religion* (Englewood Cliffs, NJ: Prentice-Hall, 1966) has become a classic in the field. Other authors to note are John B. Cobb, Jr., David Ray Griffin, Marjorie Suchocki, and Catherine Keller.

PART TWO

Scientists of Our Time

A religion, old or new, that stressed the
magnificence of the universe as revealed by
modern science, might be able to draw forth
reserves of reverence and awe tapped by the
conventional faiths. Sooner or later, such a
religion will emerge.
—Carl Sagan

9 Rachel Carson
(1907–1964)

Introduction

Rachel Carson, the ardent naturalist whose classic work *Silent Spring* launched the environmental movement, was a resolutely intellectual and formidably precise biologist. She also possessed a profound natural piety that suffuses her writings. As her biographer Paul Brooks rightly points out, "her attitude toward the natural world was that of a deeply religious person."[1] Carson's fresh voice—both objective and lyrical at once—could give the processes of nature spiritual meaning without sacrificing the scientific accuracy of the biological facts or behaviors. Nature, she held, is necessary for spiritual growth: "I believe natural beauty has a necessary place in the spiritual development of any individual or any society. I believe that whenever we substitute something man-made and artificial for a natural feature of the earth, we have retarded some part of man's spiritual growth."[2]

[1] Paul Brooks, *The House of Life: Rachel Carson at Work, with Selections from Her Writings* (Boston: Houghton Mifflin, 1972), 9.

[2] Quoted in Linda Lear, *Rachel Carson: Witness for Nature* (New York: Henry Holt, 1997), 259.

Carson found in dunes and water and leaves, in silence and in changing seasons, all that the ancients called absolute or miraculous. Her life and writings are powerful evidence that naturalism—whether as a complex belief system or, more simply, as a devotion to nature—can satisfy what many have regarded as an instinctive religious craving for meaning. Nature itself gives joy and satisfaction and coherence to brief human life spans. It is sufficient, she said.

Awe and wonder are as vital a part of our response to the natural world as laughter or grief is to the social world. If we do not exactly define religion exclusively in terms of awe and wonder, we still recognize these as integral to spiritual renewal. Rachel Carson believed that there was spiritual value in contemplating with awe the beauty of nature, and that it led to the renewal of our spirits, to inner healing, and to a new depth of humanity.

Destined to become the twentieth century's preeminent interpreter of marine science, Carson was a twenty-two-year-old graduate student before she saw the sea for the first time. She had loved the sea at a distance since childhood, but it was not until that first summer in 1929, when she was working at the Marine Biological Laboratory at Woods Hole, that she could walk the beaches of Cape Cod and thrill to the ocean. Earning a master's degree in zoology, she studied genetics with H. S. Jennings and Raymond Pearl at Johns Hopkins. She also studied radiation as a cause of mutation and developed an early interest in the effects of synthetic pesticides after World War II. But for reasons related to gender, the Depression, and family financial obligations, Carson's career path was not that of an academic scientist publishing in peer-reviewed journals. From 1936 to 1952 she held a civil service job as an aquatic biologist with the U. S. Fish and Wildlife Service in Washington, D.C., and eventually found her voice writing for the public.

That voice speaks with passion and eloquence in the nine excerpts below. Their common theme is the relation of life to its environment in a panorama of ceaseless change. In the first excerpt and again in the eighth, Carson speaks of "material immortality"; she makes clear, especially in the eighth excerpt, that she viewed death, even her own, as of an entirely natural occurrence, like rivers running into the sea, or the drift of Monarch butterflies alighting briefly on the goldenrod as they make their migration south.

Carson's public career was launched when she was asked to write an introduction for one of the agency's pamphlets. Under the title "The World of Waters," she began work on "Undersea" (first excerpt) in early 1936. Finally deemed too literary for publication by the Fish and Wildlife Service, the essay was sent to *Atlantic Monthly*, which published it in 1937. Over a decade later, Carson delivered a speech on the mysteries of the sea and its scientific exploration, capturing the interest of her audience by showing pictures and playing audio recordings of such things as the clicking noises made by shrimp snapping their claws. Her study of the ocean was evoking in her an ever-deeper sense of the mystery of life.

In contemplating the sea lace, a tiny transparent wisp of protoplasm that is found by the trillion amid the rocks and weeds of the shore, Carson wrote: "The meaning haunts and ever eludes us, and in its very pursuit we approach the ultimate mystery of Life itself." Her passion for the sea and the creatures of the sea could be compared to the "feeling for the organism" that drove Nobel Prize–winning botanist Barbara McClintock's in her research on corn. Both scientists believed that only by empathizing with living beings and natural habitats can we begin to understand others and ourselves in the house of life.

Carson's religious sensibility compares with that of the famous scientist-physician Albert Schweitzer, known for formulating the cardinal principle of "reverence for life." Of the many awards Carson received, none had more meaning for her or touched her more deeply than the Schweitzer Medal of the Animal Welfare Institute. In accepting it in 1963, she said:

> In his various writings, we may read Dr. Schweitzer's philosophical interpretations of that phrase. But to many of us, the truest understanding of Reverence for Life comes, as it did to him, from some personal experience, perhaps the sudden, unexpected sight of a wild creature, perhaps some experience with a pet. Whatever it

may be, it is something that takes us out of ourselves, that makes us aware of other life. From my own memories, I think of the sight of a small crab alone on a dark beach at night, a small and fragile being waiting at the edge of the roaring surf, yet so perfectly at home in its world. To me it seemed a symbol of life, and of the way life has adjusted to the forces of its physical environment. Or I think of a morning when I stood in a North Carolina marsh at sunrise, watching flock after flock of Canada geese rise from resting places at the edge of a lake and pass low overhead. In that orange light, their plumage was like brown velvet. Or I have found that deep awareness of life and its meaning in the eyes of a beloved cat.[3]

With *The Edge of the Sea* in 1955 (fourth excerpt), Carson began to interweave ideas about the sacrality of the cycle of life with the actions of the ocean. The glimpse of some ineffable universal truths through scientific exploration, a motif that returns in Carson's personal correspondence, is found in this early essay. "Contemplating the teeming life of the shore, we have an uneasy sense of the communication of some universal truth that lies just beyond our grasp," she wrote. This sense of a "peculiar brand of magic" is explored further in Carson's posthumously published field notebooks from Saint Simon Island, off the coast of Georgia (fifth excerpt).

Writing to her friend and biographer Paul Brooks, Carson explicitly set forth her convictions in the sixth excerpt below, entitled (by Brooks) "A Statement of Belief." Finding the larger meaning of life in the natural world around her rather than in any formal creed, Carson expresses her faith movingly. She is forthright that the need for traditional ideas of heaven and God are replaced in her mind by the insatiable questioning and curiosity that suffuses the very living of life. She cannot be sure of the answers, but the natural piety she lives by is sufficient. She finds traditional religion's "certainties," on the other hand, insufficient.

Another biographer, Mary McCay writes, "Once, when her mother told her that God created the world, Rachel replied, 'Yes,

---

[3] Quoted in Brooks, 315–17.

and General Motors created my Oldsmobile. But *how* is the question.'"[4] Carson's own description of *how* the creation of the world occurred appears in *The Sea Around Us*, revised and reprinted in 1961. Here she writes a narrative of the origin of the world, and identifies the sea as the central character. The seventh excerpt here begins by describing the sea as the "great mother of life" and refers to all living beings as its "children." Just as each human passes on its genes to its offspring, the ocean is a part of every person. Human beings are the sea's progeny. The sea is within us. How could we not feel a vital and haunting connection to it? Mammals may have abandoned the sea for land millions of years ago, but the desire of humans to return to it is palpable.

In the remaining portion of the excerpt, Carson writes her own book of Genesis, sketching out in the pages of *The Sea Around Us* an account of the "gray beginnings." That she intended it as an alternative, or supplemental, version of the biblical book is suggested by her using as an epigram the familiar words: "And the earth was without form, and void; and darkness was upon the face of the deep." Carson's vision offers a radical challenge to religious reflection to come down to earth, down to the very sea, and to reclaim once again from Genesis that earthy and watery story of our humble origins. After all, we are earth creatures with salt water still flowing within us, making up 70 percent of our bodies. We can entrust our lives to the mystery of creation and allow the earth to store up our lives in death.

Finally, the primordial protoplasm from which all life eventually emerged was formed. Carson does not attempt to explain how such protoplasm came about; she simply points to the fact that the natural conditions of the environment were necessarily perfect for such a monumental biological event to take place. These conditions were in fact so perfect that no humans, from medieval alchemists to modern laboratory scientists, have been able to reproduce nature's results. The question of the origin of all life simply gives rise to a feeling of awe, not to any theological urge.

[4] Mary McCay, *Rachel Carson* (New York: Twayne Publishers, 1993), 42.

Another source of wonder for Carson in *The Sea Around Us* is the vastness of space and time. A speck in a grand universe, the human race exists for only a moment in a long, extraordinary natural history. The planet is "a water world, a planet dominated by its covering mantle of the ocean, in which continents are but transient intrusions of land above the surface of the all-encircling sea." Carson describes the ocean as an omnipresent, controlling force. One consequence of this control is that humans cannot exist in the sea for any length of time. People are not the most significant beings in the universe or even on the planet, and neither universe nor planet exist specifically to provide for human existence, as some anthropic views currently maintain.

Carson shows a great deal of reverence for natural processes in her description of the island of Krakatoa, on which a volcanic eruption decimated almost all forms of life. One visitor to the island reported finding only a single microscopic spider after the eruption. Carson notes that practically nothing lived on the island for twenty-five years, but then different species of creatures slowly began to arrive and inhabit it. As life returned to Krakatoa, the small number of individuals present from each species led to smaller gene pools, which resulted in a deviation from the norm of the species and caused life to develop in what Carson describes as a "remarkable manner." Quoting Darwin's words that the "mystery of mysteries" is "the first appearance of new beings on earth," Carson agrees. According to one of her biographers, "if Carson was unimpressed with the fact that God made the world, she was certainly impressed with the ingenuity with which the sea endured; her tone throughout *The Sea Around Us* implies a reverence for the ocean that borders on the religious."[5]

The seventh excerpt concludes with Carson's recognition that everything will eventually return to the sea, including the land, which has already begun to erode. That process is natural since everything on earth has been influenced by the sea in one way or another and seeks to return to it. Carson writes, "For all at last

[5] McCay, 43.

return to the sea—to Oceanus, the ocean river, like the ever-flowing stream of time, the beginning and the end." This idea of "material immortality" regarding aspects of the sea is important to Carson: the ocean lives forever, while everything else exists and returns to it in cycles.[6]

In the letters selected for the eighth excerpt, Carson is writing to Dorothy Freeman, her neighbor on Southport Island, Maine, where Carson had purchased a summer cottage in July 1953. Here her heart speaks.

One of the most beautiful pieces of nature writing in the English language is Carson's essay "Helping Your Child to Wonder," in which she recounts adventures with her young nephew, Roger, as they enjoy walks along the rocky coast of Maine and through dense forests and fields. Observing wildlife, exotic plants, full moons, and storm clouds, Carson teaches Roger to listen for the "living music" of insects in the underbrush. She asks in closing, "What is the value of preserving and strengthening this sense of awe and wonder, this recognition of something beyond the boundaries of human existence? Is the exploration of the natural world just a pleasant way to pass the golden hours of childhood or is there something deeper?" Carson's eloquent answer is contained in the last excerpt and is suggestive of what religious naturalists like Ursula Goodenough in chapter 21 recognize as profoundly spiritual. When she died in 1964, Carson was turning this essay into a book, *The Sense of Wonder.*

✑ Carson's Contribution to Science

Rachel Carson developed the idea for Silent Spring *(1962) when a friend complained that pesticide spraying had killed the birds in her yard as well as the intended insects. Research and observation revealed that long-lasting chemical pesticides, including DDT, caused immense damage. Evidence also indicated that pesticide residue triggered physiological changes in human beings. With*

[6] McCay, 42.

more than fifty pages of supporting citations from the scientific literature, Silent Spring *did not call for a complete pesticide ban but rather for more prudent use and further study of their environmental effects. The book engendered an almost immediate grass-roots sentiment for improvement of environmental quality and passage of related federal legislation.*

Carson in Her Own Words

From "Undersea"[7]

Thus we see the parts of the plan fall into place: the water receiving from earth and air the simple materials, storing them up until the gathering energy of the spring sun wakens the sleeping plants to a burst of dynamic activity, hungry swarms of planktonic animals growing and multiplying upon the abundant plants, and themselves falling prey to the shoals of fish; all, in the end, to be redissolved into their component substances when the inexorable laws of the sea demand it. Individual elements are lost to view, only to reappear again and again in different incarnations in a kind of material immortality. Kindred forces to those which, in some period inconceivably remote, gave birth to that primeval bit of protoplasm tossing on the ancient seas continue their mighty and incomprehensible work. Against this cosmic background the life span of a particular plant or animal appears, not as a drama complete in itself, but only as a brief interlude in a panorama of endless change.

From Under the Sea-Wind[8]

To stand at the edge of the sea, to sense the ebb and the flow of the tides, to feel the breath of a mist moving over a great salt marsh, to

---

[7] Rachel Carson, "Undersea," *Atlantic Monthly*, September 1937, 325.

[8] Rachel Carson, *Under the Sea-Wind: A Naturalist's Picture of Ocean Life* (New York: Simon and Schuster, 1941), xviii.

watch the flight of shore birds that have swept up and down the surf lines of the continents for untold thousands of years, to see the running of the old eel and the young shad to the sea, is to have knowledge of things that are as nearly eternal as any earthly life can be.

From the New York Herald-Tribune *Book and Author Luncheon Speech*[9]

That is part of the fascination of the ocean. But most of all, the sea is a place of mystery. One by one, the mysteries of yesterday have been solved. But the solution seems always to bring with it another, perhaps a deeper mystery. I doubt that the last, final mysteries of the sea will ever be resolved. In fact, I cherish a very unscientific hope that they will not be.

A century is a very short time. Yet only a century ago men thought nothing could live in the deep waters of the ocean. They believed that, at most, there could be only a "few sparks" of life in the black waters of the oceanic abyss. Now, of course, we know better. In the year 1860 a surveying vessel was looking for the best route for the trans-Atlantic cable. When the sounding line was brought up from a depth of about a mile and a half, there were starfish clinging to the line. The same year a cable was brought up for repairs from the bottom of the Mediterranean. It was heavily encrusted with corals and other animals that evidently had been living on it for months or years. Such discoveries gave our grandfathers and our great-grandfathers their first proof that the floor of the deep sea is inhabited by living creatures.

Now, in our own time, another mystery of the sea is engaging the attention of scientists. This is the nature of the life of those strange, middle regions—far below the surface, but also far above the bottom.

[9] Rachel Carson, "*The New York Herald Tribune* Book and Author Luncheon Speech," in *Lost Woods: The Discovered Writings of Rachel Carson*, ed. Linda Lear (Boston: Beacon Press, 1998), 80.

From The Edge of the Sea[10]

On all these shores there are echoes of past and future: of the flow of time, obliterating yet containing all that has gone before; of the sea's eternal rhythms—the tides, the beat of surf, the pressing rivers of the currents—shaping, changing, dominating; of the stream of life, flowing as inexorably as any ocean current, from past to unknown future. For as the shore configuration changes in the flow of time, the pattern of life changes, never static, never quite the same from year to year. Whenever the sea builds a new coast, waves of living creatures surge against it, seeking a foothold, establishing their colonies. And so we come to perceive life as a force as tangible as any of the physical realities of the sea, a force strong and purposeful, as incapable of being crushed or diverted from its ends as the rising tide.

Contemplating the teeming life of the shore, we have an uneasy sense of the communication of some universal truth that lies just beyond our grasp. What is the message signaled by the hordes of diatoms, flashing their microscopic lights in the night sea? What truth is expressed by the legions of the barnacles, whitening the rocks with their habitations, each small creature within finding the necessities of its existence in the sweep of the surf? And what is the meaning of so tiny a being as the transparent wisp of protoplasm that is a sea lace, existing for some reason inscrutable to us—a reason that demands its presence by the million amid the rocks and weeds of the shore? The meaning haunts and ever eludes us, and in its very pursuit we approach the ultimate mystery of Life itself.

"Dunes," from the Fragments of Carson's Field Notebooks on Saint Simon Island, Georgia[11]

What peculiar brand of magic is inherent in that combination of sand and sky and water it is hard to say. It is bleak and stark. But

[10] Rachel Carson, *The Edge of the Sea* (Boston: Houghton Mifflin, 1955), 250.
[11] In *Lost Woods*, 130–32.

somehow it is not forbidding. Its bleakness is part of its quiet, calm strength.

The dune land is a place of overwhelming silence, or so it seems at first. But soon you realize that what you take for silence is an absence of human-created sound. For the dunes have a voice of their own, which you may hear if you will but sit down and listen to it. It is compounded of many natural sounds which are never heard in the roar of a city or even in the stir of a small town. A soft, confused, hollow rustling fills the air. In part it is the sound of surf on the beach half a mile away—a wide sand cause [sic] they show the wind to be blowing alternately from different quarters. I cannot say as to that; but the scribblings of the dune grass always enchant me, though I cannot read their meaning.

I knew the history of that land, and there, under the wind and beside the surf that had carved it, I recalled the story—I stood where a new land was being built out of the sea, and I came away deeply moved. Although our intelligence forbids the idea, I believe our deeply rooted attitude toward the creation of the earth and the evolution of living things is a feeling that it all took place in a time infinitely remote. Now I understood. Here, as if for the benefit of my puny human understanding, the processes of creation—of earth building—had been speeded up so that I could trace the change within the life of my own contemporaries. The changes that were going on before my eyes were part and parcel of the same processes that brought the first dry land emerging out of the ancient and primitive ocean; or that led the first living creatures step by step out of the sea into the perilous new world of earth.

Water and wind and sand were the builders, and only the gulls and I were there to witness this act of creation.

Strange thoughts come to a man or woman who stands alone in that bleak and barren world. It is a world stripped of the gracious softness of the trees, the concealing mercies of abundant vegetation, the refreshment of a quiet lake, the beguilement of shade. It is a world stripped to the naked elements of life. And it is, after all, so newly born of the sea that it could hardly be otherwise. And then there is the voice of the sand itself—the quick sharp sibilance of a gust of sand blown over a dune crest by a sudden shift of the breeze, the all but silent sound of the never ending, restless shifting of the individual grains, one over another.

I am not sure that I can recommend the dunes as a tonic for all souls, nor for all moods. But I can say that anyone who will go alone into the dune lands for a day, or even for an hour, will never forget what he has seen and felt there.

A Statement of Belief[12]

A large part of my life has been concerned with some of the beauties and mysteries of this earth about us, and with the even greater mysteries of the life that inhabits it. No one can dwell long among such subjects without thinking rather deep thoughts, without asking himself searching and often unanswerable questions, and without achieving a certain philosophy.

There is one quality that characterizes all of us who deal with the sciences of the earth and its life—we are never bored. We can't be. There is always something new to be investigated. Every mystery solved brings us to the threshold of a greater one.

I like to remember the wonderful old Swedish oceanographer, Otto Petterson. He died a few years ago at the age of ninety-three, in full possession of his keen mental powers. His son, also a distinguished oceanographer, tells us in a recent book how intensely his father enjoyed every new experience, every new discovery concerning the world about him. "He was an incurable romantic," the son wrote, "intensely in love with life and with the mysteries of the Cosmos which, he was firmly convinced, he had been born to unravel." When, past ninety, Otto Petterson realized he had not much longer to enjoy the earthly scene, he said to his son: "What will sustain me in my last moments is an infinite curiosity as to what is to follow."

---

[12] Fom a speech Carson gave to Theta Sigma Phi, April 21, 1954, much of which became part of *The Sense of Wonder* (reprinted in Brooks, 324–26).

The pleasures, the values of contact with the natural world, are not reserved for the scientists. They are available to anyone who will place himself under the influence of a lonely mountain top— or the sea—or the stillness of a forest; or who will stop to think about so small a thing as the mystery of a growing seed.

I am not afraid of being thought a sentimentalist when I say that I believe natural beauty has a necessary place in the spiritual development of any individual or any society. I believe that whenever we destroy beauty, or whenever we substitute something man-made and artificial for a natural feature of the earth, we have retarded some part of man's spiritual growth . . .

We see the destructive trend on a national scale in proposals to invade the national parks with commercial schemes such as the building of power dams. The parks were placed in trust for all the people, to preserve for them just such recreational and spiritual values as I have mentioned. Is it the right of this, our generation, in its selfish materialism, to destroy these things because we are blinded by the dollar sign? Beauty—and all the values that derive from beauty—are not measured and evaluated in terms of the dollar.

Years ago I discovered in the writings of the British naturalist Richard Jefferies a few lines that so impressed themselves upon my mind that I have never forgotten them.

> The exceeding beauty of the earth, in her splendor of life, yields a new thought with every petal. The hours when the mind is absorbed by beauty are the only hours when we really live. All else is illusion, or mere endurance.

Those lines are, in a way, a statement of the creed I have lived by . . . I have had the privilege of receiving many letters from people who, like myself, have been steadied and reassured by contemplating the long history of the earth and sea, and the deeper meanings of the world of nature . . . In contemplating "the exceeding beauty of the earth" these people have found calmness and courage. For there is symbolic as well as actual beauty in the migration of birds; in the ebb and flow of the tides; in the folded bud ready for the spring. There is something infinitely healing in these repeated refrains of nature—the assurance that dawn comes after night, and spring after the winter.

Mankind has gone very far into an artificial world of his own creation . . . But I believe that the more clearly we can focus our attention on the wonders and realities of the universe about us, the less taste we shall have for destruction.

From The Sea Around Us[13]

Beginnings are apt to be shadowy, and so it is with the beginnings of that great mother of life, the sea. Many people have debated how and when the earth got its ocean, and it is not surprising that their explanations do not always agree. For the plain and inescapable truth is that no one was there to see, and in the absence of eyewitness accounts there is bound to be a certain amount of disagreement. So if I tell here the story of how the young planet Earth acquired an ocean, it must be a story pieced together from many sources and containing whole chapters the details of which we can only imagine. The story is founded on the testimony of the earth's most ancient rocks, which were young when the earth was young; on other evidence written on the face of the earth's satellite, the moon; and on hints contained in the history of the sun and the whole universe of star-filled space. For although no man was there to witness this cosmic birth, the stars and the moon and the rocks were there, and, indeed, had much to do with the fact that there is an ocean.

❧

That primeval ocean, growing in bulk as the rains slowly filled its basins, must have been only faintly salt. But the falling rains were the symbol of the dissolution of the continents. From the

[13] Rachel Carson, *The Sea Around Us* (New York: Oxford University Press, 1961), 1, 6–7, 14–15, 72–73, 88–89, 208–9.

moment the rains began to fall, the lands began to be worn away and carried to the sea. It is an endless, inexorable process that has never stopped—the dissolving of the rocks, the leaching out of their contained minerals, the carrying of the rock fragments and the dissolved minerals to the ocean. And over the eons of time, the sea has grown ever more bitter with the salt of the continents.

In what manner the sea produced the mysterious and wonderful stuff called protoplasm we cannot say. In its warm, dimly lit waters the unknown conditions of temperature and pressure and saltiness must have been the critical ones for the creation of life from non-life. At any rate they produced the result that neither the alchemists with their crucibles nor modern scientists in their laboratories have been able to achieve.

Before the first living cell was created, there may have been many trials and failures. It seems probable that, within the warm saltiness of the primeval sea, certain organic substances were fashioned from carbon dioxide, sulphur, nitrogen, phosphorus, potassium, and calcium. Perhaps these were transition steps from which the complex molecules of protoplasm arose—molecules that somehow acquired the ability to reproduce themselves and begin the endless stream of life. But at present no one is wise enough to be sure.

Those first living things may have been simple microorganisms rather like some of the bacteria we know today—mysterious borderline forms that were not quite plants, not quite animals, barely over the intangible line that separates the non-living from the living. It is doubtful that this first life possessed the substance chlorophyll, with which plants in sunlight transform lifeless chemicals into the living stuff of their tissues. Little sunshine could enter their dim world, penetrating the cloud banks from which fell the endless rains. Probably the sea's first children lived on the organic substances then present in the ocean waters, or, like the iron and sulphur bacteria that exist today, lived directly on inorganic food.

All the while the cloud cover was thinning, the darkness of the nights alternated with palely illumined days, and finally the sun for the first time shone through upon the sea. By this time some of the living things that floated in the sea must have developed the magic of chlorophyll.

~

Some of the land animals later returned to the ocean. After perhaps 50 million years of land life, a number of reptiles entered the sea about 170 million years ago, in the Triassic period. They were huge and formidable creatures. Some had oarlike limbs by which they rowed through the water; some were web-footed, with long, serpentine necks. These grotesque monsters disappeared millions of years ago, but we remember them when we come upon a large sea turtle swimming many miles at sea, its barnacle-encrusted shell eloquent of its marine life. Much later, perhaps no more than 50 million years ago, some of the mammals, too, abandoned a land life for the ocean. Their descendants are the sea lions, seals, sea elephants, and whales of today.

Among the land mammals there was a race of creatures that took to an arboreal existence. Their hands underwent remarkable development, becoming skilled in manipulating and examining objects, and along with this skill came a superior brain power that compensated for what these comparatively small mammals lacked in strength. At last, perhaps somewhere in the vast interior of Asia, they descended from the trees and became again terrestrial. The past million years have seen their transformation into beings with the body and brain and spirit of man.

Eventually man, too, found his way back to the sea. Standing on its shores, he must have looked out upon it with wonder and curiosity, compounded with an unconscious recognition of his lineage. He could not physically re-enter the ocean as the seals and whales had done. But over the centuries, with all the skill and ingenuity and reasoning powers of his mind, he has sought to explore and investigate even its most remote parts, so that he might re-enter it mentally and imaginatively.

He built boats to venture out on its surface. Later he found ways to descend to the shallow parts of its floor, carrying with him the air that, as a land mammal long unaccustomed to aquatic life, he needed to breathe. Moving in fascination over the deep sea he could not enter, he found ways to probe its depths, he let down nets to capture its life, he invented mechanical eyes and ears that could re-create for his senses a world long lost, but a world that, in the deepest part of his subconscious mind, he had never wholly forgotten.

And yet he has returned to his mother sea only on her own terms. He cannot control or change the ocean as, in his brief tenancy of earth, he has subdued and plundered the continents. In the artificial world of his cities and towns, he often forgets the true nature of his planet and the long vistas of its history, in which the existence of the race of men has occupied a mere moment of time. The sense of all these things comes to him most clearly in the course of a long ocean voyage, when he watches day after day the receding rim of the horizon, ridged and furrowed by waves; when at night he becomes aware of the earth's rotation as the stars pass overhead; or when, alone in this world of water and sky, he feels the loneliness of his earth in space. And then, as never on land, he knows the truth that his world is a water world, a planet dominated by its covering mantle of ocean, in which the continents are but transient intrusions of land above the surface of the all-encircling sea.

➤

The rains, the eroding away of the earth, the rush of sediment-laden waters have continued, with varying pulse and tempo, throughout all of geologic time. In addition to the silt load of every river that finds its way to the sea, there are other materials that compose the sediments. Volcanic dust, blown perhaps halfway around the earth in the upper atmosphere, comes eventually to rest on the ocean, drifts in the currents, becomes waterlogged, and sinks. Sands from coastal deserts are carried seaward on offshore winds, fall to the sea, and sink. Gravel, pebbles, small boulders, and shells are carried by icebergs and drift ice, to be released to the water when the ice melts. Fragments of iron, nickel, and other

meteoric debris that enter the earth's atmosphere over the sea—
these, too, become flakes of the great snowfall. But most widely
distributed of all are the billions upon billions of tiny shells and
skeletons, the limy or silicious remains of all the minute creatures
that once lived in the upper waters.

The sediments are a sort of epic poem of the earth. When we
are wise enough, perhaps we can read in them all of past history.
For all is written here. In the nature of the materials that compose
them and in the arrangement of their successive layers the sediments reflect all that has happened in the waters above them and
on the surrounding lands. The dramatic and the catastrophic in
earth history have left their trace in the sediments—the outpour-
ings of volcanoes, the advance and retreat of the ice, the searing
aridity of desert lands, the sweeping destruction of floods.

❧

The catastrophe of Krakatoa gave naturalists a perfect opportunity to observe the colonization of an island. With most of the island itself destroyed, and the remnant covered with a deep layer
of lava and ash that remained hot for weeks, Krakatoa after the
explosive eruptions of 1883 was, from a biological standpoint, a
new volcanic island. As soon as it was possible to visit it, scientists
searched for signs of life, although it was hard to imagine how
any living thing could have survived. Not a single plant or animal
could be found. It was not until nine months after the eruption
that the naturalist Cotteau was able to report: "I only discovered
one microscopic spider—only one. This strange pioneer of the
renovation was busy spinning its web." Since there were no insects on the island, the web-spinning of the bold little spider was
presumably in vain, and except for a few blades of grass, practically nothing lived on Krakatoa for a quarter of a century. Then
the colonists began to arrive—a few mammals in 1908; a number
of birds, lizards, and snakes; various mollusks, insects, and earth-
worms. Ninety per cent of Krakatoa's new inhabitants, Dutch scientists found, were forms that could have arrived by air.

Isolated from the great mass of life on the continents, with no opportunity for the crossbreeding that tends to preserve the average and to eliminate the new and unusual, island life has developed in a remarkable manner. On these remote bits of earth, nature has excelled in the creation of strange and wonderful forms. As though to prove her incredible versatility, almost every island has developed species that are endemic—that is, they are peculiar to it alone and are duplicated nowhere else on earth.

It was from the pages of earth's history written on the lava fields of the Galapagos that young Charles Darwin got his first inkling of the great truths of the origin of species. Observing the strange plants and animals—giant tortoises, black, amazing lizards that hunted their food in the surf, sea lions, birds in extraordinary variety—Darwin was struck by their vague similarity to mainland species of South and Central America, yet was haunted by the differences, differences that distinguish them not only from the mainland species but from those on other islands of the archipelago. Years later he was to write in reminiscence: "Both in space and time, we seem to be brought somewhat near to that great fact—that mystery of mysteries—the first appearance of new beings on earth."

Of the "new beings" evolved on islands, some of the most striking examples have been birds. In some remote age before there were men, a small, pigeonlike bird found its way to the island of Mauritius, in the Indian Ocean. By processes of change at which we can only guess, this bird lost the power of flight, developed short, stout legs, and grew larger until it reached the size of a modern turkey. Such was the origin of the fabulous dodo, which did not long survive the advent of man on Mauritius. New Zealand was the sole home of the moas. One species of these ostrich-like birds stood twelve feet high. Moas had roamed New Zealand from the early part of the Tertiary; those that remained when the Maoris arrived soon died out.

Other island forms besides the dodo and the moas have tended to become large. Perhaps the Galapagos tortoise became a giant after its arrival on the islands, although fossil remains on the continents cast doubt on this. The loss of wing use and even of the wings themselves (the moas had none) are common results of insular life. Insects on small, wind-swept islands tend to lose the power of flight—those that retain it are in danger of being blown out to sea. The Galapagos Islands have a flightless cormorant. There have been at least fourteen species of flightless rails on the islands of the Pacific alone.

$\sim$

And the ultra-modern *United States Pilot* for Antarctica says:

> Navigators should observe the bird life, for deductions may often be drawn from the presence of certain species. Shags are . . . a sure sign of the close proximity of land . . . The snow petrel is invariably associated with ice and is of great interest to mariners as an augury of ice conditions in their course . . . Blowing whales usually travel in the direction of open water.

Sometimes the Pilots for remote areas of the sea can report only what the whalers or sealers or some old-time fisherman has said about the navigability of a channel or the set of the tidal currents; or they must include a chart prepared half a century ago by the last vessel to take soundings in the area. Often they must caution the navigator not to proceed without seeking information of those having "local knowledge." In phrases like these we get the feel of the unknown and the mysterious that never quite separates itself from the sea: "It is said that there was once an island there . . . such information as could be secured from reports of men with local knowledge . . . their position has been disputed . . . a bank reported by an old-time sealer."

So here and there, in a few out-of-the-way places, the darkness of antiquity still lingers over the surface of the waters. But it is rapidly being dispelled and most of the length and breadth of the ocean is known; it is only in thinking of its third dimension that we can still apply the concept of the Sea of Darkness. It took centuries to chart the surface of the sea; our progress in delineating the unseen world beneath it seems by comparison phenomenally rapid. But even with all our modern instruments for probing and sampling the deep ocean, no one now can say that we shall ever resolve the last, the ultimate mysteries of the sea.

In its broader meaning, that other concept of the ancients remains. For the sea lies all about us. The commerce of all lands must cross it. The very winds that move over the lands have been cradled on its broad expanse and seek ever to return to it. The continents themselves dissolve and pass to the sea, in grain after grain of eroded land. So the rains that rose from it return again in rivers. In its mysterious past it encompasses all the dim origins of life and receives in the end, after, it may be, many transmutations, the dead husks of that same life. For all at last return to the sea— to Oceanus, the ocean river, like the ever-flowing stream of time, the beginning and the end.

Letters from Carson to Dorothy Freeman[14]

March 27, 1963

There are three things I want to talk about as I can, my plans for Roger, your writing, and your dear letter in which you talked about your new thoughts on immortality. Of course, darling, it touched me deeply that this new conviction has come to you through me. I have never formulated my own belief and feeling in words and am not sure I can now. Of two things I am certain. One is the kind of "material immortality" of which I wrote in the concluding paragraphs of "Undersea," and which is expressed in one of Charles Alldredge's poems which I am sending you. That is purely a biologist's philosophy. For me it has great meaning and beauty—but it is not wholly satisfying. Then, the immortality

[14] *Always, Rachel: The Letters of Rachel Carson and Dorothy Freeman, 1952–1964*, ed. Martha Freeman (Boston: Beacon Press, 1994), 446–47. The September 10 letter was written seven months before her death of cancer at the age of fifty-six.

through memory is real and, in a personal way, far more satisfying. It is good to know that I shall live on even in the minds of many who do not know me, and largely through association with things that are beautiful and lovely. When E. B. White wrote me last summer that he would always think of me when he heard his hermit thrushes, I told him I could think of no more lovely memorial. And I know, darling, that as between you and me, the one who goes first will always speak to the other through many things— the songs of the veeries and hermits, and a sleepy white throat at midnight—moonlight on the bay—ribbons of waterfowl in the sky. But, as you ask, is that enough? No, it isn't. For one thing, the concept of nothingness is hard to accept. How could that which is truly one's self cease to exist? And if not, then what kind of spiritual existence can there be? If we try to form a definite concept we are, of course, only guessing, but it seems to me that if we say we do not know and can't even imagine, this doesn't mean we disbelieve in personal immortality. Because I cannot understand something doesn't mean it doesn't exist. The marvels of atomic or nuclear physics, and the mathematical concepts of astronomy are wholly beyond my ability to grasp. Yet I know these concepts deal with proven realities, so it is no more difficult to believe there is some sort of life beyond that "horizon," and to accept the fact we cannot now know what it is. Perhaps you remember what I wrote in "Help Your Child—" about the old Swedish oceanographer Otto Petterson—how, as he neared the end of his long life, he said to his son that in his last moments he would be sustained "by an infinite curiosity as to what was to follow." To me, that sort of feeling is an acceptable substitute for the old-fashioned "certainties" as to heaven and what it must be like. I know that we do not really "know" and I'm content that it should be so. . . .

September 10, 1963

This is a postscript to our morning at Newagen, something I think I can write better than say. For me it was one of the loveliest of the summer hours, and all the details will remain in my memory: that blue September sky, the sounds of wind in the spruces and surf on the rocks, the gulls busy with their foraging, alighting with deliberate grace, the distant views of Griffiths Head and Todd Point, today so clearly etched, though once seen in swirling fog. But most of all I shall remember the Monarchs, that unhurried drift of one small winged form after another, each drawn by some invisible force. We talked a little about their life history. Did they return? We thought not; for most, at least, this was the closing journey of their lives.

But it occurred to me this afternoon, remembering, that it had been a happy spectacle, that we had felt no sadness when we spoke of the fact that there would be no return. And rightly— for when any living thing has come to the end of its cycle we accept that end as natural. For the Monarch butterfly, that cycle is measured in a known span of months. For ourselves, the measure is something else, the span of which we cannot know. But the thought is the same: when that intangible cycle has run its course it is a natural and no unhappy thing that a life comes to its end.

That is what those brightly fluttering bits of life taught me this morning. I found a deep happiness in it—so, I hope, may you. Thank you for this morning.

From The Sense of Wonder[15]

What is the value of preserving and strengthening this sense of awe and wonder, this recognition of something beyond the boundaries of human existence? Is the exploration of the natural world just a pleasant way to pass the golden hours of childhood or is there something deeper?

I am sure there is something much deeper, something lasting and significant. Those who dwell, as scientists or laymen, among

---

[15] Rachel Carson, *The Sense of Wonder* (New York: HarperCollins, 1998), 85. An earlier version first appeared in *Woman's Home Companion,* under the title "Help your Child to Wonder" (1956).

the beauties and mysteries of the earth are never alone or weary of life. Whatever the vexations or concerns of their personal lives, their thoughts can find paths that lead to inner contentment and to renewed excitement in living. Those who contemplate the beauty of the earth find reserves of strength that will endure as long as life lasts. There is symbolic as well as actual beauty in the migration of the birds, the ebb and flow of the tides, the folded bud ready for the spring. There is something infinitely healing in the repeated refrains of nature—the assurance that dawn comes after night, and spring after the winter.

I like to remember the distinguished Swedish oceanographer, Otto Petterson, who died a few years ago at the age of ninety-three, in full possession of his keen mental powers. His son, also world-famous in oceanography, has related in a recent book how intensely his father enjoyed each new experience, every new discovery concerning the world around him.

"He was an incurable romantic," the son wrote, "intensely in love with life and with the mysteries of the cosmos." When he realized he had not much longer to enjoy the earthly scene, Otto Petterson said to his son: "What will sustain me in my last moments is an infinite curiosity as to what is to follow."

In my mail recently was a letter that bore eloquent testimony to the lifelong durability of a sense of wonder. It came from a reader who asked advice on choosing a seacoast spot for a vacation, a place wild enough that she might spend her days roaming beaches unspoiled by civilization, exploring that world that is old but ever new.

Regretfully she excluded the rugged northern shores. She had loved the shore all her life, she said, but climbing over the rocks of Maine might be difficult, for an eighty-ninth birthday would soon arrive. As I put down her letter I was warmed by the fires of wonder and amazement that still burned brightly in her youthful mind and spirit, just as they must have done fourscore years ago.

The lasting pleasures of contact with the natural world are not reserved for scientists but are available to anyone who will place himself under the influence of earth, sea, and sky and their amazing life.

Further Reading

While working as a government employee Carson wrote *Under the Sea-Wind: A Naturalist's Picture of Ocean Life* (New York: Simon and Schuster, 1941) and *The Sea Around Us* (New York: Oxford University Press, 1951). In 1955 she published *The Edge of the Sea* (Boston: Houghton Mifflin). Controversial when it first appeared, *Silent Spring* (Boston: Houghton Mifflin, 1962) is now considered far ahead of its time. Her last book, *The Sense of Wonder* (New York: Harper and Row, 1965), was published posthumously and has gone through several editions, some with beautiful photographs. Two biographies are exceptionally interesting: Paul Brooks, *The House of Life: Rachel Carson at Work* (Boston: Houghton Mifflin, 1972) and Linda Lear, *Rachel Carson: Witness for Nature* (New York: Henry Holt, 1997). See also Mary McCay, *Rachel Carson* (New York: Twayne Publishers, 1993). Martha E. Freeman has collected over 750 of her grandmother's letters to and from Rachel Carson in *Always, Rachel: The Letters of Rachel Carson and Dorothy Freeman, 1952–1964* (Boston: Beacon Press, 1994). See also the important work edited by Linda Lear; *Lost Woods: The Discovered Writings of Rachel Carson* (Boston: Beacon Press, 1998).

10 Carl Sagan
(1934–1996)

Introduction

Carl Sagan, astronomer, public intellectual, and creator of the popular television series *Cosmos*, expresses in his writings a far more complex view of religion—and far more complex religious views—than his critics or even his admirers acknowledged during his lifetime. Sometimes severe in his assessment of religion's history, Sagan is always fair in his depiction of the different future that the world's religions might yet help to promote.

Labels or "isms" such as agnosticism do not begin to do justice to Sagan's own sense of "the numinous." He revered the universe. He was utterly imbued with awe, wonder, and a marvelous sense of belonging to a planet, a galaxy, a cosmos that inspires devotion as much as it does discovery. Ann Druyan has described the most important part of her late husband's work as providing "a new sense of the sacred," and it is surely this aspect of Sagan's writings that continues to edify and uplift his readers. "Uplift" is exactly the perspective Sagan aimed to achieve. He invites us to shift our frame of reference up and off of planet Earth so that we might turn around and regard it. He leads us—in our imaginations—far out into space with the *Voyager* spacecraft and, in that mission's only photograph of the earth, taken at Sagan's insistence, he bids us to look down on that "pale blue dot," seeing its beauty, its obscurity, and its fragility. A single pixel in the context of the vast cosmos, planet Earth swirls outward to the stars.

When Druyan speaks of the pale blue dot, she dares us to ". . . stare at this image of our tiny planet in its larger context and do your best to remain a militant nationalist, a zealot willing to drench this tiny mote in blood, or a capitalist who places the bottom line above all. Is this piece of scientific evidence really value-free, lacking in moral and spiritual implications?"[1]

For Sagan, the consequences of science always carried moral and spiritual implications. Among celebrity scientists of the twentieth century, Sagan stands apart as an *activist* public intellectual who helped raise our awareness of the perils of the nuclear age and the threats to the planet of environmental degradation. In 1990 he spearheaded a joint appeal to the religious and scientific communities for environmental action on behalf of humankind. The open letter he drafted was signed by thirty-two Nobel laureate and other scientists. It was presented on January 1990 to the Global Forum of Spiritual and Parliamentary Leaders Conference in Moscow. The following paragraph from the closing portions of the letter gives a sense of the alliance between science and religion that Sagan had come to see as valuable:

> As scientists, many of us have had profound experiences of awe and reverence before the universe. We understand that what is regarded as sacred is more likely to be treated with care and respect. Our planetary home should be so regarded. Efforts to safeguard and cherish the environment need to be infused with a vision of the sacred. At the same time, a much wider and deeper understanding of science and technology is needed. If we do not understand the problem, it is unlikely we will be able to fix it. Thus, there is a vital role for both religion and science.[2]

[1] Ann Druyan, "A New Sense of the Sacred," *Humanist* 60, no. 6 (2000): 24.
[2] http://earthrenewal.org/Open_letter_to_the_religious_.htm.

The environmental degradations that alarmed Sagan were many: depletion of the protective ozone layer; a global warming unprecedented in the last 150 millennia; the obliteration of an acre of forest every second; the rapid-fire extinction of species; and the prospect of a global nuclear war which would put at risk most of the population of the earth. In the words of the 1990 open letter: "We are close to committing—many would argue we are already committing—what in religious language is sometimes called Crimes against Creation."

Toward conventional religions, Sagan's attitude was usually one of dismissal. As the stuff of myths, they were not to be believed. He thought that extraordinary claims require extraordinary evidence, and he could find none. In *Cosmos* Sagan was combative toward religion. By the time he wrote *Contact* he had mellowed somewhat to a stance of dialogue. In the last book he wrote before his death, *The Demon-Haunted World,* he argued that "science is not only compatible with spirituality; it is a profound source of spirituality."[3] These are the words of a scientist who finds in science not simply the best explanation of phenomena but also a source of amazement, reverence, and humility. Modern science provides for the first time in human history something superior to anything provided by traditional religion: an accurate understanding of our human place in the universe. And this understanding itself carries spiritual significance.

As Sagan wrote in *Cosmos*, we are the ". . . starstuff pondering the stars; organized assemblages of ten billion billion billion atoms considering the evolution of atoms; tracing the long journey by which, here at least, consciousness arose." Our oneness with the cosmos is science's revelation to us in the last century, more powerful than any prescientific religion in helping us locate our place. When it comes to evolution, natural selection elicits a far more

[3] Carl Sagan, *The Demon-Haunted World: Science as a Candle in the Dark* (New York: Random House, 1995), 29.

inspiring response than the hypothesis of a Designer. "A Designer," Sagan concedes, "is a natural, appealing and altogether human explanation of the biological world. But, as Darwin and Wallace showed, there is another way, equally appealing, equally human, and far more compelling: natural selection, which makes the music of life more beautiful as the aeons pass."[4]

In removing us from our older, privileged, Apollo-photograph position at the center of the cosmos and placing us in the anonymity of the "pale blue dot," Sagan did not see himself as rendering human life or planet Earth insignificant. In fact, the new view increased our significance. Nothing in the universe is privileged. We are part of a much larger, connected whole. The one sense in which we are special (although not likely unique in the cosmos) is that unlike the stars, the planets, or even our closest relatives on earth, we alone are conscious, and we alone have the capacity to perceive the universe and appreciate its majesty, "For we are the local embodiment of a Cosmos grown to self-awareness."[5] He never waivered from the conviction that "We make our world significant by the courage of our questions and by the depth of our answers."[6]

It is striking that Sagan's greatest scientific achievements were discoveries that disproved the possibility of life on Venus (he determined that surface temperatures are in excess of 900 degrees Celsius) and discredited possible evidence for life on Mars (he showed that seasonal color changes of the surface of the planet are due not to vegetation, as some claimed, but to dust storms)—findings that flew in the face of his own most cherished expectations. A crucial flaw of most religions, according to Sagan, is their refusal to accept putative evidence against anything that flies in the face of cherished beliefs. The Fourteenth Dalai Lama pleased and surprised Sagan when he acknowledged in conversation that

[4] Carl Sagan, *Cosmos* (New York: Random House, 1980), 345, 29.
[5] *Cosmos*, 345.
[6] *Cosmos*, 193.

Tibetan Buddhism would have to abandon any doctrine disproved by science.

In the passages that follow, the reader will find a sampling of Sagan's most astute and eloquent observations. Included are some of his reflections on religion and science, both philosophically considered and fictionally imagined. *Contact*, his only published novel, proves to be one of the best representations of Sagan's own faith as a scientist, put into the mouth of his female protagonist. Waving aside the usual dangers of attributing a fictional character's beliefs to the author, in this case it is clear that Ellie Arroway speaks for Carl Sagan. The final selection records his reflections from his hospital bed as he was dying at the age of sixty two after a long and difficult fight with myelodysplasia.

✌ Sagan's Contribution to Science

As a planetary astronomer, Carl Sagan made significant contributions to the fields of chemical evolution, Martian topography, and Venusian meteorology. He discovered the true nature of the atmosphere and surface conditions on Venus. He later made important discoveries about the Martian atmosphere and the moons of Saturn. He served as an official adviser to NASA on the Mariner, Voyager, *and* Viking *unmanned space missions. He led the charge both to the public and in the Congressional halls of government for funding of space research and particularly SETI, the Search for Extra-Terrestrial Intelligence. He predicted or anticipated global climate change, biodiversity loss, genetic engineering, artificial intelligence, space-based weapons, and the Internet. He taught at Stanford University and Harvard University and was a staffer at the Smithsonian Astrophysical Observatory. In 1968, he became director of the Laboratory for Planetary Studies at Cornell University, where he also taught classes. Standing room only crowds thronged his lectures. Carl Sagan may have persuaded more people to read, study, teach, and do science than any other single individual in history.*

Sagan in His Own Words

Our Place in the Universe[7]

The pioneering psychologist William James called religion a "feeling of being at home in the Universe." Our tendency has been, as I described in the early chapters of this book, to pretend that the Universe is how we wish our home would be, rather than to revise our notion of what's homey so it embraces the Universe. If, in considering James' definition, we mean the *real* Universe, then we have no true religion yet. That is for another time, when the sting of the Great Demotions is well behind us, when we are acclimatized to other worlds and they to us, when we are spreading outward to the stars.

The Cosmos extends, for all practical purposes, forever. After a brief sedentary hiatus, we are resuming our ancient nomadic way of life. Our remote descendants, safely arrayed on many worlds through the Solar System and beyond, will be unified by their common heritage, by their regard for their home planet, and by the knowledge that, whatever other life may be, the only humans in all the Universe come from Earth.

They will gaze up and strain to find the blue dot in their skies. They will love it no less for its obscurity and fragility. They will marvel at how vulnerable the repository of all our potential once was, how perilous our infancy, how humble our beginnings, how many rivers we had to cross before we found our way.

On the Historical Use of Religion[8]

In attempting to understand who we are, every human culture has invented a corpus of myth. The contradictions within us are

---

[7] Carl Sagan, *Pale Blue Dot: A Vision of the Human Future in Space* (New York: Random House, 1994), 405.

[8] Carl Sagan and Ann Druyan, *Shadows of Forgotten Ancestors* (New York: Random House, 1992), 4, 6, 35.

ascribed to a struggle between contending but equally matched deities; or to an imperfect Creator; or, paradoxically, to a rebellious angel and the Almighty; or to the even more unequal struggle between an omnipotent being and disobedient humans.

❧

Insecure, we clung to these stories, imposing the strictest penalties on any who dared to doubt them. It was better than nothing, better than admitting our ignorance of our own origins, better than acknowledging that we had been left naked and helpless, a foundling on a doorstep. . . .

. . . We were once sure, not just of our central position, but that the Universe was *made* for us. This old, comfortable conceit, this safe view of the world has been crumbling for five centuries. The more we understood of how the world is put together, the less we needed to invoke a God or gods, and the more remote in time and causality any divine intervention had to be. . . .

The distasteful prospect of an indifferent Universe—or worse, a meaningless Universe—has generated fear, denial, ennui, and the sense that science is an instrument of alienation. The cold truths of our scientific age are uncongenial to many. We feel stranded and alone. We crave a purpose to give meaning to our existence. We do not want to hear that the world was not made for us. We are unimpressed with moral codes contrived by mere mortals; we want one handed down from on high.

❧

The world and everything in it was made for us, as we were made for God:

For the last few thousand years, and especially since the end of the Middle Ages, this proud, self-confident assertion was increasingly common belief, held by Emperor and slave, Pope and parish priest. The Earth was a lavishly decorated stage set, designed by an ingenious if inscrutable Director, who had managed to round up, from only He knew where, a multitudinous supporting cast of toucans and mealy bugs, eels, voles, elms, yaks, and much, much more ... For thousands of years, virtually everyone, theologian and scientist alike, found this, both emotionally and intellectually, a satisfying account.

On Science over God and Cosmos over Creation[9]

Many people were scandalized—some still are—at both ideas, evolution and natural selection. Our ancestors looked at the elegance of life on Earth, at how appropriate the structures of organisms are to their functions, and saw evidence for a Great Designer.... There seemed to be no way in which atoms and molecules could somehow spontaneously fall together to create organisms of such awesome complexity and subtle functioning as grace every region of the Earth. The idea that every organism was meticulously constructed by a Great Designer provided a significance and order to nature and an importance to human beings that we crave still. A Designer is a natural, appealing and altogether human explanation of the biological world. But, as Darwin and Wallace showed, there is another way, equally appealing, equally human, and far more compelling: natural selection, which makes the music of life more beautiful as the aeons pass ... The fossil record implies trial and error, an inability to anticipate the future, features inconsistent with an efficient Great Designer (although not with a Designer of a more remote and indirect temperament).

In many cultures it is customary to answer that God created the universe out of nothing. But this is mere temporizing. If we wish courageously to pursue the question, we must, of course ask next where God comes from. And if we decide this to be unanswerable,

[9] *Cosmos*, 28–29, 257, 175.

why not save a step and decide that the origin of the universe is an unanswerable question? Or, if we say that God has always existed, why not save a step and conclude that the universe has always existed?

✌

The early Greeks had believed that the first being was Chaos, corresponding to the phrase in Genesis in the same context, "without form." ... A universe created from Chaos was in perfect keeping with the Greek belief in an unpredictable Nature run by capricious gods. But in the sixth century B.C., in Ionia, a new concept developed, one of the great ideas of the human species. The universe is knowable, the ancient Ionians argued, because it exhibits an internal order: there are regularities in Nature that permit its secrets to be uncovered. Nature is not entirely unpredictable; there are rules even she must obey. This ordered and admirable character of the universe was called Cosmos.

On Natural Selection and God[10]

In astronomy, we no longer believe that an angel pushes each planet around the Sun; the inverse square law of gravitation and Newton's laws of motion suffice. But no one considers this a demonstration of the nonexistence of God, and Newton himself—except for a private reservation about the notion of the Trinity—was close to the conventional Christianity of his day. We are free to posit, if we wish, that God is responsible for the laws of Nature, and that the divine will is worked through secondary causes. In biology those causes would have to include mutation and natural selection. (Many people would find it unsatisfying, though, to worship the law of gravity.)

[10] *Shadows*, 63, 66–67.

Evolution in no way *implies* atheism, although it is *consistent* with atheism. But evolution is clearly inconsistent with the literal truth of certain revered books. If we believe the Bible was written by people, and not dictated word-for-word to a flawless stenographer by the Creator of the Universe, or if we believe God might on occasion resort to metaphor for clarity, then evolution should pose no theological problem. But whether it poses a problem or not, the evidence for evolution—*that* it has happened, apart from the debate on whether uniformitarian natural selection fully explains *how* it happened—is overwhelming. . . .

Evolution suggests that if God exists, God is fond of secondary causes and factotum processes: getting the Universe going, establishing the laws of Nature, and then retiring from the scene. A hands-on Executive seems to be absent; power has been delegated. Evolution suggests that God will not intervene, whether beseeched or not, to save us from ourselves. Evolution suggests we're on our own—that if there is a God, that God must be very far away. This is enough to explain much of the emotional anguish and alienation that evolution has worked. We long to believe that there's someone at the helm.

On the Real Difference between Science and Religion[11]

Think of how many religions attempt to validate themselves with prophecy. Think of how many people rely on these prophecies, however vague, however unfulfilled to support or prop up their beliefs. Yet has there ever been a religion with the prophetic accuracy and reliability of science? There isn't a religion on the planet that doesn't long for a comparable ability—precise, and repeatedly demonstrated before committed skeptics—to foretell future events. No other human institution comes close.

[11] *The Demon-Haunted World*, 30–31; 34–35.

Is this worshiping at the altar of science? Is this replacing one faith by another, equally arbitrary? In my view, not at all. The directly observed success of science is the reason I advocate its use. If something else worked better, I would advocate the something else. Does science insulate itself from philosophical criticism? Does it define itself as having a monopoly on the "truth"? . . . Compare as many doctrines as you can think of, note what predictions they make of the future, which ones are vague, which ones are precise, and which doctrines—every one of them subject to human fallibility—have error-correcting mechanisms built in. Take account of the fact that not one of them is perfect. Then simply pick the one that in a fair comparison works (as opposed to feels) best. If different doctrines are superior in quite separate and independent fields, we are of course free to choose several—but not if they contradict one another. Far from being idolatry, this is the means by which we can distinguish the false idols from the real thing. . . .

This is one of the reasons that the organized religions do not inspire me with confidence. Which leaders of the major faiths acknowledge that their beliefs might be incomplete or erroneous and establish institutes to uncover possible doctrinal deficiencies? Beyond the test of everyday living, who is systematically testing the circumstances in which traditional religious teachings may no longer apply? (It is certainly conceivable that doctrines and ethics that may have worked fairly well in patriarchal or patristic or medieval times might be thoroughly invalid in the very different world we inhabit today.) What sermons even-handedly examine the God hypothesis? What rewards are religious skeptics given by the established religions—or, for that matter, social and economic skeptics by the society in which they swim?

Science, Ann Druyan notes, is forever whispering in our ears, "Remember, you're very new at this. You might be mistaken. You've been wrong before." Despite all the talk of humility, show me something comparable in religion. Scripture is said to be divinely inspired—a phrase with many meanings. But what if it's simply made up by fallible humans? Miracles are attested, but what if they're instead some mix of charlatanry, unfamiliar states of consciousness, misapprehensions of natural phenomena, and mental illness? No contemporary religion and no New Age belief seems to me to take sufficient account of the grandeur, magnificence, subtlety and intricacy of the Universe revealed by science. The fact that so little of the findings of modern science is prefigured in Scripture to my mind casts further doubt on its divine inspiration.

But of course I might be wrong.

On Criticizing Scientists for Their Religious Views[12]

The historians Joyce Appleby, Lynn Hunt, and Margaret Jacob (in *Telling the Truth About History*, 1994) criticize Isaac Newton: He is said to have rejected the philosophical position of Descartes because it might challenge conventional religion and lead to social chaos and atheism. Such criticisms amount only to the charge that scientists are human. How Newton was buffeted by the intellectual currents of his time is of course of interest to the historian of ideas; but it has little bearing on the truth of his propositions. For them to be generally accepted, they must convince atheists and theists alike. This is just what happened.

Appleby and her colleagues claim that "When Darwin formulated his theory of evolution, he was an atheist and a materialist," and suggest that evolution was a product of a purported atheist agenda. They have hopelessly confused cause and effect. Darwin was about to become a minister of the Church of England when the opportunity to sail on H.M.S. *Beagle* presented itself. His religious ideas, as he himself described them, were at the time highly conventional. He found every one of the Anglican Articles of Faith entirely believable. Through his interrogation of Nature, through science, it slowly dawned on him that at least some of his religion was false. That's why he changed his religious views.

[12] *The Demon-Haunted World*, 258–59.

Answering Charges That Science is Too Reductionist in Relying on a Small Number of "Laws of Nature"[13]

We hear—for example from the theologian Langdon Gilkey in his *Nature, Reality and the Sacred*—that the notion of the laws of Nature being everywhere the same is simply a preconception imposed on the Universe by fallible scientists and their social milieu. He longs for other kinds of "knowledge," as valid in their contexts as science is in its. But the order of the Universe is not an assumption; it's an observed fact. We detect the light from distant quasars only because the laws of electromagnetism are the same ten billion light-years away as here. The spectra of those quasars are recognizable only because the same chemical elements are present there as here, and because the same laws of quantum mechanics apply. The motion of galaxies around one another follows familiar Newtonian gravity. Gravitational lenses and binary pulsar spin-downs reveal general relativity in the depths of space. We *could* have lived in a Universe with different laws in every province, but we do not. This fact cannot but elicit feelings of reverence and awe.

Of course, we may make mistakes in applying a reductionist program to science. There may be aspects which, for all we know, are not reducible to a few comparatively simple laws. But in light of the findings in the last few centuries, it seems foolish to complain about reductionism. It is not a deficiency but one of the chief triumphs of science. And, it seems to me, its findings are perfectly consonant with many religions (although it does not *prove* their validity). Why should a few simple laws of Nature explain so much and hold sway throughout this vast Universe? Isn't this just what you might expect from a Creator of the Universe? Why should some religious people oppose the reductionist program in science, except out of some misplaced love of mysticism?

---

[13] *The Demon-Haunted World*, 273–74.

On Reconciling Religion and Science[14]

Attempts to reconcile religion and science have been on the religious agenda for centuries—at least for those who did not insist on Biblical and Qu'ranic literalism with no room for allegory or metaphor. The crowning achievements of Roman Catholic theology are the *Summa Theologica* and the *Summa Contra Gentiles* ("Against the Gentiles") of St. Thomas Aquinas. Out of the maelstrom of sophisticated Islamic philosophy that tumbled into Christendom in the twelfth and thirteenth centuries were the books of the ancient Greeks, especially Aristotle—works even on casual inspection of high accomplishment. Was this ancient learning compatible with God's Holy Word? In the *Summa Theologica*, Aquinas set himself the task of reconciling 631 questions between Christian and classical sources. But how to do this where a clear dispute arises?. . . Often, Aquinas appealed to common sense and the natural world—i.e., science used as an error-correcting device. With some contortion of both common sense and Nature, he managed to reconcile all 631 problems. (Although when push came to shove, the desired answer was simply assumed. Faith always got the nod over Reason.) Similar attempts at reconciliation permeate Talmudic and post-Talmudic Jewish literature and medieval Islamic philosophy. But tenets at the heart of religion can be tested scientifically. This in itself makes some religious bureaucrats and believers wary of science. Is the Eucharist, as the Church teaches, in fact, and not just as productive metaphor, the flesh of Jesus Christ, or is it—chemically, microscopically, and in other ways—just a wafer handed to you by a priest? Will the world be destroyed at the end of the 52-year Venus cycle unless humans are sacrificed to the gods? Does the occasional uncircumcised Jewish man fare worse than his co-religionists who abide by the ancient covenant in which God demands a piece of foreskin from every

---

[14] *The Demon-Haunted World*, 274–78; Carl Sagan, *Billions and Billions: Thoughts on Life and Death at the Brink of the Millennium* (New York: Random House, 1997), 139.

male worshiper? . . . By making pronouncements that are, even if only in principle, testable, religions, however unwillingly, enter the arena of science. Religions can no longer make unchallenged assertions about reality—so long as they do not seize secular power, provided they cannot coerce belief. This, in turn, has infuriated some followers of some religions. Occasionally they threaten skeptics with the direst imaginable penalties. . . . Of course many religions—devoted to reverence, awe, ethics, ritual, community, family, charity, and political and economic justice—are in no way challenged, but rather uplifted, by the findings of science. There is no necessary conflict between science and religion. On one level, they share similar and consonant roles, and each needs the other. Open and vigorous debate, even the consecration of doubt, is a Christian tradition going back to John Milton's *Areopagitica* (1644). . . . The religious traditions are often so rich and multi-variate that they offer ample opportunity for renewal and revision, again especially when their sacred books can be interpreted metaphorically and allegorically. There is thus a middle ground of confessing past errors—as the Roman Catholic Church did in its 1992 acknowledgment that Galileo was right after all, that the Earth does revolve around the Sun: three centuries late, but courageous and most welcome nonetheless. . . .

In theological discussion with religious leaders, I often ask what their response would be if a central tenet of their faith were disproved by science. When I put this question to the current, Fourteenth, Dalai Lama, he unhesitatingly replied as no conservative or fundamentalist religious leaders do: In such a case, he said, Tibetan Buddhism would have to change.

Even, I asked, if it's a *really* central tenet, like (I searched for an example) reincarnation?

Even then, he answered.

However—he added with a twinkle—it's going to be hard to disprove reincarnation.

Plainly, the Dalai Lama is right. Religious doctrine that is insulated from disproof has little reason to worry about the advance of science. The grand idea, common to many faiths, of a Creator of the Universe is one such doctrine—difficult alike to demonstrate or to dismiss.

❧

The methods and ethos of science and religion are profoundly different. Religion frequently asks us to believe without question, even (or especially) in the absence of hard evidence. Indeed, this is the central meaning of faith. Science asks us to take nothing on faith, to be wary of our penchant for self-deception, to reject anecdotal evidence. Science considers deep skepticism a prime virtue. Religion often sees it as a barrier to enlightenment. So, for centuries, there has been a conflict between the two fields—the discoveries of science challenging religious dogmas, and religion attempting to ignore or suppress the disquieting findings.

But times have changed. Many religions are now comfortable with an Earth that goes around the Sun, with an Earth that's 4.5 billion years old, with evolution, and with the other discoveries of modern science. Pope John Paul II has said, "Science can purify religion from error and superstition; religion can purify science from idolatry and false absolutes. . . . Each can draw the other into a wider world, a world in which both can flourish. . . . Such bridging ministries must be nurtured and encouraged."

Contact[15]

[Editor's note: Sagan's novel Contact is based on a hypothetical situation in which scientists detect a signal from extraterrestrials, in the form of a return broadcast of the first powerful television signal that ever left Earth: Hitler's opening of the 1936 Olympic Games in Berlin. In the excerpt below, the scientist who discovered the signal, Ellie Arroway, frankly describes her position on science and religion to a colleague, der Heer, and discusses the theological

[15] Carl Sagan, *Contact* (New York: Simon and Schuster, 1985), 166–76.

implications of her scientific discovery with two evangelical Christian theologians, Joss and Rankin.]

"I suppose you want a reply," she found herself saying. "There isn't an 'official' scientific position on any of these questions, and I can't pretend to talk for all scientists or even for the Argus Project. But I can make some comments, if you'd like."

Rankin nodded his head vigorously, smiling encouragement. Languidly, Joss merely waited.

"I want you to understand that I'm not attacking anybody's belief system. As far as I'm concerned, you're entitled to any doctrine you like, even if it's demonstrably wrong. And many of the things you're saying, and that the Reverend Joss has said—I saw your talk on television a few weeks ago—can't be dismissed instantly. It takes a little work. But let me try to explain why I think they're improbable."

So far, she thought, I've been the soul of restraint.

"You're uncomfortable with scientific skepticism. But the reason it developed is that the world is complicated. It's subtle. Everybody's first idea isn't necessarily right. Also, people are capable of self-deception. Scientists, too. All sorts of socially abhorrent doctrines have at one time or another been supported by scientists, well-known scientists, famous brand-name scientists. And, of course, politicians. And respected religious leaders. Slavery, for instance, or the Nazi brand of racism. Scientists make mistakes, theologians make mistakes, everybody makes mistakes. It's part of being human. You say it yourselves: 'To err is.'

"So the way you avoid the mistakes, or at least reduce the chance that you'll make one, is to be skeptical. You test the ideas. You check them out by rigorous standards of evidence. I don't think there is such a thing as a received truth. But when you let the different opinions debate, when any skeptic can perform his or her own experiment to check some contention out, then the truth tends to emerge. That's the experience of the whole history of science. It isn't a perfect approach, but it's the only one that seems to work.

"The major religions on the Earth contradict each other left and right. You can't all be correct. And what if all of you are wrong? It's a possibility, you know. You must care about the truth, right? Well, the way to winnow through all the differing contentions is to be skeptical. I'm not any more skeptical about your religious beliefs than I am about every new scientific idea I hear about. But in my line of work, they're called hypotheses, not inspiration and not revelation."

Joss now stirred a little, but it was Rankin who replied.

"The revelations, the confirmed predictions by God in the Old Testament and the New are legion. The coming of the Saviour is foretold in Isaiah fifty-three, in Zechariah fourteen, in First Chronicles seventeen. That He would be born in Bethlehem was prophesied in Micah five. That He would come from the line of David was foretold in Matthew one and—"

"In Luke. But that ought to be an embarrassment for you, not a fulfilled prophecy. Matthew and Luke give Jesus totally different genealogies. Worse than that, they trace the lineage from David to Joseph, not from David to Mary. Or don't you believe in God the Father?"

Rankin continued smoothly on. Perhaps he hadn't understood her. ". . . the Ministry and Suffering of Jesus are foretold in Isaiah fifty-two and fifty-three, and the Twenty-second Psalm. That He would be betrayed for thirty pieces of silver is explicit in Zechariah eleven. If you're honest, you can't ignore the evidence of fulfilled prophecy.

"And the Bible speaks to our own time. Israel and the Arabs, Gog and Magog, America and Russia, nuclear war—it's all there in the Bible. Anybody with an ounce of sense can see it. You don't have to be some fancy college professor."

"Your trouble," she replied, "is a failure of the imagination. These prophecies are—almost every one of them—vague, ambiguous, imprecise, open to fraud. They admit lots of possible interpretations. Even the straightforward prophecies direct from the top you try to weasel out of—like Jesus' promise that the Kingdom of God would come in the lifetime of some people in his audience. And don't tell me the Kingdom of God is within me. His audience understood him quite literally. You only quote the passages that seem to you fulfilled, and ignore the rest. And don't forget there was a hunger to see prophecy fulfilled.

"But imagine that your kind of god—omnipotent, omniscient, compassionate—really wanted to leave a record for future generations, to make his existence unmistakable to, say, the remote descendants of Moses. It's easy, trivial. Just a few enigmatic phrases, and some fierce commandment that they be passed on unchanged . . ."

Joss leaned forward almost imperceptibly. "Such as . . . ?"

"Such as 'The Sun is a star.' Or 'Mars is a rusty place with deserts and volcanoes, like Sinai.' Or 'A body in motion tends to remain in motion.' Or—let's see now"—she quickly scribbled some numbers on a pad—"'The Earth weighs a million million million million times as much as a child.' Or—I recognize that both of you seem to have some trouble with special relativity, but it's confirmed every day routinely in particle accelerators and cosmic rays—how about 'There are no privileged frames of reference'? Or even 'Thou shalt not travel faster than light.' Anything they couldn't possibly have known three thousand years ago."

"Any others?" Joss asked.

"Well, there's an indefinite number of them—or at least one for every principle of physics. Let's see . . . 'Heat and light hide in the smallest pebble.' Or even 'The way of the Earth is as two, but the way of the lodestone is as three.' I'm trying to suggest that the gravitational force follows an inverse square law, while the magnetic dipole force follows an inverse cube law. Or in biology"—she nodded toward der Heer, who seemed to have taken a vow of silence—"how about 'Two strands entwined is the secret of life?'"

"Now that's an interesting one," said Joss. "You're talking, of course, about DNA. But you know the physician's staff, the symbol of medicine? Army doctors wear it on their lapels. It's called the caduceus. Shows two serpents intertwined. It's a perfect double helix. From ancient times that's been the symbol of preserving life. Isn't this exactly the kind of connection you're suggesting?"

"Well, I thought it's a spiral, not a helix. But if there are enough symbols and enough prophecies and enough myth and folklore, eventually a few of them are going to fit some current scientific understanding purely by accident. But I can't be sure. Maybe you're right. Maybe the caduceus *is* a message from God. Of course, it's not a Christian symbol, or a symbol of any of the major religions today. I don't suppose you'd want to argue that the gods talked only to the ancient Greeks. What I'm saying is, if God wanted to send us a message, and ancient writings were the only way he could think of doing it, he could have done a better job. And he hardly had to confine himself to writings. Why isn't there a monster crucifix orbiting the Earth? Why isn't the surface of the Moon covered with the Ten Commandments? Why should God be so clear in the Bible and so obscure in the world?"

Joss had apparently been ready to reply a few sentences back, a look of genuine pleasure unexpectedly on his face, but Ellie's rush of words was gathering momentum, and perhaps he felt it impolite to interrupt.

"Also, why would you think that God has abandoned us? He used to chat with patriarchs and prophets every second Tuesday, you believe. He's omnipotent, you say, and omniscient. So it's no particular effort for him to remind us directly, unambiguously, of his wishes at least a few times in every generation. So how come, fellas? Why don't we see him with crystal clarity?"

"We *do*." Rankin put enormous feeling in this phrase. "He is all around us. Our prayers are answered. Tens of millions of people in this country have been born again and have witnessed God's glorious grace. The Bible speaks to us as clearly in this day as it did in the time of Moses and Jesus."

"Oh, come off it. You know what I mean. Where are the burning bushes, the pillars of fire, the great voice that says 'I am that I am' booming down at us out of the sky? Why should God manifest himself in such subtle and debatable ways when he can make his presence completely unambiguous?"

"But a voice from the sky is just what you say you found." Joss made this comment casually while Ellie paused for breath. He held her eyes with his own.

Rankin quickly picked up the thought. "Absolutely. Just what I was going to say. Abraham and Moses, they didn't have radios or telescopes. They couldn't have heard the Almighty talking on FM. Maybe today God talks to us in new ways and permits us to have a new understanding. Or maybe it's not God—"

"Yes, Satan. I've heard some talk about that. It sounds crazy. Let's leave that one alone for a moment, if it's okay with you. You think maybe the Message is the Voice of God, your God. Where in your religion does God answer a prayer by repeating the prayer back?"

"I wouldn't call a Nazi newsreel a prayer, myself," Joss said. "You say it's to attract our attention."

"Then why do you think God has chosen to talk to scientists? Why not preachers like yourself?"

"God talks to *me* all the time." Rankin's index finger audibly thumped his sternum. "And the Reverend Joss here. God has told me that a revelation is at hand. When the end of the world is nigh, the Rapture will be upon us, the judgment of sinners, the ascension to heaven of the elect—"

"Did he tell you he was going to make that announcement in the radio spectrum? Is your conversation with God recorded somewhere, so we can verify that it really happened? Or do we have only your say-so? Why would God choose to announce it to radio astronomers and not to men and women of the cloth? Don't you think it's a little strange that the first message from God in two thousand years or more is prime numbers ... and Adolf Hitler at the 1936 Olympics? Your God must have quite a sense of humor."

"My God can have any sense He wants to have."

❦

"That's another thing." She interrupted her own train of thought as well as der Heer's. "If that signal is from God, why does it come from just one place in the sky—in the vicinity of a particularly bright nearby star? Why doesn't it come from all over the sky at once, like the cosmic black-body background radiation? Coming from one star, it looks like a signal from another civilization.

Coming from everywhere, it would look much more like a signal from your God."

"God can make a signal come from the bunghole of the Little Bear if He wants." Rankin's face was becoming bright red. "Excuse me, but you've gotten me riled up. God can do *anything*."

"Anything you don't understand, Mr. Rankin, you attribute to God. God for you is where you sweep away all the mysteries of the world, all the challenges to our intelligence. You simply turn your mind off and say God did it."

꒜

[Editor's note: The discussion becomes exceptionally rancorous, and so they agree to a break for lunch. In private during the break, Arroway discusses the debate thus far with der Heer.]

Outside the library conference room, leaning on the railing surrounding the Foucault pendulum, Ellie began a brief whispered exchange with der Heer.

"I'd like to punch out that cocksure, know-it-all, holier-than-thou . . ."

"Why, exactly, Ellie? Aren't ignorance, and error painful enough?"

"Yes, if he'd shut up. But he's corrupting millions."

"Sweetheart, he thinks the same about you."

꒜

[Editor's note: After the break, the discussion resumes with Joss asking Arroway a pointed question.]

"I was struck by one or two things you said this morning. You called yourself a Christian. May I ask? In what sense are you a Christian?"

"You know, this wasn't in the job description when I accepted the directorship of the Argus Project." She said this lightly. "I'm a Christian in the sense that I find Jesus Christ to be an admirable historical figure. I think the Sermon on the Mount is one of the greatest ethical statements and one of the best speeches in history. I think that 'Love your enemy' might even be the long-shot solution to the problem of nuclear war. I wish he was alive today. It would benefit everybody on the planet. But I think Jesus was only a man. A great man, a brave man, a man with insight into unpopular truths. But I don't think he was God or the son of God or the grandnephew of God."

"You don't *want* to believe in God." Joss said it as a simple statement. "You figure you can be a Christian and not believe in God. Let me ask you straight out: *Do* you believe in God?"

"The question has a peculiar structure. If I say no, do I mean I'm convinced God *doesn't* exist, or do I mean I'm not convinced he *does* exist? Those are two very different statements."

"Let's see if they are so different, Dr. Arroway. May I call you 'Doctor'? You believe in Occam's Razor, isn't that right? If you have two different, equally good explanations of the same experience, you pick the simplest. The whole history of science supports it, you say. Now, if you have serious doubts about whether there *is* a God—enough doubts so you're unwilling to commit yourself to the Faith—then you must be able to imagine a world *without* God: a world that comes into being without God, a world that goes about its everyday life without God, a world where people die without God. No punishment. No reward. All the saints and prophets, all the faithful who have ever lived—why, you'd have to believe they were foolish. Deceived themselves, you'd probably say. That would be a world in which we weren't here on Earth for any good reason—I mean for any purpose. It would all be just complicated collisions of atoms—is that right? Including the atoms that are inside human beings.

"To me, that would be a hateful and inhuman world. I wouldn't want to live in it. But if *you* can imagine that world, why straddle? Why occupy some middle ground? If you believe all that already, isn't it much simpler to say there's no God? You're not being true to Occam's Razor. I think you're waffling. How can a thoroughgoing conscientious scientist be an agnostic if you can even *imagine* a world without God? Wouldn't you just *have* to be an atheist?"

"I thought you were going to argue that God is the simpler hypothesis," Ellie said, "but this is a much better point. If it were only a matter of scientific discussion, I'd agree with you, Reverend Joss. Science is essentially concerned with examining and correcting hypotheses. If the laws of nature explain all the available facts without supernatural intervention, or even do only as well as the God hypothesis, then for the time being I'd call myself an atheist. Then, if a single piece of evidence was discovered that doesn't fit, I'd back off from atheism. We're fully able to detect some breakdown in the laws of nature. The reason I don't call myself an atheist is because this isn't mainly a scientific issue. It's a religious issue and a political issue. The tentative nature of scientific hypothesis doesn't extend into these fields. *You* don't talk about God as a hypothesis. You think you've cornered the truth, so I point out that you may have missed a thing or two. But if you ask, I'm happy to tell you: I can't be *sure* I'm right."

"I've always thought an agnostic is an atheist without the courage of his convictions."

"You could just as well say that an agnostic is a deeply religious person with at least a rudimentary knowledge of human fallibility. When I say I'm an agnostic, I only mean that the evidence isn't in. There isn't compelling evidence that God exists—at least your kind of god—and there isn't compelling evidence that he doesn't. Since more than half the people on the Earth aren't Jews or Christians or Muslims, I'd say that there aren't any compelling arguments for your kind of god. Otherwise, everybody on Earth would have been converted. I say again, if your God wanted to convince us, he could have done a much better job.

"Look at how clearly authentic the Message is. It's being picked up all over the world. Radio telescopes are humming away in countries with different histories, different languages, different politics, different religions. Everybody's getting the same kind of data from the same place in the sky, at the same frequencies with the same polarization modulation. The Muslims, the Hindus, the Christians, and the atheists are all getting the same message. Any skeptic can hook up a radio telescope—it doesn't have to be very big—and get the identical data."

"You're not suggesting that your radio message *is* from God," Rankin offered.

"Not at all. Just that the civilization on Vega—with powers infinitely less than what you attribute to your God—was able to make things very clear. If your God wanted to talk to us through the unlikely means of word-of-mouth transmission and ancient writings over thousands of years, he could have done it so there was no room left for debate about his existence."

She paused, but neither Joss nor Rankin spoke, so she tried again to steer the conversation to the data.

"Why don't we just withhold judgment for a while until we make some more progress on decrypting the Message? Would you like to see some of the data?"

This time they assented, readily enough it seemed. But she could produce only reams of zeros and ones, neither edifying nor inspirational.

His Perspective on Death[16]

I would love to believe that when I die I will live again, that some thinking, feeling, remembering part of me will continue. But as much as I want to believe that, and despite the ancient and world-wide cultural traditions that assert an afterlife, I know of nothing to suggest that it is more than wishful thinking ... the world is so exquisite, with so much love and moral depth, that there is no reason to deceive ourselves with pretty stories for which there's little good evidence. Far better, it seems to me, in our vulnerability, is to look death in the eye and to be grateful every day for the brief but magnificent opportunity that life provides. . . . Five thousand

---

[16] *Billions and Billions*, 214, 215, 221.

people prayed for me at an Easter service at the Cathedral of St. John the Divine in New York City, the largest church in Christendom. A Hindu priest described a large prayer vigil for me held on banks of the Ganges. The Imam of North America told me about his prayers for my recovery. Many Christians and Jews wrote me to tell about theirs. While I do not think that, if there is a god, his plan for me will be altered by prayer, I'm more grateful than I can say to those—including so many whom I've never met—who have pulled for me during my illness.

Many of them have asked me how it is possible to face death without the certainty of an afterlife. I can only say that it hasn't been a problem. With reservations about "feeble souls," I share the view of a hero of mine, Albert Einstein: "I cannot conceive of a god who rewards and punishes his creatures or has a will of the kind that we experience in ourselves. Neither can I, nor would I want to, conceive of an individual that survives his physical death; let feeble souls, from fear or absurd egotism, cherish such thoughts. I am satisfied with the mystery of the eternity of life and a glimpse of the marvelous structure of the existing world, together with the devoted striving to comprehend a portion, be it ever so tiny, of the Reason that manifests itself in nature."

Further Reading

Author or editor of 31 books and some 1,380 articles, Sagan's best-known works are *The Cosmic Connection: An Extraterrestrial Perspective* (Garden City, NJ: Anchor Press, 1973); *Broca's Brain: Reflections of the Romance of Science* (New York: Random House, 1974); *Other Worlds* (New York: Bantam Books, 1975); *The Dragons of Eden: Speculations on the Origin of Human Intelligence* (New York: Random House, 1977); *Cosmos* (New York: Random House, 1980); *Contact: A Novel* (New York: Simon and Schuster, 1985); *Pale Blue Dot: A Vision of the Human Future in Space* (New York: Random House, 1994); *The Demon-Haunted World: Science as a Candle in the Dark* (New York: Random House, 1995); *Billions and Billions: Thoughts on Life and Death at the Brink of the Millennium* (New York: Random House, 1997). With Ann Druyan he coauthored *Comet* (New York: Random

House, 1986) and *Shadows of Forgotten Ancestors: A Search for Who We Are* (New York: Random House, 1992). See also *Carl Sagan's Universe*, edited by Yervant Terzian and Elizabeth Bilson (1997). His Gifford Lectures were edited by Ann Druyan and published under the title *The Varieties of Scientific Experience: A Personal View of the Search for God* (New York: Penguin Books, 2006). For a biography, see Keay Davidson, *Carl Sagan: A Life* (New York: John Wiley, 1999).

11 Stephen Jay Gould
(1941–2002)

Introduction

In the tradition of Thomas Henry Huxley, who was known as Darwin's bulldog, Stephen Jay Gould ranged widely over philosophy, history, science, art, and literature—all from the perspective of an evolutionary biologist, paleontologist, and snail geneticist. At the start of Gould's career, the neo-Darwinian synthesis of nineteenth-century natural selection with twentieth-century mathematical population genetics reigned. Predicting smooth and gradual change, neo-Darwinism, orchestrated by Ernst Mayr at Harvard, was challenged by the work of Gould and Niles Eldredge who called their theory "punctuated equilibrium."

Also in the tradition of Huxley, Gould could describe his own personal religious views as agnostic: "I am not a believer. I am an agnostic in the wise sense of T. H. Huxley, who coined the word in identifying such open-minded skepticism as the only rational position because, truly, one cannot know."[1] The sense of open-minded questioning is evident in all of Gould's writings, along

[1] Stephen Jay Gould, *Rocks of Ages: Science and Religion in the Fullness of Life* (New York: Ballantine Publishing Group, 1999), 8.

with a great respect for the practice of religion, a subject that fascinated him beyond almost all others (the few exceptions were evolution, paleontology, and baseball). Although Gould could call himself an agnostic inclined toward atheism, his book *Rocks of Ages* is a passionate plea for tolerance between the two realms of science and religion. In the first excerpt below, he contends that science and religion are examples of a principle he calls NOMA, or Non-Overlapping Magisteria. By the notion of a "magisterium" Gould means "a domain where one finds one form of teaching holds the appropriate tools for meaningful discourse and resolution."

Gould was especially clear about the way that science and religion should interact in the world. In its simplest form, NOMA says that science and religion each has its own sphere of influence and that the two should never overlap. Science is limited to observing facts and attempting to formulate theories to explain those facts while religion is to be concerned with "the equally important, but utterly different, realm of human purposes, meanings, and values."[2] While the two will never overlap, they will often interact closely, since each offers unique insight into the world.

This view, as we have seen in previous chapters, is as old as Galileo and Bacon. Nothing is more conducive to peace between believers and nonbelievers than the idea that religion deals with matters in the realm of the unseen world (salvation, values, morals) while science deals with the observable, physical world. The two cannot conflict because they deal with different subject matters. In Gould's witty formula: "science gets the age of the rocks, and religion retains the rock of ages; science studies how the heavens go, and religion determines how to go to heaven."[3]

Less interested in being peacekeepers, scholars of religion have some bones to pick with this theory. First, Gould's proposal makes

[2] *Rocks of Ages*, 8.
[3] *Rocks of Ages*, 6.

little allowance for the plain fact that religions throughout history have claimed and continue to claim knowledge of facts and truth, not just values, meanings, and purposes. They may be mistaken in these matters, but a proper understanding of the history of religions and of the contemporary cultural and political scene requires an understanding of religious actors as putting forth claims to knowledge, facts, and truths of a literal kind, including the real—not merely symbolic or metaphorical—existence of superhuman beings. Such claims, however, can never be proved false, if the NOMA principle prevails. A second problematic aspect appears when we recall that many scientists are themselves deeply religious and regard the objects of their belief as constituted not only by values and morals but by facts as well. To faithful scientists, as well as to their skeptical counterparts, the very notion of non-overlapping magisteria is an invitation to schizoid thinking. And third, when the factual content of religious claims and beliefs is considered, it very often turns out to have a scientific or empirical element. To take only the major doctrines of the Christian religion—the Virgin Birth, the resurrection of Jesus, eternal life—these are claims involving scientific questions.

Even so, it cannot be denied that Gould's NOMA proposal currently enjoys great popularity. It has become the default position for most public commentary on religion and science. Its very prevalence is indicative of two major shifts occurring in the way intellectuals and academics think about religion, faith, and spirituality. First, we are seeing the gradual erosion of the old warfare metaphor that viewed science and religion as irreconcilable, a claim defended in two classic works: *The Conflict between Religion and Science* (1877), by the American scientist John William Draper, and the two-volume *History of the Warfare of Science and Theology* (1894), by historian Andrew Dickson White, first president of Cornell. Both books, which Gould discusses at length in *Rocks of Ages*, regard science and religion, especially Roman Catholicism, as locked in eternal combat. This is a view that certainly survives today among creationists and others who associate religion only with supernaturalist claims. Increasingly, however, among educated groups religion is viewed as a spiritual path, a ritual way, a set of symbolic performances or moral judgments that may or may not involve cognitive claims. With this, the second shift, already alluded to, is evident. "Religion," taken in a broader and less precise sense than scholars of religion use, is coming to mean for educated liberals something akin to a philosophical theism free of supernaturalism, or a secular humanism grounded on ethical norms and accompanied by optional ritual participation. Whether this will be the embrace that revives or the kiss of death for religion in an age of science we cannot yet say.

More rich than his view of religion is Gould's vision of what a "wonderful life" it is. Anyone who reads Stephen Jay Gould discovers that his faith, in the strongest sense of that term, is reserved for the meaningfulness of human life as the offspring of evolution, a detail in a vast universe not evidently designed for our presence, but offering great fascination and intellectual challenge. Gould's view of evolution is best summed up in a passage from the book of Ecclesiastes: "For the race is not to the swift, nor the battle to the strong, neither bread to the wise man, nor yet riches to men of understanding . . . but time and chance happeneth to all." Compared to Einstein's God, who does not play at dice with the universe, the Gouldian god is an inveterate crapshooter, but the game of life is not for that reason any less sublime. Like Darwin, Gould rejected the notion of progress in evolution. Advances toward complexity can be balanced by regression from complexity (e.g., parasites), and progress is a statistical illusion, bolstered by anthropomorphic projections. "Nature is amoral," Gould writes, "not immoral. . . . [It] existed for eons before we arrived, didn't know we were coming, and doesn't give a damn about us. . . . Nature betrays no statistical preference for being either warm and fuzzy, or ugly and disgusting. Nature just is—in all her complexity and diversity, in all her sublime indifference to our desires. Therefore we cannot use nature for our moral instruction, or for answering any question within the magisterium of religion."[4] In his 1989 *Wonderful Life*, we find the real faith by which Stephen Jay Gould lived: "We are the offspring of history, and must establish our own paths in this most diverse and interesting of conceivable universes—one indifferent to our suffering, and therefore offering us maximal freedom to thrive, or to fail, in our own chosen way."[5]

✌ Gould's Contribution to Science

Stephen Jay Gould—evolutionary biologist, paleontologist, and snail geneticist; professor of zoology at Harvard University; MacArthur Fellow; Pulitzer Prize finalist—is famous as one of the developers, with Niles Eldredge, of the theory of punctuated equilibrium. This view of evolution emphasizes that the fossil record reveals not so much gradual development as long periods of equilibrium punctuated by sudden extinctions or the apparently sudden emergence (in geologic time) of new species. He also advocated the concept that the evolutionary process does not have a predetermined outcome. If a portion of the evolutionary record could be replayed, some large-brained, intelligent species would probably still exist, but that species might not be human and might not even evolve from the line of primates.

Gould in His Own Words

On the Principle of Non-Overlapping Magisteria[6]

People of goodwill wish to see science and religion at peace, working together to enrich our practical and ethical lives. From this worthy premise, people often draw the wrong inference that

---

[4] *Rocks of Ages*, 195.

[5] Stephen Jay Gould, *Wonderful Life: The Burgess Shale and the Nature of History* (New York: W. W. Norton, 1989), 323.

[6] *Rocks of Ages*, 4, 6, 8, 9, 20, 64ff.

joint action implies common methodology and subject matter—
in other words, that some grand intellectual structure will bring
science and religion into unity, either by infusing nature with
a knowable factuality of godliness, or by tooling up the logic of
religion to an invincibility that will finally make atheism impossible. But just as human bodies require both food and sleep for sustenance, the proper care of any whole must call upon disparate
contributions from independent parts. We must live the fullness of
a complete life in many mansions of a neighborhood that would
delight any modern advocate of diversity.

I do not see how science and religion could be unified, or
even synthesized, under any common scheme of explanation or
analysis; but I also do not understand why the two enterprises
should experience any conflict. Science tries to document the factual character of the natural world, and to develop theories that
coordinate and explain these facts. Religion, on the other hand,
operates in the equally important, but utterly different, realm of
human purposes, meanings, and values—subjects that the factual
domain of science might illuminate, but can never resolve. Similarly, while scientists must operate with ethical principles, some
specific to their practice, the validity of these principles can never
be inferred from the factual discoveries of science.

❧

I propose that we encapsulate this central principle of respectful noninterference—accompanied by intense dialogue between
the two distinct subjects, each covering a central facet of human
existence—by enunciating the Principle of NOMA, or Non-
Overlapping Magisteria.

❧

To summarize, with a tad of repetition, the net, or magisterium, of science covers the empirical realm: what is the universe

made of (fact) and why does it work this way (theory). The magisterium of religion extends over questions of ultimate meaning and moral value. These two magisteria do not overlap, nor do they encompass all inquiry (consider, for example, the magisterium of art and the meaning of beauty). To cite the old cliches, science gets the age of rocks, and religion the rock of ages; science studies how the heavens go, religion how to go to heaven.

✦

I am not a believer. I am an agnostic in the wise sense of T. H. Huxley, who coined the word in identifying such open-minded skepticism as the only rational position because, truly, one cannot know. Nonetheless, in my own departure from parental views (and free, in my own upbringing, from the sources of their rebellion), I have great respect for religion. The subject has always fascinated me, beyond almost all others (with a few exceptions, like evolution, paleontology, and baseball). Much of this fascination lies in the stunning historical paradox that organized religion has fostered, throughout Western history, both the most unspeakable horrors and the most heartrending examples of human goodness in the face of personal danger.

✦

I believe, with all my heart, in a respectful, even loving, concordat between the magisteria of science and religion—the NOMA concept. NOMA represents a principled position on moral and intellectual grounds, not a merely diplomatic solution. NOMA also cuts both ways. If religion can no longer dictate the nature of factual conclusions residing properly within the magisterium of science, then scientists cannot claim higher insight into moral truth from any superior knowledge of the world's empirical constitution. This mutual humility leads to important practical consequences in a world of such diverse passions. We would do well to embrace the principle and enjoy the consequences.

❧

Burnet followed the common view of a remarkable group of men, devout theists all, who set the foundations of modern science in late-seventeenth-century Britain—including Newton, Halley, Boyle, Hooke, Ray, and Burnet himself. Invoking a convenient trope of English vocabulary, these scientists argued that God would permit no contradiction between his *words* (as recorded in scripture) and his *works* (the natural world). This principle, in itself, provides no rationale for science, and could even contradict my central claim for science and religion as distinct magisteria—for if works (the natural world) must conform to words (the scriptural text), then doesn't science become conflated with, constrained by, and subservient to religion? Yes, under one possible interpretation, but not as these men defined the concept. (Always look to nuance and actual utility, not to a first impression about an ambiguous phrase.) God had indeed created nature at some inception beyond the grasp of science; but he also established invariant laws to run the universe without interference forever after. (Surely omnipotence must operate by such a principle of perfection, and not by frequent subsequent correction, i.e., by special miracle, to fix some unanticipated bungle or wrinkle—to make extra water, for example, when human sin required punishment.)

Thus, nature works by invariant laws subject to scientific explanation. The natural world cannot contradict scripture (for God, as author of both, cannot speak against himself). So—and now we come to the key point—if some contradiction seems to emerge between a well-validated scientific result and a conventional reading of scripture, then we had better reconsider our exegesis, for the natural world does not lie, but words can convey many meanings, some allegorical or metaphorical. (If science clearly indicates an ancient world, then the "days" of creation must represent periods longer than twenty-four hours.) In this crucial sense, the magisteria become separate, and science holds sway over the factual character of the natural world. A scientist may be pious and devout—as all these men were, with utmost sincerity—and still hold a conception of God (as an imperial clockwinder at time's beginning in this version of NOMA) that leaves science entirely free in its own proper magisterium.

 ❧

Finally, how far apart do the magisteria of science and religion stand? Do their frames surround pictures at opposite ends of our mental gallery, with miles of minefields between? If so, why should we even talk about dialogue between such distantly non-overlapping magisteria, and of their necessary integration to infuse a fulfilled life with wisdom?

I hold that this non-overlapping runs to completion only in the important logical sense that standards for legitimate questions, and criteria for resolution, force the magisteria apart on the model of immiscibility—the oil and water of a common metaphorical image. But, like those layers of oil and water once again, the contact between magisteria could not be more intimate and pressing over every square micrometer (or upon every jot and tittle, to use an image from the other magisterium) of contact. Science and religion do not glower at each other from separate frames on opposite walls of the Museum of Mental Arts. Science and religion interdigitate in patterns of complex fingering, and at every fractal scale of self-similarity.

Still, the magisteria do not overlap–but then, neither do spouses fuse in the best of marriages. Any interesting problem, at any scale (hence the fractal claim above, meant more than metaphorically), must call upon the separate contributions of both magisteria for any adequate illumination. The logic of inquiry prevents true fusion, as stated above. The magisterium of science cannot proceed beyond the anthropology of morals–the documentation of what people believe, including such important information as the relative frequency of particular moral values among distinct cultures, the correlation of those values with ecological and economic conditions, and even (potentially) the adaptive value of certain beliefs in specified Darwinian situations–although my intense skepticism about speculative work in this last area has been well aired in other publications. But science can say nothing about the morality of morals. That is, the potential discovery by anthropologists that murder, infanticide, genocide, and xenophobia may have characterized many human societies, may have arisen preferentially in certain social situations, and may even be adaptively beneficial in certain contexts, offers no support whatever for the moral proposition that we ought to behave in such a manner.

Still, only the most fearful and parochial moral philosopher would regard such potential scientific information as useless or uninteresting. Such facts can never validate a moral position, but we surely want to understand the sociology of human behavior, if only to recognize the relative difficulty of instituting various consensuses reached within the magisterium of morals and meaning. To choose a silly example, we had better appreciate the facts of mammalian sexuality, if only to avoid despair if we decide to advocate uncompromising monogamy as the only moral path for human society, and then become confused when our arguments, so forcefully and elegantly crafted, fare so poorly in application.

Similarly, scientists would do well to appreciate the norms of moral discourse, if only to understand why a thoughtful person without expert knowledge about the genetics of heredity might justly challenge an assertion that some particular experiment in the controlled breeding of humans should be done because we now have the technology to proceed, and the results would be interesting within the internal logic of expanding information and explanation.

From Mutt and Jeff to yin and yang, all our cultures, in their full diversity of levels and traditions, include images of the absolutely inseparable but utterly different. Why not add the magisteria of science and religion to this venerable and distinguished list?

Two Myths Science Must Give Up[7]

I criticize the myth that science itself is an objective enterprise, done properly only when scientists can shuck the constraints of their culture and view the world as it really is.

Among scientists, few conscious ideologues have entered these debates on either side. Scientists needn't become explicit apologists for their class or culture in order to reflect these pervasive aspects of life. My message is not that biological determinists were bad scientists or even that they were always wrong. Rather, I believe that science must be understood as a social phenomenon, a gutsy, human enterprise, not the work of robots programmed to collect pure information. I also present this view as an upbeat for science, not as a gloomy epitaph for a noble hope sacrificed on the altar of human limitations.

Science, since people must do it, is a socially embedded activity. It progresses by hunch, vision, and intuition. Much of its change through time does not record a closer approach to absolute truth, but the alteration of cultural contexts that influence it so strongly. Facts are not pure and unsullied bits of information; culture also influences what we see and how we see it. Theories, moreover, are not inexorable inductions from facts. The most creative theories are often imaginative visions imposed upon facts; the source of imagination is also strongly cultural.

This argument, although still anathema to many practicing scientists, would, I think, be accepted by nearly every historian of science. In advancing it, however, I do not ally myself with an overextension now popular in some historical circles: the purely relativistic claim that scientific change only reflects the modification of social contexts, that truth is a meaningless notion outside cultural assumptions, and that science can therefore provide no enduring answers. As a practicing scientist, I share the credo of

---

[7] Stephen Jay Gould, *The Mismeasure of Man* (New York: W. W. Norton, 1981), 21–23.

my colleagues: I believe that a factual reality exists and that science, though often in an obtuse and erratic manner, can learn about it. Galileo was not shown the instruments of torture in an abstract debate about lunar motion. He had threatened the Church's conventional argument for social and doctrinal stability: the static world order with planets circling about a central earth, priests subordinate to the Pope and serfs to their lord. But the Church soon made its peace with Galileo's cosmology. They had no choice; the earth really does revolve about the sun.

Yet the history of many scientific subjects is virtually free from such constraints of fact for two major reasons. First, some topics are invested with enormous social importance but blessed with very little reliable information. When the ratio of data to social impact is so low, a history of scientific attitudes may be little more than an oblique record of social change. The history of scientific views on race, for example, serves as a mirror of social movements . . . . This mirror reflects in good times and bad, in periods of belief in equality and in eras of rampant racism. The death knell of the old eugenics in America was sounded more by Hitler's particular use of once-favored arguments for sterilization and racial purification than by advances in genetic knowledge.

Second, many questions are formulated by scientists in such a restricted way that any legitimate answer can only validate a social preference. Much of the debate on racial differences in mental worth, for example, proceeded upon the assumption that intelligence is a thing in the head. Until this notion was swept aside, no amount of data could dislodge a strong Western tradition for ordering related items into a progressive chain of being.

Science cannot escape its curious dialectic. Embedded in surrounding culture, it can, nonetheless, be a powerful agent for questioning and even overturning the assumptions that nurture it. Science can provide information to reduce the ratio of data to social importance. Scientists can struggle to identify the cultural assumptions of their trade and to ask how answers might be formulated under different assertions. Scientists can propose creative theories that force startled colleagues to confront unquestioned procedures.

But science's potential as an instrument for identifying the cultural constraints upon it cannot be fully realized until scientists give up the twin myths of objectivity and inexorable march toward truth. One must, indeed, locate the beam in one's own eye before interpreting correctly the pervasive motes in everybody else's. The beams can then become facilitators, rather than impediments.

On Biblical Literalism[8]

But the seventeenth century marked the golden age in this enterprise of scouring historical records to set the limits of time. We tend to scoff at these efforts today, branding them as the last holdout of an unthinking and anti-intellectual biblical idolatry. I will not, needless to say, defend the enterprise for any factual acuity. These scholars made a crucial error in choosing to regard the Bible as literally true. Since the "week" of creation is too short by several orders of magnitude, the calculated dates obviously bear no relationship to the true extent of geological history! But we cannot fairly invoke our present knowledge to castigate past scholarship based on different and honorable (if incorrect) premises. The calendrical counters of the seventeenth century included the brightest and most learned scholars of the time. Their efforts marked a high point in traditions of humanism, for these scholars committed themselves to an exclusive use of data and reason (though we now view their data as insufficiently accurate, and their reasoning as crucially misguided on the fundamental issue of biblical literalism).

Why Humans Exist[9]

And so, if you wish to ask the question of the ages—why do humans exist?—a major part of the answer, touching those aspects

---

[8] Stephen Jay Gould, *Questioning the Millennium: A Rationalist's Guide to a Precisely Arbitrary Countdown* (New York: Harmony Books, 1997), 88.
[9] *Wonderful Life*, 323.

of the issue that science can treat at all, must be: because *Pikaia* survived the Burgess decimation. This response does not cite a single law of nature; it embodies no statement about predictable evolutionary pathways, no calculation of probabilities based on general rules of anatomy or ecology. The survival of *Pikaia* was a contingency of "just history." I do not think that any "higher" answer can be given, and I cannot imagine that any resolution could be more fascinating. We are the offspring of history, and must establish our own paths in this most diverse and interesting of conceivable universes—one indifferent to our suffering, and therefore offering us maximal freedom to thrive, or to fail, in our own chosen way.

Scientific Knowledge Is Helpful to Religion[10]

But the myth of a war between science and religion remains all too current, and continues to impede a proper bonding and conciliation between these two utterly different and powerfully important institutions of human life. How can a war exist between two vital subjects with such different appropriate turfs—science as an enterprise dedicated to discovering and explaining the factual basis of the empirical world and religion as an examination of ethics and values?

I do understand, of course, that this territorial separation is a modern decision—and that differing past divisions did entail conflict in subsequent adjustment of boundaries. After all, when science was weak to nonexistent, religion did extend its umbrella into regions now properly viewed as domains of natural knowledge. But shall we blame religion for these overextensions? As thinking beings, we are internally compelled to ponder the great issues of human origins and our relationship with the earth and other creatures; we have no other option but ignorance. If science

---

[10] Stephen Jay Gould, *Dinosaur in a Haystack: Reflections in Natural History* (New York: Harmony Books, 1995), 48.

once had no clue about these subjects, then they fell, albeit uncomfortably and inappropriately, into the domain of religion by default. No one gives up turf voluntarily, and the later expansion of science into rightful territory temporarily occupied by religion did evoke some lively skirmishes and portentous battles. These tensions were also exacerbated by particular circumstances of contingent history—including the resolute and courageous materialism of Darwin's personal theory, and the occupation (at the same time) of the Holy See by one of the most fascinating and enigmatic figures of the nineteenth century: the strong, embittered, and increasingly conservative pope Pio Nono (Pius IX).

But these adjustments, however painful, do not justify a simplistic picture of history as continual warfare between science and theology. Exposure of the flat-earth myth should teach us the fallacy of such a view and help us to recognize the complexity of interaction between these institutions. Irrationality and dogmatism are always the enemies of science, but they are no true friends of religion either. Scientific knowledge has always been helpful to more generous views of religion—as preservation, by ecclesiastical scholars, of classical knowledge about the earth's shape aided religion's need for accurate calendars, for example.

On Creationism[11]

These two stories illustrate a cardinal point, frequently unrecognized but absolutely central to any understanding of the status and impact of the politically potent, fundamentalist doctrine known by its self-proclaimed oxymoron as "scientific creationism"—the claim that the Bible is literally true, that all organisms were created during six days of twenty-four hours, that the earth is only a few thousand years old, and that evolution must therefore be false. Creationism does not pit science against religion (as my opening

---

[11] Stephen Jay Gould, *Leonardo's Mountain of Clams and the Diet of Worms: Essays on Natural History* (New York: Harmony Books, 1998), 270.

stories indicate), for no such conflict exists. Creationism does not raise any unsettled intellectual issues about the nature of biology or the history of life. Creationism is a local and parochial movement, powerful only in the United States among Western nations, and prevalent only among the few sectors of American Protestantism that choose to read the Bible as an inerrant document, literally true in every jot and tittle.

I do not doubt that one could find an occasional nun who would prefer to teach creationism in her parochial school biology class, or an occasional rabbi who does the same in his yeshiva, but creationism based on biblical literalism makes little sense either to Catholics or Jews, for neither religion maintains any extensive tradition for reading the Bible as literal truth, rather than illuminating literature based partly on metaphor and allegory (essential components of all good writing), and demanding interpretation for proper understanding. Most Protestant groups, of course, take the same position—the fundamentalist fringe notwithstanding.

A New Rapprochement between Science and Religion[12]

In conclusion, Pius had grudgingly admitted evolution as a legitimate hypothesis that he regarded as only tentatively supported and potentially (as he clearly hoped) untrue. John Paul, nearly fifty years later, reaffirms the legitimacy of evolution under the NOMA principle—no news here—but then adds that additional data and theory have placed the factuality of evolution beyond reasonable doubt. Sincere Christians must now accept evolution not merely as a plausible possibility, but also as an effectively proven fact. In other words, official Catholic opinion on evolution has moved from "say it ain't so, but we can deal with it if we have to" (Pius's grudging view of 1950) to John Paul's entirely welcoming "it has been proven true; we always celebrate nature's factuality, and we

[12] *Leonardo's Mountain of Clams*, 280ff.

look forward to interesting discussions of theological implications." I happily endorse this turn of events as gospel; literally good news. I may represent the magisterium of science, but I welcome the support of a primary leader from the other major magisterium of our complex lives. And I recall the wisdom of King Solomon: "As cold waters to a thirsty soul, so is good news from a far country" (Proverbs 25:25).

Just as religion must bear the cross of its hard-liners, I have some scientific colleagues, including a few in prominent enough positions to wield influence by their writings, who view this rapprochement of the separate magisteria with dismay. To colleagues like me—agnostic scientists who welcome and celebrate the rapprochement, especially the Pope's latest statement—they say, "C'mon, be honest; you know that religion is addlepated, superstitious, old-fashioned BS. You're only making those welcoming noises because religion is so powerful, and we need to be diplomatic in order to buy public support for science." I do not think that many scientists hold this view, but such a position fills me with dismay—and I therefore end this essay with a personal statement about religion, as a testimony to what I regard as a virtual consensus among thoughtful scientists (who support the NOMA principle as firmly as the Pope does).

❧

Religion is too important for too many people to permit any dismissal or denigration of the comfort still sought by many folks from theology. I may, for example, privately suspect that papal insistence on divine infusion of the soul represents a sop to our fears, a device for maintaining a belief in human superiority within an evolutionary world offering no privileged position to any creature. But I also know that the subject of souls lies outside the magisterium of science. My world cannot prove or disprove such a notion, and the concept of souls cannot threaten or impact my domain. Moreover, while I cannot personally accept the Catholic view of souls, I surely honor the metaphorical value of such a concept both for grounding moral discussion, and for expressing what we most value about human potentiality: our decency, our care, and all the ethical and intellectual struggles that the evolution of consciousness imposed upon us.

As a moral position (and therefore not as a deduction from my knowledge of nature's factuality), I prefer the "cold bath" theory that nature can be truly "cruel" and "indifferent"—in the utterly inappropriate terms of our ethical discourse—because nature does not exist for us, didn't know we were coming (we are, after all, interlopers of the latest geological moment), and doesn't give a damn about us (speaking metaphorically). I regard such a position as liberating, not depressing, because we then gain the capacity to conduct moral discourse—and nothing could be more important—in our own terms, free from the delusion that we might read moral truth passively from nature's factuality.

But I recognize that such a position frightens many people, and that a more spiritual view of nature retains broad appeal (acknowledging the factuality of evolution, but still seeking some intrinsic meaning in human terms, and from the magisterium of religion). I do appreciate, for example, the struggles of a man who wrote to *The New York Times* on November 3, 1996, to declare both his pain and his endorsement of John Paul's statement:

> Pope John Paul II's acceptance of evolution touches the doubt in my heart. The problem of pain and suffering in a world created by a God who is all love and light is hard enough to bear, even if one is a creationist. But at least a creationist can say that the original creation, coming from the hand of God, was good, harmonious, innocent and gentle. What can one say about evolution, even a spiritual theory of evolution? Pain and suffering, mindless cruelty and terror are its means of creation. Evolution's engine is the grinding of predatory teeth upon the screaming, living flesh and bones of prey. . . . If evolution be true, my faith has rougher seas to sail.

I don't agree with this man, but we could have a terrific argument. I would push the "cold bath" theory; he would (presumably) advocate the theme of inherent spiritual meaning in nature, however opaque the signal. But we would both be enlightened and filled with better understanding of these deep and ultimately unanswerable issues. Here, I believe, lies the greatest strength and necessity of NOMA, the non-overlapping magisteria of science and religion. NOMA permits—indeed enjoins—the prospect of respectful discourse, of constant input from both magisteria toward the common goal of wisdom. If human beings can lay claim to anything special, we evolved as the only creatures that must ponder and talk. Pope John Paul II would surely point out to me that his magisterium has always recognized this uniqueness, for John's gospel begins by stating *in principio erat verbum"*—in the beginning was the word.

Further Reading

Stephen Jay Gould published 22 books, 101 book reviews, 479 scientific papers, and 300 *Natural History* essays during a career cut short by his death from cancer at age sixty. Gould's primary analysis of science and religion is found in *Rocks of Ages* (New York: Ballantine Publishing Group, 1999). His last works in natural history were *The Lying Stones of Marrakech* (New York: Harmony Books, 2000) and *I Have Landed: The End of a Beginning in Natural History* (New York, 2002). In history of science/science studies, see, among many of his publications, his *Questioning the Millennium* (New York: Harmony Books, 1997). In evolutionary theory Gould's chief contributions were *Ontogeny and Phylogeny* (Cambridge, MA: Belknap Press of Harvard University Press, 1977); *The Book of Life* (New York: W. W. Norton, 1993); *Full House* (New York: Harmony Books, 1996); and *The Structure of Evolutionary Theory* (Cambridge, MA: Belknap Press of Harvard University Press, 2002). In paleontology/geology he wrote *Time's Arrow, Time's Cycle* (Cambridge, MA: Harvard University Press, 1987) and *Wonderful Life* (New York: W. W. Norton, 1989). Critics of Gould have included Daniel Dennett, in *Darwin's Dangerous Idea* (New York: Simon and Schuster, 1995), and Richard Dawkins, in *The Blind Watchmaker* (New York: W. W. Norton, 1986).

12 Richard Dawkins
(1941–)

Introduction

Richard Dawkins is the Charles Simonyi Professor for the Public Understanding of Science at Oxford University. Regarded by many as the world's leading evolutionary biologist, he works tirelessly to make scientific knowledge accessible to general audiences. He offers a bracing alternative to Stephen Jay Gould's views in the last chapter. Disputing the idea of "non-overlapping magisteria," Dawkins believes that science and religion really do conflict in their methods of obtaining and testing knowledge and in their crucial truth-claims. Religion's truth-claims are false, or very improbable, while those of science are testable and corrigible in principle. The question of the existence of God is, for Dawkins, a hypothesis like any other, and should be tested by evidence, like a scientific hypothesis.

At first glance harsh, Dawkins' critique of Western religion in his best-selling book, *The God Delusion*, offers an instructive point. Dawkins takes seriously the truth-claims implicit in the faith of priests, mullahs, rabbis, and millions of ordinary believers. He understands that the God of the philosophers and of the postmodernist theologians is light years away from the interventionist, miracle-performing, sin-punishing, prayer-answering God of Abraham, Isaac, Jacob, Jesus, Mohammed, and most religious believers the world over even today. Actual religions from Texas to the Taliban do in fact assert as true such beliefs as "Jesus rose from the dead" and "eternal punishment awaits sinners." By refusing to paper over the literal meaning of religious beliefs with a symbolic veneer that is said to be its "true" meaning, Dawkins thus presents an interesting case of a scientist who is more willing than are many liberal theologians to take the religious assertions of ordinary believers at face value. He speaks for all those who find an inescapable tension between science and religion.

What readers may not realize is that Dawkins's definition of religion in terms of belief in superhuman beings conforms to a long-standing intellectualist-rationalist school in the study of religion, beginning with E. B. Tylor and continuing through Robin Horton, Melford Spiro, Rodney Stark, and Pascal Boyer. These scholars all advise against flouting the actor's point of view by assuming that religious people are using something called "symbolic" language rather than asserting beliefs that are literal statements-held-as-true in ordinary language. Moreover, they agree that the defining characteristic of "religion" is beliefs and practices having to do with superhuman agents. In this light, Dawkins is no different from a host of other neo-Tylorean scholars of religion in taking the truth-value of traditional religious assertions to be false, thus raising the question, Why do so many rational human beings hold beliefs that are false? As he makes clear in the excerpts below, Dawkins rejects several popular theoretical answers in favor of a clear and concise Darwinian explanation of religion.

By contrast, the symbolic-expressivist school of religious interpretation argues that religious beliefs are best taken as symbolic truths if their proper meaning is to be understood. Members of this school often take a tough line against interpreters like Dawkins, portraying them as theologically illiterate or as lacking an appreciation for a special symbolic, allegorical, or metaphorical truth. Yet Dawkins asks, What precisely is the "real" meaning of religious language as opposed to its apparent meaning? At this point his critics are often remarkably silent or offer contradictory interpretations that Dawkins finds evasive and vacuous.

The proper contrast in this debate may not be "crude and facile" versus "sophisticated and symbolic" readings of religious claims. Dawkins argues that there was never any underlying symbolic truth in the first place. Semantically, either an assertion is true, literally, or it is not true, literally.

In the first selection below, Dawkins elaborates his view that those who think that science and religion are converging do so because they do not give much of a propositional content to religious assertions. In effect, they have already conceded the two-valued logic of true/false and have gone over to the symbolic-expressivist camp. But, according to Richard Dawkins's analysis, religion without propositional content is empty, and symbolic truth without literal semantic mooring is blind.

In the second selection, Dawkins demonstrates what he calls the Ultimate Boeing 747 gambit. This is his variation on a standard creationist argument. By tweaking that argument in an original way, he can claim that it now leads to a conclusion quite the opposite of the traditional creationist one.

✌ Dawkins's Contribution to Science

Richard Dawkins was educated at Oxford University, completing his doctorate under the Nobel Prize–winning ethologist Niko Tinbergen. He has been a fellow of New College since 1970. Beginning his career as an ethologist, Dawkins then mutated into an evolutionary biologist. Permanently changing the face of biology, Dawkins has redefined the fundamental mechanics of living systems by postulating a series of powerful ideas. First, biology can ask the same questions about the genome and its genes that ethologists ask about chimpanzees and chickens. How do genes communicate? How do genes behave differently in groups than they do as individuals? Why do genes cooperate? How do genes compete? Second, genes are the basic unit of evolution. "Selfish genes" provide a basis for understanding the otherwise paradoxical phenomenon of altruism. Third, "memes," or viruses of the mind, are to cultural inheritance what genes are to biological heredity: natural selection operates on both. Fourth, both genes and memes are "replicators" that effect change in their world so that they can reproduce; the replicating code beneath the organism is a more fundamental unit of evolution than the individual gene or meme. Fifth, the "extended phenotype" of the replicating code embraces the whole family of the organism, its social group, the tools and environments it creates. A recipient of the Zoological Society Silver Medal, the Faraday Award, and the Kistler Prize, among many other honors, Dawkins is a Fellow of the Royal Society.

Dawkins in His Own Words

Snake Oil and Holy Water[1]

Are science and religion converging? No.

🐍

If you count Einstein and Hawking as religious, if you allow the cosmic awe of Goodenough, Davies, Sagan, and me as true religion, then religion and science have indeed merged, especially when you factor in such atheistic priests as Don Cupitt and many university chaplains. But if the term *religion* is allowed such a flabbily elastic definition, what word is left for conventional religion, religion as the ordinary person in the pew or on the prayer mat understands it today—indeed, as any intellectual would have understood it in previous centuries, when intellectuals were religious like everybody else?

[1] Richard Dawkins, "Snake Oil and Holy Water," *Forbes ASAP*, October 4, 1999, available at http://www.simonyi.ox.ac.uk/dawkins/WorldOfDawkins-archive/Dawkins/Work/Articles/1999–10–04snakeoil.shtml.

If *God* is a synonym for the deepest principles of physics, what word is left for a hypothetical being who answers prayers, intervenes to save cancer patients or helps evolution over difficult jumps, forgives sins or dies for them? If we are allowed to re-label scientific awe as a religious impulse, the case goes through on the nod. You have redefined science as religion, so it's hardly surprising if they turn out to "converge."

Another kind of marriage has been alleged between modern physics and Eastern mysticism. The argument goes as follows: Quantum mechanics, that brilliantly successful flagship theory of modern science, is deeply mysterious and hard to understand. Eastern mystics have always been deeply mysterious and hard to understand. Therefore, Eastern mystics must have been talking about quantum theory all along.

Similar mileage is made of Heisenberg's uncertainty principle ("Aren't we all, in a very real sense, uncertain?"), fuzzy logic ("Yes, it's okay for you to be fuzzy, too"), chaos and complexity theory (the butterfly effect, the Platonic, hidden beauty of the Mandelbrot Set—you name it, somebody has mysticized it and turned it into dollars). You can buy any number of books on "quantum healing," not to mention quantum psychology, quantum responsibility, quantum morality, quantum immortality, and quantum theology. I haven't found a book on quantum feminism, quantum financial management, or Afro-quantum theory, but give it time.

The whole dippy business is ably exposed by the physicist Victor Stenger in his book, *The Unconscious Quantum*, from which the following gem is taken. In a lecture on "Afrocentric healing," the psychiatrist Patricia Newton said that traditional healers "are able to tap that other realm of negative entropy—that superquantum velocity and frequency of electromagnetic energy—and bring them as conduits down to our level. It's not magic. It's not mumbo jumbo. You will see the dawn of the 21st century, the new medical quantum physics really distributing these energies and what they are doing."

Sorry, but mumbo jumbo is precisely what it is. Not African mumbo jumbo but pseudoscientific mumbo jumbo, down to the trademark misuse of the word *energy*. It is also religion, masquerading as science in a cloying love feast of bogus convergence.

In 1996 the Vatican, fresh from its magnanimous reconciliation with Galileo, a mere 350 years after his death, publicly announced that evolution had been promoted from tentative hypothesis to accepted theory of science. This is less dramatic than many American Protestants think it is, for the Roman Catholic Church has never been noted for biblical literalism—on the contrary, it has treated the Bible with suspicion, as something close to a subversive document, needing to be carefully filtered through priests rather than given raw to congregations. The pope's recent message on evolution has, nevertheless, been hailed as another example of late-20th-century convergence between science and religion.

Responses to the pope's message exhibited liberal intellectuals at their worst, falling over themselves in their eagerness to concede to religion its own magisterium, of equal importance to that of science, but not opposed to it. Such agnostic conciliation is, once again, easy to mistake for a genuine meeting of minds.

At its most naive, this appeasement policy partitions the intellectual territory into "how questions" (science) and "why questions" (religion). What are "why questions," and why should we feel entitled to think they deserve an answer? There may be some deep questions about the cosmos that are forever beyond science. The mistake is to think that they are therefore not beyond religion, too.

I once asked a distinguished astronomer, a fellow of my college, to explain the big bang theory to me. He did so to the best of his (and my) ability, and I then asked what it was about the fundamental laws of physics that made the spontaneous origin of space and time possible. "Ah," he smiled, "now we move beyond the realm of science. This is where I have to hand you over to our good friend, the chaplain." But why the chaplain? Why not the gardener or the chef? Of course chaplains, unlike chefs and gardeners, claim to have some insight into ultimate questions. But what reason have we ever been given for taking their claims seriously? Once again, I suspect that my friend, the professor of astronomy, was using the Einstein/Hawking trick of letting "God" stand for "That which we don't understand." It would be a harmless trick if it were not continually misunderstood by those hungry to misunderstand it. In any case, optimists among scientists, of whom I am one, will insist, "That which we don't understand" means only "That which we don't yet understand." Science is still working on the problem. We don't know where, or even whether, we ultimately shall be brought up short.

Agnostic conciliation, which is the decent liberal bending over backward to concede as much as possible to anybody who shouts loud enough, reaches ludicrous lengths in the following common piece of sloppy thinking. It goes roughly like this: You can't prove a negative (so far so good). Science has no way to disprove the existence of a supreme being (this is strictly true). Therefore, belief or disbelief in a supreme being is a matter of pure, individual inclination, and both are therefore equally deserving of respectful attention! When you say it like that, the fallacy is almost self-evident; we hardly need spell out the reductio ad absurdum. As my colleague, the physical chemist Peter Atkins, puts it, we must be equally agnostic about the theory that there is a teapot in orbit around the planet Pluto. We can't disprove it. But that doesn't mean the theory that there is a teapot is on level terms with the theory that there *isn't*.

Now, if it be retorted that there actually are reasons X, Y, and Z for finding a supreme being more plausible than a teapot, then X, Y, and Z should be spelled out—because, if legitimate, they are proper scientific arguments that should be evaluated. Don't protect them from scrutiny behind a screen of agnostic tolerance. If religious arguments are actually better than Atkins' teapot theory, let us hear the case. Otherwise, let those who call themselves agnostic with respect to religion add that they are equally agnostic about orbiting teapots. At the same time, modern theists might acknowledge that, when it comes to Baal and the golden calf, Thor and Wotan, Poseidon and Apollo, Mithras and Ammon Ra, they are actually atheists. We are all atheists about most of the gods that humanity has ever believed in. Some of us just go one god further.

In any case, the belief that religion and science occupy separate magisteria is dishonest. It founders on the undeniable fact that religions still make claims about the world that on analysis turn out to be scientific claims. Moreover, religious apologists try to have it both ways. When talking to intellectuals, they carefully keep off science's turf, safe inside the separate and invulnerable religious magisterium. But when talking to a nonintellectual mass audience, they make wanton use of miracle stories—which are blatant intrusions into scientific territory.

The Virgin Birth, the Resurrection, the raising of Lazarus, even the Old Testament miracles, all are freely used for religious propaganda, and they are very effective with an audience of unsophisticates and children. Every one of these miracles amounts to a violation of the normal running of the natural world. Theologians should make a choice. You can claim your own magisterium, separate from science's but still deserving of respect. But in that case, you must renounce miracles. Or you can keep your Lourdes and your miracles and enjoy their huge recruiting potential among the uneducated. But then you must kiss goodbye to separate magisteria and your high-minded aspiration to converge with science.

The desire to have it both ways is not surprising in a good propagandist. What is surprising is the readiness of liberal agnostics to go along with it, and their readiness to write off, as simplistic, insensitive extremists, those of us with the temerity to blow the whistle. The whistle-blowers are accused of imagining an outdated caricature of religion in which God has a long white beard and lives in a physical place called heaven. Nowadays, we are told, religion has moved on. Heaven is not a physical place, and God does not have a physical body where a beard might sit. Well, yes, admirable: separate magisteria, real convergence. But the doctrine of the Assumption was defined as an Article of Faith by Pope Pius XII as recently as November 1, 1950, and is binding on all Catholics. It clearly states that the body of Mary was taken into heaven and reunited with her soul. What can that mean, if not that heaven is a physical place containing bodies? To repeat, this is not a quaint and obsolete tradition with just a purely symbolic significance. It has officially, and recently, been declared to be literally true.

Convergence? Only when it suits. To an honest judge, the alleged marriage between religion and science is a shallow, empty, spin-doctored sham.

From The God Delusion[2]

An Interlude at Cambridge

At a recent Cambridge conference on science and religion, where I put forward the argument I am here calling the Ultimate 747 argument, I encountered what, to say the least, was a cordial failure to achieve a meeting of minds on the question of God's simplicity. The experience was a revealing one, and I'd like to share it.

❧

. . . I challenged the theologians to answer the point that a God capable of designing a universe, or anything else, would have to be complex and statistically improbable. The strongest response I heard was that I was brutally foisting a scientific epistemology upon an unwilling theology. Theologians had always defined God as simple. Who was I, a scientist, to dictate to theologians that their God had to be complex? Scientific arguments, such as those I was accustomed to deploying in my own field, were inappropriate since theologians had always maintained that God lay outside science.

I did not gain the impression that the theologians who mounted this evasive defense were being willfully dishonest. I think they were sincere. Nevertheless, I was irresistibly reminded of Peter Medawar's comment on Father Teilhard de Chardin's *The Phenomenon of Man*, in the course of what is possibly the greatest

[2] Richard Dawkins, *The God Delusion* (London: Bantam Press, 2006), 153–59, 166–69, 172–79.

negative book review of all time: "its author can be excused of dishonesty only on the grounds that before deceiving others he has taken great pains to deceive himself."[3] The theologians of my Cambridge encounter were *defining* themselves into an epistemological Safe Zone where rational argument could not reach them because they had *declared by fiat* that it could not. Who was I to say that rational argument was the only admissible kind of argument? There are other ways of knowing besides the scientific, and it is one of these other ways of knowing that must be deployed to know God.

The most important of these other ways of knowing turned out to be personal, subjective experience of God. Several discussants at Cambridge claimed that God spoke to them, inside their heads, just as vividly and as personally as another human might. I have dealt with illusion and hallucination in Chapter 3 ("The argument from personal experience"), but at the Cambridge conference I added two points. First, that if God really did communicate with humans that fact would emphatically not lie outside science. *God* comes bursting through from whatever other-worldly domain is his natural abode, crashing through into our world where his messages can be intercepted by human brains—and that phenomenon has nothing to do with science? Second, a God who is capable of sending intelligible signals to millions of people simultaneously, and of receiving messages from all of them simultaneously, cannot be, whatever else he might be, simple. Such bandwidth! God may not have a brain made of neurones, or a CPU made of silicon, but if he has the powers attributed to him he must have something far more elaborately and non-randomly constructed than the largest brain or the largest computer we know.

Time and again, my theologian friends returned to the point that there had to be a reason why there is something rather than nothing. There must have been a first cause of everything, and we might as well give it the name God. Yes, I said, but it must have

---

[3] P. B. Medawar, review of *The Phenomenon of Man*, repr. in Medawar, *Pluto's Republic* (Oxford University Press, 1982). —RD *as modified by Ed.*

been simple and therefore, whatever else we call it, God is not an appropriate name (unless we very explicitly divest it of all the baggage that the word "God" carries in the minds of most religious believers). The first cause that we seek must have been the simple basis for a self-bootstrapping crane which eventually raised the world as we know it into its present complex existence. To suggest that the original prime mover was complicated enough to indulge in intelligent design, to say nothing of mindreading millions of humans simultaneously, is tantamount to dealing yourself a perfect hand at bridge. Look around at the world of life, at the Amazon rainforest with its rich interlacement of lianas, bromeliads, roots and flying buttresses; its army ants and its jaguars, its tapirs and peccaries, treefrogs and parrots. What you are looking at is the statistical equivalent of a perfect hand of cards (think of all the other ways you could permute the parts, none of which would work)—except that we know how it came about: by the gradualistic crane of natural selection. It is not just scientists who revolt at mute acceptance of such improbability arising spontaneously; common sense balks too. To suggest that the first cause, the great unknown which is responsible for something existing rather than nothing, is a being capable of designing the universe and of talking to a million people simultaneously, is a total abdication of the responsibility to find an explanation. It is a dreadful exhibition of self-indulgent, thought-denying skyhookery.

I am not advocating some sort of narrowly scientistic way of thinking. But the very least that any honest quest for truth must have in setting out to explain such monstrosities of improbability as a rainforest, a coral reef, or a universe is a crane and not a skyhook. The crane doesn't have to be natural selection. Admittedly, nobody has ever thought of a better one. But there could be others yet to be discovered. Maybe the "inflation" that physicists postulate as occupying some fraction of the first yoctosecond of the universe's existence will turn out, when it is better understood, to be a cosmological crane to stand alongside Darwin's biological one. Or maybe the elusive crane that cosmologists seek will be a version of Darwin's idea itself: either Smolin's model or something

similar. Or maybe it will be the multiverse plus anthropic principle espoused by Martin Rees and others. It may even be a superhuman designer—but, if so, it will most certainly *not* be a
designer who just popped into existence, or who always existed. If
(which I don't believe for a moment) our universe was designed,
and *a fortiori* if the designer reads our thoughts and hands out
omniscient advice, forgiveness and redemption, the designer himself must be the end product of some kind of cumulative escalator
or crane, perhaps a version of Darwinism in another universe.

🐌

I left the conference stimulated and invigorated, and reinforced
in my conviction that the argument from improbability—the "Ultimate 747" gambit—is a very serious argument against the existence of God, and one to which I have yet to hear a theologian give
a convincing answer despite numerous opportunities and invita-
tions to do so. Dan Dennett rightly describes it as "an unrebuttable
refutation, as devastating today as when Philo used it to trounce
Cleanthes in Hume's Dialogues two centuries earlier. A sky-hook
would at best simply postpone the solution to the problem, but
Hume couldn't think of any cranes, so he caved in."[4] Darwin, of
course, supplied the vital crane. How Hume would have loved it.

This chapter has contained the central argument of my book,
and so, at the risk of sounding repetitive, I shall summarize it as a
series of six numbered points.

1. One of the greatest challenges to the human intellect, over the
   centuries, has been to explain how the complex, improbable
   appearance of design in the universe arises.

2. The natural temptation is to attribute the appearance of design
   to actual design itself. In the case of a man-made artifact such
   as a watch, the designer really was an intelligent engineer. It is

---

[4] Daniel Dennett, *Darwin's Dangerous Idea* (New York: Simon and Schuster,
1995), 155. —*R.D. as modified by Ed.*

tempting to apply the same logic to an eye or a wing, a spider or a person.

3. The temptation is a false one, because the designer hypothesis immediately raises the larger problem of who designed the designer. The whole problem we started out with was the problem of explaining statistical improbability. It is obviously no solution to postulate something even more improbable. We need a "crane," not a "skyhook," for only a crane can do the business of working up gradually and plausibly from simplicity to otherwise improbable complexity.

4. The most ingenious and powerful crane so far discovered is Darwinian evolution by natural selection. Darwin and his successors have shown how living creatures, with their spectacular statistical improbability and appearance of design, have evolved by slow, gradual degrees from simple beginnings. We can now safely say that the illusion of design in living creatures is just that—an illusion.

5. We don't yet have an equivalent crane for physics. Some kind of multiverse theory could in principle do for physics the same explanatory work as Darwinism does for biology. This kind of explanation is superficially less satisfying than the biological version of Darwinism, because it makes heavier demands on luck. But the anthropic principle entitles us to postulate far more luck than our limited human intuition is comfortable with.

6. We should not give up hope of a better crane arising in physics, something as powerful as Darwinism is for biology. But even in the absence of a strongly satisfying crane to match the biological one, the relatively weak cranes we have at present are, when abetted by the anthropic principle, self-evidently better than the self-defeating skyhook hypothesis of an intelligent designer.

If the argument of this chapter is accepted, the factual premise of religion—the God Hypothesis—is untenable. God almost certainly does not exist. This is the main conclusion of the book so far. Various questions now follow. Even if we accept that God doesn't exist, doesn't religion still have a lot going for it? Isn't it consoling? Doesn't it motivate people to do good? If it weren't for religion, how would we know what is good? Why, in any case, be so hostile? Why, if it is false, does every culture in the world have religion? True or false, religion is ubiquitous, so where does it come from? It is to this last question that we turn next.

The Darwinian Imperative

Everybody has their own pet theory of where religion comes from and why all human cultures have it. It gives consolation and comfort. It fosters togetherness in groups. It satisfies our yearning to understand why we exist. I shall come to explanations of this kind in a moment, but I want to begin with a prior question, one that takes precedence for reasons we shall see: a Darwinian question about natural selection.

Knowing that we are products of Darwinian evolution, we should ask what pressure or pressures exerted by natural selection originally favoured the impulse to religion. The question gains urgency from standard Darwinian considerations of economy. Religion is so wasteful, so extravagant; and Darwinian selection habitually targets and eliminates waste. Nature is a miserly accountant, grudging the pennies, watching the clock, punishing the smallest extravagance. Unrelentingly and unceasingly, as Darwin explained, "natural selection is daily and hourly scrutinizing, throughout the world, every variation, even the slightest; rejecting that which is bad, preserving and adding up all that is good; silently and insensibly working, whenever and wherever opportunity offers, at the improvement of each organic being." If a wild animal habitually performs some useless activity, natural selection will favour rival individuals who devote the time and energy, instead, to surviving and reproducing. Nature cannot afford frivolous *jeux d'esprit*. Ruthless utilitarianism trumps, even if it doesn't always seem that way.

On the face of it, the tail of a peacock is a *jeu d'esprit par excellence*. It surely does no favours to the survival of its possessor. But it does benefit the genes that distinguish him from his less spectacular rivals. The tail is an advertisement, which buys its place in the economy of nature by attracting females. The same is true of the labour and time that a male bower bird devotes to his bower: a sort of external tail built of grass, twigs, colourful berries, flowers and, when available, beads, baubles and bottle caps. Or, to choose an example that doesn't involve advertising, there is "anting": the odd habit of birds, such as jays, of "bathing" in an ants' nest or otherwise applying ants to the feathers. Nobody is sure what the benefit of anting is—perhaps some kind of hygiene, cleaning out parasites from the feathers; there are various other hypotheses, none of them strongly supported by evidence. But uncertainty as to details doesn't—nor should it—stop Darwinians from presuming, with great confidence, that anting must be "for" something. In this case common sense might agree, but Darwinian logic has a particular reason for thinking that, if the birds didn't do it, their statistical prospects of genetic success would be damaged, even if we don't yet know the precise route of the damage. The conclusion follows from the twin premises that natural selection punishes wastage of time and energy, and that birds are consistently observed to devote time and energy to anting. If there is a one-sentence manifesto of this "adaptationist" principle, it was expressed—admittedly in somewhat extreme and exaggerated terms—by the distinguished Harvard geneticist Richard Lewontin: "That is the one point which I think all evolutionists are agreed upon, that it is virtually impossible to do a better job than an organism is doing in its own environment."[5] If anting wasn't positively useful for survival and reproduction, natural selection would long ago have favoured individuals who refrained from it. A Darwinian might be tempted to say the same of religion; hence the need for this discussion.

To an evolutionist, religious rituals "stand out like peacocks in a sunlit glade" (Dan Dennett's phrase). Religious behaviour is a writ-large human equivalent of anting or bower-building. It is

---

[5] Quoted in Richard Dawkins, *The Extended Phenotype* (Oxford: W. H. Freeman, 1982), 30. —*RD as modified by Ed.*

time-consuming, energy-consuming, often as extravagantly ornate as the plumage of a bird of paradise. Religion can endanger the life of the pious individual, as well as the lives of others. Thousands of people have been tortured for their loyalty to a religion, persecuted by zealots for what is in many cases a scarcely distinguishable alternative faith. Religion devours resources, sometimes on a massive scale. A medieval cathedral could consume a hundred man-centuries in its construction, yet was never used as a dwelling, or for any recognizably useful purpose. Was it some kind of architectural peacock's tail? If so, at whom was the advertisement aimed? Sacred music and devotional paintings largely monopolized medieval and Renaissance talent. Devout people have died for their gods and killed for them; whipped blood from their backs, sworn themselves to a lifetime of celibacy or to lonely silence, all in the service of religion. What is it all for? What is the benefit of religion?

By "benefit," the Darwinian normally means some enhancement to the survival of the individual's genes. What is missing from this is the important point that Darwinian benefit is not restricted to the genes of the individual organism. There are three possible alternative targets of benefit. One arises from the theory of group selection, and I'll come to that. The second follows from the theory that I advocated in *The Extended Phenotype*: the individual you are watching may be working under the manipulative influence of genes in another individual, perhaps a parasite. Dan Dennett reminds us that the common cold is universal to all human peoples in much the same way as religion is, yet we would not want to suggest that colds benefit us. Plenty of examples are known of animals manipulated into behaving in such a way as to benefit the transmission of a parasite to its next host. I encapsulated the point in my "central theorem of the extended phenotype": "An animal's behaviour tends to maximize the survival of the genes 'for' that behaviour, whether or not those genes happen to be in the body of the particular animal performing it."

Third, the "central theorem" may substitute for "genes" the more general term "replicators." The fact that religion is ubiquitous probably means that it has worked to the benefit of something, but it may not be us or our genes. It may be to the benefit of only the religious ideas themselves, to the extent that they behave in a somewhat gene-like way, as replicators. I shall deal with this below, under the heading "Tread softly, because you tread on my memes." Meanwhile, I press on with more traditional interpretations of Darwinism, in which "benefit" is assumed to mean benefit to individual survival and reproduction.

Hunter-gatherer peoples such as Australian aboriginal tribes presumably live in something like the way our distant ancestors did. The New Zealand-Australian philosopher of science Kim Sterelny points up a dramatic contrast in their lives. On the one hand aboriginals are superb survivors under conditions that test their practical skills to the uttermost. But, Sterelny goes on, intelligent as our species might be, we are *perversely* intelligent. The very same peoples who are so savvy about the natural world and how to survive in it simultaneously clutter their minds with beliefs that are palpably false and for which the word "useless" is a generous understatement. Sterelny himself is familiar with aboriginal peoples of Papua New Guinea. They survive under arduous conditions where food is hard to come by, by dint of "a legendarily accurate understanding of their biological environment. But they combine this understanding with deep and destructive obsessions about female menstrual pollution and about witchcraft. Many of the local cultures are tormented by fears of witchcraft and magic, and by the violence that accompanies those fears." Sterelny challenges us to explain "how we can be simultaneously so smart and so dumb."[6]

Though the details differ across the world, no known culture lacks some version of the time-consuming, wealth-consuming, hostility-provoking rituals, the anti-factual, counter-productive fantasies of religion. Some educated individuals may have abandoned religion, but all were brought up in a religious culture from

---

[6] K. Sterelny, "The Perverse Primate," in, *Richard Dawkins: How a Scientist Changed the Way We Think*, ed. A. Grafen and M. Ridley (Oxford: Oxford University Press, 2006), 213–23. —*RD as modified by Ed.*

which they usually had to make a conscious decision to depart. The old Northern Ireland joke, "Yes, but are you a Protestant atheist or a Catholic atheist?" is spiked with bitter truth. Religious behaviour can be called a human universal in the same way as heterosexual behaviour can. Both generalizations allow individual exceptions, but all those exceptions understand only too well the rule from which they have departed. Universal features of a species demand a Darwinian explanation.

Obviously, there is no difficulty in explaining the Darwinian advantage of sexual behaviour. It is about making babies, even on those occasions where contraception or homosexuality seems to belie it. But what about religious behaviour? Why do humans fast, kneel, genuflect, self-flagellate, nod maniacally towards a wall, crusade, or otherwise indulge in costly practices that can consume life and, in extreme cases, terminate it?

Direct Advantages of Religion

There is a little evidence that religious belief protects people from stress-related diseases. The evidence is not strong, but it would not be surprising if it were true, for the same kind of reason as faith-healing might turn out to work in a few cases. I wish it were not necessary to add that such beneficial effects in no way boost the truth value of religion's claims. In George Bernard Shaw's words, "The fact that a believer is happier than a skeptic is no more to the point than the fact that a drunken man is happier than a sober one."

Part of what a doctor can give a patient is consolation and reassurance. This is not to be dismissed out of hand. My doctor doesn't literally practice faith-healing by laying on of hands. But many's the time I've been instantly "cured" of some minor ailment by a reassuring voice from an intelligent face surmounting a stethoscope. The placebo effect is well documented and not even very mysterious. Dummy pills, with no pharmacological activity at all, demonstrably improve health. That is why double-blind drug trials must use placebos as controls. It's why homoeopathic remedies appear to work, even though they are so dilute that they have the same amount of active ingredient as the placebo control— zero molecules. Incidentally, an unfortunate by-product of the encroachment by lawyers on doctors' territory is that doctors are now afraid to prescribe placebos in normal practice. Or bureaucracy may oblige them to identify the placebo in written notes to which the patient has access, which of course defeats the object. Homoeopaths may be achieving relative success because they, unlike orthodox practitioners, are still allowed to administer placebos— under another name. They also have more time to devote to talking and simply being kind to the patient. In the early part of its long history, moreover, homoeopathy's reputation was inadvertently enhanced by the fact that its remedies did nothing at all—by contrast with orthodox medical practices, such as bloodletting, which did active harm.

Is religion a placebo that prolongs life by reducing stress? Possibly, although the theory must run a gauntlet of sceptics who point out the many circumstances in which religion causes rather than relieves stress. It is hard to believe, for example, that health is improved by the semi-permanent state of morbid guilt suffered by a Roman Catholic possessed of normal human frailty and less than normal intelligence. Perhaps it is unfair to single out the Catholics. The American comedian Cathy Ladman observes that "All religions are the same: religion is basically guilt, with different holidays." In any case, I find the placebo theory unworthy of the massively pervasive worldwide phenomenon of religion. I don't think the reason we have religion is that it reduced the stress levels of our ancestors. That's not a big enough theory for the job, although it may have played a subsidiary role. Religion is a large phenomenon and it needs a large theory to explain it.

Other theories miss the point of Darwinian explanations altogether. I'm talking about suggestions like "religion satisfies our curiosity about the universe and our place in it," or "religion is consoling." There may be some psychological truth here, as we shall see in Chapter 10, but neither is in itself a Darwinian explanation. As Steven Pinker pointedly said of the consolation theory, in *How the Mind Works*: "it only raises the question of *why* a mind would evolve to find comfort in beliefs it can plainly see are false. A freezing person finds no comfort in believing he is warm; a person face-to-face with a lion is not put at ease by the conviction that it is a rabbit." At the very least, the consolation theory needs to be translated into Darwinian terms, and that is harder than you might think. Psychological explanations to the effect that people find some belief agreeable or disagreeable are proximate, not ultimate, explanations.

Darwinians make much of this distinction between proximate and ultimate. The proximate explanation for the explosion in the cylinder of an internal combustion engine invokes the sparking plug. The ultimate explanation concerns the purpose for which the explosion was designed: to impel a piston from the cylinder, thereby turning a crankshaft. The proximate cause of religion might be hyperactivity in a particular node of the brain. I shall not pursue the neurological idea of a "god centre" in the brain because I am not concerned here with proximate questions. That is not to belittle them. I recommend Michael Shermer's *How We Believe: The Search for God in an Age of Science* for a succinct discussion, which includes the suggestion by Michael Persinger and others that visionary religious experiences are related to temporal lobe epilepsy.

But my preoccupation in this chapter is with Darwinian *ultimate* explanations. If neuroscientists find a "god centre" in the brain, Darwinian scientists like me will still want to understand the natural selection pressure that favoured it. Why did those of our ancestors who had a genetic tendency to grow a god centre survive to have more grandchildren than rivals who didn't? The Darwinian ultimate question is not a better question, not a more profound question, not a more scientific question than the neurological proximate question. But it is the one I am talking about here.

Nor are Darwinians satisfied by political explanations, such as "Religion is a tool used by the ruling class to subjugate the underclass." It is surely true that black slaves in America were consoled by promises of another life, which blunted their dissatisfaction with this one and thereby benefited their owners. The question of whether religions are deliberately designed by cynical priests or rulers is an interesting one, to which historians should attend. But it is not, in itself, a Darwinian question. The Darwinian still wants to know why people are *vulnerable* to the charms of religion and therefore open to exploitation by priests, politicians and kings.

A cynical manipulator might use sexual lust as a tool of political power, but we still need the Darwinian explanation of why it works. In the case of sexual lust, the answer is easy: our brains are set up to enjoy sex because sex, in the natural state, makes babies. Or a political manipulator might use torture to achieve his ends. Once again, the Darwinian must supply the explanation for why torture is effective; why we will do almost anything to avoid intense pain. Again it seems obvious to the point of banality, but the Darwinian still needs to spell it out: natural selection has set up the perception of pain as a token of life-threatening bodily damage, and programmed us to avoid it. Those rare individuals who cannot feel pain, or don't care about it, usually die young of injuries which the rest of us would have taken steps to avoid. Whether it is cynically exploited, or whether it just manifests itself spontaneously, what ultimately explains the lust for gods?

Religion as a By-Product of Something Else

I want now to set aside group selection and turn to my own view of the Darwinian survival value of religion. I am one of an increasing number of biologists who see religion as a by-product of something else. More generally, I believe that we who speculate about Darwinian survival value need to "think by-product." When we ask about the survival value of anything, we may be asking the wrong question. We need to rewrite the question in a more helpful way. Perhaps the feature we are interested in (religion in this case) doesn't have a direct survival value of its own, but is a by-product of something else that does. I find it helpful to introduce the by-product idea with an analogy from my own field of animal behaviour.

Moths fly into the candle flame, and it doesn't look like an accident. They go out of their way to make a burnt offering of themselves. We could label it "self-immolation behaviour" and, under that provocative name, wonder how on earth natural selection could favour it. My point is that we must rewrite the question before we can even attempt an intelligent answer. It isn't suicide. Apparent suicide emerges as an inadvertent side-effect or by-product of something else. A by-product of . . . what? Well, here's one possibility, which will serve to make the point.

Artificial light is a recent arrival on the night scene. Until recently, the only night lights on view were the moon and the stars. They are at optical infinity, so rays coming from them are parallel. This fits them for use as compasses. Insects are known to use celestial objects such as the sun and the moon to steer accurately in a straight line, and they can use the same compass, with reversed sign, for returning home after a foray. The insect nervous system is adept at setting up a temporary rule of thumb of this kind: "Steer a course such that the light rays hit your eye at an angle of 30 degrees." Since insects have compound eyes (with straight tubes or light guides radiating out from the centre of the eye like the spines of a hedgehog), this might amount in practice to something as simple as keeping the light in one particular tube or ommatidium.

But the light compass relies critically on the celestial object being at optical infinity. If it isn't, the rays are not parallel but diverge like the spokes of a wheel. A nervous system applying a 30-degree (or any acute angle) rule of thumb to a nearby candle, as though it were the moon at optical infinity, will steer the moth, via a spiral trajectory, into the flame. Draw it out for yourself, using some particular acute angle such as 30 degrees, and you'll produce an elegant logarithmic spiral into the candle.

Though fatal in this particular circumstance, the moth's rule of thumb is still, on average, a good one because, for a moth, sightings of candles are rare compared with sightings of the moon. We don't notice the hundreds of moths that are silently and effectively steering by the moon or a bright star, or even the glow from a distant city. We see only moths wheeling into our candle, and we ask the wrong question: Why are all these moths committing suicide? Instead, we should ask why they have nervous systems that steer by maintaining a fixed angle to light rays, a tactic that we notice only where it goes wrong. When the question is rephrased, the mystery evaporates. It never was right to call it suicide. It is a misfiring by-product of a normally useful compass.

Now, apply the by-product lesson to religious behaviour in humans. We observe large numbers of people—in many areas it amounts to 100 per cent—who hold beliefs that flatly contradict demonstrable scientific facts as well as rival religions followed by others. People not only hold these beliefs with passionate certitude, but devote time and resources to costly activities that flow from holding them. They die for them, or kill for them. We marvel at this, just as we marvelled at the "self-immolation behaviour" of the moths. Baffled, we ask why. But my point is that we may be asking the wrong question. The religious behaviour may be a misfiring, an unfortunate by-product of an underlying psychological propensity which in other circumstances is, or once was, useful. On this view, the propensity that was naturally selected in our ancestors was not religion *per se*; it had some other benefit, and it only incidentally manifests itself as religious behaviour. We shall understand religious behaviour only after we have renamed it.

If, then, religion is a by-product of something else, what is that something else? What is the counterpart to the moth habit of navigating by celestial light compasses? What is the primitively advantageous trait that sometimes misfires to generate religion? I shall offer one suggestion by way of illustration, but I must stress that it is only an example of the *kind* of thing I mean, and I shall come on to parallel suggestions made by others. I am much more wedded to the general principle that the question should be properly put, and if necessary rewritten, than I am to any particular answer.

My specific hypothesis is about children. More than any other species, we survive by the accumulated experience of previous generations, and that experience needs to be passed on to children for their protection and well-being. Theoretically, children might learn from personal experience not to go too near a cliff edge, not to eat untried red berries, not to swim in crocodile-infested waters. But, to say the least, there will be a selective advantage to child brains that possess the rule of thumb: believe, without question, whatever your grown-ups tell you. Obey your parents; obey the tribal elders, especially when they adopt a solemn, minatory tone. Trust your elders without question. This is a generally valuable rule for a child. But, as with the moths, it can go wrong.

I have never forgotten a horrifying sermon, preached in school chapel when I was little. Horrifying in retrospect, that is: at the time, my child brain accepted it in the spirit intended by the preacher. He told us a story of a squad of soldiers, drilling beside a railway line. At a critical moment the drill sergeant's attention was distracted, and he failed to give the order to halt. The soldiers were so well schooled to obey orders without question that they carried on marching, right into the path of an oncoming train. Now, of, course, I don't believe the story and I hope the preacher didn't either. But I believed it when I was nine, because I heard it from an adult in authority over me. And whether he believed it or not, the preacher wished us children to admire and model ourselves on the soldiers' slavish and unquestioning obedience to an order, however preposterous, from an authority figure. Speaking for myself, I think we *did* admire it. As an adult I find it almost impossible to credit that my childhood self wondered whether I would have had the courage to do my duty by marching under the train. But that, for what it is worth, is how I remember my feelings. The sermon obviously made a deep impression on me, for I have remembered it and passed it on to you.

To be fair, I don't think the preacher thought he was serving up a religious message. It was probably more military than religious, in the spirit of Tennyson's "Charge of the Light Brigade," which he may well have quoted. . . . Soldiers are drilled to become as much like automata, or computers, as possible.

Computers do what they are told. They slavishly obey any instructions given in their own programming language. This is how they do useful things like word processing and spreadsheet calculations. But, as an inevitable by-product, they are equally robotic in obeying bad instructions. They have no way of telling whether an instruction will have a good effect or a bad. They simply obey, as soldiers are supposed to. It is their unquestioning obedience that makes computers useful, and exactly the same thing makes them inescapably vulnerable to infection by software viruses and worms. A maliciously designed program that says, "Copy me and send me to every address that you find on this hard disk" will simply be obeyed, and then obeyed again by the other computers down the line to which it is sent, in exponential expansion. It is difficult, perhaps impossible, to design a computer which is usefully obedient and at the same time immune to infection.

If I have done my softening-up work well, you will already have completed my argument about child brains and religion. Natural selection builds child brains with a tendency to believe whatever their parents and tribal elders tell them. Such trusting obedience is valuable for survival: the analogue of steering by the moon for a moth. But the flip side of trusting obedience is slavish gullibility. The inevitable by-product is vulnerability to infection by mind viruses. For excellent reasons related to Darwinian survival, child brains need to trust parents, and elders whom parents tell them to trust. An automatic consequence is that the truster has no way of distinguishing good advice from bad. The child cannot know that "Don't paddle in the crocodile-infested Limpopo" is good advice but "You must sacrifice a goat at the time of the full moon, otherwise the rains will fail" is at best a waste of time and goats. Both admonitions sound equally trustworthy. Both come from a respected source and are delivered with a solemn earnestness that commands respect and demands obedience. The same goes for propositions about the world, about the cosmos, about morality and about human nature. And, very likely, when the child grows up and has children of her own, she will naturally pass the whole lot on to her own children—nonsense as well as sense—using the same infectious gravitas of manner.

On this model we should expect that, in different geographical regions, different arbitrary beliefs, none of which have any factual basis, will be handed down, to be believed with the same conviction as useful pieces of traditional wisdom such as the belief that manure is good for the crops. We should also expect that superstitions and other non-factual beliefs will locally evolve—change over generations—either by random drift or by some sort of analogue of Darwinian selection, eventually showing a pattern of significant divergence from common ancestry. Languages drift apart from a common progenitor given sufficient time in geographical separation (I shall return to this point in a moment). The same seems to be true of baseless and arbitrary beliefs and injunctions, handed down the generations—beliefs that were perhaps given a fair wind by the useful programmability of the child brain. . . .

. . . But remember, my specific suggestion about the useful gullibility of the child mind is only an example of the *kind* of thing that might be the analogue of moths navigating by the moon or the stars. The ethnologist Robert Hinde, in *Why Gods Persist*, and the anthropologists Pascal Boyer, in *Religion Explained*, and Scott Atran, in *In Gods We Trust*, have independently promoted the general idea of religion as a by-product of normal psychological dispositions—many by-products, I should say, for the anthropologists especially are concerned to emphasize the diversity of the world's religions as well as what they have in common. The findings of anthropologists seem weird to us only because they are unfamiliar. All religious beliefs seem weird to those not brought up in them. Boyer did research on the Fang people of Cameroon, who believe . . .

> . . . that witches have an extra internal animal-like organ that flies away at night and ruins other people's crops or poisons their blood. It is also said that these witches sometimes assemble for huge banquets, where they devour their victims and plan future attacks. Many will tell you that a friend of a friend actually saw

witches flying over the village at night, sitting on a banana leaf and throwing magical darts at various unsuspecting victims.

Boyer continues with a personal anecdote:

> I was mentioning these and other exotica over dinner in a Cambridge college when one of our guests, a prominent Cambridge theologian, turned to me and said: "That is what makes anthropology so fascinating and so difficult too. You have to explain *how people can believe such nonsense*." Which left me dumbfounded. The conversation had moved on before I could find a pertinent response—to do with kettles and pots.

Assuming that the Cambridge theologian was a mainstream Christian, he probably believed some combination of the following:

- In the time of the ancestors, a man was born to a virgin mother with no biological father being involved.
- The same fatherless man called out to a friend called Lazarus, who had been dead long enough to stink, and Lazarus promptly came back to life.
- The fatherless man himself came alive after being dead and buried three days.
- Forty days later, the fatherless man went up to the top of a hill and then disappeared bodily into the sky.
- If you murmur thoughts privately in your head, the fatherless man, and his "father" (who is also himself) will hear your thoughts and may act upon them. He is simultaneously able to hear the thoughts of everybody else in the world.
- If you do something bad, or something good, the same fatherless man sees all, even if nobody else does. You may be rewarded or punished accordingly, including after your death.
- The fatherless man's virgin mother never died but "ascended" bodily into heaven.
- Bread and wine, if blessed by a priest (who must have testicles), "become" the body and blood of the fatherless man.

What would an objective anthropologist, coming fresh to this set of beliefs while on fieldwork in Cambridge, make of them?

Further Reading

Richard Dawkins's other bestsellers are *The Selfish Gene* (Oxford and New York: Oxford University Press, 1976; 30th anniversary ed., 2006); *The Extended Phenotype* (Oxford and San Francisco: W. H. Freeman, 1982); *The Blind Watchmaker* (New York: W. W. Norton, 1986); *River Out of Eden* (New York: Basic Books, 1995); *Climbing Mount Improbable* (New York: W. W. Norton, 1996); *Unweaving the Rainbow* (New York: Houghton Mifflin, 1998); *A Devil's Chaplain* (New York: Houghton Mifflin, 2003); and *The Ancestor's Tale* (New York: Houghton Mifflin, 2004). Related studies of religion are Sam Harris, *The End of Faith* (New York: W. W. Norton, 2004); Daniel C. Dennett, *Breaking the Spell: Religion as a Natural Phenomenon* (New York: Viking, 2006); and Victor Stenger, *God: The Failed Hypothesis* (Amherst, NY: Prometheus Books, 2007). For an anthology of twenty-five essays on Dawkins and his work, see *Richard Dawkins: How a Scientist Changed the Way We Think*, edited by Alan Grafen and Mark Ridley (New York and Oxford: Oxford University Press, 2006). For theological critiques of Dawkins, see Alister McGrath, *Dawkins' God: Genes, Memes and the Meaning of Life* (Oxford: Blackwell Publishing, 2005), and Alister McGrath and Joanna Collicutt McGrath, *The Dawkins Delusion? Atheist Fundamentalism and the Denial of the Divine* (Downers Grove, IL: IVP Books, 2007). For an indication of the nature of his replies to his critics, see Richard Dawkins, "Is Science a Religion?" *Humanist* (January/February 1997), and "My Critics Are Wrong to Call Me Dogmatic," *London Times*, February 12, 2007.

13 Jane Goodall
(1934–)

Introduction

In the summer of 1960, the young Englishwoman Jane Goodall arrived on the shores of Lake Tanganyika in Tanzania, East Africa. With the encouragement of Dr. Louis Leakey and with her mother as a companion, she was about to venture into the African forest to study chimpanzees—quite an unconventional activity for a former secretary from Bournemouth. Three years earlier she had fulfilled her dream of coming to Africa, but she had not yet made it her home. Almost from the start, the mountains and valley forests of the Gombe Stream Chimpanzee Reserve became for her not only a home but also a spiritual dwelling, a place where she would find healing and reason to hope.

Goodall's scientific work at Gombe over more than four decades redefined the relationship between humans and animals. Stephen Jay Gould considered Jane Goodall's work with chimpanzees "one of the Western world's greatest scientific achievements." In her pioneering role, Goodall had no formal training at first, returning to study in England only later and earning a Ph.D. from the University of Cambridge in 1965. One of her most significant discoveries came in the first year at Gombe, when she saw chimps stripping leaves off stems to make them useful for fishing termites out of nearby mounds. This and subsequent observations of Gombe chimps making and using tools called into question the prevalent criterion that separated humans from other animals. "Man the toolmaker" was no longer so dramatically different from chimpanzees, whose DNA, we would learn, differs from ours by only a little over 1 percent. The widespread belief that chimpanzees were primarily vegetarians was also dispelled by Goodall's observations. On the question of whether the chimps had distinct personalities, minds, and emotions, she was adamant: they did. Convinced of the validity of her observations, Goodall gave the chimpanzees names instead of numbers. Indeed, some of the most vivid writing in her numerous books brings to life the unique personalities and lasting family bonds of Flo and Fifi, Gilka and Gigi, Melissa and Gremlin, Goliath and Mike, Fian and Goblin, and her early favorite, David Greybeard. Her studies revealed that chimpanzees are capable of a range of behaviors previously thought unique to humans: reasoned thought, abstraction, generalization, symbolic representation, and concept of self.

One incident stands out as the most important turning point in her career—an exchange Goodall had with David Greybeard. She had been tracking him through the jungle, at a distance. At one point she thought she had lost him, and then, suddenly, as she entered a clearing, he was sitting there, looking at her, as if he had been waiting for her. Not sure what to do, Goodall approached him, very gingerly, and then noticed there was a pinenut on the ground. Picking it up, she very slowly and gently held it out to him. David Greybeard pushed her hand away, but he didn't run away. She tried again, and this time he took the pinenut from her. Then he did something remarkable, Goodall recounts. He reached out his hand and covered hers with it and just held it for a moment, in the same gesture that chimpanzees use to reassure each other. Realizing that this wild animal was communicating with her just as he would with a member of his own species, Goodall knew at that moment that the evolutionary gap between humans and chimpanzees was not, after all, so very wide.

Had she stayed only for the ten years Louis Leakey predicted would be needed to complete the research, Goodall says she would have continued to believe that chimpanzees, "though very like us in behavior, were rather nicer." Then came the series of events that began in 1971 and became known as the "Four-Year War" of the Gombe chimpanzees. In 1975, Goodall's station recorded the first observed cannibalistic attacks made by a high-ranking female chimpanzee and her young adult daughter upon an infant chimp. Food was not at issue. Over the course of four years one group of chimps set about systematically annihilating a smaller group that had become isolated from it. Between 1974 and 1977 Goodall experienced her most intellectually and emotionally challenging years. They changed forever her view of chimpanzee nature. In the first ten years of her study, when she believed that the Gombe chimpanzees were, for the most part, "rather nicer" than human beings, she knew, of course, that aggression could flare up and that chimpanzees could be volatile. But that they could also be brutal, that they had a dark side to their nature, could wage war and commit murder, was hard to discover.

That discovery prompts Goodall's reflections in a number of the excerpts that follow, as she ponders the meaning of the human propensity for violence and warfare. She concludes that, unfortunately, humans are probably hard-wired for violence. In the events of September 11, the answer to the question "What does it mean to be human?" is amply illustrated for Goodall. It means, in short, having the capacity both for far greater evil and far greater good than chimpanzees or any other animal. "Our brain has enabled us to be both better and worse," Goodall says. "We have inherited aggressive behavior, but we have also inherited the ability to do good." Human warfare, however, may not be a biologically predetermined inevitability, even if we have inherited aggressive tendencies. Chimpanzees show love, compassion, and altruism; we have inherited those things too. With our huge brains, we have far more ability to control our genetic inheritance than any other creature. Neither war nor human aggression is inevitable, Goodall says.

She also writes about observing what could be interpreted as a precursor to an animist religion among the chimps when they come upon a spectacular waterfall in the jungle. The chimps seem to exhibit a sense of awe, standing in the stream below for fifty minutes at a time and staring at the falling water, even though they don't normally like to get wet. They will sometimes sit on a rock and watch the cascade or swing from a vine into the mist caused by the falling water. "We find that chimps do have a sense of wonder, of awe," Goodall said. "I think we can see the roots of some kind of religion from chimp behavior—[inhibited] by their lack of language."

Jane Goodall's own religious sensibilities lean toward the mystical. "Thinking back over my life," she writes, "it seems to me that there are different ways of looking out and trying to understand the world around us. There's a very clear scientific window. And it does enable us to understand an awful lot about what's out there. There's another window; it's the window through which the wise men, the holy men, the masters of the different and great religions look as they try to understand the meaning in the world. My own preference is the window of the mystic." Yet her window opens out upon the world of nature and living creatures to reveal kinship and responsibility. Like Rachel Carson, Goodall speaks for an ecological spirituality that is as much concerned with moral evolution as with the physical evolution of species. The whole purpose of spiritual energy and insight, as Goodall sees it, is to hasten human moral progress. Either we evolve into saints or into extinction.

Hope is the leitmotif of her spiritual journey. In our time, hope may indeed be the quintessential religious virtue, more elemental than faith, more fragile even than love. Jane Goodall's faith is all about hope, as the titles of her books and essays attest. In the first excerpt below, found on her website, Goodall states four reasons she faces the new millennium with hope. The remaining excerpts, all found in Goodall's memoir, *Reason for Hope: A Spiritual Journey*, capture her spiritual reflections as she looks back over her first sixty-five years of life.

✒ Goodall's Contribution to Science

Primatologist, ethnologist, and anthropologist, Jane Goodall conducted a forty-five-year study of chimpanzee social and family life, as scientific director of the Jane Goodall Institute in Gombe Stream National Park in Tanzania. There, her scientific discoveries—including the observation of chimpanzees making and using tools—laid the foundation for all future primate studies. Considered the world's foremost authority on chimpanzees, Goodall has redefined our understanding of what makes humans distinct from animals.

Goodall in Her Own Words

My Four Reasons for Hope[1]

It is easy to be overwhelmed by feelings of hopelessness as we look around the world. Is there, in fact, hope for Africa's future? Yes. Provided human populations develop programs that will stabilize, or optimize, their growth rate. It is very important to implement child healthcare programs along with family planning so that women can expect that their children will live—instead of knowing, as they do today, that many of them will die.

There are many signs of hope. Along a lakeshore in Tanzania, for example, villagers are planting trees where all the trees had disappeared. Women are taking more control over their lives, and, once they become better educated, then the birth rate begins to drop. And the children are being taught about the dire effects of habitat destruction. There is the terrible pollution around the world, the balance of nature is disturbed, and we are destroying our beautiful planet. There are fears of new epidemics for which there will be no drugs, and, rather than fight the cause, we torture

---

[1] Jane Goodall, "My Four Reasons for Hope," accessed July 5, 2005 at www.janegoodall.org.

millions of animals in the name of medical progress. But in spite of all this I do have hope. And my hope is based on three factors.

The Human Brain

Firstly, we have at last begun to understand and face up to the problems that threaten us and the survival of life on Earth as we know it. Surely, then, we can use our problem-solving abilities, our brains, and, joining hands around the world, find ways to live that are in harmony with nature. Indeed, many companies have begun "greening" their operations, and millions of people world-wide are beginning to realize that each one of us has a responsibility to the environment and our descendants, and that the way each one of us lives our life does matter, does make a difference.

The Determination of Young People

My second reason for hope lies in the tremendous energy, enthusiasm and commitment of a growing number of young people around the world. As they find out about the environmental and social problems that are now part of their heritage, they want to fight to right the wrongs. Of course they do—they have a vested interest in this, for it will be their world tomorrow. They will be moving into leadership positions, into the work force, becoming parents themselves. Young people, when informed and empowered, when they realize that what they do truly makes a difference, can indeed change the world.

The Indomitable Human Spirit

My third reason for hope lies in the indomitable nature of the human spirit. There are so many people who have dreamed seemingly unattainable dreams and, because they never gave up, achieved their goals against all the odds, or blazed a path along which others could follow. As I travel around the world I meet so many incredible and amazing human beings. They inspire me. They inspire those around them.

The Resilience of Nature

My fourth reason for hope is the incredible resilience of nature. I have visited Nagasaki, site of the second atomic bomb that ended World War II. Scientists had predicted that nothing could grow there for at least 30 years. But, amazingly, greenery grew very quickly. One sapling actually managed to survive the bombing, and today it is a large tree, with great cracks and fissures, all black inside; but that tree still produces leaves. I carry one of those leaves with me as a powerful symbol of hope. I have seen such renewals time and again, including animal species brought back from the brink of extinction.

So let us move into the next millennium with hope, for without it all we can do is eat and drink the last of our resources as we watch our planet slowly die. Instead, let us have faith in ourselves, in our intellect, in our staunch spirit. Let us develop respect for all living things. Let us try to replace impatience and intolerance with understanding and compassion. And love.

Thinking about Ultimate Questions[2]

There are really only two ways, it seems to me, in which we can think about our existence here on earth. We either agree with Macbeth that life is nothing more than a "tale told by an idiot," a purposeless emergence of life-forms including the clever, greedy, selfish, and unfortunately destructive species that we call *Homo sapiens*—the "evolutionary goof." Or we believe that, as Pierre Teilhard de Chardin put it, "There is something afoot in the universe, something that looks like gestation and birth." In other words, a plan, a purpose to it all.

As I thought about these ultimate questions during the trying time of my divorce, I realized that my experience in the forest, my

---

[2] All subsequent excerpts are from Jane Goodall, *Reason for Hope: A Spiritual Journey* (with Philip Berman; New York: Warner Books, 1999), xi–xiii, 92–94, 152, 173–79, 190–94, 198–200, 250–51. I have supplied the headings.

understanding of the chimpanzees, had given me a new perspective. I personally was utterly convinced that there was a great spiritual power that we call God, Allah, or Brahma, although I knew, equally certainly, that my finite mind could never comprehend its form or nature. But even if there was no God, even if human beings had no soul, it would still be true that evolution had created a remarkable animal—the human animal—during its millions of years of labor. So very like our closest biological relatives, the chimpanzees, yet so different. For our study of the chimpanzees had helped to pinpoint not only the similarities between them and us, but also those ways in which we are most different. Admittedly we are not the only beings with personalities, reasoning powers, altruism, and emotions like joy and sorrow; nor are we the only beings capable of mental as well as physical suffering. But our intellect has grown mightily in complexity since the first true men branched off from the ape-man stock some two million years ago. And we, and only we, have developed a sophisticated spoken language. For the first time in evolution, a species evolved that was able to teach its young about objects and events not present, to pass on wisdom gleaned from the successes—and the mistakes—of the past, to make plans for the distant future, to discuss ideas so that they could grow, sometimes out of all recognition, through the combined wisdom of the group.

With language we can ask, as can no other living being, those questions about who we are and why we are here. And this highly developed intellect means, surely, that we have a responsibility toward the other life-forms of our planet whose continued existence is threatened by the thoughtless behavior of our own human species—*quite regardless of whether or not we believe in God*. Indeed, those who acknowledge no God, but are convinced that we are in this world as an evolutionary accident, may well be more active in environmental responsibility—for if there is no God, then, obviously, it is entirely up to us to put things right. On the other hand, I have encountered a number of people with a strong faith in God who shrug off their own human responsibilities, believing that everything is safely "in God's hands."

I was brought up to believe that "God helps those who help themselves."

On Death and Dying

I do not believe that [chimpanzees] have a concept of death. And most surely they can have no concept of life after death. I personally have never been afraid of death itself for I have never wavered in believing that a part of us, the spirit or soul, continues on. It is the process of *dying* that I shy away from.

On Parapsychological Phenomena

It is so easy in a skeptical, reductionistic scientific world to explain away these sorts of things as coincidental dreams, hallucinations, or psychological reactions triggered by the onset of pain, stress, or loss. But I have never been able to discount such experiences so easily—there have been too many events in my life, and in the lives of my friends, which have defied any kind of scientific explanation. Science does not have appropriate tools for the dissection of the spirit.

An Experience of Spiritual Ecstasy

Lost in awe [in the Gombe forest] at the beauty around me, I must have slipped into a state of heightened awareness. It is hard—impossible, really—to put into words the moment of truth that suddenly came upon me then. Even the mystics are unable to describe their brief flashes of spiritual ecstasy. It seemed to me, as I struggled afterward to recall the experience, that *self* was utterly absent: I and the chimpanzees, the earth and trees and air, seemed to merge, to become one with the spirit power of life itself. The air was filled with a feathered symphony, the evensong of birds.

I heard new frequencies in their music and also in the singing insects' voices—notes so high and sweet I was amazed. Never had I been so intensely aware of the shape, the color of the individual leaves, the varied patterns of the veins that made each one unique. Scents were clear as well, easily identifiable: fermenting, overripe fruit; waterclogged earth; cold, wet bark; the damp odor of chimpanzee hair and, yes, my own too. And the aromatic scent of young, crushed leaves was almost overpowering. I sensed a new presence, then saw a bushbuck, quietly browsing upward, his spiraled horns gleaming and his chestnut coat dark with rain.

Suddenly a distant chorus of pant-hoots elicited a reply from Fifi. As though wakening from some vivid dream I was back in the everyday world, cold, yet intensely alive. When the chimpanzees left, I stayed in that place—it seemed a most sacred place—scribbling some notes, trying to describe what, so briefly, I had experienced. I had not been visited by the angels or other heavenly beings that characterize the visions of the great mystics or the saints, yet for all that I believe it truly was a mystical experience.

Time passed. Eventually I wandered back along the forest trail and scrambled down behind my house to the beach. The sun was a huge red orb just vanishing behind the Congo hills and I sat on the beach watching the everchanging sunset as it painted the sky red and gold and dark purple. The surface of the lake, calm after the storm, glinted with gold and violet and red ripples below the flaming sky.

Later, as I sat by my little fire, cooking my little dinner of beans, tomatoes, and an egg, I was still lost in the wonder of my experience. Yes, I thought, there are many windows through which we humans, searching for meaning, can look out into the world around us. There are those carved out by Western science, their panes polished by a succession of brilliant minds. Through them we can see ever farther, ever more clearly, into areas which until recently were beyond human knowledge. Through such a scientific window I had been taught to observe the chimpanzees. For more than twenty-five years I had sought, through careful recording and critical analysis, to piece together their complex social behavior, to understand the workings of their minds. And this had not only helped us to understand their place in nature but also helped us to understand a little better some aspects of our own human behavior, our own place in the natural world. Yet there are other windows through which we humans can look out into the world around us, windows through which the mystics and holy men of the East, and the founders of the great world religions, have gazed as they searched for the meaning and purpose of our life on earth, not only in the wondrous beauty of the world, but also in its darkness and ugliness. And those Masters contemplated the truths that they saw, not with their minds only but with their hearts and souls too. From those revelations came the spiritual essence of the great scriptures, the holy books, and the most beautiful mystic poems and writings. That afternoon, it had been as though an unseen hand had drawn back a curtain and, for the briefest moment, I had seen through such a window. In a flash of "outsight" I had known timelessness and quiet ecstasy, sensed a truth of which mainstream science is merely a small fraction. And I knew that the revelation would be with me for the rest of my life, imperfectly remembered yet always within. A source of strength on which I could draw when life seemed harsh or cruel or desperate.

Inside Notre Dame Cathedral

Many years ago, in the spring of 1974, I visited the cathedral of Notre Dame in Paris. There were not many people around, and it was quiet and still inside. I gazed in silent awe at the great Rose Window, glowing in the morning sun. All at once the cathedral was filled with a huge volume of sound: an organ playing magnificently for a wedding taking place in a distant corner. Bach's Toccata and Fugue in D Minor. I had always loved the opening theme; but in the cathedral, filling the entire vastness, it seemed to enter and possess my whole self. It was as though the music itself was alive.

That moment, a suddenly captured moment of eternity, was perhaps the closest I have ever come to experiencing ecstasy, the ecstasy of the mystic. How could I believe it was the chance gyrations of bits of primeval dust that had led up to that moment in time—the cathedral soaring to the sky; the collective inspiration and faith of those who caused it to be built; the advent of Bach himself; the brain, his brain, that translated truth into music; and the mind that could, as mine did then, comprehend the whole inexorable progression of evolution? Since I cannot believe that this was the result of chance, I have to admit anti-chance. And so I must believe in a guiding power in the universe—in other words, I must believe in God.

I was taught, as a scientist, to think logically and empirically, rather than intuitively or spiritually. When I was at Cambridge University in the early 1960's most of the scientists and science students working in the Department of Zoology, so far as I could tell, were agnostic or even atheist. Those who believed in a God kept it hidden from their peers.

Fortunately, by the time I got to Cambridge I was twenty-seven years old and my beliefs had already been molded so that I was not influenced by these opinions. I believed in the spiritual power that, as a Christian, I called God. But as I grew older and learned about different faiths I came to believe that there was, after all, but One God with different names: Allah, Tao, the Creator, and so on. God, for me, was the Great Spirit in Whom "we live and move and have our being." There have been times during my life when this belief wavered, when I questioned—even denied—the existence of God. And then there have been times when I have despaired that we humans can ever get out of the environmental and social mess which we have created for ourselves and other life-forms on the planet. Why is the human species so destructive? So selfish and greedy and, sometimes, truly evil? At such times I feel there can be no underlying meaning to the emergence of life on earth. And if there is no meaning, doesn't this suggest, as a bitter New York skinhead once put it, that the human species is simply an "evolutionary goof?"

Still, for me those periods of doubt have been relatively rare, triggered by a variety of circumstances—such as when my second husband died of cancer; when the ethnic hatred erupted in the little country of Burundi and I heard terrible tales of torture and mass killings that reminded me of the unspeakable evils of the Holocaust; when four of my students studying in Gombe National Park in Tanzania were kidnapped and held for ransom. How, I asked myself on such occasions, how can I be expected to believe in some divine plan in the face of so much suffering, so much hatred, so much destruction? Yet somehow I overcame those periods of doubt; most of the time I am optimistic about the future. There are, however, many people today who have lost whatever faith and hope they had, whether in God or human destiny.

On Religion and Science

How sad that so many people seem to think that science and religion are mutually exclusive. Science has used modern technology and modern techniques to uncover so much about the formation and the development of life-forms on Planet Earth and about the solar system of which our little world is but a minute part. In recent times astronomers have charted the atmosphere of planets and identified new solar systems; neurologists have learned astounding truths about the workings of our brains; physicists have divided the atom into smaller and smaller particles; a sheep has been cloned; a little robot has been sent to wander about on the surface of Mars; the whole miraculous world of cyberspace has been opened up. Truly the human intellect is awesome. Alas, all of these amazing discoveries have led to a belief that every wonder of the natural world and of the universe—indeed, of infinity and time—can, in the end, be understood through the logic and the reasoning of a finite mind. And so, for many, science has taken the place of religion.

. . . But not all scientists believe thus. There are quantum physicists who have concluded that the concept of God is not, after all, merely wishful thinking. Physicist John C. Eccles, although he felt that questions regarding the human soul were matters beyond science, warned scientists that they should not give definitive negative answers when asked about the continuity of the conscious self after death. There are those exploring the human brain who feel that no matter how much they discover about this extraordinary structure it will never add up to a complete understanding of the human mind—that the whole is, after all, greater than the sum of the parts. The Big Bang theory is yet another example of the incredible, the awe-inspiring ability of the human mind to learn about seemingly unknowable phenomena in the beginning of time. Time as we know it, or think we know it. But what about before time? And what about beyond space?

Reply to a Young Man Working at Her Hotel in Dallas, Texas

He had watched all my documentaries, read my books. He was fascinated, and he thought that what I did was great. But I talked about evolution. Was I religious? Did I believe in God? If so, how did that square with evolution? Had we really descended from chimpanzees? All these questions, asked with frank sincerity and genuine concern.

And so I tried to answer him as truthfully as I could, to explain my own beliefs. I told him that no one thought humans had descended from chimpanzees. I explained that I did believe in Darwinian evolution and told him of my time at Olduvai, when I had held the remains of extinct creatures in my hands. That I had traced, in the museum, the various stages of the evolution of, say, a horse: from a rabbit-sized creature that gradually, over thousands of years, changed, became better and better adapted to its environment and eventually was transformed into the modern horse. I told him I believed that millions of years ago there had been a primitive, apelike, humanlike creature, one branch of which had gone on to become the chimpanzee, another branch of which had eventually led to us.

"But that doesn't mean I don't believe in God," I said. And I told him something of my beliefs, and those of my family. How my grandfather had been a Congregational minister. I told him that I had always thought that the description of God creating the world in seven days might well have been an attempt to explain evolution in a parable. In that case, each of the days would have been several million years. . . . I ended by telling him that it honestly didn't matter how we humans got to be the way we are, whether evolution or special creation was responsible. What mattered and mattered desperately was our future development. Were we going to go on destroying God's creation, fighting each other, hurting the other creatures of His planet? Or were we going to find ways to live in greater harmony with each other and with the natural world?

On Moral Evolution

[Lecomte] du Noüy suggested that we try to view our moral progress in the time frame of human evolution. Our physical form has evolved slowly over the aeons. From the first living specks of protoplasm it took billions of years before the first mammals appeared during Paleolithic times. *Homo sapiens*, modern man, has walked the planet for only a couple of million years. And so, although there always has been and still is a great deal that is clearly unethical and often downright evil in human practices everywhere, a growing number of people around the globe are more aware than ever before of what is wrong, what needs to change.

As I contemplated du Noüy's arguments, our moral behavior—or the lack of it—could be seen in a new light. It was indeed tragic that our selfish instincts so often dominated our loving and altruistic ones, but, nevertheless, we had come a long way in a very short time—by evolutionary standards, that is. Less than a hundred years ago, for example, in my own country of England (and in other Western countries too), conditions for the poor were unspeakably terrible. Women and children—and ponies—were sent down into the mines to work in the near dark, in horrific conditions and for incredibly long periods, with very little rest between shifts, and but little food. Children, as well as adults, shivered in the winter with bare feet and few clothes in the unspeakable slums. Diseases such as tuberculosis and rickets were commonplace. Slavery was an accepted form of labor. . . . How different things had become in the U.K. by the 1980s, I reflected. Theoretically everyone had access to welfare. Conditions were still bad in some inner-city areas, but local governments and social workers were at least trying to improve them. The welfare state, for all its drawbacks, had sprung from ethical concerns for those who were unable to care for themselves and their families. Many charitable organizations were working to improve the condition of minority groups. Slavery had been banished, and when it became known that industry was making use of cheap slave labor in developing countries, there was massive public condemnation, which at least sometimes led to improved conditions for the workers.

Similar kinds of reforms had taken place in other democracies around the globe. Moreover, changes in thinking were taking place that would lead, thanks to the leadership of Mikhail Gorbachev, to the breakdown of the repressive communist dictatorship of the Soviet bloc and eventually to the collapse of communist regimes in other parts of the world. Human dignity and human rights were increasingly topics of concern, and even animal rights movements around the world were gaining more recognition and support. The violence, cruelty, oppression, and suppression that still plagued our world had, in and of themselves, led to international organizations such as the United Nations. And although this had not lived up to the expectations of its founders in such matters as preserving peace and preventing genocide, the very fact that it had been formed was a major step in the right direction. Gradually, it seemed to me, human beings were reaching out and trying to help beyond the borders of their own nations. We had a long, long road ahead of us, but we were slowly moving in the right direction.

On the Depletion of the Natural Environment

But was there going to be time, I wondered, for us to complete the journey? No thinking, rational person could feel anything but dismay at the rate at which humanity was destroying nature—destroying that which had, for millions of years, nurtured our birth and development as a species. In recent times, as modern beliefs and modern technology had swept away ancient beliefs and traditions and as human populations had increased in number, needing more and ever more land, countless people, particularly in the Western world, had lost, or were rapidly losing, all sense of our rightful place in the great scheme of things. My own spirit had been nourished and strengthened by nature and I had developed a very real understanding of and respect for the fascinating diversity of life-forms on earth, and their interdependence. And now forests, grasslands, prairies, wetlands—all wild habitats—were disappearing at a terrifying rate. So too were many species of animals and plants—each unique, each slowly evolved over the millennia. Even in the last wilderness strongholds, such as the North and South Poles, there were signs of our human poisons and debris.

On Greed and Blight

Most of this destruction was due to the greedy, wasteful societies of the affluent world, which, in order to maintain their absurd, materialistic, luxurious standards of living, were, to all intents and purposes, stealing food from the mouths of the poor in the developing world. The poor became poorer and both infant mortality and birth rates soared. The developing world struggled to cultivate the eroded soils of the spreading deserts, to get water from the ever lower water tables, while Western societies covered thousands of square miles of rich agricultural land with concrete, cut down thousands of square miles of rain forest to create grazing or grow grain for cattle in order to feed meat to overweight citizens, and paid (scandalously inadequately) Third World farmers to grow cash crops such as coffee and tea, so that there was even less land available for subsistence farming.

Indigenous Peoples and Spiritual Values

I thought about the quickening of interest in the lifestyles and spiritual values of the indigenous people of the world, especially in North America. What a perfect solution for the environmental crisis if we could go back to the ways of the American Indians—the Native Americans or First Nation peoples—who, for hundreds of years, had lived in harmony with nature, taking only what they needed to live, and giving thanks, and giving back. I knew that there were Elders who still lived by the old values, the old sense of reverence for the Great Spirit, the Creator. But while it sounded attractive, very few Westerners, I thought, could tolerate such a way of life—for it would mean having to forgo the luxuries which we had come to think of as necessities. It would be hard to endure the vagaries of mother nature without the soft protective cocoon that was wrapped around us—at least the economically privileged among us—at birth. I thought, half sadly, half with amusement, of the archaeologist of the future who would analyze the physical makeup of these cocoons: cars—many of them, since the custom is to trade one in every few years; a series of apartments and/or houses, as families grew or moved around the country; washing machines; household effects; dishwashers; hi-fis, CD players, countless TVs and computers and cell phones; zillions of gadgets varying with the interests and occupations of the inhabitants of the cocoons; enough clothing and footwear to keep an African village clad for years. . . . The measure of *outward* success. And if some priest or monk were to sift through the inner lives of those same people, and lay out the spiritual acquisitions, the measure of success of the soul, how, I wondered, would the tallies compare, material versus spiritual acquisitions?

On Achieving Spiritual Insight

I contemplated my own record, somewhat ruefully. I didn't like a lot of what I found. I had always been puzzled by the admonition to "love thy neighbor as thyself." How could I love myself, when so often I failed to live up to the standards that I set? But suddenly it seemed clearer, and I thought I understood. The "self" that we had to love was not our ego, not the everyday person who went around behaving thoughtlessly, selfishly, sometimes unkindly, but the flame of pure spirit that is in each and every one of us, that is part of the Creator; what the Buddhists call *Kernal*. That which is loved, I realized, can grow. We had to learn to understand and love this Spirit within in order to find peace within. And only then could we reach out beyond the narrow prison of our own lives, seeking reunion with the Spiritual Power that we call God, or Allah, the Tao, Brahma, the Creator, or whatever our personal belief prescribes. Once we had attained that goal, our power to connect with others, so that together we could create a better world, would be immeasurably greater.

The ability to reach beyond their upbringing, their culture, and their immediate surroundings has always, I realized, been a characteristic of the greatest spiritual leaders and the saints. Our task, then, if we would hasten our moral evolution, progress a little more quickly toward our human destiny, is obvious—formidable, but in the long run not impossible. We will have to evolve, all of us, from ordinary, everyday human beings—into saints! Ordinary people, like you and me, will have to become saints, or at least mini-saints. The great saints and the Masters were not supernatural beings; they were mortals like us, made of flesh and blood. They, like us, needed air to breathe, and food and drink (though not in abundance). And they all believed in a Spiritual Power, in God. That enabled them to tap into the great spiritual energy "in which we live and move and have our being." They lived on this energy, breathed it into their lungs so that it ran in the blood, giving them strength. We must strive, each of us, to join them. I imagine them standing as though on a bridge, suspended between God and earth.

On Atheists

And what about those, and there are many, who do not believe in a God—those who are atheists? It does not make any difference, I thought. A life lived in the service of humanity, a love of and respect for all living things—those attributes are the essence of saintlike behavior.

The Ultimate Destiny of Our Species

I shall conclude this chapter with a symbolic story. It is about an American, Rick Swope, a zoo visitor who rescued an adult male chimpanzee from drowning in the moat around his enclosure. And this despite the dire warning of a keeper and the threats of other adult male chimpanzees of the group. When asked what had made him risk his life he answered: "I looked into his eyes. It was like looking into the eyes of a man. And the message was: Won't *anybody* help me?"

That is the look I have seen in the eyes of the chimpanzees tied up in the African markets, from under the frills of the circus chimp, from behind the steel bars of the laboratory animals. And in the eyes of little children from Burundi who saw their parents slaughtered in the ethnic violence. In the eyes of the street children, and those that are caught up in the violence of our inner cities. Indeed, that appeal is all around us. Albert Schweitzer wrote: "A man who possesses a veneration of life will not simply say his prayers. He will throw himself into the battle to preserve life, if for no other reason than that he is himself an extension of life around him."

I truly believe that more and more people are seeing the appeal in the eyes around them, feeling it in their hearts, and throwing themselves into the battle. Herein lies the real hope for our future; we are moving toward the ultimate destiny of our species—a state of compassion and love. Yes, I do have hope. I do believe we can look forward to a world in which our great-grandchildren and their children after them can live in peace. A world in which there will still be trees and chimpanzees swinging through them, and blue skies and birds singing, and the drumbeats of indigenous peoples reminding us powerfully of our link to Mother Earth and the Great Spirit—the God we worship. But, as I've stated repeatedly, we don't have much time. The planet's resources are running out. And so if we truly care about the future of our planet we must stop leaving it to "them" out there to solve all the problems. It is up to *us* to save the world for tomorrow: it's up to you and me.

Further Reading

Jane Goodall's books include *My Friends the Wild Chimpanzees* (Washington, DC: National Geographic Society, 1970); *Innocent Killers*, with H. van Lawick (New York: Ballantine Publishing Group, 1971); *In the Shadow of Man* (Boston: Houghton Mifflin, 1971); *The Chimpanzees of Gombe: Patterns of Behavior* (Cambridge, MA: Belknap Press of Harvard University Press, 1986); *Through a Window: Thirty Years Observing the Gombe Chimpanzees* (Boston: Houghton Mifflin, 1990); *Visions of Caliban*, with Dale Peterson (New York: Houghton Mifflin, 1993); *Brutal Kinship*, with Michael Nichols (New York: Aperture, 1999); *Reason for Hope: A Spiritual Journey*, with Phillip Berman (New York: Warner Books, 1999); *40 Years at Gombe* (New York: Stewart, Tabori and Chang, 2000); *Africa in My Blood: An Autobiography in Letters: The Early Years*, edited by Dale Peterson (New York: Houghton Mifflin, 2000); *Beyond Innocence: An Autobiography in Letters: The Later Years*, edited by Dale Peterson (New York: Houghton Mifflin, 2001); *The Ten Trusts: What We Must Do to Care for the Animals We Love*, with Marc Bekoff (San Francisco: HarperSanFrancisco: 2002). Goodall has also written a "guide to mindful eating" under the title *Harvest for Hope* (New York: Warner Books, 2005).

14 Steven Weinberg
(1933–)

Introduction

Steven Weinberg's faith is devoutly humanistic, realistic, and rationalistic. He believes that "humanity must choose an earthly kingdom because there isn't any heavenly kingdom."[1] He believes in the importance of a moral order independent of all religious doctrine. And he believes that one of the great social functions of science is to free people from superstition. Science writer Paul Hogan sees Weinberg, and most other particle physicists, as possessed of "a profound faith in the power of physics to achieve absolute truth." "But what makes Weinberg such an interesting spokesperson for his tribe," according to Hogan, "is that he . . . is acutely aware that his faith is just that, a faith; Weinberg knows that he is speaking with a philosophical accent."[2]

Weinberg's vision of science is propelled by a simple faith that physics will discover a complete explanation of nature's particles and forces. Only then will we be able to address the vexed question, What happened before the big bang? In 1997 he could

---

[1] "Steven Weinberg 2002 Humanist of the Year," *Humanist* 62, no. 5 (2002): 21.
[2] Paul Hogan, *The End of Science* (Addison-Wesley Publishing Co., 1996), 72.

write: "About one thing I am sure. Those who think that an infinitely old universe is absurd, so there must have been a first moment in time, and those who think that a first moment is absurd,
so the universe must be infinitely old, have one thing in common:
whichever side happens to be right about the origin of the universe, the reasoning of both sides is wrong. We don't know if the
universe is infinitely old or if there was a first moment; but neither
view is absurd, and the choice between them will not be made by
intuition, or by philosophy or theology, but by the ordinary methods of science."[3] The faith of this Nobel laureate is every bit as
demanding as that of religious ascetics who forego the pleasant
and the comfortable for the sake of a higher truth. Weinberg for-
sakes more pleasant and comfortable pictures of human life in
favor of the conviction that the ultimate laws of the universe are
quite impersonal, with no hint of a divine plan or any special
place for humans.

Readers of Weinberg's elegant essays in the pages of the *New
York Review of Books* and elsewhere know how deserving a recipient he was of the Lewis Thomas Prize, awarded to the researcher
who best embodies "the scientist as poet." Both the scientist and
the poet are on display in this chapter. In the last of the three selections below, an interview on the PBS series *Faith and Reason*,
Weinberg explains what he meant by the famous, perhaps infa-
mous, statement in his book *The First Three Minutes* that "the
more the universe seems comprehensible, the more it also seems
pointless." He also comments on the use of God as an explanation, the dialogue between religion and science, and the overall
value of religion.

The second selection consists of excerpts from the chapter
"What About God?" in *Dreams of a Final Theory*, where Weinberg
makes an important critique of revisionist uses of the term "God,"
such as we see in Einstein and other authors in part 2 of this volume. His point is that by "God" the vast majority of religious folk

---

[3] Steven Weinberg, "Before the Big Bang," *New York Review of Books*, 44,
no. 10 (June 12, 1997).

throughout history have meant a personal being who is concerned about humans and intervenes in human life, not an abstract principle of harmony and order or a placeholder for "fundamental laws of nature." From the standpoint of philosophers and theologians who have labored in the modern period to rehabilitate the concept of God, sometimes even to revise its meaning in entirely naturalistic terms, Weinberg's premise may seem to involve an unfair catch-22: more plausible, revisionist notions of God are not what people really mean by "God," and what they really mean by "God" is not plausible. However, from the standpoint of recent work in the academic study of religion, Weinberg's determination to hold theists to the distinctive supernatural definition is methodologically important. How else can we identify anything as specifically religious, unless in connection with beliefs having to do with superhuman gods, goddesses, ancestors, ghosts, water spirits, and other powers? These beliefs may be judged false, but their truth-value is irrelevant in identifying the proper object of the study of religion, and that involves the distinguishing characteristic "belief in superhuman beings." The scholar of religion does not need to believe in God, but she does need to believe that religious folk believe in superhuman beings. Otherwise, the object of study becomes so expansive that it should be handed over to the desk of the philosopher or the scientist.

The very first selection below is "A Designer Universe?" Here Weinberg explains in the space of fifteen compelling pages why he thinks physics gives us a more satisfying explanation of the world than do religious theories of design. Confessing that he cannot conceive of any set of laws of nature whose discovery would not leave him with an unsatisfied sense of wonder, he says, "So there seems to be an irreducible mystery that science will not eliminate." When physicists have found a final unified theory of everything (TOE), it will still be possible to ask, why *this* theory rather than some other theory? Likewise, those who believe in an intelligent designer God who governs the universe cannot explain why this should be so. Why *this* sort of God and not some other? By acknowledging an irreducible mystery, Weinberg appears to position science in the same boat in which religion sinks or swims. However, as he goes on to argue, physics is able to show why its governing laws are not *slightly* different than they are, whereas religious theories appear to be infinitely flexible. Weinberg has a ready reply to those who cite evidence of conscious design, such as the just-right radioactive state of carbon or the very low energy density of empty space (the small "cosmological constant"). Without these and other unlikely conditions, the design proponents observe, life would be impossible. Weinberg asks why we should be surprised to find perfect conditions for life. In all other parts of the universe, where perfect conditions do not exist, "there is no one to raise the question."

From beginning to end, Weinberg's essay "A Designer Universe?" is a masterpiece of concise reasoning and scientific argument. That he would be challenged was inevitable. The first response came from fellow physicist John Polkinghorne and is reprinted in chapter 15 of the present volume. Three other responses appeared in Letters to the Editor.[4] A Jesuit wanted to know how Weinberg could fail to see the way the why-question takes on a whole new dimension when applied to God, who by definition is the ground that makes possible all why-questions whatsoever. A sociologist wanted to know whether the argument against intelligent design of the universe is effectively unfalsifiable—that is, something that could never be proved wrong, and hence can't be considered part of science. A third response came from a poet, who chided Weinberg for declaring that his life had been happy rather than simply fortunate, since "happiness cannot easily abide alongside a consciousness of the misery and misfortunes of others" (Herodotus, *Histories*). In reply, Weinberg argued that the Jesuit, in ruling out the application of the "why" question to the nature of God, in effect is claiming that he feels no sense of wonder about why the God in which he believes is the way He is. A mere definition may suffice for reaching this happy state, Weinberg said, but it is a

---

[4] The letters to the editor and Steven Weinberg's reply appeared in *New York Review of Books*, 47, no. 1 (January 20, 2000): 64.

psychological state and not a logical resting place that prohibits further "why" questions. Furthermore, his argument against the designer God is eminently falsifiable. "All that's needed," Weinberg answered, "is a miracle or two." Finally, to support what he calls "our right to consider ourselves happy" despite the warnings of the poet, Weinberg called upon the words of another poet, William Butler Yeats in "Lapis Lazuli":

> All perform their tragic play
> There struts Hamlet, there is Lear;
> That's Ophelia, that Cordelia;
> Yet they, should the last scene be there,
> The great stage curtain about to drop,
> If worthy their prominent part in the play,
> Do not break up their lines to weep.
> They know that Hamlet and Lear are gay;
> Gaiety transfiguring all that dread.

✌ Weinberg's Contribution to Science

Steven Weinberg holds the Josey Regental Chair in Science at the University of Texas at Austin. He has been awarded the Nobel Prize in physics and the National Medal of Science and is a foreign member of the Royal Society. A major proponent of the idea that physics is working toward a "final theory" that will, when discovered, serve as a complete explanation of nature's particles and forces, Weinberg took the first conceptual steps toward this goal in 1967, when he realized that it might be possible to use the idea of "broken symmetry" to find the underlying unity between two of nature's four known forces or interactions: electromagnetism and the weak nuclear force. He proposed that the same equations could be used to describe the two interactions if a kind of energy called a "scalar field" permeated all of space. While physicists are still looking for evidence that such a field exists, they have largely accepted Weinberg's idea, which has since been dubbed the electroweak theory. This conceptual experimentation is regarded as the first step toward finding an ultimate unified theory.

Weinberg in His Own Words

A Designer Universe?[5]

I have been asked to comment on whether the universe shows signs of having been designed.[6] I don't see how it's possible to talk about this without having at least some vague idea of what a designer would be like. Any possible universe could be explained as the work of some sort of designer. Even a universe that is completely chaotic, without any laws or regularities at all, could be supposed to have been designed by an idiot.

The question that seems to me to be worth answering, and perhaps not impossible to answer, is whether the universe shows signs of having been designed by a deity more or less like those of traditional monotheistic religions—not necessarily a figure from the ceiling of the Sistine Chapel, but at least some sort of personality, some intelligence, who created the universe and has some special concern with life, in particular with human life. I expect that this is not the idea of a designer held by many here. You may tell me that you are thinking of something much more abstract, some cosmic spirit of order and harmony, as Einstein did. You are certainly free to think that way, but then I don't know why you use words like "designer" or "God," except perhaps as a form of protective coloration.

It used to be obvious that the world was designed by some sort of intelligence. What else could account for fire and rain and lightning

⁵ Originally published in *New York Review of Books* 46, no. 16 (October 21, 1999): 46–48. Also printed in *Cosmic Questions*, ed. James B. Miller, Annals of the New York Academy of Sciences, vol. 950 (New York: New York Academy of Sciences, 2001), 169–74.

⁶ This article is based on a talk given in April 1999 at the Conference on Cosmic Design of the American Association for the Advancement of Science in Washington, D.C. —*SW*.

and earthquakes? Above all, the wonderful abilities of living things seemed to point to a creator who had a special interest in life. Today we understand most of these things in terms of physical forces acting under impersonal laws. We don't yet know the most fundamental laws, and we can't work out all the consequences of the laws we do know. The human mind remains extraordinarily difficult to understand, but so is the weather. We can't predict whether it will rain one month from today, but we do know the rules that govern the rain, even though we can't always calculate their consequences. I see nothing about the human mind any more than about the weather that stands out as beyond the hope of understanding as a consequence of impersonal laws acting over billions of years.

There do not seem to be any exceptions to this natural order, any miracles. I have the impression that these days most theologians are embarrassed by talk of miracles, but the great monotheistic faiths are founded on miracle stories—the burning bush, the empty tomb, an angel dictating the Koran to Mohammed—and some of these faiths teach that miracles continue at the present day. The evidence for all these miracles seems to me to be considerably weaker than the evidence for cold fusion, and I don't believe in cold fusion. Above all, today we understand that even human beings are the result of natural selection acting over millions of years of breeding and eating.

I'd guess that if we were to see the hand of the designer anywhere, it would be in the fundamental principles, the final laws of nature, the book of rules that govern all natural phenomena. We don't know the final laws yet, but as far as we have been able to see, they are utterly impersonal and quite without any special role for life. There is no life force. As Richard Feynman has said, when you look at the universe and understand its laws, "the theory that it is all arranged as a stage for God to watch man's struggle for good and evil seems inadequate."

True, when quantum mechanics was new, some physicists thought that it put humans back into the picture, because the principles of quantum mechanics tell us how to calculate the probabilities of various results that might be found by a human observer. But, starting with the work of Hugh Everett forty years ago, the tendency of physicists who think deeply about these things has been to reformulate quantum mechanics in an entirely objective way, with observers treated just like everything else. I don't know if this program has been completely successful yet, but I think it will be.

I have to admit that, even when physicists will have gone as far as they can go, when we have a final theory, we will not have a completely satisfying picture of the world, because we will still be left with the question "why?" Why this theory, rather than some other theory? For example, why is the world described by quantum mechanics? Quantum mechanics is the one part of our present physics that is likely to survive intact in any future theory, but there is nothing logically inevitable about quantum mechanics; I can imagine a universe governed by Newtonian mechanics instead. So there seems to be an irreducible mystery that science will not eliminate.

But religious theories of design have the same problem. Either you mean something definite by a God, a designer, or you don't. If you don't, then what are we talking about? If you do mean something definite by "God" or "design," if for instance you believe in a God who is jealous, or loving, or intelligent, or whimsical, then you still must confront the question "why?" A religion may assert that the universe is governed by that sort of God, rather than some other sort of God, and it may offer evidence for this belief, but it cannot explain why this should be so.

In this respect, it seems to me that physics is in a better position to give us a partly satisfying explanation of the world than religion can ever be, because although physicists won't be able to explain why the laws of nature are what they are and not something completely different, at least we may be able to explain why they are not slightly different. For instance, no one has been able to think of a logically consistent alternative to quantum mechanics that is only slightly different. Once you start trying to make small changes in quantum mechanics, you get into theories with negative probabilities or other logical absurdities. When you combine quantum mechanics with relativity you increase its logical fragility. You find that unless you arrange the theory in just the right way you get nonsense, like effects preceding causes, or infinite probabilities. Religious theories, on the other hand, seem to be infinitely flexible, with nothing to prevent the invention of deities of any conceivable sort.

Now, it doesn't settle the matter for me to say that we cannot see the hand of a designer in what we know about the fundamental principles of science. It might be that, although these principles do not refer explicitly to life, much less human life, they are nevertheless craftily designed to bring it about.

Some physicists have argued that certain constants of nature have values that seem to have been mysteriously fine-tuned to just the values that allow for the possibility of life, in a way that could only be explained by the intervention of a designer with some special concern for life. I am not impressed with these supposed instances of fine-tuning. For instance, one of the most frequently quoted examples of fine-tuning has to do with a property of the nucleus of the carbon atom. The matter left over from the first few minutes of the universe was almost entirely hydrogen and helium, with virtually none of the heavier elements like carbon, nitrogen, and oxygen that seem to be necessary for life. The heavy elements that we find on earth were built up hundreds of millions of years later in a first generation of stars, and then spewed out into the interstellar gas out of which our solar system eventually formed.

The first step in the sequence of nuclear reactions that created the heavy elements in early stars is usually the formation of a carbon nucleus out of three helium nuclei. There is a negligible chance of producing a carbon nucleus in its normal state (the state of lowest energy) in collisions of three helium nuclei, but it would be possible to produce appreciable amounts of carbon in stars if the carbon nucleus could exist in a radioactive state with an energy roughly 7 million electron volts (MeV) above the energy of the normal state, matching the energy of three helium nuclei, but (for reasons I'll come to presently) not more than 7.7 MeV above the normal state.

This radioactive state of a carbon nucleus could be easily formed in stars from three helium nuclei. After that, there would be no problem in producing ordinary carbon; the carbon nucleus in its radioactive state would spontaneously emit light and turn into carbon in its normal nonradioactive state, the state found on earth. The critical point in producing carbon is the existence of a radioactive state that can be produced in collisions of three helium nuclei.

In fact, the carbon nucleus is known experimentally to have just such a radioactive state, with an energy 7.65 MeV above the normal state. At first sight this may seem like a pretty close call; the energy of this radioactive state of carbon misses being too high to allow the formation of carbon (and hence of us) by only 0.05 MeV, which is less than one percent of 7.65 MeV. It may appear that the constants of nature on which the properties of all nuclei depend have been carefully fine-tuned to make life possible.

Looked at more closely, the fine-tuning of the constants of nature here does not seem so fine. We have to consider the reason why the formation of carbon in stars requires the existence of a radioactive state of carbon with an energy not more than 7.7 MeV above the energy of the normal state. The reason is that the carbon nuclei in this state are actually formed in a two-step process: first, two helium nuclei combine to form the unstable nucleus of a beryllium isotope, beryllium 8, which occasionally, before it falls apart, captures another helium nucleus, forming a carbon nucleus in its radioactive state, which then decays into normal carbon. The total energy of the beryllium 8 nucleus and a helium nucleus at rest is 7.4 MeV above the energy of the normal state of the carbon nucleus; so if the energy of the radioactive state of carbon were more than 7.7 MeV it could only be formed in a collision of a helium nucleus and a beryllium 8 nucleus if the energy of motion of these two nuclei were at least 0.3 MeV—an energy which is extremely unlikely at the temperatures found in stars.

Thus the crucial thing that affects the production of carbon in stars is not the 7.65 MeV energy of the radioactive state of carbon above its normal state, but the 0.25 MeV energy of the radioactive state, an unstable composite of a beryllium 8 nucleus and a helium nucleus, above the energy of those nuclei at rest.[7] This energy misses being too high for the production of carbon by a fractional amount of 0.05 MeV/0.25 MeV, or 20 percent, which is not such a close call after all.

This conclusion about the lessons to be learned from carbon synthesis is somewhat controversial. In any case, there is one constant whose value does seem remarkably well adjusted in our favor. It is the energy density of empty space, also known as the cosmological constant. It could have any value, but from first principles one would guess that this constant should be very large, and could be positive or negative. If large and positive, the cosmological constant would act as a repulsive force that increases with distance, a force that would prevent matter from clumping together in the early universe, the process that was the first step in forming galaxies and stars and planets and people. If large and negative the cosmological constant would act as an attractive force increasing with distance, a force that would almost immediately reverse the expansion of the universe and cause it to recollapse, leaving no time for the evolution of life. In fact, astronomical observations show that the cosmological constant is quite small, very much smaller than would have been guessed from first principles.

It is still too early to tell whether there is some fundamental principle that can explain why the cosmological constant must be this small. But even if there is no such principle, recent developments in cosmology offer the possibility of an explanation of why the measured values of the cosmological constant and other physical constants are favorable for the appearance of intelligent life. According to the "chaotic inflation" theories of André Linde

---

[7] This was pointed out in a 1989 paper by M. Livio, D. Hollowell, A. Weiss, and J. W. Truran ("The anthropic significance of the existence of an excited state of 12C," *Nature*, vol. 340, no. 6231 [July 27, 1989]). They did the calculation quoted here of the 7.7 MeV maximum energy of the radioactive state of carbon, above which little carbon is formed in stars. —*SW*.

and others, the expanding cloud of billions of galaxies that we call the big bang may be just one fragment of a much larger universe in which big bangs go off all the time, each one with different values for the fundamental constants.

In any such picture, in which the universe contains many parts with different values for what we call the constants of nature, there would be no difficulty in understanding why these constants take values favorable to intelligent life. There would be a vast number of big bangs in which the constants of nature take values unfavorable for life, and many fewer where life is possible. You don't have to invoke a benevolent designer to explain why we are in one of the parts of the universe where life is possible: in all the other parts of the universe there is no one to raise the question.[8] If any theory of this general type turns out to be correct, then to conclude that the constants of nature have been fine-tuned by a benevolent designer would be like saying, "Isn't it wonderful that God put us here on earth, where there's water and air and the surface gravity and temperature are so comfortable, rather than some horrid place, like Mercury or Pluto?" Where else in the solar system other than on earth could we have evolved?

Reasoning like this is called "anthropic." Sometimes it just amounts to an assertion that the laws of nature are what they are so that we can exist, without further explanation. This seems to me to be little more than mystical mumbo jumbo. On the other hand, if there really is a large number of worlds in which some constants take different values, then the anthropic explanation of why in our world they take values favorable for life is just common sense, like explaining why we live on the earth rather than Mercury

---

[8] The same conclusion may be reached in a more subtle way when quantum mechanics is applied to the whole universe. Through a reinterpretation of earlier work by Stephen Hawking, Sidney Coleman has shown how quantum mechanical effects can lead to a split of the history of the universe (more precisely, in what is called the wave function of the universe) into a huge number of separate possibilities, each one corresponding to a different set of fundamental constants. See Sidney Coleman, "Black Holes as Red Herrings: Topological fluctuations and the loss of quantum coherence," *Nuclear Physics*, Vol. B307 (1988): 867. —SW.

or Pluto. The actual value of the cosmological constant, recently measured by observations of the motion of distant supernovas, is about what you would expect from this sort of argument: it is just about small enough so that it does not interfere much with the formation of galaxies. But we don't yet know enough about physics to tell whether there are different parts of the universe in which what are usually called the constants of physics really do take different values. This is not a hopeless question; we will be able to answer it when we know more about the quantum theory of gravitation than we do now.

It would be evidence for a benevolent designer if life were better than could be expected on other grounds. To judge this, we should keep in mind that a certain capacity for pleasure would readily have evolved through natural selection, as an incentive to animals who need to eat and breed in order to pass on their genes. It may not be likely that natural selection on any one planet would produce animals who are fortunate enough to have the leisure and the ability to do science and think abstractly, but our sample of what is produced by evolution is very biased, by the fact that it is only in these fortunate cases that there is anyone thinking about cosmic design. Astronomers call this a selection effect.

The universe is very large, and perhaps infinite, so it should be no surprise that, among the enormous number of planets that may support only unintelligent life and the still vaster number that cannot support life at all, there is some tiny fraction on which there are living beings who are capable of thinking about the universe, as we are doing here. A journalist who has been assigned to interview lottery winners may come to feel that some special providence has been at work on their behalf, but he should keep in mind the much larger number of lottery players whom he is not interviewing because they haven't won anything. Thus, to judge whether our lives show evidence for a benevolent designer, we have not only to ask whether life is better than would be expected in any case from what we know about natural selection, but we need also to take into account the bias introduced by the fact that it is we who are thinking about the problem.

This is a question that you all will have to answer for yourselves. Being a physicist is no help with questions like this, so I have to speak from my own experience. My life has been remarkably happy, perhaps in the upper 99.99 percentile of human happiness, but even so, I have seen a mother die painfully of cancer, a father's personality destroyed by Alzheimer's disease, and scores of second and third cousins murdered in the Holocaust. Signs of a benevolent designer are pretty well hidden.

The prevalence of evil and misery has always bothered those who believe in a benevolent and omnipotent God. Sometimes God is excused by pointing to the need for free will. Milton gives God this argument in *Paradise Lost*:

> I formed them free, and free they must remain
> Till they enthral themselves: I else must change
> Their nature, and revoke the high decree
> Unchangeable, eternal, which ordained
> Their freedom; they themselves ordained their fall.

It seems a bit unfair to my relatives to be murdered in order to provide an opportunity for free will for Germans, but even putting that aside, how does free will account for cancer? Is it an opportunity of free will for tumors?

I don't need to argue here that the evil in the world proves that the universe is not designed, but only that there are no signs of benevolence that might have shown the hand of a designer. But in fact the perception that God cannot be benevolent is very old. Plays by Aeschylus and Euripides make a quite explicit statement that the gods are selfish and cruel, though they expect better behavior from humans. God in the Old Testament tells us to bash the heads of infidels and demands of us that we be willing to sacrifice our children's lives at His orders, and the God of traditional Christianity and Islam damns us for eternity if we do not worship him in the right manner. Is this a nice way to behave? I know, I know, we are not supposed to judge God according to human standards, but you see the problem here: If we are not yet convinced of

His existence, and are looking for signs of His benevolence, then what other standards can we use?

The issues that I have been asked to address here will seem to many to be terribly old-fashioned. The "argument from design" made by the English theologian William Paley is not on most people's minds these days. The prestige of religion seems today to derive from what people take to be its moral influence, rather than from what they may think has been its success in accounting for what we see in nature. Conversely, I have to admit that, although I really don't believe in a cosmic designer, the reason that I am taking the trouble to argue about it is that I think that on balance the moral influence of religion has been awful.

This is much too big a question to be settled here. On one side, I could point out endless examples of the harm done by religious enthusiasm, through a long history of pogroms, crusades, and jihads. In our own century it was a Muslim zealot who killed Sadat, a Jewish zealot who killed Rabin, and a Hindu zealot who killed Gandhi. No one would say that Hitler was a Christian zealot, but it is hard to imagine Nazism taking the form it did without the foundation provided by centuries of Christian anti-Semitism. On the other side, many admirers of religion would set countless examples of the good done by religion. For instance, in his recent book *Imagined Worlds*, the distinguished physicist Freeman Dyson has emphasized the role of religious belief in the suppression of slavery. I'd like to comment briefly on this point, not to try to prove anything with one example but just to illustrate what I think about the moral influence of religion.

It is certainly true that the campaign against slavery and the slave trade was greatly strengthened by devout Christians, including the Evangelical layman William Wilberforce in England and the Unitarian minister William Ellery Channing in America. But Christianity, like other great world religions, lived comfortably with slavery for many centuries, and slavery was endorsed in the New Testament. So what was different for anti-slavery Christians like Wilberforce and Channing? There had been no discovery of new sacred scriptures, and neither Wilberforce nor Channing claimed to have received any supernatural revelations. Rather, the eighteenth century had seen a widespread increase in rationality and humanitarianism that led others—for instance, Adam Smith, Jeremy Bentham, and Richard Brinsley Sheridan—also to oppose slavery, on grounds having nothing to do with religion. Lord Mansfield, the author of the decision in Somersett's Case, which ended slavery in England (though not its colonies), was no more than conventionally religious, and his decision did not mention religious arguments. Although Wilberforce was the instigator of the campaign against the slave trade in the 1790s, this movement had essential support from many in Parliament like Fox and Pitt, who were not known for their piety. As far as I can tell, the moral tone of religion benefited more from the spirit of the times than the spirit of the times benefited from religion.

Where religion did make a difference, it was more in support of slavery than in opposition to it. Arguments from scripture were used in Parliament to defend the slave trade. Frederick Douglass told in his Narrative how his condition as a slave became worse when his master underwent a religious conversion that allowed him to justify slavery as the punishment of the children of Ham. Mark Twain described his mother as a genuinely good person, whose soft heart pitied even Satan, but who had no doubt about the legitimacy of slavery, because in years of living in antebellum Missouri she had never heard any sermon opposing slavery, but only countless sermons preaching that slavery was God's will. With or without religion, good people can behave well and bad people can do evil; but for good people to do evil—that takes religion.

In an e-mail message from the American Association for the Advancement of Science I learned that the aim of this conference is to have a constructive dialogue between science and religion. I am all in favor of a dialogue between science and religion, but not a constructive dialogue. One of the great achievements of science has been, if not to make it impossible for intelligent people to be religious, then at least to make it possible for them not to be religious. We should not retreat from this accomplishment.

What about God?[9]

Of course, like any other word, the word "God" can be given any meaning we like. If you want to say that "God is energy," then you can find God in a lump of coal. But if words are to have any value to us, we ought to respect the way that they have been used historically, and we ought to preserve distinctions that prevent the meanings of words from merging with the meanings of other words.

&

In this spirit, it seems to me that if the word "God" is to be of any use, it should be taken to mean an interested God, a creator and lawgiver who has established not only the laws of nature and the universe but also standards of good and evil, some personality that is concerned with our actions, something in short that it is appropriate for us to worship. This is the God that has mattered to men and women throughout history. Scientists and others sometimes use the word "God" to mean something so abstract and unengaged that He is hardly to be distinguished from the laws of nature. Einstein once said that he believed in "Spinoza's God who reveals Himself in the orderly harmony of what exists, not in a God who concerns himself with fates and actions of human beings." But what possible difference does it make to anyone if we use the word "God" in place of "order" or "harmony," except perhaps to avoid the accusation of having no God? Of course, anyone is free to use the word "God" in that way, but it seems to me that it makes the concept of God not so much wrong as unimportant.

&

The inconsistency between the modern theory of evolution and belief in an interested God does not seem to me one of logic—one can imagine that God established the laws of nature and set the

[9] Steven Weinberg, *Dreams of a Final Theory* (New York: Pantheon Books, 1992), 195, 244–45, 248, 250, 250–51.

mechanism of evolution in motion with the intention that through natural selection you and I would someday appear—but there is real inconsistency in temperament. After all, religion did not arise in the minds of men and women who speculated about infinitely prescient first causes but in the hearts of those who longed for the continual intervention of an interested God.

❧

Judging from this historical experience, I would guess that, though we shall find beauty in the final laws of nature, we will find no special status for life or intelligence. *A fortiori*, we will find no standards of value or morality. And so we will find no hint of any God who cares about such things. We may find these things elsewhere, but not in the laws of nature.

❧

Religious people have grappled for millennia with theodicy, the problem posed by the existence of suffering in a world that is supposed to be ruled by a good God. They have found ingenious solutions in terms of various supposed divine plans. I will not try to argue with these solutions, much less to add one more of my own. Remembrance of the Holocaust leaves me unsympathetic to attempts to justify the ways of God to man. If there is a God that has special plans for humans, then He has taken very great pains to hide His concern for us. To me it would seem impolite if not impious to bother such a God with our prayers.

A Pointless Universe?[10]

QUESTION: You have written that the more comprehensible the universe becomes the more pointless it seems. Could you explain what you mean by that?

---

[10] "Steven Weinberg," *Faith and Reason*, PBS, transcript, accessed May 11, 2005. http://www.pbs.org/faithandreason/transcript/wein-body.html.

MR. WEINBERG: Years ago I wrote a book about cosmology, and near the end I tried to summarize the view of the expanding universe and the laws of nature. And I made the remark—I guess I was foolish enough to make the remark—that the more the universe seems comprehensible the more it seems pointless. And that remark has been quoted more than anything else I've ever said. It's even in *Bartlett's Quotations*. I think it's been the truth in the past that it was widely hoped that by studying nature we will find the sign of a grand plan, in which human beings play a particularly distinguished starring role. And that has not happened. I think that more and more the picture of nature, the outside world, has been one of an impersonal world governed by mathematical laws that are not particularly concerned with human beings, in which human beings appear as a chance phenomenon, not the goal toward which the universe is directed. And for some this has no effect on their religion. Their religion never looked for any kind of point in nature. For others this is appalling, the idea that all of the stars and galaxies and atoms are going about their business, and it's just by accident that here on this solar system the peculiar chemical properties of DNA acting over billions of years have produced these people who have been able to talk and look around and enjoy life. For some people that picture is antithetical to the view of nature and the world that their religion had given them.

QUESTION: Do you believe then there is no overall point to the universe?

MR. WEINBERG: I believe that there is no point in the universe that can be discovered by the methods of science. I believe that what we have found so far, an impersonal universe in which it is not particularly directed toward human beings is what we are going to continue to find. And that when we find the ultimate laws of nature they will have a chilling, cold impersonal quality about them.

I don't think this means [however] there's no point to life. Usually the remark is quoted just as it stands. But if anyone read the next paragraph, they would see that I went on to say that if there is no point in the universe that we discover by the methods of science, there is a point that we can give the universe by the way we live, by loving each other, by discovering things about nature, by creating works of art. And that—in a way, although we are not the stars in a cosmic drama, if the only drama we're starring in is one that we are making up as we go along, it is not entirely ignoble that faced with this unloving, impersonal universe we make a little island of warmth and love and science and art for ourselves. That's not an entirely despicable role for us to play.

QUESTION: What is your response to scientists like Paul Davies, who say they do see a point to the universe and they think that science itself supports that?

MR. WEINBERG: I think it's true that there is a mystery about nature which is not likely to be cleared up in any way that I can now foresee. That is, we can look forward to a theory which encompasses all existing theories, which unifies all the forces, all the particles, and at least in principle is capable of serving as the basis of an explanation of everything. We can look forward to that, but then the question will always arise, "Well, what explains that? Where does that come from?" And then we—looking at—standing at that brink of that abyss, we have to say we don't know, and how could we ever know, and how can we ever get comfortable with this sort of a world ruled by laws which just are what they are without any further explanation?

And coming to that point which I think we will come to, some would say, well, then the explanation is God made it so. And I suppose that's a natural reaction to this dilemma. Unfortunately to me it seems quite unsatisfactory. Either by God you mean something definite or you don't mean something definite. If by God you mean a personality who is concerned about human beings, who did all this out of love for human beings, who watches us and who intervenes, then I would have to say in the first place, how do you know, what makes you think so? And in the second place, is that really an explanation? If that's true, what explains that? Why is there such a God? It isn't the end of the chain of whys, it just is another step, and you have to take the step beyond that.

I think much more often, however, when a physicist says, "Well, then the explanation is God," they don't mean anything particular by it. That's just the word they apply. Einstein said that he didn't believe in a God who was concerned with human affairs, who intervenes in human life, but a God who was simply an abstract principle of harmony and order.

And so then I rather grieve that they use the word "God," because I do think one should have some loyalty to the way words are used historically, and that's not what people have historically meant by "God"—not an abstract principle of harmony and order. If that's all you mean by it, if God is practically synonymous with the laws of nature, then we don't need the word. Why not just say the laws of nature? It isn't that it's wrong, because after all G-O-D is just a set of letters of the alphabet, and you can let it mean anything you like. But if language is to be of any use to us, we ought to try to preserve the meanings of words, and "God" historically has not meant the laws of nature. It has meant an interested personality. And that's not something we're finding scientifically. It's not something for which I see any evidence.

QUESTION: In some sense do you think this quest for a "final theory" of physics—a theory that would unite all the forces of nature under one unified umbrella—in some sense is that like a religious quest? Is it like a quest for the ultimate source of order and creation, which is one aspect of God in traditional Judeo-Christianity?

MR. WEINBERG: I think a lot of intellectual energy over the centuries has gone into religious matters. Think of all the monks devoting themselves to fine points of theological doctrine—monks and rabbis and bonzes and Moabs, imams, down through the years devoting so much talent and energy to questions of theology. In a way science provides an alternative way of using your mind. This is something else where you can use human intelligence. It has several advantages. It has the advantage that we have ways of finding out we're wrong about things. I've had that experience in my life—most scientists have—of having a theory that I thought was bound to be right shown to be wrong by experiments—it's a very cleansing experience.

We scientists also have ways of coming to solutions about things. There are things about which now there is universal agreement as compared with the situation in theology. So in a way the same kind of intellectual activity goes on in science as has historically been devoted to religion. But I think with several distinct advantages.

QUESTION: What do you think about this new dialogue between science and religion that's taking place now?

MR. WEINBERG: I know there's been a lot of talk about a reconciliation between science and religion, of ending the old conflict. And in a way it's a good thing. Certainly science in trying to get public support doesn't need to have a conflict with religion going on at the same time. In another sense I tend to deplore it. I think that part of the historical mission of science has been to teach us that we are not the playthings of supernatural intervention, that we can make our own way in the universe, and that we have to find our own sense of morality. We have to find our own sense of what we should love. And I would hate to have those gains made by science vitiated by a misguided reconciliation with religious life.

QUESTION: Do you think religion has value?

MR. WEINBERG: I think there's much to be said on both sides of that. I mean, certainly religion has produced great art. Where would architecture be without the great cathedrals and wonderful Japanese temples, and mosques?

On the moral side, however, I'm less sure about it. Certainly good causes have sometimes been mobilized under the banner of religion, but you find the opposite I think more often the case. It's more often been the motivation for us to kill each other—not only for people of one religion to kill those of another, but even within religions. After all, it was a Moslem who killed Sadat. It was a devout Jew who killed Rabin. It was a devout Hindu who killed Gandhi. And this has been going on for centuries and centuries.

I think in many respects religion is a dream—a beautiful dream often. Often a nightmare. But it's a dream from which I think it's about time we awoke. Just as a child learns about the tooth fairy and is incited by that to leave a tooth under the pillow—and you're glad that the child believes in the tooth fairy. But eventually you want the child to grow up. I think it's about time that the human species grew up in this respect.

Further Reading

For general readers, two of Weinberg's books, *The First Three Minutes: A Modern View of the Origin of the Universe* (New York: Basic Books, 1993[1977]) and *Dreams of a Final Theory* (New York: Pantheon Books, 1992), deal with the origin of the universe and the ultimate laws of nature in a clear and accessible manner. *Facing Up: Science and Its Cultural Adversaries* (Cambridge, MA: Harvard University Press, 2001) is a collection of twenty-three essays written by Weinberg over a fifteen-year period, "facing up" to the facts that the laws of nature are impersonal, there is no discernible divine plan, and human beings do not have a starring role in the drama of the universe. See also "An Exchange between Steven Weinberg and John Polkinghorne," in *Cosmic Questions*, edited by James B. Miller, Annals of the New York Academy of Sciences 950 (New York: NYAS, 2001), 183–90, reprinted in the next chapter of this volume; Steven Weinberg, "Free People from Superstition," *Freethought Today* 17 (2000); "Steven Weinberg 2002 Humanist of the Year," *Humanist* 62 (2002); and Steven Weinberg, "Can Science Explain Everything? Anything?" *New York Review of Books*, May 31, 2001.

15 John Polkinghorne
(1930–)

Introduction

Regarded by some as the C. S. Lewis of science-religion dialogues, John Polkinghorne, physicist, priest, and prolific author, is the finest British theologian/scientist of our time. His career path began with an appointment as professor of mathematical physics at the University of Cambridge, a position he held for twenty-five years. Resigning this chair in 1979 in order to study for ordination in the Church of England, he worked as a parish priest for a period before eventually returning to Cambridge in 1986 as dean of Trinity Hall. Subsequently, Polkinghorne was appointed president of Queen's College, a post which he held till his retirement in 1997. Like many traditional Christians, Polkinghorne believes in the Trinity, the virgin birth, the empty tomb, and the post-resurrection appearances of Christ. Introducing his book *The Faith of a Physicist*, he observed, "I do not find that a Trinitarian and incarnational theology needs to be abandoned in favor of a toned-down theology of a Cosmic Mind and an Inspired Teacher, alleged to be more accessible to the modern mind."[1]

---

[1] John Polkinghorne, *The Faith of a Physicist: Reflections of a Bottom-Up Thinker* (Minneapolis: Fortress Press, 1996), 1.

Many of Polkinghorne's books address the general looseness and bagginess of nature as revealed by chaos theory and its significance in thinking about the mode of divine action. Rather than explore the idea of divine action by way of the loophole of quantum uncertainty, he is interested in dynamical systems on a macro scale. All complex systems, as we know, display a double nature, as part energy and part pattern. They have an orderly disorder. They evolve in a somewhat haphazard manner, but one that involves only a certain number of possible patterns of motion called "strange attractors." These patterns differ in the details of how they will evolve, but not in the amount of energy they contain. "Bottom-up" analysis describes the energy exchanged between the parts of the system, while "top-down" descriptions have to do with an agency that forms patterns out of possibilities left indeterminate at the lower level. According to Polkinghorne, God interacts with the world through information input into open physical process, a kind of selection agency among options. Unlike creatures, however, God's information input expends no energy, and so God should not be thought of as an invisible actor on the cosmic stage. More like the director of a vast improvisatory troupe, God is the improviser of unsurpassed ingenuity.

A longstanding motif in Polkinghorne's writings is the question from whence the ordering of the world comes. His answer rests upon a version of the anthropic principle, which says biological life in its lowest as well as its most highly evolved forms is the whole point and purpose of the cosmos. Polkinghorne believes that physics should not determine metaphysics, although it may constrain it. The central metaphysical question, he says, is one of scope. In a Theory of Everything is the realm of the personal as important to take into account as that of the impersonal? Polkinghorne affirms that it is. Science raises questions of intelligibility and anthropic fine-tuning that go beyond its own self-limited power to answer. Theism, he believes, provides a coherent response, as well as furnishing a foundation for the human encounter with value. Evolutionary understanding affords some insight into the problems of physical evil emphasized by unbelievers, but the prospect of eventual cosmic futility can only find an answer in what Polkinghorne calls the faithfulness of a Creator whose purposes are not frustrated by death.

In the previous chapter, Steven Weinberg's faith in an undesigned universe was featured. This chapter consists of the entirety of John Polkinghorne's reply to Weinberg as part of their celebrated debate on the question of design at the American Association for the Advancement of Science in 1999. It is followed by an interview with the two physicists conducted by the eminent astronomer Owen Gingerich.

ꙮ Polkinghorne's Contribution to Science

John Polkinghorne distinguished himself in the field of elementary particle physics, creating mathematical models to calculate the paths of quantum particles. He played a significant role in the discovery of the quark and authored two technical scientific books, The Analytic S-Matrix *(jointly with R. J. Eden, P. V. Landshoff and D. I. Olive, 1966) and* Models of High Energy Processes *(1980). Since resigning his post as professor of mathematical physics at Cambridge University and turning to theology, his books and articles on the relationship between science and theology have earned him an international reputation as one of the leading thinkers attempting to correlate the conundrums of quantum physics with the mysteries of the Christian faith. In 1997 Queen Elizabeth II knighted him for distinguished service to science, religion, learning, and medical ethics.*

Polkinghorne in His Own Words

Understanding the Universe[2]

Is the universe designed? If it is, we shall not learn about it by looking for items trademarked "The Heavenly Construction

---

[2] John Polkinghorne, "Understanding the Universe," in *Cosmic Questions*, ed. James B. Miller. Annals of the New York Academy of Sciences, vol. 950 (New York: New York Academy of Sciences, 2001): 175–90.

Company," any more than, if it is not designed, we shall learn that by finding objects stamped "Blind Chance Rules." Science by itself will not tell us the answer to this question, either in the positive or in the negative. The reason for this is simple. The question of design is a metaphysical question, a question that goes "beyond" *(meta)* physics, and metaphysical questions must receive metaphysical answers, given for metaphysical reasons. Physics—or science generally—constrains metaphysics, but it does not determine it, just as the foundations of a house constrain what can be built on them, but they do not determine the actual form of the edifice. You can get the idea by thinking about another metaphysical issue: the nature of causality. Take non-relativistic quantum mechanics. Is it an indeterministic theory or not? Niels Bohr says Yes; David Bohm says No. Their interpretations are completely contrasting, but their radically different theories both lead to the same physical consequences. There is no empirical scientific test that can settle the matter between them. Whether they are aware of it or not, the 99.9% of physicists (among whom I number myself) who take the conventional view of an indeterministic quantum mechanics, do so for metascientific reasons. Chief among these is the belief that Bohm's very clever ideas are, in fact, too clever by half, for they have a metaphysically unattractive air of contrivance about them.

That judgment illustrates the sort of considerations that are relevant to assessing metaphysical proposals. The criteria include a variety of desirable properties, many of which we also associate with a successful fundamental physical theory: economy, elegance, naturalness, and adequacy to experience. As we know in the case of science itself, these characteristics are not always easy to define in a watertight way, but it is often not difficult to find agreement in a truth-seeking community about when they have been fulfilled. There is greater possibility for disagreement in metaphysics than in science, and one reason for that is that a very significant metaphysical criterion is that of *scope*. How wide-embracing should be the understanding that the theory will afford us? What range of experience should it take into account? I shall be arguing today for a generously conceived metaphysic that takes personal experience as seriously as impersonal, and I shall be rejecting what I see as a narrow scientism. Some of the disagreements among us will certainly stem from this question of the breadth of phenomena we are trying to understand.

Although we are rightly impressed by the many things that science can account for satisfactorily, we should also recognize that this great success has been purchased by a degree of modesty of ambition. Science limits itself to considering only certain kinds of experience. Broadly speaking, its concern is with the impersonal dimension of reality. Galileo had the brilliant idea, followed so strictly by successive generations of physicists, of confining attention to the primary quantities of matter and motion, and to set aside what he called the secondary characteristics of human perception, such as color. This neglect of what the philosophers call *qualia* (that is to say, feelings such as seeing red or judging someone to be trustworthy) was an immensely successful technique of investigation. It would, however, be a very bad mistake to equate Galileo's methodological strategy with an act of ontological judgment—that is to say, a verdict on the nature of reality. Such a confusion would, in my view, result in a woefully inadequate metaphysics. Physics may tell us that music is vibrations in the air, and neurophysiology may describe the consequent patterns of neuron excitation that result from those airwaves impinging on the eardrum, but to suppose that this discourse is adequate to the phenomenon of music would be totally misleading. The mystery and reality of music slips through the wide meshes of the scientific net.

Metaphysics cannot tolerate such an impoverished scientism, for its grand aim is truly to be a Theory of Everything, obtained, not by Procrustean truncation of experience until it has been reduced to a scale so limited that it can be condensed into a formula that can be written on a T-shirt, but by taking absolutely seriously the many-layered richness of the reality in which we live. It will not grant an automatic priority of the objective over the subjective, of the impersonal over the personal, of the repeatable over the unique.

Interestingly enough, some of these wider issues that a true metaphysics must consider relate to questions that arise from our experience as scientists, but that go beyond the merely scientific. They center round two great metaquestions: Why is science possible at all? Why is the universe so special?

Those of us privileged to be scientists are so excited by the quest to understand the workings of the physical world that we seldom stop to ask ourselves why we are so fortunate. Human powers of rational comprehension vastly exceed anything that could be simply an evolutionary necessity for survival, or plausibly construed as some sort of collateral spin-off from such a necessity. How could that kind of argument possibly relate to our amazing ability to understand the strange and counterintuitive quantum world of subatomic physics, or to comprehend the cosmic structure of curved space? The point is reinforced by considering what the Nobel Prize–winning physicist, Eugene Wigner, called "the unreasonable effectiveness of mathematics." Wigner's brother-in-law, Paul Dirac, one of the founding fathers of quantum mechanics, said that his fundamental belief was that the laws of physics are expressed in "beautiful equations." The relentless and highly successful pursuit of a beautiful equation was how Dirac discovered the relativistic equation of the electron, and consequently antimatter. Einstein discovered the equations of general relativity in a similar fashion.

Mathematics is abstract human thinking. When this most austere of subjects proves to be the key to unlock the secrets of the physical universe, something very unexpected is happening. The unreasonable effectiveness of mathematics is a phenomenon that the mathematicians, in their modest way of speaking, would call "non-trivial." Non-trivial is a mathematical word meaning "highly significant." This raises the metaquestion of why this is the case.

In dealing with a question of that kind, I want first of all to say two things by way of preliminaries. One is that it is a question that should be pressed. My instinct as a scientist is to seek understanding through and through and it seems to me that it would be intolerably intellectually lazy just to shrug one's shoulders and say

"That's just the way it is—and a bit of good luck for you people who are good at mathematics." The second thing I want to say is that deep metaphysical questions of this kind are too profound to have simple knockdown answers to them. When we enter the realm of metaphysical enquiry, we are in a domain where no one has access to absolute rational certainty. For that reason, I could not use so curt and categorical a title for my talk as that chosen by Steve Weinberg for his. This character of metaphysical argument does not mean that we shall not have reasons for the answers that we propose, for stating them will involve invoking the metaphysically desirable properties I have already discussed, particularly that of scope. However, none of us can pretend that our answers are logically coercive in a $2 + 2 = 4$ way. I am going to propose theistic responses to the questions we are concerned with. I think I have good reasons for my beliefs, but I do not for a moment suppose that my atheistic friends are simply stupid not to see it my way. I do believe, however, that religious belief can explain more than unbelief can do.

Back then to the metaquestion of why science is possible at all in the deep way that it is. I have described a physical world whose rational transparency makes theoretical physics possible and whose rational beauty guides and rewards those who inquire into its structure. In a phrase, it is a world shot through "with signs of mind." I believe that it is an attractive, coherent, and intellectually satisfying explanation of this fact that there is indeed a divine Mind behind the scientifically discerned rational order of the universe. In fact, I believe that science is possible because the physical world is a creation and we are, to use an ancient and powerful phrase, creatures "made in the image" of the Creator (Genesis 1:26). I regard this insight as the primary ground for believing that the universe is designed. I make no apology for speaking in theistic terms, for if the universe is designed, who could be its designer other than a Creator-God?

A second reason for that belief can be found in the answer to my second metaquestion: Why is the universe so special? Of course, here I am referring to the findings of the Anthropic Principle.

Other contributors to this volume have already outlined the many considerations that lead us to conclude that the laws of nature as we observe them in our universe are precisely those that permit the development of carbon-based life, in the sense that even very small changes in intrinsic force strengths would have broken links in the long, delicate and beautiful chain of consequences linking the early universe to the existence of life today here on Earth. I agree with John Leslie's analysis, presented in his book *Universes*, that suggests, firstly that it would be irrational just to shrug this off as a happy accident, and secondly that there are two broad categories of possible explanation: either many universes with a vast variety of different natural laws instantiated in them, of which ours is the one that by chance has allowed us to appear within its history; or a single universe that is the way it is because it is not "any old world," but a creation that has been endowed by its Creator with just the circumstances that will allow it to have a fruitful history. I simply want to make two comments on this analysis.

The first is to emphasize that *both* proposals are metaphysical in character. That is clear enough in the case of creation, but it is also true of a many-universes proposal that is wide enough in scope actually to serve as an explanation. Of course, an inflation-expanded structure, containing many domains with differing consequences of spontaneous symmetry breaking, could give vast regions in which effective force constants differed and in one of which they might take the anthropically desirable values, but that would still require that the overall Grand Unified Theory was constrained in its character in order to permit this to happen. Something specific and requiring explanation would remain. I regard quantum cosmology and baby universes as being too precarious and speculative in character at present to rely on. In any case, the underlying theory would again have to take an appropriate form. One might comment that quantum theory, general relativity and suitable matter fields do not "come for free," so to speak. It is important to recognize that anthropic fruitfulness requires the right kinds of laws as well as the right values for the parameters appearing in those laws. It is very difficult to see what could ensure this right character of fundamental physical law, realizing the necessary combination of flexibility and stability required to make fruitful evolution possible, other than a strictly metaphysical proposal.

The second point is to agree with Leslie that, in relation to the Anthropic Principle, it is a metaphysically even-handed choice between many universes and creation. It seems to be six of one and half a dozen of the other, neatly illustrating the point I made that these kinds of argument are not knockdown in their character. However, I believe that, while the many-universes hypothesis seems to have only one explanatory piece of work that it can do, there are other kinds of explanation that the thesis of theism can afford, such as granting an understanding of the intelligibility of the universe, and also providing the ground for the widely attested phenomena of religious experience. (Of course, the history of religions is a tangled tale. Weinberg is right to draw our attention to the sad fact that religion can cause good people to do bad things, but we should also recognize that religious conversion has often led to bad people becoming able to do good things.) My conclusion is to prefer the explanation of anthropic fruitfulness in terms of a Creator, which strikes me as being more economic and forming part of a cumulative case for theism.

There are a number of other considerations that can be held to be relevant to the discussion of whether the universe is designed. One concerns what seems to me to be the most astonishing (and most significant) event known to us that has happened since the Big Bang. I refer, of course, to the dawning of self-consciousness here on Earth (and perhaps elsewhere). In us, the universe has become aware of itself. You remember that Blaise Pascal said that human beings are thinking *reeds*, so insubstantial on the grand scale of the cosmos, but we are *thinking* reeds, and so greater than all the stars, for we know them and ourselves and they know nothing. With, for example, Paul Davies in his book *The Mind of God*, I cannot regard this dawning of consciousness as being just a fortunate accident in the course of an essentially meaningless cosmic history. We know from the Anthropic Principle that the potentiality for this happening was present in the ground rules of the universe from the beginning. I see this striking emergence as a signal of meaningfulness, amounting to an intimation of intrinsic design. Something is going on in what is happening in cosmic process. Of course, I am talking in terms of a propensity to great fruitfulness. There is much that is contingent in the way that this has been realized. I am not claiming that it was laid down from all eternity that *Homo sapiens* should have five fingers! I will return later to the matter of contingency.

Meanwhile, let us recognize that our human self-consciousness enables us to look through many different windows onto reality. We are not confined to the impersonal scientific perspective of Galileo's primary quantities, but we have access to those personal qualities that Galileo set aside. I take with the greatest seriousness our human encounters with beauty and with moral imperative. I see them as affording us windows onto the reality within which we live and not, as I think Steven Weinberg does, as being internally constructed human attitudes through which we defy an intrinsically meaningless and hostile universe.

I have already drawn attention to science's inadequacy in relation to music. Its reductionist strategy can never do justice to a work of art, for a Leonardo painting is much more than a collection of specks of paint of known chemical composition. It would be a disastrous mistake to throw away the insights of aesthetics, for they must find their proper place in a true Theory of Everything.

I believe that the same is true of our ethical intuitions. I know something about what the anthropologists tell us about the cultural tricks of perspective that different societies impose upon their discernment of moral issues. Of course, we must pay attention to these matters but, when all is said and done, I personally cannot believe that my conviction that torturing children is wrong is just a convention of my society. It is a fact about reality, the way things are. We have access to moral knowledge, which is knowledge of a totally different kind from scientific knowledge, for ethical insights are more than disguised genetic survival strategies. If that were not so, what would be the grounds on which Richard Dawkins could, on the last page of *The Selfish Gene*, urge us to rebel against their influence?

A true cosmology—an adequate account of reality—will have to take these issues into account. The physical world that science describes is the carrier of beauty and the arena of moral decision, value-laden aspects of reality that science does not describe. One of the attractions of theism is that it offers a way of tying these different levels of experience together, which otherwise might seem so unconnected with each other. Just as we can understand the rational order of the world that science discovers, as being a reflection of the mind of its creator, so we can understand our aesthetic experience as being a sharing in the Creator's joy in creation, and our moral intuitions as being intimations of God's good and perfect will. And, I would want to add that dimension of human experience that testifies to a meeting with the sacred as being encounter with the divine presence.

But is there not a fatal flaw in all this argument? I refer to the greatest difficulty for theism, namely the problem of the evil and suffering so manifestly present in the world. I think that this problem holds more people back from religious belief than any other, and those of us who are believers can never be unaware of it, or untroubled by the challenge it presents. Could one really claim that so apparently dysfunctional a universe was one that exhibited design? Does not our very sense of value, to which I have appealed, make us rebel against a strange and bitter "creation"?

The questions proliferate. Is not evolutionary history a tale of struggle and competition, of death as the necessary cost of life, of the blind alleys of extinction that have dealt death blows to 99.9% of the species that have ever lived? Is not the role of chance, in the evolutionary interplay of chance and necessity, the conclusive sign that the universe's history is, as Macbeth said, "a tale told by an idiot, full of sound and fury, signifying nothing"?

I do not wish to deny that these are serious questions. But, in an unexpected way, science's insights have been moderately helpful to theology in its wrestling with the problem. The key concept, in fact, is evolution itself. It is historically ignorant to suppose, as the modern myth does, that Darwin was opposed by solid ranks of obscurantist clergymen when *The Origin of Species* was published in 1859. In both Britain and the United States there were Christians, like Charles Kingsley and Asa Gray, who welcomed his insights. Kingsley coined the phrase that, in a nutshell, sums up a theological understanding of evolution. He said that God had done something cleverer than producing a ready-made creation, for God had created a world "that could make itself." If there is a God who is the God of love, then creation could never be just the divine puppet theatre. The gift of love is always the gift of a due independence, as wise parents know in relation to their children. The God of love must be one who allows creatures to be themselves, and to make themselves by exploring the endowment of potentiality given to creation. "Chance" simply means historical contingency—this happens rather than that. It is not automatically to be given the tendentious adjective "blind," as if it were an unambiguous sign of meaninglessness. Rather, it may be seen as signifying the shuffling exploration and realization of fertile possibilities, by which creation makes itself. This due independence of process is a good gift, but it has a necessary cost attached to it. Raggednesses and blind alleys, as well as fruitful outcomes, are inescapable accompaniments of this evolving self-realization. Biology even helps theology a little with the deep question of theodicy, the problem of the evil and suffering of the world. Exactly the same biochemical processes that enable some cells to mutate and produce new forms of life—in other words, the very engine that has driven the stupendous four billion year history of life on Earth—these same processes will inevitably allow other cells to mutate and become malignant. In a non-magic world, it could not be different, and the world is not magic because its Creator is not a capricious Magician. I do not pretend for a moment that this insight removes all the perplexities posed by the sufferings of creation. Yet it affords some mild help, in that it suggests that the existence of cancer is not gratuitous, as if it were due to the Creator's callousness or incompetence. We all tend to think that if we had been in charge of creation we would have made a better job of it. We would have kept the nice things (flowers and sunsets) and got rid of the nasty (disease and disaster). The more science helps us to understand the process of the universe, the more, it seems to me, to cohere into a single "package deal." The light and the dark are two sides of the same coin.

One final threat to any claim that the universe is designed, as the expression of a divine purpose, needs to be considered. In a sense, it is the ultimate difficulty, for it concerns how things will end. As cosmologists peer into the universe's future, they tell us that the only honest answer is "badly." There are the two possible alternative scenarios of collapse or decay, but either way carbon-based life will prove to have been a transient cosmic episode, and eventually all is condemned to futility. We know about built-in obsolescence in car design, but surely Creatorly design should be able to do better than that? Can one wonder that Steven Weinberg notoriously said that the more he understood the universe, the more it seemed pointless to him? We have to consider what response theology can make to this.

I do not think that the problem posed by cosmic death on a time-scale of tens of billions of years is altogether different from the problem posed by the even more certain knowledge of our own deaths on a time-scale of tens of years. In each case, what seems to be put in question is the genuineness of the Creator's concern for creatures. Do they—do *we*—matter to God only transiently? Those of us who believe in the steadfast faithfulness of God must reply that creatures matter to God for ever. What cosmic and human death remind us of is that an evolutionary optimism, based on total fulfillment in terms of unfolding present process, is an illusion. Death is a real end, but it is not the ultimate end, because only God is ultimate. As a Christian speaking in this season of Easter, I affirm my belief in a destiny beyond death. Such a destiny could never arise naturally, but it can only be the outcome of a great divine redeeming act. To trust that that is God's ultimate purpose is an exciting and mysterious belief, which I cannot find time to explain and defend on this occasion, though I have sought to do so in some of my writings (*The Faith of a Physicist*).

I agree with Steve Weinberg that the issue of apparent cosmic futility is one of paramount importance. In reality, it is the question of whether the universe makes *total* sense or not. We disagree about the answer to that. Such disagreement is possible because, as I have repeatedly acknowledged in this paper, none of us has access to logical certainty in metaphysical matters. What I have sought to show is that religious believers who see a divine Mind and Purpose behind the universe are not shutting their eyes and irrationally believing impossible things. We have reasons for our beliefs. They have come to us through that search for motivated understanding that is so congenial to the scientist. That search, however, needs to be pursued in the widest possible context, including the insights of science but going beyond them, in the direction of the deepest and most comprehensive encounter with reality.

An Exchange between Steven Weinberg and John Polkinghorne Moderated by Owen Gingerich[3]

WEINBERG: First, let me respond to the parts of John's eloquent talk that dealt with a few scientific issues. I don't agree that the two metaphysical approaches to quantum mechanics are the probabilistic theory of Bohr and the deterministic theory of Bohm. With John, I don't think much of Bohm's reworking of quantum mechanics. What I would take as an alternative to the probabilistic view of quantum mechanics is a thoroughly deterministic view. After all, quantum mechanics in its basic equations is completely deterministic. The Schrodinger Equation tells us that if we know the wave function in any instant, we know precisely what it is at any future instant. There is no chaos, as in Newtonian mechanics, because the equations are perfectly linear. The problem always has been how to represent the observer

[3] *Cosmic Questions*, 183–90.

in the deterministic evolution of the wave function. This is a problem that is increasingly being solved, although not yet completely. But that's the opposition I would make: between the modern deterministic view, which sees the observer as part of the reality described by the wave function, and Bohr's view, in which the observer was something separate.

POLKINGHORNE: That is another way of setting it up, but you would agree that it is a metaphysical argument about . . .

WEINBERG: Yes, that's right and . . . it's just I don't think you should take David Bohm, as the representative of . . .

POLKINGHORNE: . . . but, of course, you are right.

WEINBERG: Another scientific question is about fine-tuning. As I said in my talk, I am not terribly impressed by the examples of fine-tuning of constants of nature that have been presented. To be a little bit more precise: the energy levels of carbon are the most notorious example of fine-tuning that is cited: there is an energy level that is 7.65 MeV above the ground state of carbon. If it was 0.06 of an MeV higher, then carbon production would be greatly diminished and there would be much less chance of life forming. That looks like a 1% fine-tuning of the constants of nature. If the energy level were lower, then there would be even more carbon produced. But it is striking that it could not be more than a percent higher. However, as has been realized subsequently after this "fine-tuning" was pointed out, you should really measure the energy level not above the ground state of carbon, but above the state of the nucleus beryllium 8 (^{8}Be) plus a helium nucleus. And it is only 0.28 MeV above that. In other words, the fine-tuning is not 1% but it's something like 25%. So, it's not very impressive fine-tuning at all. I'm not saying that none of these examples of fine-tuning will survive or that we won't discover others. I'm also not saying that the many-universe picture has been established. These are open questions. Are the constants of nature remarkably well adjusted to allow for the presence of life? We don't really know. And can they be explained by having many sub-universes? We don't really know that either. And indeed at any moment we may get evidence of a supernatural supervisor of the universe.

I mean suddenly in this auditorium a flaming sword may come and strike me for my impiety, and then we will know the answer.

POLKINGHORNE: Actually, we won't. But that's by the way.

WEINBERG: I don't agree that this is a metaphysical question. If there are these many terms in the wave function as Coleman[4] describes or many separate big bangs, as Linde[5] would have it, this is something that will appear in our scientific theories. It hasn't yet. We don't know this for sure. It has appeared as a possibility but it is not something that's going to remain a matter of metaphysical choice. Either our theories will show us that this is the case or they will not. And it will not be a matter of personal taste. At this moment the question is open.

To answer the question John raised—another question, one that he has raised before in his writings and that I thought I had answered in my talk. He asked "Why is it that we are so fortunate to be able to do quantum mechanics and to do mathematics? Is it really necessary from evolution that we should be able to do this?" And I would answer: no, it is not, that we are able to have such abstract thoughts and to be able to have the leisure to sit around talking about it. It may be, as I explained, that in the great majority of planets where life arises and evolves, only that measure of intelligence evolves that is strictly necessary for breeding and eating. However, those animals are not discussing the issue and the fact that we are discussing the issue creates a bias and naturally the people who are discussing the issue have intelligence and the leisure to discuss it.

Now, the points I have covered so far are, I think, minor points, but John also makes the big point that science is not everything. There is metaphysics in addition to physics—I agree, but I do look differently at the examples he gave.

---

[4] Sidney Coleman, *Nuclear Physics* B, vol. 310 (1988): 643. —*SW as modified by Ed.*

[5] Andre Linde, "The self-reproducing inflationary universe," in *The Magnificent Cosmos*, a *Scientific American* special issue (March 1998). —*SW as modified by Ed.*

It is certainly true that scientists are helped in their work by non-rational processes including an aesthetic sense of beauty, which is very well developed among mathematicians. Mathematics is the science of order and they see order in an abstract, inner-directed way, which often turns out, quite spookily, to be relevant to the real world. This poses a problem. I would try to explain it as the sort of learning that goes on whenever one has long experience—one learns things that one cannot express in words. Our long experience is the many centuries of experience of scientific work in which we have learned what sort of thing is beautiful; we've learned what sort of mathematics is possible. Not all forms of order are possible. And we've learned what sort of ideas might be relevant to the real world. I think that's what we mean by beauty and, in fact, our sense of beauty has changed.

Today, beauty based on symmetry, on invariance under some group of transformations of change of point of view, is regarded as a highly beautiful part of a theory—something you would be proud to base a theory on. At the beginning of this century that wasn't true; in fact, Lorenz criticized Einstein for basing his special theory of relativity on a principle of symmetry, which is not something that he thought should be taken as a starting point of a physical theory. So, in this sense, I think, we are in the grip of a learning machine which is gradually beating into us a sense of beauty, which is a very important part of the work of science.

Finally, though, I must admit that science isn't everything. It certainly isn't. There are things that are outside the scope of science and that are still terribly important to human beings. There is metaphysics of a sort that goes beyond the kind of learning processes I mentioned. There is also aesthetics and morality. It seems to me that there's an unbridgeable gulf between statements with the word "is" and statements with the word "ought." There is no way science can ever tell you how you ought to behave. It may tell you, if you have some fundamental moral principles, how you can satisfy them, how you can bring about what you take as a desired goal. But it can never tell you what your goals ought to be.

There is a moral order. It is wrong to torture children. And the reason it is wrong to torture children is because I say so, and John says so, and probably most of us say so—but it is not a moral order out there. It is something we impose on others, and bully for us. In this respect I think religion is no better. Suppose you knew that the universe had been created by a designer who watched our progress and intervened and behaved very much like the god of the Old or the New Testament. That has no moral implications. That god may set down moral principles which are wrong. Wrong from what point of view? Our own point of view—what other point of view could there be? And indeed, that is what I would say is the case. I don't believe in torturing children but god apparently, according to many religious faiths, believes that children who were not baptized or who, when they got older did not accept god or come to him through Christ or through the Koran are subject to eternal damnation. I think that even those who believe in a god still have the responsibility to answer the question, "What is right?" And they have to answer it for themselves and, if they accept the morality provided by god, that is their choice, so that they, like the atheist scientist, have to make a free choice of moral behavior which is not dictated by a theory of the universe, religious or scientific.

POLKINGHORNE: I want to make a few comments on your remarks. This question of the nature of morality is a very important issue. I don't think we just make it up. I don't think that Steve and I make up one sort of morality and Hitler and Stalin make up another sort of morality. On what basis does Steve say, "Bully for us," and deny them. There has to be something that transcends human construction, otherwise these senses of value would not function the way they do.

Theology does make progress, very slowly. That's one of the reasons why I swapped out of physics and into theology. It is a more stately subject. But in the 19th century Christians first began to question and have continued to question and dispose of the question really, most of them anyway, that the god of love would condemn people to infinite torment for finite transgressions. That doesn't mean that Hell is gone, but that Hell is no longer thought of as a place of torment into which an angry God has cast people. Rather it is thought of as colored gray rather than red, as a place of boredom to which people have condemned themselves by their own choice of excluding the divine life. That's just a little point on Hell and I think that is actual progress in theology to have reached that.

But, Steve, I think the fundamental difference between you and me is this: We both want to take human persons seriously, but we take them seriously in radically different ways. You see human persons as constructing a world of meaning that is a sort of oasis in a vast desert of a hostile and meaningless universe. I see us not constructing meaning—although, of course, there is a constructive element in it—but as *discovering* meaning also, which for me is a clue to the nature of reality more generally. It is not an internal good of the human community, of sections of the human community; it's a perception of the real. And therefore I see that as a clue that we are not defiant inhabitants of an island of meaning in an ocean of meaninglessness, but that in fact the world has a meaning that extends beyond us. That is the basic difference between us, I think.

WEINBERG: Well, I don't disagree with that and I don't disagree with your characterization. If, in fact, there is out there, built into the structure of the universe, an objective meaning, an objective moral order, that would be really quite wonderful. And perhaps part of my passion about this arises from regret that it isn't true. But, if it isn't true, then surely it's better that we not kid ourselves into thinking that it is. It's better that we at least salvage what we can from the satisfaction of creating some meaning around us.

POLKINGHORNE: I would agree with you that, if it isn't true, then it is better that we know it. The central religious question is the question of truth. Religion can do all sorts of things for you, console you in life and at the approach of death, but it can't really do any of those things unless it's actually true—not in some knock-down sense—because, of course, the divine reality will always exceed our finite thoughts. But if there isn't a benevolent divine will or purpose behind the world, it is better for us to know that than to live in a sort of happy illusion. I don't see religion as a way of keeping our spirits up and keeping us through life in a happy illusion in that way.

WEINBERG: Yes, in this respect I think John and I represent what must be in today's world a minority—we are probably the wrong people to be debating each other. I often find that many people who claim to be religious actually have no beliefs to speak of. They have, to quote Susan Sontag, "piety without content." I spoke to some Buddhists a while ago and asked, "So, do you really believe in reincarnation?" And they said no, they didn't think they believed in reincarnation. And I couldn't imagine what it meant to be a Buddhist and not to believe in reincarnation: for them Buddhism was just a flag, rather than a belief. So, in this respect John and I are not the right people to argue.

GINGERICH: Steve Weinberg, what meaning, if any, do you see in the fact that many scientists see their own work, solutions to problems, as coming from outside themselves and even perhaps having a religious dimension?

WEINBERG: I don't think that's true of most scientists: my experience, just talking to my fellow physicists at lunch, I find that most of them have not only no religious faith, but also no interest in the issue. I am a little unusual in being interested in the question. I think again there is a selection effect. Scientists who do talk about supernatural influences on their work are the ones who are likely to get published and win prizes endowed by Mr. Templeton. But, I think the public is getting a rather misleading view. I think most scientists are not atheists because they don't think about it enough to be atheists. There are scientists who are quite religious, my friend here and others, but I think they are thin on the ground.

POLKINGHORNE: Can I just briefly comment on that? This is anecdote swapping. My impression is somewhat different. I certainly agree that the majority of scientists are not religious believers in some traditional sense. The majority, in my view, and I'm thinking of my friends, are people who can neither take religion or throw it away. They are slightly wistful in relation to religion. They'd like to think there is a deeper meaning and purpose behind things. But they're wary of religion because they think religion involves accepting things on authority. I want to always say that religious belief isn't shutting your eyes, gritting your teeth, believing six impossible things before breakfast because the Bible tells you that's what you have to do. It is a search for motivated belief. The search is difficult, and different people will reach different conclusions about it. But you don't have to commit intellectual suicide to be a religious believer; otherwise I wouldn't be one.

GINGERICH: The questions which have come in are quite interesting but I think many of them are what you would consider simply debating points and not genuine questions. But here is one for both of you. What is the point of continuing to live in a universe that has no ultimate purpose? That's for you, Steve.

WEINBERG: Well, if you don't see the point then, too bad for you. I feel there is a point. How can I say it? There's nothing in science that says we should look at life as not worth living any more than there is something that tells what there is about life that is worth living. It is left as an open question for us to decide on any grounds we like. I enjoy life and there are things I value very much about being alive and that's the point it has. I remember in the preface to one of his plays, I think it was *Heartbreak House*, George Bernard Shaw said, "Darwin has knocked centuries of dusty theology out of the room and now we don't have any of that anymore but at the same time he has knocked out morality. And now because of Darwin's work there is no basis of any moral principle." I disagree. I don't think Shaw was right about that. I think Darwin—and science in general— perhaps took away the idea that there was a supernatural plan which imposes a moral order, but it did not say that we must behave immorally. We are left to make moral choices or not and we are free to make them. And, in fact, not only to make moral choices for ourselves but for others just as we would condemn someone else who tortured children. We're free to find a point and to make moral choices. We don't get them from an objective supernatural world order.

POLKINGHORNE: There was a German atheist philosopher, Max Horkheimer, who said there was a deep longing in the human heart that the murderer should not triumph over his innocent victim. And some of us entertain that hope that the murderer will not ultimately triumph. But those that can't entertain that hope and who live a life of austere nobility in the face of a hostile world, I believe their position to be quite admirable.

GINGERICH: Here is a question for you, John. Could you imagine an ultimate argument that God is not existent? If we cannot refute this mode of explanation, then it is just a matter of belief. But how can we be sure or convinced that it is not just wishful thinking?

POLKINGHORNE: That's a very interesting question. I think that certainty, in the sense of logical proof, is a pretty spare quantity. There isn't too much of it around. Kurt Godel has told us that even mathematics has its *aporia*, as the theologians say, its uncertainties. And I think it is also the case that there is a sort of complementary relationship between things that are really interesting and things that can be proved. So, I think we shouldn't worry about proof and certainty.

That doesn't mean that anything goes. We should search for motivated beliefs. But I think this is true of both science and religion and everything that lies between them: we will attain beliefs that are motivated, but we will never be certain. One of the best books on the philosophy of science written in the 20th century is Michael Polanyi's *Personal Knowledge*. Polanyi was a distinguished physical chemist before he became a philosopher. That means he's not been very well accepted in the philosophical community, I am afraid to say. He wrote in this book—and he was talking in relation to his scientific beliefs—to explain how I can hold to what I believe to be true knowing that it might be false. And that is the human condition, whether it concerns science, religion, or anything else. So, I think we shouldn't become fixated upon certainty. I don't think that you can prove God exists; I don't think you can prove that God does not exist.

GINGERICH: Steve, you stated that there is a mysterious realm that science will never explain and that a similar statement is true about religion. What do you see as the nature of this mysterious realm? How is it different from your conception of a religious realm?

WEINBERG: The realm I refer to is something that may be discovered in the next century. I am not certain about this, but I do believe that sometime in the next century or so we're going to find that all our physical theories converge to a fundamental theory, maybe something like the string theories that people are talking about today, or maybe something deeper, from which, in principle, all other scientific generalizations that don't simply rely on historical accidents can be inferred. The mystery will then be: why is that true? The theory will be something very specific, crystallized into a clear scientific statement. We will then wonder why it is true. As I said there may be a chance of answering the question why it's not slightly different, but we probably will not ever know why the truth is not totally different.

There is the possibility that we may be able to show that there is no other logically consistent theory that would allow a rich enough universe for people to be raising the issue. That doesn't completely satisfy me, but it may give some satisfaction. For instance, when you look for alternatives to quantum mechanics, you think of Newtonian mechanics, which don't allow for atoms, and I can hardly imagine how life could evolve in a purely Newtonian world.

But, on the other hand, the religious mystery is a mystery: we will never know whether any of it is true. Unless the flaming sword descends, and unless miracles start happening again in a reproducible way that they haven't . . . there'll never be any way of being certain about religion, and the truth, as the religious thinker finds it, will always be flexible, it will always be something that can vary indefinitely.

POLKINGHORNE: May I just say that, God forbid, if a flaming sword were to come and decapitate Steve before our very eyes that would pose a very big theological problem. Because that would be the capricious act of a magical, vengeful god and that's not the God of my belief. You see the problem with miracles . . .

WEINBERG: . . . it is the god, however, of your religious tradition.

POLKINGHORNE: I wouldn't say that the religious tradition is un-sullied, but it's certainly not the sole strand within that belief. The problem with miracles is the problem of divine consistency. God is not capricious, but God is not condemned equally to dreary uniformity.

WEINBERG: Well, it would pose not only a theological problem but a janitorial problem as well . . .

GINGERICH: Steve, here's a final question for you. You completely reject any notion of a divine designer, but on what basis beyond faith can you justify the idea of multiple universes being more valid?

WEINBERG: I thought I had answered that, but I would be happy to say it again. I don't maintain that that idea is true—it's a possibility that has emerged and it remains a possibility. When I become convinced of its truth, it will be because the equations of physics that unify the various forces—the equations of quantum mechanics, relativity, all that—have that as a consequence. It won't be an act of faith. It will be a deduction from laws which we, unfortunately, at present don't know. Now you may say that it is an act of faith because we will not be able to observe these other big bangs, or these other terms in the wave function. But that's the dilemma that science has been in for a long time. We don't really observe quarks and we never will see the track of a quark. And yet we believe in quarks because the theories that have quarks in them work. And in the same way, if we come to that—and we have not yet come to that—we will believe in these other big bangs or these other terms in the wave function because the theories in which they appear work.

GINGERICH: Ladies and gentlemen, let me just remind you that this is the very room in which in April of 1920 the very famous

Shapley/Curtis debate on the scale of the universe took place; a debate that has gone down in astronomical lore ever since. You have been privileged to have been present at this debate today, which may also assume mythic proportions.

Further Reading

Sir John Polkinghorne's most recent books are *Quantum Physics and Theology* (New Haven: Yale University Press, 2007); *Science and the Trinity* (New Haven: Yale University Press, 2004); *The God of Hope and the End of the World* (New Haven: Yale University Press, 2002); *Faith in the Living God* (Minneapolis: Fortress Press, 2001); *The End of the World and the Ends of God*, edited with Michael Welker (Harrisburg, PA: Trinity Press International, 2000); *Faith, Science, and Understanding* (New Haven: Yale University Press, 2000); *Science and Theology* (Minneapolis: Fortress Press, 1998); *Belief in God in an Age of Science* (New Haven: Yale University Press, 1998); *The Faith of a Physicist* (Princeton: Princeton University Press, 1994); and *Quarks, Chaos and Christianity* (London: Triangle, 1994). Highly recommended secondary sources are Kevin Sharpe, "Nudging John Polkinghorne," *Quodlibet Journal* 5 nos. 2–3 (July 2003), at http://www.Quodlibet.net; and Wolfhart Pannenberg, "Response to John Polkinghorne," *Zygon* 36, no. 4 (2001): 799–800.

16 **Freeman Dyson**
(1923–)

Introduction

Freeman Dyson is a modern-day William James. He has the mind of a scientist, the pen of a master prose stylist, the heart of a humanist, and the irreverence and wit of genius. James the psychologist and Dyson the physicist, scientists both, never doubt the value and variety of the spiritual life. Neither has any place for exclusiveness or dogmatism in religion. James joyfully extolled his "pluralistic hypothesis" as Dyson does his "principle of maximum diversity." Both look at religion from inside it, attuned to what real people, not academic theologians, make of it. In *The Varieties of Religious Experience* (1902) and then again in his essays on *Pragmatism* (1907), William James declares for a "finite God," one who is limited in power or in knowledge or in both. He could not abide the "metaphysical monster" offered by scholastic theology—"an absolutely worthless invention of the scholarly mind," he scoffed. In *Infinite in All Directions*, Freeman Dyson too opts for a Jamesian finite God, under the label, however, of "Socinianism."

In the first excerpt below, Dyson reports an exchange of views he had at a conference once with the American philosopher Charles Hartshorne, a leading interpreter of Alfred North Whitehead and process theology. Hartshorne told Dyson his theological standpoint sounded "Socinian" to him. Faustus Socinus (1539–1604) was an Italian theologian judged a heretic by Rome for holding the view, like William James, that God is neither omniscient nor omnipotent. His reasons for doing so seem to be identical to James's. Believing that human beings have genuine freedom, Socinus denied that God either determines or eternally knows our free acts. Rather, we determine the acts, and God knows them only after the fact or as they occur. The traditional idea of God as an unmoved mover, an immutable and all-determining power, thus gives way to the conclusion that there is real novelty in the divine consciousness. We cause changes in God. In a bold break with tradition, Socinus anticipated not only William James but also current process theology. Dyson decided that the idea that God "learns and grows as the universe unfolds" was "congenial and consistent with scientific common sense." An emergent God who changes and becomes with the universe is a more appropriate conception in this century than a monarch who rules over nature. Modestly, Dyson is not saying that his personal theology is supported or proved by scientific evidence, only that it is consistent with scientific evidence.

The evidence that impresses him is apparent in the second excerpt below, from *Disturbing the Universe*. The most astounding fact in the universe to Dyson is the power of mind. Even more astounding than the flight of the monarch butterfly, as Dyson has written elsewhere, is the fact that "somehow, by natural processes still totally mysterious, a million butterfly brains working together in a human skull have the power to dream, to calculate, to see and to hear, to speak and to listen, to translate feelings into marks on paper which other brains can interpret."[1] Through the long course of biological evolution, and here on this small planet, mind has infiltrated matter and taken control. In part as a reaction to biochemist Jacques Monod's dark vision in *Chance and Necessity*,

---

[1] Freeman J. Dyson, *Infinite in All Directions* (New York: Harper and Row, 1988), 118.

Dyson defines mind as the capacity for choice and sees it as implicated at three levels. The first lesson he takes from quantum mechanics is that an observer's mind is inextricably involved in the description of events. Quantum entities, such as electrons, are active, decision-making agents, forced by experiments to make particular choices from the many options open to them. Human consciousness, at the second level, is aware of itself and of other minds, including animal minds, that appear to amplify the quantum choices made by the molecules inside heads. Dyson has a reasonable faith, therefore, in the existence of a third level of mind, a mental component of the universe that can be called God. Could the tendency of mind to infiltrate matter be a law of nature? Could it spread all over the galaxy, led, if not by our species, then perhaps by others? Might mind, no longer in the form of flesh and blood but perhaps as clouds of charged particles, expand its physical reach by many powers of ten beyond the human scale? What will mind choose to do, Dyson wonders, when it informs and controls the universe?

This very ancient idea that, simply put, God is the mind of the universe, and the universe is the body of God, calls for subtleties of expression that do not interest Freeman Dyson. He makes no clear distinction between mind and God, he tells us in the fifth excerpt below. Clearly, when it comes to the meaning of God, Dyson does not indulge many "overbeliefs," as William James called them. He does not say whether God is one or many, or perhaps the one who includes the many. The latter version of theism was systematically developed by Charles Hartshorne into a position known as panentheism, literally, "all-in-God." Conceived as the all-inclusive whole of the universe, Dyson's conception of God could be "more than" the world in the same way any emergent whole is "more than" the sum of its parts; at the same time, God would be nothing apart from or without the concrete atoms, molecules, and minds that comprise the ongoing divine life as it grows and changes. But what is the manner of the divine "inclusiveness"? Is it like marbles in a box? Too non-organic and impersonal. Like thoughts contained in a mind? This might be Dyson's drift. Or more like cells in a living body? This would be Hartshorne's preference. With fewer domes and spirals on his philosophy than Hartshorne's, William James could offer Dyson another conceptual option: "pluralistic pantheism," in which God is not the name of the all-inclusive whole but of a finite power that needs human allegiance and cooperation in a struggle against discord, triviality, and evil.

Whatever he would make of this twentieth-century pragmatic-processive philosophy of God as an upgrade of Socinius, in the years since his conversation with Hartshorne, Dyson's doubts about the very enterprise of theology seem to have deepened. In excerpts seven and eight, he discusses the theology of John Polkinghorne (chapter 15) in a way that some readers may find delightfully barbed and others, irreverently off-base.

Further distancing himself from speculative and intellectual approaches to faith, Dyson describes himself in a 1998 interview as "a Christian without the theology" (excerpt six). What does this leave that is still Christian? For Dyson, it leaves a community of people taking care of each other and a great deal of beautiful language and music. In excerpt seven he traces the trouble with theology in the Christian religion to the influence of Greek metaphysics on the early Jesus movement as it developed in a Hellenistic culture, a diagnosis confirmed in Hartshorne's critique of classical theism. In his Templeton Award address (excerpt five) he makes the exceptionally incisive point—one that is becoming increasingly rare in many public discussions of religion—that "progress in religion" should be measured not by intellectual reconciliation but by social action aimed at creating a more just, equitable, and humane society. More important than theology is religion, and religion for Dyson is about good works, social justice, abolishing slavery, and spreading peace. Progress in religion means taking the side of "the victims against the oppressed," sharing burdens, and fostering human bonding. In its entirety, this address ranks as one of the most powerful pleas delivered by a scientist on the way in which "science and religion should work together to abolish the gross inequalities that prevail in the modern world."

The moral influence of religion—for good or for evil—is the topic of the final excerpt. It represents Freeman Dyson's riposte to Steven Weinberg (chapter 14) and all those who convict religion of causing serious sins more than recuperating sinners or caring for widows, orphans, and the poor.

The excerpts in this chapter range from acerbic to eloquent to inspirational. They do little, however, to acquaint readers with the scientific side of this world-renowned astrophysicist, who has been a professor of physics at the Institute for Advanced Study in Princeton, a member of the nuclear reactor design team in 1956, a chief theoretician for propulsion studies on the Orion Project, an arms control consultant, and a member of the National Academy of Sciences. Not since William James has America had a public intellectual who combines a distinctive voice on science and religion issues with such magnanimous humanity and capacious intellect.

✌ Dyson's Contribution to Science

Freeman J. Dyson, professor of physics emeritus at the Institute for Advanced Study in Princeton, was born in England and worked as a civilian scientist for the Royal Air Force in World War II. He graduated from Cambridge University in 1945 with a B.A. degree in mathematics. He went on to Cornell University as a graduate student in 1947 and worked with Hans Bethe and Richard Feynman. His most useful contribution to science was the unification of the three versions of quantum electrodynamics invented by Feynman, Schwinger, and Tomonaga. He was called "midwife to the birth of electrodynamics." Subsequently, he worked on nuclear reactors, solid state physics, ferromagnetism, astrophysics, and biology, looking for problems where elegant mathematics could be usefully applied. Dyson is a fellow of the American Physical Society, a member of the U.S. National Academy of Sciences, and a fellow of the Royal Society of London.

Dyson in His Own Words

A Socinian Theology[2]

Like the majority of scientists in this century, I have not concerned myself with theology. Theology is a foreign language, which we have not taken the trouble to learn. My personal theology is the theology of an amateur. But I did once have some help from a professional theologian in formulating my ideas in an intellectually coherent fashion. I happened to meet Charles Hartshorne at a meeting in Minnesota and we had a serious conversation. After we had talked for a while he informed me that my theological standpoint is Socinian. Socinus was an Italian heretic who lived in the sixteenth century. If I remember correctly what Hartshorne said, the main tenet of the Socinian heresy is that God is neither omniscient nor omnipotent. He learns and grows as the universe unfolds. I do not pretend to understand the theological subtleties to which this doctrine leads if one analyzes it in detail. I merely find it congenial, and consistent with scientific common sense. I do not make any clear distinction between mind and God. God is what mind becomes when it has passed beyond the scale of our comprehension. God may be considered to be either a world-soul or a collection of world-souls. We are the chief inlets of God on this planet at the present stage of his development. We may later grow with him as he grows, or we may be left behind. As Bernal said: "That may be an end or a beginning, but from here it is out of sight." If we are left behind, it is an end. If we keep growing, it is a beginning.

The great virtue of my version of the Socinian theology is that it leaves room at the top for diversity. Just as the greatness of the creation lies in its diversity, so does also the greatness of the creator. Many world-souls are better than one. When mind grows to fill the universe, it comes as a diversifier as well as a unifier.

[2] *Infinite in All Directions*, 119–20, 294.

Another theologian, with whom I have a more distant acquaintance, is St. Paul. St. Paul had some good things to say about diversity. "Now there are diversities of gifts, but the same spirit. And there are differences of administrations, but the same Lord. And there are diversities of operations, but it is the same God which worketh all in all." . . . I am describing the universe as I encounter it in my life as a scientist and as a politically engaged citizen. I should not pretend to agree with St. Paul when in fact I find his point of view alien. For St. Paul, the diversity of the creation is less important than the unity of the creator. For me, it is the other way round. I do not know or particularly care whether the same God is working all in all. I care deeply for the diversity of his working.

꙳

My own faith . . . is similar to the faith of [H. G.] Wells. I believe that we are here to some purpose, that the purpose has something to do with the future, and that it transcends altogether the limits of our present knowledge and understanding. I do not wish to go beyond this simple statement into a discussion of theology. My ignorance of theology would quickly become obvious. If you like, you can call the transcendent purpose God. If it is God, it is a Socinian God, inherent in the universe and growing in power and knowledge as the universe unfolds. Our minds are not only expressions of its purpose but are also contributions to its growth.

The Power of Mind in Nature[3]

Monod's dogma, "The cornerstone of the scientific method is the postulate that nature is objective," turns out to be untrue. . . .

[3] Freeman J. Dyson, *Disturbing the Universe* (New York: Harper and Row, 1979), 249–51.

The laws of subatomic physics cannot even be formulated without some reference to the observer. "Chance" cannot be defined except as a measure of the observer's ignorance of the future. The laws leave a place for mind in the description of every molecule.

It is remarkable that mind enters into our awareness of nature on two separate levels. At the highest level, the level of human consciousness, our minds are somehow directly aware of the complicated flow of electrical and chemical patterns in our brains. At the lowest level, the level of single atoms and electrons, the mind of an observer is again involved in the description of events. . . . But I, as a physicist, cannot help suspecting that there is a logical connection between the two ways in which mind appears in my universe. I cannot help thinking that our own awareness of our own brains has something to do with the process which we call "observation" in atomic physics. That is to say, I think our consciousness is not just a passive epiphenomenon carried along by the chemical events in our brains, but is an active agent forcing the molecular complexes to make choices between one quantum state and another. In other words, mind is already inherent in every electron, and the processes of human consciousness differ only in degree but not in kind from the processes of choice between quantum states which we call "chance" when they are made by electrons.

Jacques Monod has a word for people who think as I do and for whom he reserves his deepest scorn. He calls us "animists," believers in spirits. "Animism," he says, "established a covenant between nature and man, a profound alliance outside of which seems to stretch only terrifying solitude. Must we break this tie because the postulate of objectivity requires it?" Monod answers yes: "The ancient covenant is in pieces; man knows at last that he is alone in the universe's unfeeling immensity, out of which he emerged only by chance." I answer no. I believe in the covenant. It is true that we emerged in the universe by chance, but the idea of chance is itself only a cover for our ignorance. I do not feel like an alien in this universe. The more I examine the universe and study the details of its architecture, the more evidence I find that the universe in some sense must have known that we were coming.

🙢

I conclude from the existence of these [lucky] accidents of physics and astronomy that the universe is an unexpectedly hospitable place for living creatures to make their home in. Being a scientist, trained in the habits of thought and language of the twentieth century rather than the eighteenth, I do not claim that the architecture of the universe proves the existence of God. I claim only that the architecture of the universe is consistent with the hypothesis that mind plays an essential role in its functioning.

We had earlier found two levels on which mind manifests itself in the description of nature. On the level of subatomic physics, the observer is inextricably involved in the definition of the objects of his observations. On the level of direct human experience, we are aware of our own minds, and we find it convenient to believe that other human beings and animals have minds not altogether unlike our own. Now we have found a third level to add to these two. The peculiar harmony between the structure of the universe and the needs of life and intelligence is a third manifestation of the importance of mind in the scheme of things. This is as far as we can go as scientists. We have evidence that mind is important on three levels. We have no evidence for any deeper unifying hypothesis that would tie these three levels together. As individuals, some of us may be willing to go further. Some of us may be willing to entertain the hypothesis that there exists a universal mind or world soul which underlies the manifestations of mind that we observe. If we take this hypothesis seriously, we are, according to Monod's definition, animists. The existence of a world soul is a question that belongs to religion and not to science.

Reconciling Points of Tension between Faith and Reason[4]

In the no-man's-land between science and theology, there are five specific points at which faith and reason may appear to clash. The five points are the origin of life, the human experience of free will, the prohibition of teleological explanations in science, the argument from design as an explanatory principle, and the question of ultimate aims. Each of these points could be the subject of a whole chapter, but fortunately I have only a few pages for all five. I will deal with each of them in turn as well as I can in a few lines.

First, the origin of life. This is not the most difficult problem from a philosophical point of view. Life in its earliest stages was little removed from ordinary chemistry. We can at least imagine life originating by ordinary processes which chemists know how to calculate. Much more serious problems for philosophy arise at a later stage with the development of mind and consciousness and language. As the physicist Wigner once said: "Where in the Schrödinger equation do you put the joy of being alive?" The problem with the origin of life is only this: How do you reconcile a theory which makes life originate by a process of chance with the doctrine that life is a part of God's plan for the universe? There are three possible answers to this question. Answer 1. Deny that God has a plan and say that everything is accidental. This is the answer of Jacques Monod, and of the majority of modern biologists. But then Wigner will ask: Is consciousness also an accident? Answer 2. Deny that chance exists and say that God knows how the dice will fall. This is the answer of Einstein, who believed that chance is a human concept arising from our ignorance of the exact working of nature. But then, why do statistical laws play such a fundamental role in physics, if chance is only a cover for our ignorance? Answer 3. Say that chance exists because God shares our ignorance. This is the answer of Hartshorne, the Socinian heresy. God is not omniscient. He grows with the universe and learns as it

[4] *Infinite in All Directions*, 294–99.

develops. Chance is a part of his plan. He uses it as we do to achieve his ends.

The second clash between faith and reason is the problem of free will. It was formulated most clearly by Schrödinger in the epilogue at the end of his little book *What Is Life?* The problem is to reconcile the direct human experience of free will with a belief in scientific causality. Here again we have the same three alternative answers to deal with the conflict. But now both narrow-minded science and narrow-minded theology stand opposed to free will. The Jacques Monod view of the universe as pure "Chance and Necessity" denies free will. The orthodox theology of an omniscient and omnipotent God also denies it. For those of us who would like to believe both in God and in free will, the Socinian answer is the best way out. The philosophical problems of chance and of free will are closely related. The Socinian theology deals with both together. Free will is the coupling of a human mind to otherwise random processes inside a brain. God's will is the coupling of a universal mind to otherwise random processes in the world at large.

My third problem is the problem of forbidden teleology, the conflict between human notions of purpose and the operational rules of science. Science does not accept Aristotelian styles of explanation, that stone falls because its nature is earthy and so it likes to be on Earth, or that man's brain evolves because man's nature is to be intelligent. Within science, all causes must be local and instrumental. Purpose is not acceptable as an explanation of scientific phenomena. Action at a distance, either in space or time, is forbidden. Especially, teleological influences of final goals upon phenomena are forbidden. How do we reconcile this prohibition with our human experience of purpose and with our faith in a universal purpose? I make the reconciliation possible by restricting the scope of science. The choice of laws of nature, and the choice of initial conditions for the universe, are questions belonging to meta-science and not to science. Science is restricted to the explanation of phenomena within the universe. Teleology is not forbidden when explanations go beyond science into meta-science.

The most familiar example of a meta-scientific explanation is the so-called Anthropic Principle. The Anthropic Principle says that laws of nature are explained if it can be established that they must be as they are in order to allow the existence of theoretical physicists to speculate about them. We know that theoretical physicists exist: ergo, the laws of nature must be such as to allow their existence. This mode of explanation is frankly teleological. It leads to non-trivial consequences, restrictions on the possible building blocks of the universe, which I have no space to discuss in detail. Many scientists dislike the Anthropic Principle because it seems to be a throwback to a pre-Copernican, Aristotelian style of reasoning. It seems to imply an anthropocentric view of the cosmos. Whether you like the Anthropic Principle or not is a matter of taste. I personally find it illuminating. It accords with the spirit of modern science that we have two complementary styles of explanation, the teleological style allowing a role for purpose in the universe at large, and the non-teleological style excluding purpose from phenomena within the strict jurisdiction of science.

The argument from design is the fourth on my short list of philosophical problems. The argument was one of the classic proofs of the existence of God. The existence of a watch implies the existence of a watchmaker. This argument was at the heart of the battle between creationists and evolutionists in nineteenth-century biology. The evolutionists won the battle. Random genetic variations plus Darwinian selection were shown to be sufficient causes of biological evolution. The argument from design was excluded from science because it makes use of teleological causes. For a hundred years the biologists have been zealously stamping out all attempts to revive the old creationist doctrines. Nevertheless, the argument from design still has some merit as a philosophical principle. I propose that we allow the argument from design the same status as the Anthropic Principle, expelled from science but tolerated in meta-science.

The argument from design is a theological and not a scientific argument. It is a mistake to try to squeeze theology into the mold of science. I consider the argument from design to be valid in the following sense. The universe shows evidence of the operations of mind on three levels. The first level is the level of elementary physical processes in quantum mechanics. Matter in quantum mechanics is not an inert substance but an active agent, constantly making choices between alternative possibilities according to probabilistic laws. Every quantum experiment forces nature to make choices. It appears that mind, as manifested by the capacity to make choices, is to some extent inherent in every electron. The second level at which we detect the operations of mind is the level of direct human experience. Our brains appear to be devices for the amplification of the mental component of the quantum choices made by molecules inside our heads. We are the second big step in the development of mind. Now comes the argument from design. There is evidence from peculiar features of the laws of nature that the universe as a whole is hospitable to the growth of mind. The argument here is merely an extension of the Anthropic Principle up to a universal scale. Therefore it is reasonable to believe in the existence of a third level of mind, a mental component of the universe. If we believe in this mental component and call it God, then we can say that we are small pieces of God's mental apparatus.

The last of the five philosophical problems is the problem of final aims. The problem here is to try to formulate some statement of the ultimate purpose of the universe. In other words, the problem is to read God's mind. Previous attempts to read God's mind have not been notably successful. One of the more penetrating of such attempts is recorded in the Book of Job. God's answer to Job out of the whirlwind was not encouraging. Nevertheless I stand in good company when I ask again the questions Job asked. Why do we suffer? Why is the world so unjust? What is the purpose of pain and tragedy? I would like to have answers to these questions, answers which are valid at our childish level of understanding even if they do not penetrate far into the mind of God. My answers are based on a hypothesis which is an extension both of the Anthropic Principle and of the argument from design. The hypothesis is that the universe is constructed according to a principle of maximum diversity. The principle of maximum diversity operates both at the physical and at the mental level. It says that the laws of nature and the initial conditions are such as to make the universe as interesting as possible. As a result, life is possible but not too easy. Always when things are dull, something new turns up to challenge us and to stop us from settling into a rut. Examples of things which make life difficult are all around us: comet impacts, ice ages, weapons, plagues, nuclear fission, computers, sex, sin and death. Not all challenges can be overcome, and so we have tragedy. Maximum diversity often leads to maximum stress. In the end we survive, but only by the skin of our teeth.

The expansion of life and of mankind into the universe will lead to a vast diversification of ecologies and of cultures. As in the past, so in the future, the extension of our living space will bring opportunities for tragedy as well as achievement. To this process of growth and diversification I see no end. It is useless for us to try to imagine the varieties of experience, physical and intellectual and religious, to which mankind may attain. To describe the metamorphosis of mankind as we embark on our immense journey into the universe, I return to the humble image of the butterfly. All that can be said was said long ago by Dante in Canto 10 of the *Purgatorio*:

> O you proud Christians, wretched souls and small,
> Who by the dim lights of your twisted minds
> Believe you prosper even as you fall,
> Can you not see that we are worms, each one
> Born to become the angelic butterfly
> That flies defenseless to the Judgment Throne?

The Authority of Religion[5]

I do not claim that the voice of science speaks with unique authority. Religion has at least an equal claim to authority in defining

[5] Freeman J. Dyson, *Imagined Worlds* (Cambridge, MA: Harvard University Press, 1997), 7, 8.

human destiny. Religion lies closer to the heart of human nature and has a wider currency than science. Like the human nature that it reflects, religion is often cruel and perverted. When science achieved power to equal the power of religion, science often became cruel and perverted, too.

Everywhere, religion and ethics are strongly coupled . . . . We may hope that groups of citizens united by ethical concerns may gain sufficient strength to shape history in the future, as they have done in the past. But ethical considerations can prevail over short-sighted self-interest only if the voice of religion is added to the voice of science. Both must be heard, if our ethical choices are to be at the same time rational and humane.

Progress in Religion[6]

. . . To me, good works are more important than theology. We all know that religion has been historically, and still is today, a cause of great evil as well as great good in human affairs. We have seen terrible wars and terrible persecutions conducted in the name of religion. We have also seen large numbers of people inspired by religion to lives of heroic virtue, bringing education and medical care to the poor, helping to abolish slavery and spread peace among nations. Religion amplifies the good and evil tendencies of individual souls. Religion will always remain a powerful force in the history of our species. To me, the meaning of progress in religion is simply this, that as we move from the past to the future the good works inspired by religion should more and more prevail over the evil. . . .

Even in the gruesome history of the twentieth century, I see some evidence of progress in religion. The two individuals who epitomized the evils of our century, Adolf Hitler and Joseph Stalin, were both avowed atheists. Religion cannot be held responsible

---

[6] Freeman J. Dyson, "Progress in Religion," 2000 Templeton Speech (online), http://www.edge.org/documents/archive/edge68.html, accessed June 2, 2005.

for their atrocities. And the three individuals who epitomized the good, Mahatma Gandhi, Martin Luther King and Mother Teresa, were all in their different ways religious. One of the great but less famous heroes of World War Two was André Trocmé, the Protestant pastor of the village of Le Chambon-sur-Lignon in France, which sheltered and saved the lives of five thousand Jews under the noses of the Gestapo. Forty years later Pierre Sauvage, one of the Jews who was saved, recorded the story of the village in a magnificent documentary film with the title, "Weapons of the Spirit." The villagers proved that civil disobedience and passive resistance could be effective weapons, even against Hitler. Their religion gave them the courage and the discipline to stand firm. Progress in religion means that, as time goes on, religion more and more takes the side of the victims against the oppressors.

For Ian Barbour, who won the Templeton Prize last year, religion is an intellectual passion. For me it is simply a part of the human condition. Recently I visited the Imani church in Trenton because my daughter, who is a Presbyterian minister, happened to be preaching there. Imani is an inner-city church with a mostly black congregation and a black minister. The people come to church, not only to worship God, but also to have a good time. The service is informal and the singing is marvelous. While I was there they baptized seven babies, six black and one white. Each baby in turn was not merely shown to the congregation but handed around to be hugged by everybody. Sociological studies have shown that violent crimes occur less frequently in the neighborhood of Imani church than elsewhere in the inner city. After the two hour service was over, the congregation moved into the adjoining assembly room and ate a substantial lunch. Sharing the food is to me more important than arguing about beliefs. Jesus, according to the gospels, thought so too.

I am content to be one of the multitude of Christians who do not care much about the doctrine of the Trinity or the historical truth of the gospels. Both as a scientist and as a religious person, I am accustomed to living with uncertainty. Science is exciting because it is full of unsolved mysteries, and religion is exciting for the same reason. The greatest unsolved mysteries are the mysteries of our existence as conscious beings in a small corner of a vast universe. Why are we here? Does the universe have a purpose? Whence comes our knowledge of good and evil? These mysteries, and a hundred others like them, are beyond the reach of science. They lie on the other side of the border, within the jurisdiction of religion.

My personal theology is described in the Gifford Lectures that I gave at Aberdeen in Scotland in 1985, published under the title, *Infinite in All Directions*. Here is a brief summary of my thinking. The universe shows evidence of the operations of mind on three levels. The first level is elementary physical processes, as we see them when we study atoms in the laboratory. The second level is our direct human experience of our own consciousness. The third level is the universe as a whole. Atoms in the laboratory are weird stuff, behaving like active agents rather than inert substances. They make unpredictable choices between alternative possibilities according to the laws of quantum mechanics. It appears that mind, as manifested by the capacity to make choices, is to some extent inherent in every atom. The universe as a whole is also weird, with laws of nature that make it hospitable to the growth of mind. I do not make any clear distinction between mind and God. God is what mind becomes when it has passed beyond the scale of our comprehension. God may be either a world-soul or a collection of world-souls. So I am thinking that atoms and humans and God may have minds that differ in degree but not in kind. We stand, in a manner of speaking, midway between the unpredictability of atoms and the unpredictability of God. Atoms are small pieces of our mental apparatus, and we are small pieces of God's mental apparatus. Our minds may receive inputs equally from atoms and from God. This view of our place in the cosmos may not be true, but it is compatible with the active nature of atoms as revealed in the experiments of modern physics. I don't say that this personal theology is supported or proved by scientific evidence. I only say that it is consistent with scientific evidence.

I do not claim any ability to read God's mind. I am sure of only one thing. When we look at the glory of stars and galaxies in the sky and the glory of forests and flowers in the living world around us, it is evident that God loves diversity. Perhaps the universe is constructed according to a principle of maximum diversity. The principle of maximum diversity says that the laws of nature, and the initial conditions at the beginning of time, are such as to make the universe as interesting as possible. As a result, life is possible but not too easy. Maximum diversity often leads to maximum stress. In the end we survive, but only by the skin of our teeth. This is the confession of faith of a scientific heretic. Perhaps I may claim as evidence for progress in religion the fact that we no longer burn heretics.

✌

Now I have five minutes left to give you a message to take home. The message is simple. "God forbid that we should give out a dream of our own imagination for a pattern of the world." This was said by Francis Bacon, one of the founding fathers of modern science, almost four hundred years ago. Bacon was the smartest man of his time, with the possible exception of William Shakespeare. Bacon saw clearly what science could do and what science could not do. He is saying to the philosophers and theologians of his time: look for God in the facts of nature, not in the theories of Plato and Aristotle. I am saying to modern scientists and theologians: don't imagine that our latest ideas about the Big Bang or the human genome have solved the mysteries of the universe or the mysteries of life. Here are Bacon's words again: "The subtlety of nature is greater many times over than the subtlety of the senses and understanding." In the last four hundred years, science has fulfilled many of Bacon's dreams, but it still does not come close to capturing the full subtlety of nature. To talk about the end of science is just as foolish as to talk about the end of religion. Science and religion are both still close to their beginnings, with no ends in sight. Science and religion are both destined to grow and change in the millennia that lie ahead of us, perhaps solving some old mysteries, certainly discovering new mysteries of which we yet have no inkling. After sketching his program for the scientific revolution that he foresaw, Bacon ends his account with a prayer: "Humbly we pray that this mind may be steadfast in us, and that through these our hands, and the hands of others to whom thou shalt give the same spirit, thou wilt vouchsafe to endow the human family with new mercies." That is still a good prayer for all of us as we begin the twenty-first century.

Science and religion are two windows that people look through, trying to understand the big universe outside, trying to understand why we are here. The two windows give different views, but they look out at the same universe. Both views are one-sided, neither is complete. Both leave out essential features of the real world. And both are worthy of respect.

Trouble arises when either science or religion claims universal jurisdiction, when either religious dogma or scientific dogma claims to be infallible. Religious creationists and scientific materialists are equally dogmatic and insensitive. By their arrogance they bring both science and religion into disrepute. The media exaggerate their numbers and importance. The media rarely mention the fact that the great majority of religious people belong to moderate denominations that treat science with respect, or the fact that the great majority of scientists treat religion with respect so long as religion does not claim jurisdiction over scientific questions. In the little town of Princeton where I live, we have more than twenty churches and at least one synagogue, providing different forms of worship and belief for different kinds of people. They do more than any other organizations in the town to hold the community together. Within this community of people, held together by religious traditions of human brotherhood and sharing of burdens, a smaller community of professional scientists also flourishes.

I look out from the pampered little community of Princeton, which Einstein described in a letter to a friend in Europe as "a quaint and ceremonious village, peopled by demi-gods on stilts." I look out from this community of bankers and professors to ask, what can we do for the suffering multitudes of humanity in the world outside? The great question for our time is, how to make sure that the continuing scientific revolution brings benefits to everybody rather than widening the gap between rich and poor. To lift up poor countries, and poor people in rich countries, from poverty, to give them a chance of a decent life, technology is not enough. Technology must be guided and driven by ethics if it is to do more than provide new toys for the rich. Scientists and business leaders who care about social justice should join forces with environmental and religious organizations to give political clout to ethics. Science and religion should work together to abolish the gross inequalities that prevail in the modern world. That is my vision, and it is the same vision that inspired Francis Bacon four hundred years ago, when he prayed that through science God would "endow the human family with new mercies."

From Wired *Interview*[7]

> FD: Lately, I've become a tame scientist for the theologians. I get invited to a number of meetings on what they call "Science and Religion" or "Science and Theology," and I talk with theologians. I don't find it very helpful. I take my religion without theology.
>
> INTERVIEWER: What does that mean, you take your religion without theology?
>
> [FD:] Theology didn't even come from Jesus. It was an accident. The Greek world was heavily philosophical at the time Christianity was developing, and so the Christians adopted all this jargon from Greek philosophy and incorporated it into their religion; that became theology. I've never found it essential to my religion . . . It's given rise to this profession of theologians who would like to make the subject into a science, particularly John Templeton. He organizes these conferences I go to, and he has a strong belief that he can make theology scientific and make religion into a force for progress.

[7] Stewart Brand, "Freeman Dyson's Brain," *Wired Magazine*, 1998 (online), http://www.wired.com/wired/6.02/dyson.html?pg=1&topic?=, accessed June 2, 2005.

INTERVIEWER: What is your religion?

FD: Christianity, but of a very watered-down kind—essentially, what's left over after you get rid of the theology. The Church of England is pretty close to it.

The Religion of Jesus versus Christian Theology [8]

Polkinghorne argues from the detailed concordance of the two struggles that science and theology are two aspects of a single intellectual adventure. He sees theology as dealing with God in essentially the same way as science is dealing with nature. This is a grand vision. The historical evidence that he brings to support it is impressive. But I have to say that, much as I admire Polkinghorne's vision, I cannot share it. To share it, you must disregard a crucial difference between science and theology. When all is said and done, science is about things and theology is about words. Things behave in the same way everywhere, but words do not. Quantum mechanics works equally in all countries and in all cultures. Quantum mechanics gives plants the power to turn the energy of sunlight into leaves and fruit, and it gives animals the power to turn the energy of sunlight into neural images in retinas and brains, whether they are living in Tokyo or in Timbuktu. Theology works in one culture alone. If you have not grown up in Polkinghorne's culture, where words such as "incarnation" and "trinity" have a profound meaning, you cannot share his vision.

The prominence of theology in the Christian world has had two important consequences for the history of science. On the one hand, Western science grew out of Christian theology. It is probably

[8] Freeman J. Dyson, "Is God in the Lab?" *New York Review of Books*, 45, no. 9 (May 28, 1998): 8–10. This essay reviews two books: *The Meaning of It All: Thoughts of a Citizen Scientist*, by Richard P. Feynman, and *Belief in God in an Age of Science*, by John Polkinghorne.

not an accident that modern science grew explosively in Christian Europe and left the rest of the world behind. A thousand years of theological disputes nurtured the habit of analytical thinking that could also be applied to the analysis of natural phenomena. On the other hand, the close historical relations between theology and science have caused conflicts between science and Christianity that do not exist between science and other religions. It is more difficult for a modern scientist to be a serious Christian, like John Polkinghorne, than to be a serious Muslim, like the Nobel Prize–winning physicist Abdus Salam.

The common root of modern science and Christian theology was Greek philosophy. The historical accident that caused the Christian religion to become heavily theological was the fact that Jesus was born in the eastern part of the Roman Empire at a time when the prevailing culture was profoundly Greek.

[T]wo facts are certain. First, Jesus was no simple peasant, but grew up in intimate contact with an urban and overwhelmingly Greek culture. And second, he intended to lead a spiritual regeneration of his people, based on a total repudiation of Greek culture. In all his preaching, he quotes from the Law and the Prophets, the old Hebrew scriptures. After seeing what the Greek culture had to offer, he went back to his Hebrew roots.

When Jesus died, he left behind a mass movement that rapidly grew into a new religion. The new religion moved fast from Jerusalem to other cities that were easily accessible to travelers, cities where Greek culture was even more predominant. The followers of Jesus first called themselves Christians in the Greek city of Antioch. And the man who took charge of the new religion, Saint Paul of Tarsus, was a thoroughly Hellenized Jew. Saint Paul preached to the learned men of Athens in their own language. In his writings he laid the foundations for what became orthodox Christian doctrine. Christianity became a religion for people ignorant of Hebrew and educated in the Greek tradition. Within a century, the Greek culture had swept over Christianity, and Greek philosophy had metamorphosed into Christian theology.

This history has left Western civilization with a strangely divided legacy. On the one hand, the religion of Jesus as we find it in his teachings recorded in the Gospels, a religion for ordinary people trying to find their way in a harsh world. On the other hand, the theology that turned the Christian religion into a demanding intellectual discipline, a breeding ground for scholars and ultimately for scientists. . . . There is not much connection between them. It is one of the great ironies of history that Jesus gave rise to them both.

Describing John Polkinghorne's View of the Afterlife[9]

For theories of the afterlife, scientific verification is impossible. But for a theologian, eschatological verification can be an effective substitute for scientific verification. Eschatological verification occurs when you arrive in the afterlife and verify the hypotheses with which you traveled there. At the end of the day, [Polkinghorne writes] "Belief in the faithfulness of God is the ground of eschatological hope. Equally, eschatological experience will provide the ultimate vindication of belief in that God."

Polkinghorne's book is written for the general public, but it grew out of discussions with the author's theological colleagues who share his vocabulary and his way of thinking. His arguments make sense if you accept the rules of theological argument, rules which are different from the rules of scientific argument. The way a scientific argument goes is typically as follows: We have a

---

[9] Freeman J. Dyson, "Science & Religion: No Ends in Sight," *New York Review of Books* 49, no. 5 (March 28, 2002). This essay reviews *The God of Hope and the End of the World*, by John Polkinghorne.

number of theories to explain what we have observed. Most of the theories are probably wrong or irrelevant. Then somebody does a new experiment or a new calculation that proves that Theory A is wrong. As a result, Theory B now has a better chance of being right. The way a theological argument goes is the other way round. We have a number of theories to explain what we believe. Different theologians have different theories. Then somebody, in this case Polkinghorne, declares that Theory A is right. As a result, Theory B now has a better chance of being wrong.

I am myself a Christian, a member of a community that preserves an ancient heritage of great literature and great music, provides help and counsel to young and old when they are in trouble, educates children in moral responsibility, and worships God in its own fashion. But I find Polkinghorne's theology altogether too narrow for my taste. I have no use for a theology that claims to know the answers to deep questions but bases its arguments on the beliefs of a single tribe. I am a practicing Christian but not a believing Christian. To me, to worship God means to recognize that mind and intelligence are woven into the fabric of our universe in a way that altogether surpasses our comprehension. When I listen to Polkinghorne describing the afterlife, I think of God answering Job out of the whirlwind, "Who is this that darkeneth counsel by words without knowledge? . . . Where wast thou when I laid the foundations of the earth? Declare, if thou hast understanding. . . . Have the gates of death been opened unto thee? Or hast thou seen the doors of the shadow of death?" God's answer to Job is all the theology I need. As a scientist, I live in a universe of overwhelming size and mystery. The mysteries of life and language, good and evil, chance and necessity, and of our own existence as conscious beings in an impersonal cosmos are even greater than the mysteries of physics and astronomy. Behind the mysteries that we can name, there are deeper mysteries that we have not even begun to explore.

Science and religion are both still close to their beginnings, with no ends in sight. Science and religion are both destined to grow and change in the millennia that lie ahead of us, perhaps solving some old mysteries, certainly discovering new mysteries of which we yet have no inkling. Bacon was the first writer to understand the greatness of the revolution that science would bring to human history. He was the first to see that science would lead to a future radically different from the past. He was aware that he stood at the beginning of an age of exploration that has not yet ended. "I do not think ourselves yet learned or wise enough to wish reasonably for man," he wrote. "I wait for harvest time, nor attempt to reap green corn."

Reply to Steven Weinberg on What Religion Makes You Do[10]

[About] the famous remark of the physicist Steven Weinberg: "Good people will do good things, and bad people will do bad things. But for good people to do bad things—that takes religion." Weinberg's statement is true as far as it goes, but it is not the whole truth. To make it the whole truth, we must add an additional clause: "And for bad people to do good things—that takes religion." The main point of Christianity is that it is a religion for sinners. Jesus made that very clear. When the Pharisees asked his disciples, "Why eateth your Master with publicans and sinners?" he said, "I come to call not the righteous but sinners to repentance." Only a small fraction of sinners repent and do good things, but only a small fraction of good people are led by their religion to do bad things.

I see no way to draw up a balance sheet, to weigh the good done by religion against the evil and decide which is greater by some impartial process. My own prejudice, looking at religion from the inside, leads me to conclude that the good vastly outweighs the evil. In many places in the United States, with widening gaps between rich and poor, churches and synagogues are almost the

---

[10] Freeman J. Dyson, "Religion from the Outside," *New York Review of Books* 53, no. 11 (June 22, 2006). This excerpt appears in the context of Dyson's review of *Breaking the Spell: Religion as a Natural Phenomenon*, by Daniel C. Dennett.

only institutions that bind people together into communities. In church or in synagogue, people from different walks of life work together in youth groups or adult education groups, making music or teaching children, collecting money for charitable causes, and taking care of each other when sickness or disaster strikes. Without religion, the life of the country would be greatly impoverished. I know nothing at first hand about Islam, but by all accounts the mosques in Islamic countries, and to some extent in America too, play a similar role in holding communities together and taking care of widows and orphans.

Further Reading

Dyson has written a number of illuminating and absorbing books for the general public about science, scientists, politics, arms control, nature, human nature, and religion. *Disturbing the Universe* (New York: Harper and Row, 1974) is a portrait gallery of people he has known during his career as a scientist. *Weapons and Hope* (New York: Harper and Row, 1984) is a study of ethical problems of war and peace, and a landmark book on nuclear arms and the human predicament. *Infinite in All Directions* (New York: Harper and Row, 1988) is a philosophical meditation based on Dyson's Gifford Lectures on Natural Theology given at the University of Aberdeen in Scotland. *Origins of Life* (Cambridge and New York: Cambridge University Press, 1999 [1986]) is a study of one of the major unsolved problems of science. *From Eros to Gaia* (New York: Pantheon Books, 1992) is a collection of essays ranging from 1933 to 1990; the chapter called "The Face of Gaia" touches on religious themes. *The Sun, the Genome and the Internet* (New York: New York Public Library, Oxford University Press, 1999) discusses the question of whether modern technology could be used to narrow the gap between rich and poor rather than widen it. *The Scientist as Rebel* (New York: New York Review of Books Collection, 2006) contains many of Dyson's reviews, essays, and lectures. Most nonspecialists will profit from reading Dyson's trailblazing article "Time without End: Physics and Biology in an Open Universe," *Reviews of Modern Physics* 51, no. 3 (July 1979): 447–60. Also recommended are Dyson's-review essays in the *New York Review of Books*, especially "Is God in the Lab?" (vol. 45, no. 9 [May 28, 1998]); "Science and Religion: No Ends in Sight" (vol. 49, no. 5

[March 28, 2002]); and "Religion from the Outside" (vol. 53, no. 11 [June 22, 2006]). For Dyson's 2000 Templeton Speech, see "Progress in Religion" at http://www.edge.org/documents/archive/edge68.html. For a 1998 interview with Dyson in *Wired*, see Stewart Brand, "Freeman Dyson's Brain" in *Wired Magazine* (at http://www.wired.com/wired/6.02/dyson.html?pg=1&topic=. For an acclaimed double biography of Freeman Dyson and his son George Dyson, see Kenneth Brower, *The Starship and the Canoe* (New York: Harper Perennial, 1983).

17 Stephen Hawking
(1942–)

Introduction

Isaac Newton was born in the same year that Galileo died, and Stephen Hawking was born exactly three hundred years from the day Galileo died. Hawking is now Lucasian Professor of Mathematics at Cambridge University, the same chair that Newton held. He has been hailed as "Einstein's heir," "the greatest genius of the late twentieth century," "the finest mind alive," and even "Master of the Universe," by one adoring journalist.[1] The extraordinary success of Hawking's books is testimony both to the "genius factor" and to the public's admiration for his fortitude in the face of amyotrophic lateral sclerosis. More than that, it is an indication of the widespread interest we have today in the big questions: What is the nature of the universe? What is our place in it and where did it and we come from? Why is it the way it is?

Those who have wrestled with *A Brief History of Time* know that Hawking talks about God from beginning to end. What does he mean by God? At first glance, Hawking appears to retain the idea of

---

[1] Michael White and John Gribbin, *Stephen Hawking: A Life in Science* (Washington, DC: Joseph Henry Press, 2002), 4.

God the Creator as the final answer to the ancient question, Why is there something rather than nothing? Yet he goes on to propose a model of the universe as "completely self-contained and not affected by anything outside itself," a universe that is "neither created nor destroyed" but just *is*. So one might suppose that if the universe is eternal and uncreated, it makes no sense to ask why it exists. In the seventeenth century, however, Leibniz saw the intelligibility of asking why even an eternal something exists, rather than nothing. He concluded that only a metaphysically necessary being would satisfy the principle of sufficient reason that prompts us to ask "why" questions. A "necessary being" is one whose nature is such that if it exists, it exists in all possible worlds without cause or ground of being. The best way of reading Hawking is to say that he feels the force of Leibniz's reasoning concerning a sufficient reason for the universe, while rejecting the notion of a temporal First Cause.

Hawking's achievement is to have shown for the first time the possibility of a cosmology based on a fusion of general relativity and quantum mechanics. His model yields a finite universe that has neither spatial nor temporal bounds. Classical big bang cosmology refers to the big bang explosion as a "singularity," that is, an ultimate boundary or edge, a state of infinite density where space-time has ceased. But if all physical theories are formulated in the context of space and time, it is not possible to speculate about conditions before or beyond these categories, so Hawking's quantum cosmology does without an initial state. There is no singularity. Hawking tells us that space-time has no boundary, no edge at which we might have to appeal to God or some new law to set the initial or boundary conditions for the universe.

If the universe is in the no-boundary state, and there are no singularities at which the laws of physics would break down, then no appeal to anything "outside" the universe is needed. The universe is a completely self-contained system that is not determined by anything outside itself because "outside" would have no meaning. The no-boundary proposal, then, posits something that is the cause of itself without existing prior to itself. Using a powerful mathematical device known as "imaginary time," Hawking considers space and "imaginary time" together as finite in extent. According to equations too complex for most of us to grasp, time might be multidimensional or imaginary, in which case one asymptotically approaches an initial singularity but never reaches it. In this remarkable scenario, the universe has no instant at which it began, and without a beginning, the universe requires no cause. The best one can say is that the universe is finite with respect to the past, not that it had some beginning event. Asking what caused it to exist or what existed before it is like asking what lies north of the North Pole, Hawking says. There is no way to travel north of the North Pole, but there is no boundary there either.

A historic moment occurred in 1992 when the Cosmic Background Explorer satellite, COBE, found irregularities in the microwave background radiation. Scientists saw back deep into the earliest universe. The form of the fluctuations in the microwave background agrees closely with the predictions of the Hawking-Hartle no-boundary proposal. These very slight irregularities in the universe would have caused some regions to expand less fast than others. Eventually, they would have stopped expanding and would have collapsed in on themselves, to form stars and galaxies. Many physicists believe that the Hartle-Hawking no-boundary condition, speculative as it is, can explain the rich and varied structure of the world we live in and account for all experimental observations to date.

In the last analysis, this physics simply dissolves the question about how the universe could begin to exist without being caused. As Hawking notes in the first excerpt below, the idea of a finite universe without a beginning in time bears a striking similarity to Augustine's famous response in the early fifth century to the question about what God was doing before God made the universe. Such a question, Augustine argued, involves a false assumption about time. God did not create the world in time, but rather created time along with the world. Hawking makes the same dismissal of questions about "before" or "outside" the universe. There *was* no time before the instant of the big bang, and therefore no "pre"-existent cause for which the big bang could be the effect. The difference is that for Augustine "the beginning" was an event, hidden from view, while for Hawking there is no such event as "the beginning."

All of this makes sense if causation only involves temporal priority of cause to effect. God could not be a First Cause "before" or "outside" the universe because "before" and "outside" have no meaning in terms of contemporary cosmology. It is in this sense that Hawking is right to wonder, "What place, then, for a Creator?" The mythological picture of a God, alone, splendid in the divine aseity, deciding to create a world, is incoherent and obsolete.

On the other hand, Hawking's theological naïveté is evident in the same passage. Sophisticated theists regard God as sustainer, not only as creator. God is not an existent object, they say, but the source of all existing objects. Theologians and philosophers after Augustine have certainly understood the perils of saying things such as "before God created the world. . . ."[2] In that light, we may still be haunted by the question, why does something exist instead of nothing? We may even be tempted to answer this question as Leibniz did by arguing that something exists rather than nothing because a necessary being exists which carries within itself its reason for existence and is the sufficient reason for the existence of all contingent beings. Here, too, Hawking's speculations have something original to contribute. He gives us a new, twenty-first century candidate for the role of "necessary being": the universe itself, via the Hawking no-boundary proposal. The universe would be its own First Cause, not in the sense of chronologically first, but as ultimate buck-stopper.

In both cases, an unexplained given is posited, whether God or universe. Perhaps they are equivalent. Can the universe itself now play the role of ultimate buck-stopper that God formerly played? That depends on whether one sees God as the embodiment of the laws of physics or as the source of them. Einstein leaned toward the first, and Hawking the second, especially when he asks in the excerpt below, "What is it that breathes fire into the equations and

[2] For the theological and philosophical history, see David Burrell, *Freedom and Creation in Three Traditions* (Notre Dame, IN: University of Notre Dame Press, 1993).

makes a universe for them to describe?" If with Einstein one gives the name God to the fundamental rationality underpinning the laws of physics and mathematical consistency, then the buck stops there. On the other hand, if with Hawking one sees that laws explain why empty space at t-0 produced matter-energy at t-1, but they do not explain why there is a universe of matter-energy at all, rather than nothing, then one is left with two possibilities. Either the universe is its own ground, *causa sui*, or it is an irrational efflorescence out of the void. As an opponent of irrationality, Hawking must choose the first possibility.

Having decided that God *does* play dice with the universe, even throwing them sometimes where they can't be seen, Hawking accepts Heisenberg's uncertainty principle rather than Einstein's determinism. We *may* come to know the mind of God, according to Hawking, but this could not be a *deus ex machina*, a God of the gaps, or the personal God of classical Western theism. Knowing the elusive mind of God means knowing why and how the universe and we ourselves exist. Einstein thought it impossible for us to know the mind of God, even if we succeeded in forging a theory that unified the four forces. More confident than Einstein, Hawking is nonetheless not lacking in humility in his quest for the mind of God. "I think I may find out 'how,'" he has said, "but I'm not so optimistic about finding out 'why.' If I knew that, I would know everything important."[3]

In other words, he would know the answer to the abiding mystery, What is it that breathes fire into the equations? What makes a universe for scientists to describe? To those who would simply answer "God," Hawking's reply is ready: "Why does the universe bother to exist? One can of course define God as the answer to the question, but that does not advance one much unless one accepts the other connotations that are usually attached to the word 'God.'"[4] Without attaching the traditional connotations to the

[3] Quoted in M. Mitchell Waldrop, "The Quantum Wave Function of the Universe," *Science* 242, no. 2 (December 1988): 1250.

[4] Stephen W. Hawking, "In Defense of 'A Brief History,'" *Cambridge Review*, March 1992, 16.

notion of a Supreme Being, Hawking gave his own verdict on the theological implications of his *Brief History of Time*. In a letter to the editor of *American Scientist*, he declared, "I thought I had left the question of the existence of a Supreme Being completely open. . . . It would be perfectly consistent with all we know to say that there was a Being who was responsible for the laws of physics."[5] Readers are advised to keep in mind that Hawking's cosmology would preclude deism but allow theism in the sense of finding the source and ground of all things in God, where "God" is something more than a *façon de parler* and something less than a traditionally conceived personal Supreme Being.

✌ Hawking's Contribution to Science

Stephen Hawking, Roger Penrose, and George Ellis demonstrated that every solution to the equations of general relativity guarantees the existence of a singular boundary for space and time in the past. This is now known as the "singularity theorem." In 1974 Hawking began to formulate ideas about the quantum evaporation of exploding black holes, the now famous "Hawking radiation." In 2004 he modified his theory of black holes, concluding that information is not lost but conserved in a garbled form when matter is swallowed.

Hawking in His Own Words

The Idea of Creation from Nothing[6]

But time is defined only within the universe, and does not exist outside it, as was pointed out by Saint Augustine (400): "What

---

[5] Stephen W. Hawking, "Letters to the Editor: Time and the Universe," *American Scientist* 73 (1985): 12.

[6] Stephen W. Hawking, "Quantum Cosmology," in *Three Hundred Years of Gravitation*, ed. S. W. Hawking and W. Israel (Cambridge: Cambridge University Press, 1987), 651.

did God do before He made Heaven and Earth? I do not answer as one did merrily: He was preparing Hell for those that ask such questions. For at no time had God not made anything because time itself was made by God."

The modern view is very similar. In general relativity, time is just a co-ordinate that labels events in the universe. It does not have any meaning outside the spacetime manifold. To ask what happened before the universe began is like asking for a point on Earth at 91 degrees north latitude; it just is not defined. Instead of talking about the universe being created, and maybe coming to an end, one should just say: the universe is.

The Nature of God and the Universe[7]

We are used to the idea that events are caused by earlier events, which in turn are caused by still earlier events. There is a chain of causality stretching back into the past. But suppose this chain has a beginning. Suppose there was a first event. What caused it? This was not a question that many scientists wanted to address. They tried to avoid it, either by claiming, like the Russians, that the universe didn't lie within the realm of science but belonged to metaphysics or religion. In my opinion, this is not a position any true scientist should take. If the laws of science are suspended at the beginning of the universe, might not they fail at other times also? . . . *We must try to understand the beginning of the universe on the basis of science. It may be a task beyond our powers, but we should at least make the attempt. . . .*

. . . [T]he reason general relativity broke down near the big bang is that it did not incorporate the uncertainty principle, the random element of quantum theory that Einstein had objected to on the grounds that God does not play dice. However, all the evidence is that God is quite a gambler. One can think of the universe

---

[7] Stephen W. Hawking, *The Universe in a Nutshell* (New York: Bantam Books, 2001), 79–80, 107.

as being like a giant casino, with dice being rolled or wheels being spun on every occasion. You might think that operating a casino is a very chancy business, because you risk losing money each time dice are thrown or the wheel is spun. But over a large number of bets, the gains and losses average out to a result that *can* be predicted. . . . The casino operators make sure the odds average out in their favor. That is why casino operators are so rich. . . .

It is the same with the universe. When the universe is big, as it is today, there are a very large number of rolls of the dice, and the results average out to something one can predict. That is why classical laws work for large systems. But when the universe is very small, as it was near in time to the big bang, there are only a small number of rolls of the dice, and the uncertainty principle is very important.

Because the universe keeps on rolling the dice to see what happens next, it doesn't have just a single history, as one might have thought. Instead, the universe must have every possible history, each with its own probability. . . .

We are now working to combine Einstein's general theory of relativity and Feynman's idea of multiple histories into a complete unified theory that will describe everything that happens in the universe. . . . But the unified theory will not in itself tell us how the universe began or what its initial state was. For that, we need what are called boundary conditions, rules that tell us what happens on the frontiers of the universe, the edges of space and time.

᠅

So the description of a particle by a wave function does not have a well-defined position or velocity. It satisfies the uncertainty principle. We now realize that the wave function is *all* that can be well defined. We cannot even suppose that the particle has a position and velocity that are known to God but are hidden from us. Such "hidden-variable" theories predict results that are not in agreement with observation. Even God is bound by the uncertainty principle and cannot know the position and velocity; He can only know the wave function.

From A Brief History of Time[8]

[The Pope] told us that it was all right to study the evolution of the universe after the big bang, but we should not inquire into the big bang itself because that was the moment of Creation and therefore the work of God. I was glad then that he did not know the subject of the talk I had just given at the conference—the possibility that space-time was finite but had no boundary, which means that it had no beginning, no moment of Creation. I had no desire to share the fate of Galileo, with whom I feel a strong sense of identity, partly because of the coincidence of having been born exactly 300 years after his death!

❧

The general theory of relativity, on its own, cannot explain these features or answer these questions because of its prediction that the universe started off with infinite density at the big bang singularity. At the singularity, general relativity and all other physical laws would break down: one couldn't predict what would come out of the singularity. As explained before, this means that one might as well cut the big bang, and any events before it, out of the theory, because they can have no effect on what we observe. Space-time *would* have a boundary—a beginning at the big bang. Science seems to have uncovered a set of laws that, within the limits set by the uncertainty principle, tell us how the universe will develop with time, if we know its state at any one time. These laws may have originally been decreed by God, but it appears that he has since left the universe to evolve according to them and does not now intervene in it. But how did he choose the initial state or configuration of the universe? What were the "boundary conditions" at the beginning of time?

[8] Stephen W. Hawking, *A Brief History of Time*, updated and expanded 10th anniversary edition (New York: Bantam Books, 1998), 120, 126–27, 129, 130, 131, 138, 141, 145–46, 190, 191.

One possible answer is to say that God chose the initial configuration of the universe for reasons that we cannot hope to understand. This would certainly have been within the power of an omnipotent being, but if he had started it off in such an incomprehensible way, why did he choose to let it evolve according to laws that we could understand? The whole history of science has been the gradual realization that events do not happen in an arbitrary manner, but that they reflect a certain underlying order, which may or may not be divinely inspired. It would be only natural to suppose that this order should apply not only to the laws, but also to the conditions at the boundary of space-time that specify the initial state of the universe.

*

According to [a strong anthropic principle], there are either many different universes or many different regions of a single universe, each with its own initial configuration and, perhaps, with its own set of laws of science. In most of these universes the conditions would not be right for the development of complicated organisms; only in the few universes that are like ours would intelligent beings develop and ask the question, "Why is the universe the way we see it?" The answer is then simple: if it had been different, we would not be here!

*

Most sets of values would give rise to universes that, although they might be very beautiful, would contain no one able to wonder at that beauty. One can take this either as evidence of a divine purpose in Creation and the choice of the laws of science or as support for the strong anthropic principle.

*

[A] universe that developed from some sort of random initial conditions should contain a number of regions that are smooth and uniform and are suitable for the evolution of intelligent life. On the other hand, if the initial state of the universe had to be chosen extremely carefully to lead to something like what we see around us, the universe would be unlikely to contain any region in which life would appear. In the hot big bang model described above, there was not enough time in the early universe for heat to have flowed from one region to another. This means that the initial state of the universe would have to have had exactly the same temperature everywhere in order to account for the fact that the microwave background has the same temperature in every direction we look. The initial rate of expansion also would have had to be chosen very precisely for the rate of expansion still to be so close to the critical rate needed to avoid recollapse. This means that the initial state of the universe must have been very carefully chosen indeed if the hot big bang model was correct right back to the beginning of time. It would be very difficult to explain why the universe should have begun in just this way, except as the act of a God who intended to create beings like us.

❧

In order to predict how the universe should have started off, one needs laws that hold at the beginning of time. If the classical theory of general relativity was correct, the singularity theorems that Roger Penrose and I proved show that the beginning of time would have been a point of infinite density and infinite curvature of space-time.

❧

God may know how the universe began, but we cannot give any particular reason for thinking it began one way rather than another. On the other hand, the quantum theory of gravity has opened up a new possibility, in which there would be no boundary to space-time and so there would be no need to specify the behavior at the boundary. There would be no singularities at which the laws of science broke down, and no edge of space-time at which one would have to appeal to God or some new law to set the boundary conditions for space-time. One could say: "The boundary condition of the universe is that it has no boundary." The universe would be completely self-contained and not affected by anything outside itself. It would neither be created nor destroyed. It would just BE.

~

The idea that space and time may form a closed surface without boundary also has profound implications for the role of God in the affairs of the universe. With the success of scientific theories in describing events, most people have come to believe that God allows the universe to evolve according to a set of laws and does not intervene in the universe to break these laws. However, the laws do not tell us what the universe should have looked like when it started—it would still be up to God to wind up the clockwork and choose how to start it off. So long as the universe had a beginning, we could suppose it had a creator. But if the universe is really completely self-contained, having no boundary or edge, it would have neither beginning nor end: it would simply be. What place, then, for a creator?

~

We find ourselves in a bewildering world. We want to make sense of what we see around us and to ask: What is the nature of the universe? What is our place in it and where did it and we come from? Why is it the way it is?

To try to answer these questions we adopt some "world picture." Just as an infinite tower of tortoises supporting the flat earth is such a picture, so is the theory of superstrings. Both are theories of the universe, though the latter is much more mathematical and precise than the former. Both theories lack observational evidence: no one has ever seen a giant tortoise with the earth on its back, but then, no one has seen a superstring either. However, the tortoise theory fails to be a good scientific theory because it predicts that people should be able to fall off the edge of the world. This has not been found to agree with experience, unless that turns out to be the explanation for the people who are supposed to have disappeared in the Bermuda Triangle!

The earliest theoretical attempts to describe and explain the universe involved the idea that events and natural phenomena were controlled by spirits with human emotions who acted in a very humanlike and unpredictable manner. These spirits inhabited natural objects, like rivers and mountains, including celestial bodies, like the sun and moon. They had to be placated and their favors sought in order to ensure the fertility of the soil and the rotation of the seasons. Gradually, however, it must have been noticed that there were certain regularities: the sun always rose in the east and set in the west, whether or not a sacrifice had been made to the sun god. Further, the sun, the moon, and the planets followed precise paths across the sky that could be predicted in advance with considerable accuracy. The sun and the moon might still be gods, but they were gods who obeyed strict laws, apparently without any exceptions, if one discounts stories like that of the sun stopping for Joshua.

At first, these regularities and laws were obvious only in astronomy and a few other situations. However, as civilization developed, and particularly in the last 300 years, more and more regularities and laws were discovered. The success of these laws led Laplace at the beginning of the nineteenth century to postulate scientific materialism, that is, he suggested that there would be a set of laws that would determine the evolution of the universe precisely, given its configuration at one time.

Laplace's determinism was incomplete in two ways. It did not say how the laws should be chosen and it did not specify the initial configuration of the universe. These were left to God. God would choose how the universe began and what laws it obeyed, but he would not intervene in the universe once it had started. In effect, God was confined to the areas that nineteenth-century science did not understand.

We now know that Laplace's hopes of determinism cannot be realized, at least in the terms he had in mind. The uncertainty principle of quantum mechanics implies that certain pairs of quantities, such as the position of and velocity of a particle, cannot both be predicted with complete accuracy.

Quantum mechanics deals with this situation via a class of quantum theories in which particles don't have well-defined positions and velocities but are represented by a wave. These quantum theories are deterministic in the sense that they give laws for the evolution of the wave with time. Thus if one knows the wave at one time, one can calculate it at any other time. The unpredictable, random element comes in only when we try to interpret the wave in terms of the positions and velocities of particles. But maybe that is our mistake: maybe there are no particle positions and velocities, but only waves. It is just that we try to fit the waves to our preconceived ideas of positions and velocities. The resulting mismatch is the cause of the apparent unpredictability.

In effect, we have redefined the task of science to be the discovery of the laws that will enable us to predict events up to the limits set by the uncertainty principle. The question remains, however: How or why were the laws and the initial state of the universe chosen?

꙰

When we combine quantum mechanics with general relativity, there seems to be a new possibility that did not arise before: that space and time together might form a finite, four-dimensional space without regularities or boundaries, like the surface of the earth but with more dimensions. It seems that this idea could explain many of the observed features of the universe, such as its large-scale uniformity and also the smaller-scale departures from homogeneity, like galaxies, stars, and even human beings. It could even account for the arrow of time that we observe. But if the universe is completely self-contained, with no singularities or boundaries, and completely described by a unified theory, that has profound implications for the role of God as Creator.

Einstein once asked the question: "How much choice did God have in constructing the universe?" If the no boundary proposal is correct, he had no freedom at all to choose initial conditions. He would, of course, still have had the freedom to choose the laws that the universe obeyed. This, however, may not really have been all that much of a choice; there may well be only one, or a small number, of complete unified theories, such as the heterotic string theory, that are self-consistent and allow the existence of structures as complicated as human beings who can investigate the laws of the universe and ask about the nature of God.

Even if there is only one possible unified theory, it is just a set of rules and equations. What is it that breathes fire into the equations and makes a universe for them to describe? The usual approach of science of constructing a mathematical model cannot answer the questions of why there should be a universe for the model to describe. Why does the universe go to all the bother of existing? Is the unified theory so compelling that it brings about its own existence? Or does it need a creator, and, if so, does he have any other effect on the universe? And who created him?

Up until now, most scientists have been too preoccupied with the development of new theories that describe *what* the universe is to ask the question *why*. On the other hand, the people whose business it is to ask *why*, the philosophers, have not been able to keep up with the advance of scientific theories. In the nineteenth and twentieth centuries, science became too technical and mathematical for the philosophers, or anyone else except a few specialists. . . .

However, if we do discover a complete theory, it should in time be understandable in broad principle by everyone, not just a few scientists. Then we shall all, philosophers, scientists, and just ordinary people, be able to take part in the discussion of the question of why it is that we and the universe exist. If we find the answer to that, it would be the ultimate triumph of human reason—for then we would know the mind of God.

On the Fate of the Universe[9]

Scientists believe that the universe is governed by well-defined laws that in principle allow one to predict the future. . . . One can therefore predict whether the universe will expand forever or whether it will recollapse eventually. This depends on the present density of the universe. In fact, the present density seems to be very close to the critical density that separates recollapse from indefinite expansion. If the theory of inflation is correct, the universe is actually on the knife edge. So I am in the well-established tradition of oracles and prophets of hedging my bets by predicting both ways.

Based on the duality arguments I mentioned earlier, I estimate the probability that Kip Thorne could go back and kill his grandfather as less than one in ten with a trillion trillion trillion trillion trillion trillion zeroes after it . . .

As gambling men, Kip and I would bet on odds like that. The trouble is, we can't bet each other because we are now both on the same side. On the other hand, I wouldn't take a bet with anyone else. He might be from the future and know that time travel worked.

I could be bounded in a nutshell and count myself a king of infinite space . . .
—Shakespeare, *Hamlet*, Act 2, Scene 2

Hamlet may have meant that although we human beings are very limited physically, our minds are free to explore the whole universe, and to go boldly where even *Star Trek* fears to tread— bad dreams permitting.

---

[9] Stephen W. Hawking, *Black Holes and Baby Universes and Other Essays* (New York: Bantam Books, 1993), 154–55; *The Universe in a Nutshell*, 153, 169.

Is the universe actually infinite or just very large? And is it ever-lasting or just long-lived? How could our finite minds comprehend an infinite universe? Isn't it presumptuous of us even to make the attempt? Do we risk the fate of Prometheus, who in classical mythology stole fire from Zeus for human beings to use, and was punished for his temerity by being chained to a rock where an eagle picked at his liver?

Despite this cautionary tale, I believe we can and should try to understand the universe. We have already made remarkable progress in understanding the cosmos, particularly in the last few years. We don't yet have a complete picture, but this may not be far off.

On Free Will and the Fundamental Laws of Science[10]

[A]re we really masters of our fate? Or is everything we do determined and preordained? The argument for preordination used to be that God was omnipotent and outside time, so God would know what was going to happen. But how then could we have any free will? And if we don't have free will, how can we be responsible for our actions? It can hardly be one's fault if one has been preordained to rob a bank. So why should one be punished for it?

❧

I now turn to . . . the question of free will and responsibility for our actions. We feel subjectively that we have the ability to choose who we are and what we do, but this may just be an illusion. Some people think they are Jesus Christ or Napoleon, but they can't all be right. What we need is an objective test that we can apply from the outside to distinguish whether an organism has free will. For example, suppose we were visited by a "little green

[10] *Black Holes and Baby Universes*, 127, 133, 134, 135, 137, 138, 139.

person" from another star. How could we decide whether it had free will or was just a robot, programmed to respond as if it were like us?

The ultimate objective test of free will would seem to be: Can one predict the behavior of the organism? If one can, then it clearly doesn't have free will but is predetermined. On the other hand, if one cannot predict the behavior, one could take that as an operational definition that the organism has free will.

One might object to this definition of free will on the grounds that once we find a complete unified theory we will be able to predict what people will do. The human brain, however, is also subject to the uncertainty principle. . . .

. . . I want to suggest that the concepts of free will and moral responsibility for our action are really an effective theory in the sense of fluid mechanics. It may be that everything we do is determined by some grand unified theory. . . . I have noticed that even people who claim that everything is predestined and that we can do nothing to change it look before they cross the road. Maybe it's just that those who don't look don't survive to tell the tale. . . .

❧

. . . The concept of free will belongs to a different arena from that of fundamental laws of science. If one tries to deduce human behavior from the laws of science, one gets caught in the logical paradox of self-referencing systems. If what one does could be predicted from the fundamental laws, then the fact of making that prediction could change what happens. It is like the problems one would get into if time travel were possible, which I don't think it will ever be. If you could see what is going to happen in the future, you could change it.

❧

. . . It doesn't make much difference whether this determinism is due to an omnipotent God or to the laws of science. Indeed, one could always say that the laws of science are the expression of the will of God.

. . . [C]an one really believe that God chose all the trivial details, like who should be on the cover of *Cosmopolitan*? The answer seems to be that the uncertainty principle of quantum mechanics means that there is not just a single history for the universe but a whole family of possible histories. . . . We happen to live in one particular history that has certain properties and details. . . .

🐟

. . . In the case of human beings, we are quite unable to use the fundamental laws to predict what people will do, for two reasons. First, we cannot solve the equations for the very large number of particles involved. Second, even if we could solve the equations, the fact of making a prediction would disturb the system and could lead to a different outcome. So as we cannot predict human behavior, we may as well adopt the effective theory that humans are free agents who can choose what to do. . . .

🐟

Is everything determined? The answer is yes, it is. But it might as well not be, because we can never know what is determined.

What Place for a Creator?[11]

I still believe the universe has a beginning in real time, at a big bang. But there's another kind of time, imaginary time, at right angles to real time, in which the universe has no beginning or end. This would mean that the way the universe began would be determined by the laws of physics. One wouldn't have to say that God chose to set the universe going in some arbitrary way that we

---

[11] *Black Holes and Baby Universes*, 172–73.

STEPHEN HAWKING — 411

couldn't understand. It says nothing about whether or not God exists—just that He is not arbitrary.

. . . Love, faith, and morality belong to a different category than physics. You cannot deduce how one should behave from the laws of physics. But one could hope that the logical thought that physics and mathematics involves would guide one also in one's moral behavior.

. . . All that my work has shown is that you don't have to say that the way the universe began was the personal whim of God. But you still have the question: Why does the universe bother to exist? If you like, you can define God to be the answer to that question.

Further Reading

Stephen Hawking's best-known and most readable books include *A Brief History of Time: From the Big Bang to Black Holes* (New York: Bantam Books, 1988; updated and expanded tenth anniversary ed., 1998); *Black Holes and Baby Universes and Other Essays* (New York: Bantam Books, 1993); and *The Universe in a Nutshell* (New York: Bantam Books, 2001). For those in a hurry, there is also *A Briefer History of Time* (New York: Bantam Books, 2005). See also Hawking's 1998 lecture "Origin of the Universe" at http://www.psyclops.com/hawking/resources. On the religious implications of Hawking's cosmology and its relation to big bang theory, see Willem Drees, *Beyond the Big Bang: Quantum Cosmologies and God* (LaSalle, Il: Open Court, 1990), and Robert John Russell, "Finite Creation without a Beginning: The Doctrine of Creation in Relation to Big Bang and Quantum Cosmologies," in *Quantum Cosmology and the Laws of Nature*, edited by Robert John Russell, Nancey Murphy, and C. J. Isham (Vatican City State: Vatican Observatory, 1993), 293–329. For philosophical criticisms of Hawking's cosmology from both theist and atheist points of view, see William Lane Craig and Quentin Smith, *Theism, Atheism and Big Bang Cosmology* (Oxford: Clarendon Press, 1993). An engaging and clear account not only of Hawking's cosmology but of other twentieth-century theories and their relation to the search for God is Kitty Ferguson's *The Fire in the Equations: Science, Religion, and the Search for God* (West Conshohocken, PA: Templeton Foundation Press, 2004).

18 Paul Davies
(1946–)

Introduction

If the faith of physicist and astrobiologist Paul Davies could be characterized in a single word, it would be "hope." His soul rebels against the popular conception that science reveals only a bleak and pointless universe in which humankind is an accidental and purposeless freak. Through scientific inquiry, he is convinced, we can glimpse a deeper meaning to physical existence than Bertrand Russell, for example, captured in his pessimistic reflections on the second law of thermodynamics. Musing on the fate of a degenerating, doomed universe, Russell saw it descending inexorably into chaos as all reserves of useful energy are squandered amidst "the vast death of the solar system." Davies flatly rejects any view that makes the aimless meandering of molecules somehow emblematic of the pointlessness of the universe. He directly challenges physicist Steven Weinberg's famous conclusion that "the more the universe appears comprehensible, the more it also appears pointless." Indeed, it is the driving purpose of Paul Davies's work to stand Weinberg's dictum on its head and to show that the more the universe seems pointless, the more it also seems incomprehensible.

Life is not a freak event. Davies thinks the universe is teeming with it. He adheres scrupulously to the same science as Weinberg (and others who see no point to the universe), but Davies believes that science overwhelmingly suggests that the universe is *about* something, that there is a point to it, and that we are part of whatever point that is. We may not yet be able to state what that point is, but science is on the brink of explaining the very origins of life, according to Davies, a development that will have profound implications for religion and philosophy. Even if science does not resolve or answer all religious questions, it will continue to have deep significance for our thinking about them. "The new physics," Davies wrote several decades ago, "has overturned so many commonsense notions of space, time, and matter that no serious religious thinker can ignore it." With only a touch of mischief he claimed: "science offers a surer path to God than religion."[1]

On the two most enduring mysteries—the origin of the universe and the origin of life—Davies believes science has much to say. He explains the origin of the universe as beginning with an unpredictable quantum fluctuation, giving rise to an inflationary expansion. In quantum cosmology, he proposes, it is not unreasonable to hold that something came out of nothing. The initial energies required to bring about the big bang came from repulsive forces in "empty space" which increased in magnitude until capable of sustaining an explosion on the order of the big bang. Along with Stephen Hawking, Davies sees no need for a Creator in the traditional sense. His interest in knowing the mind of God is focused on the question of where the fundamental laws of physics come from. And why *those* laws rather than some other set? When he uses the word "God," he means something like "that which underpins or guarantees this mathematical law–like order in the universe."

More than anything else in science, the perfect balance inherent in natural laws fascinates Davies and fuels his hope for the long-range future of life. In shifting his attention in recent years to the

---

[1] Paul Davies, *God and the New Physics* (New York: Simon and Schuster, 1983), 229, ix.

new field of astrobiology, Davies is tackling the biggest questions: What is life? Does it exist on other planets? And, if so, what form might it take? Tradition has it that the secret of life lies within the chemistry of the "stuff" it is made of, but Davies believes that what really defines it is the fact that it can replicate and process information. The question about the origin of life, therefore, concerns information—how it can be copied and transmitted and the complexity it can generate. Once the search for the essence of life has been separated from matter, it moves into the realm of physics and mathematics. Human life can now see itself as interwoven with an ancient and surprisingly intricate fabric of life. The discovery that the universe is fine-tuned for life—a discovery to which the phrase "the anthropic principle" is often applied—has prompted much speculation by philosophers, theologians, and theoretical physicists. Impressed by the underlying unity of the universe and its "felicitous dovetailing of the large and small," Davies maintains that the universe certainly *appears* to be designed, and designed for producing life. Yet he takes an original position on the anthropic principle and resists the either/or terms that usually frame questions about the ultimate nature of the cosmos: we don't have to choose between *either* design *or* chance, *either* God *or* randomness. We can have both.

Describing his vision of a self-organizing and self-complexifying universe, governed by natural laws that encourage matter to evolve toward life and consciousness, Davies sees life as part of the basic fabric of reality, written into the fundamental laws of the universe, so that it is almost bound to arise wherever earthlike conditions prevail. In that case, we human beings are living representations of a breathtakingly ingenious cosmic scheme, a set of laws that is able to coax life from nonlife and mind from unthinking matter. For Davies such a magnificent set of physical principles—which bear all the hallmarks of design—is much more impressive than the sporadic intervention of a Deity who simply conjures these marvels into existence. Davies maintains that the question of whether life was formed by law or chance can, and will, be settled by observation and experiment one day. The chance hypothesis could be disproved if life is finally made in a test tube, or discovered on Mars and shown to be completely independent of earth life. Life and mind would be revealed as integral to the cosmos, embedded in the nature of things at the deepest level of reality. Human existence, already understood as fully natural, will be seen as linked to this deep level in an intimate and purposeful way.

The difference between the law hypothesis and the chance hypothesis is a vital question for Davies not only for scientific reasons but for spiritual ones as well. On the law hypothesis, our place in the cosmos would be far more inspiring. It would not necessarily invite the hubris of seeing ourselves at the center, or the pinnacle, of creation (humility is always appropriate), but neither would human life be relegated to the status of mere moving mounds of molecules. If life and mind is discovered to have emerged as part of the natural outworking of the laws of the universe, Davies will take it as strong evidence for a deeper purpose in physical existence. Since it is easy to imagine other universes and other sets of physical laws that would prohibit life, the fact that our universe is so ingeniously bio-friendly would surely be a fact of the utmost significance. The whole drift of Paul Davies's faith is in the direction of affirming purpose and meaning in the vast panorama of life, even when no purpose or meaning is visible. Invoking neither miracles nor supernatural causality, he nonetheless sees "divine purpose" in the universe.

When Davies talks about divine purpose and the ingenious, purposeful order at the very heart of things, religious believers may easily think he is talking their language. Yet his faith in God does not fit with familiar forms of monotheism. On a spectrum of meanings that ranges all the way from an invisible, omnipotent, personal God to the nebulous notion of Being-Itself, Davies describes himself as midway on the spectrum. By "God" he means the rational ground on which the order of the universe is rooted, but—as he explains below—the rational ground is timeless. Time is part of the physical order of the world, and what Davies means by God is something that transcends space-time. It makes no sense to him that God would be "in" time or have any temporal aspects; therefore, such acts as thinking, intending, willing, knowing, et cetera, cannot be attributed to God because they all presuppose elapses of time. This understanding of God will challenge any anthropomorphic conception. A further challenge would attend the confirmation of life on Mars or elsewhere, as Davies hopes will be the case. Though it would strengthen the conclusion that the universe shows signs of some kind of a purpose behind it, it would also weaken Christian claims about the Incarnation and biblical revelation.

The excerpts below give special prominence to Davies's reflections on ultimate origins. The first selection is taken from his address upon receiving the Templeton Prize for Progress in Religion in 1995. It is probably the clearest statement of his own beliefs. In the next two excerpts, he develops his conception of God, almost, but not quite, endorses the anthropic principle as it originated with Carr and Rees, and reflects upon the overwhelming impression of design in the universe. In the last selection, Davies takes up a new topic: complexity studies and the meaning of life. Here he introduces the ideas of emergentism and self-organization, twin themes that are further developed in the work of Stuart Kauffman (chapter 20) and Ursula Goodenough (chapter 21). The religious implications of these themes imply, as Davies says here, "a radical reinterpretation of religious tradition."

✌ Davies's Contribution to Science

Paul Davies is a theoretical physicist and head of a new cosmology think tank at Arizona State University. He has been a professor at the Australian Center for Astrobiology at Macquarie University in Sydney and retired from a professorship at the University of Adelaide. His research interests are in the fields of cosmology, quantum field theory, and astrobiology. He has conducted research in the areas of quantum gravity, gravitational entropy, physics of complexity and foundations of quantum mechanics. Working in the area of quantum field theory in curved space-time, he has investigated and discovered many quantum effects associated with black holes and the early stages of the big bang and published over a hundred research papers in specialist journals. His monograph Quantum Fields in Curved Space, *co-authored with former student Nicholas Birrell, remains a seminal text in the field of quantum gravity.*

Davies in His Own Words

Physics and the Mind of God²

Although not conventionally religious, Einstein often spoke of God, and expressed a sentiment shared, I believe, by many scientists, including professed atheists. It is a sentiment best described as a reverence for nature and a deep fascination for the natural order of the cosmos. If the universe did not have to be as it is, of necessity—if, to paraphrase Einstein, God did have a choice—then the fact that nature is so fruitful, that the universe is so full of richness, diversity and novelty, is profoundly significant.

Some scientists have tried to argue that if only we knew enough about the laws of physics, if we were to discover a final theory that united all the fundamental forces and particles of nature into a single mathematical scheme, then we would find that this super-law, or theory of everything, would describe the only logically consistent world. In other words, the nature of the physical world would be entirely a consequence of logical and mathematical necessity. There would be no choice about it. I think this is demonstrably wrong. There is not a shred of evidence that the universe is logically necessary. Indeed, as a theoretical physicist I find it rather easy to imagine alternative universes that are logically consistent, and therefore equal contenders for reality.

[2] Paul Davies, "Physics and the Mind of God: The Templeton Prize Address," *First Things* 55 (August/September 1995): 31–35.

It was from the intellectual ferment brought about by the merging of Greek philosophy and Judaeo-Islamic-Christian thought, that modern science emerged, with its unidirectional linear time, its insistence on nature's rationality, and its emphasis on mathematical principles. All the early scientists such as Newton were religious in one way or another. They saw their science as a means of uncovering traces of God's handiwork in the universe. What we now call the laws of physics they regarded as God's abstract creation: thoughts, so to speak, in the mind of God. So in doing science, they supposed, one might be able to glimpse the mind of God. What an exhilarating and audacious claim!

In the ensuing three hundred years, the theological dimension of science has faded. People take it for granted that the physical world is both ordered and intelligible. The underlying order in nature—the laws of physics—are simply accepted as given, as brute facts. Nobody asks where they come from; at least they don't in polite company. However, even the most atheistic scientist accepts as an act of faith the existence of a lawlike order in nature that is at least in part comprehensible to us. So science can proceed only if the scientist adopts an essentially theological world view.

Many people want to find God in the *creation* of the universe, in the big bang that started it all off. They imagine a Superbeing who deliberates for all eternity, then presses a metaphysical button and produces a huge explosion. I believe this image is entirely misconceived. Einstein showed us that space and time are part of the physical universe, not a pre-existing arena in which the universe happens. Cosmologists are convinced that the big bang was the coming-into-being, not just of matter and energy, but of space and time as well. Time itself began with the big bang. If this sounds baffling, it is by no means new. Already in the fifth century St. Augustine proclaimed that "the world was made with time, not in time." According to James Hartle and Stephen Hawking, this coming-into-being of the universe need not be a supernatural process, but could occur entirely naturally, in accordance with the laws of quantum physics, which permit the occurrence of genuinely spontaneous events.

The origin of the universe, however, is hardly the end of the story. The evidence suggests that in its primordial phase the universe was in a highly simple, almost featureless state: perhaps a uniform soup of subatomic particles, or even just expanding empty space. All the richness and diversity of matter and energy we observe today has emerged since the beginning in a long and complicated sequence of self-organizing physical processes. What an incredible thing these laws of physics are! Not only do they permit a universe to originate spontaneously; they encourage it to self-organize and self-complexify to the point where conscious beings emerge, and can look back on the great cosmic drama and reflect on what it all means.

Now you may think I have written God entirely out of the picture. Who needs a God when the laws of physics can do such a splendid job? But we are bound to return to that burning question: Where do the laws of physics come from? And why *those* laws rather than some other set? Most especially: Why a set of laws that drives the searing, featureless gases coughed out of the big bang, towards life and consciousness and intelligence and cultural activities such as religion, art, mathematics and science?

If there is a meaning or purpose to existence, as I believe there is, we are wrong to dwell too much on the originating event. The big bang is sometimes referred to as "the creation," but in truth nature has never *ceased* to be creative. This ongoing creativity, which manifests itself in the spontaneous emergence of novelty and complexity, and organization of physical systems, is permitted through, or guided by, the underlying mathematical laws that scientists are so busy discovering.

Now the laws of which I speak have the status of timeless eternal truths, in contrast to the physical states of the universe that change with time, and bring forth the genuinely new. So we here confront in physics a re-emergence of the oldest of all philosophical and theological debates: the paradoxical conjunction of the eternal and the temporal. Early Christian thinkers wrestled with the problem of time. Is God within the stream of time, or outside of it? How can a truly timeless God relate in any way to temporal beings such as ourselves? But how can a God who relates to a changing universe be considered eternal and unchangingly perfect?

A lot of people are hostile to science because it demystifies nature. They prefer the mystery. They would rather live in ignorance of the way the world works and our place within it. For me, the beauty of science is *precisely* the demystification, because it reveals just how truly wonderful the physical universe really is. It is impossible to be a scientist working at the frontier without being awed by the elegance, ingenuity and harmony of the law-like order in nature. In my attempts to popularize science, I'm driven by the desire to share my own sense of excitement and awe with the wider community; I want to tell people the good news. The fact that we are able to do science, that we can comprehend the hidden laws of nature, I regard as a gift of immense significance. Science, properly conducted, is a wonderfully enriching and humanizing enterprise. I cannot believe that using this gift called science—using it wisely, of course—is wrong. It is good that we should know.

So where is God in this story? Not especially in the big bang that starts the universe off, nor meddling fitfully in the physical processes that generate life and consciousness. I would rather that nature can take care of itself. The idea of a God who is just another force or agency at work in nature, moving atoms here and there in competition with physical forces, is profoundly uninspiring. To me, the true miracle of nature is to be found in the ingenious and unswerving lawfulness of the cosmos, a lawfulness that permits complex order to emerge from chaos, life to emerge from inanimate matter, and consciousness to emerge from life, without the need for the occasional supernatural prod; a lawfulness that produces beings who not only ask great questions of existence, but who, through science and other methods of enquiry, are even beginning to find answers.

You might be tempted to suppose that any old rag-bag of laws would produce a complex universe of some sort, with attendant inhabitants convinced of their own specialness. Not so. It turns out that randomly selected laws lead almost inevitably either to unrelieved chaos or boring and uneventful simplicity. Our own universe is poised exquisitely between these unpalatable alternatives, offering a potent mix of freedom and discipline, a sort of restrained creativity. The laws do not tie down physical systems so rigidly that they can accomplish little, nor are they a recipe for cosmic anarchy. Instead, they encourage matter and energy to develop along pathways of evolution that lead to novel variety, what Freeman Dyson has called the principle of maximum diversity: that in some sense we live in the most interesting possible universe.

᠅

The laws that characterize our actual universe, as opposed to an infinite number of alternative possible universes, seem almost contrived—fine-tuned, some commentators have claimed—so that life and consciousness may emerge. To quote Dyson again: it is almost as if "the universe knew we were coming." I can't prove to you that that is design, but whatever it is it is certainly very clever!

Now some of my colleagues embrace the same scientific facts as I, but deny any deeper significance. They shrug aside the breathtaking ingenuity of the laws of physics, the extraordinary felicity of nature, and the surprising intelligibility of the physical world, accepting these things as a package of marvels that just happens to be. But I cannot do this. To me, the contrived nature of physical existence is just too fantastic for me to take on board as simply "given." It points forcefully to a deeper underlying meaning to existence. Some call it purpose, some design. These loaded words, which derive from human categories, capture only imperfectly what it is that the universe is about. But that it is about something, I have absolutely no doubt.

Where do we human beings fit into this great cosmic scheme? Can we gaze out into the cosmos, as did our remote ancestors, and declare: "God made all this for us"? I think not. Are we then but an accident of nature, the freakish outcome of blind and purposeless forces, incidental by-product of a mindless, mechanistic universe? I reject that, too. The emergence of life and consciousness, I maintain, are written into the laws of the universe in a very basic way. True, the actual physical form and general mental make-up of *Homo sapiens* contain many accidental features of no particular significance. If the universe were rerun a second time, there would be no solar system, no Earth, and no people. But the emergence of life and consciousness somewhere and somewhen in the cosmos is, I believe, assured by the underlying laws of nature. The origin of life and consciousness were not interventionist miracles, but nor were they stupendously improbable accidents. They were, I believe, part of the natural outworking of the laws of nature, and as such our existence as conscious enquiring beings springs ultimately from the bedrock of physical existence—those ingenious, felicitous laws. . . .

How can we test these ideas scientifically? One of the great challenges to science is to understand the nature of consciousness in general and human consciousness in particular. We still have no clue how mind and matter are related, or what process led to the emergence of mind from matter in the first place. This is an area of research that is attracting considerable attention at present, and for my part I intend to pursue my own research in this field. I expect that when we do come to understand how consciousness fits into the physical universe, my contention that mind is an emergent and in principle predictable product of the laws of the universe will be borne out.

Moreover, if I am right that the universe is fundamentally creative in a pervasive and continuing manner, and that the laws of nature encourage matter and energy to self-organize and self-complexify to the point that life and consciousness emerge naturally, then there will be a universal trend or directionality towards the emergence of great complexity and diversity. We might then expect life and consciousness to exist throughout the universe. That is why I attach such importance to the search for extraterrestrial organisms, be they bacteria on Mars or advanced technological communities on the other side of the galaxy. The search may prove hopeless—the distances and numbers are certainly daunting—but it is a glorious quest. If we are alone in the universe, if the Earth is the only life-bearing planet among countless trillions, then the choice is stark. Either we are the product of a unique supernatural event in a universe of profligate over-provision, or else an accident of mind-numbing improbability and irrelevance. On the other hand, if life and mind are universal phenomena, if they are written into nature at its deepest level, then the case for an ultimate purpose to existence would be compelling.

It is often pointed out that people are increasingly turning away from the established religions. However, it remains as true as ever that ordinary men and women yearn for some sort of deeper meaning to their lives, what is sometimes loosely referred to as a "spiritual" aspect. Our secular age has led many people to feel demoralized and disillusioned, alienated from nature, regarding their existence as a pointless charade in an indifferent, even hostile, universe, a meaningless three-score years and ten on a remote planet wandering amid the vastness of an uncaring cosmos. Many of our social ills can be traced to the bleak worldview that three hundred years of mechanistic thought have imposed on us—a worldview in which human beings are presented as irrelevant observers of nature rather than an integral part of the natural order. Some may indeed recoil from this philosophy and find comfort in ancient wisdom and revered texts that place mankind at the pinnacle of creation and the center of the universe. Others choose to put their faith in so-called New Age mysticism, or resort to bizarre religious cults.

I would like to suggest an alternative. We have to find a framework of ideas that provides ordinary people with some broader context to their lives than just the daily round, a framework that links them to each other, to nature, and to the wider universe in a meaningful way, that yields a common set of principles around which peoples of all cultures can make ethical decisions yet remains honest in the face of scientific knowledge; indeed, that celebrates that knowledge alongside other human insights and inspirations. The scientific enterprise as I have presented it may not return human beings to the center of the universe, it may reject the notion of miracles other than the miracle of nature itself, but it does not make human beings irrelevant either. A universe in which the emergence of life and consciousness is seen, not as a freak set of events, but fundamental to its lawlike workings, is a universe that can truly be called our home.

I believe that mainstream science, if we are brave enough to embrace it, offers the most reliable path to knowledge about the physical world. I am certainly not saying that scientists are infallible, and neither am I suggesting that science should be turned into a latter-day religion. But I do think that if religion is to make real progress it cannot ignore the scientific culture; nor should it be afraid to do so, for as I have argued, science reveals just what a marvel the universe is.

If religion is to progress it must confront modern scientific thought. Over the years I have enjoyed fruitful discussions on science and religion with theologians of varying persuasions—behind closed doors. What has most impressed me about my encounters with these theologians has been their open-mindedness and willingness to accept the conclusions of modern science. While the interpretation of the scientific account of the world may be contentious, there is considerable consensus on the scientific facts themselves. Basic notions like the big bang theory, the origin of life and consciousness by natural physical processes, and Darwinian evolution seem to cause these theologians little difficulty.

Yet among the general population there is a widespread belief that science and theology are forever at loggerheads, that every scientific discovery pushes God further and further out of the picture. It is clear that many religious people still cling to an image of a God-of-the-gaps, a cosmic magician invoked to explain all those mysteries about nature that currently have the scientists stumped. It is a dangerous position, for as science advances, so the

God-of-the-gaps retreats, perhaps to be pushed off the edge of space and time altogether, and into redundancy.

The position I have presented to you today is radically different. It is one that regards the universe, not as the plaything of a capricious Deity, but as a coherent, rational, elegant, and harmonious expression of a deep and purposeful meaning. I believe the time has now come for those theologians who share this vision to join me and my scientific colleagues to take the message to the people.

Discovering a Timeless God[3]

None of this, of course, rules out a creative God, but it does suggest that divine action may be no more necessary for biology than it is for, say, producing the rings of Saturn or the surface features of Jupiter. We either see the evidence of God everywhere, or nowhere. Life is not, it would seem, exceptionally different from other complex organized structures, except perhaps in degree. Our ignorance of the origin of life leaves plenty of scope for divine explanations, but that is a purely negative attitude, invoking "the God-of-the-gaps" only to risk retreat at a later date in the face of scientific advance. Instead, let us regard life, not as an isolated miracle in an otherwise clockwork universe, but as an integral part of the cosmic miracle.

❧

This raises an intriguing theological question. Does God experience the passage of time? Christians believe that God is eternal. The word "eternal" has, however, been used to mean two rather different things. In the simpler version, eternal means everlasting, or existing without beginning or end for an infinite duration. There are grave objections to such an idea of God, however. A God who

---

[3] *God and the New Physics*, 70, 133ff., 209.

is in time is subject to change. But what causes that change? If God is the cause of all existing things (as the cosmological argument of chapter 3 suggests), then does it make sense to talk about that ultimate cause itself changing?

In the earlier chapters we have seen how time is not simply there, but is itself part of the physical universe. It is "elastic" and can stretch or shrink according to well-defined mathematical laws which depend on the behaviour of matter. Also, time is closely linked to space, and space and time together express the operation of the gravitational field. In short, time is involved in all the grubby details of physical processes just as much as matter. Time is not a divine quality, but can be altered, physically, even by human manipulation. A God who is in time is, therefore, in some sense caught up in the operation of the physical universe. Indeed, it is quite likely that time will cease to exist at some stage in the future. . . . In that case God's own position is obviously insecure. Clearly, God cannot be omnipotent if he is subject to the physics of time, nor can he be considered the creator of the universe if he did not create time. In fact, because time and space are inseparable, a God who did not create time, created space neither. But as we have seen, once spacetime existed, the appearance of matter and order in the universe could have occurred automatically as the result of perfectly natural activity. Thus, many would argue that God is not really needed as a creator at all *except* to create time (strictly, spacetime).

So we are led to the other meaning of the word eternal—"timeless." The concept of a God beyond time dates at least from Augustine who . . . suggested that God created time. It has received support from many of the Christian theologians. St. Anselm expresses the idea as follows: "You [God] exist neither yesterday, today, nor tomorrow, but you exist directly right outside time."

A timeless God is free of the problems mentioned above, but suffers from the shortcomings already discussed. . . . He cannot be a personal God who thinks, converses, feels, plans, and so on, for these are all temporal activities. It is hard to see how a timeless

God can act at all in time (although it has been claimed that this is not impossible). We have also seen how the sense of the existence of the self is intimately associated with the experience of a time-flow. A timeless God could not be considered a "person" or individual in any sense that we know. Misgivings of this score have led a number of modern theologians to reject this view of an eternal God. Paul Tillich writes: "If we call God a living God, we affirm that he includes temporality and with this a relation to the modes of time." The same sentiment is echoed by Karl Barth: "Without God's complete temporality the content of the Christian message has no shape." The physics of time also has interesting implications for the belief that God is omniscient. If God is timeless, he cannot be said to think, for thinking is a temporal activity. But can a timeless being have knowledge? Acquiring knowledge clearly involves time, but knowing as such does not—provided that what is known does not itself change with time. If God knows, for example, the position of every atom today, then that knowledge will change by tomorrow. To know timelessly must therefore involve his knowing all events throughout time.

There is thus a grave and fundamental difficulty in reconciling all the traditional attributes of God. Modern physics, with its discovery of the mutability of time, drives a wedge between God's omnipotence and the existence of his personality. It is difficult to argue that God can have both these qualities.

✌

Religious adherents have learned to their cost how perilous it is to point to a phenomenon and say "That is evidence of God's work," only to find that scientific advances subsequently provide a perfectly adequate explanation. To invoke God as a blanket explanation of the unexplained is to invite eventual falsification, and to make God the friend of ignorance. If God is to be found, it must surely be through what we discover about the world, not what we fail to discover.

Nevertheless a natural, as opposed to a supernatural, God fares better in the face of this argument. The hypothesis that a natural God created life, within the laws of physics, is at least known to be possible and consistent with our scientific understanding of the physical world, if only for the reason that the creation of life by man in the laboratory is a distinct (if remote) possibility.

Explaining Apparent Design[4]

Even as recently as the mid-1970s some of the achievements described in this book would have been unthinkable. Most cosmologists held that although physics could explain the development of the universe once it had been created, the ultimate origin of the universe lay beyond the scope of science. In particular, it seemed necessary to suppose that the universe was set up in a very peculiar state initially, in order that it might evolve to the form we now observe. Thus, all-important physical structures, all matter and energy, and their large-scale distribution had to be assumed as god-given; they had to be put in "by hand" as unexplained initial conditions. With the recent breakthrough in understanding, all these features emerge naturally and automatically as a consequence of the laws of physics. The initial conditions, inasmuch as we may even make sense of the concept in a quantum context, exercise no influence on the structure of the universe which emerges subsequently. Thus the universe is seen to be a product of *law* rather than *chance*.

The fact that the present nature of the universe was bound to have developed from the big bang origin—it is written into the laws of physics—strongly suggests that these laws are not themselves accidental or haphazard, but contain an element of design. Despite the decline of traditional religion, ordinary men and women continue to search for a meaning behind existence. The

---

[4] Paul Davies, *Superforce: The Search for a Grand Unified Theory of Nature* (New York: Simon and Schuster, 1984), 9, 236, 241ff.

new physics and the new cosmology reveal that our ordered universe is far more than a gigantic accident. I believe that a study of the recent revolution in these subjects is a source of great inspiration in the search for the meaning of life.

❧

In the case of the crossword, it would never occur to us to suppose that the words just happened to fall into a consistent interlocking pattern by accident, that the subtlety and ingenuity of the clues are merely brute facts of no significance, or the product of our own minds attempting to make sense of meaningless information. Yet one frequently encounters precisely these arguments concerning the miracle of nature, which is overwhelmingly more subtle and ingenious than any crossword. If, then, we do not doubt that the order, consistency, and harmony of a crossword imply that the puzzle is the product of an ingenious, inventive mind, why are such doubts voiced in the case of the universe? Why is the evidence of design so compelling in one case but not in the other?

In the nineteenth century the existence of order and harmony in nature was frequently used by theologians as an argument for a supernatural designer. One of the most articulate proponents of the design argument was William Paley, who employed an analogy between natural mechanisms and a watch. Paley invited one to consider coming across a watch unwittingly and, after examining its intricate mechanism of interlocking components, reasonably concluding that it had been designed for a purpose by some intelligent mind. Comparing the watch with the many extraordinarily refined mechanisms in nature, such as the orderly arrangement of planets in the solar system and the complex organization of living creatures, Paley declared that the evidence for intelligent design was still more forcefully apparent than in the case of the watch.

In spite of its superficial appeal, Paley's argument—and many subsequent attempts to deduce the existence of design from the workings of nature—has been savagely attacked by philosophers and scientists.

✋

It is interesting to ask just how improbable it is that the laws of physics permit complex structures to exist. How finely must these laws be "tuned"?

In a famous article in the journal *Nature* British astrophysicists Bernard Carr and Martin Rees concluded that the world is extraordinarily sensitive to even minute changes in the laws of physics, so that if the particular set of laws we have were to be altered in any way the universe would change beyond recognition.

Carr and Rees found that the existence of complex structures seems to depend very sensitively on the numerical values that nature has assigned to the so-called fundamental constants, the numbers which determine the scale of physical phenomena. Among these constants are the speed of light, the masses of the various subatomic particles, and a number of "coupling" constants such as the elementary unit of charge, which determine how strongly the various force fields act on matter. The actual numerical values adopted by these quantities determine many of the gross features of the world, such as the sizes of atoms, nuclei, planets, and stars, the density of material in the universe, the lifetime of stars, and even the height of animals.

Most of the complex structures observed in the universe are the products of a competition or balance between competing forces. Stars, for example, while superficially quiescent, are actually a battleground in the interplay between the four forces. Gravity tries to crush the stars. Electromagnetic energy fights against it by providing an internal pressure. The energy involved is released from the nuclear processes legislated by the weak and strong force. In these circumstances, where a tightly interlocking competition occurs, the structure of the system depends delicately on the strengths of the forces, or the numerical values of the fundamental constants.

Astrophysicist Brandon Carter has studied the stellar battleground in detail, and he finds that there is an almost unbelievable delicacy in the balance between gravity and electromagnetism within a star. Calculations show that changes in the strength of either force by only one part in 10^{40} would spell catastrophe for stars like the sun.

Many other important physical structures are highly sensitive to minor alterations in the relative strengths of the forces. For example, a small percentage increase in the strength of the strong force would have caused all the hydrogen nuclei in the universe to have been consumed in the big bang, leaving a cosmos devoid of its most important stellar fuel.

In my book *The Accidental Universe* I have made a comprehensive study of all the apparent "accidents" and "coincidences" that seem to be necessary in order that the important complex structures which we observe in the universe should exist. The sheer improbability that these felicitous concurrences could be the result of a series of exceptionally lucky accidents has prompted many scientists to agree with Hoyle's pronouncement that "the universe is a put-up job."

The supreme example of complex organization in the universe is life, and so special interest attaches to the question of how dependent is our own existence on the exact form of the laws of physics. Certainly, human beings require highly special conditions for their survival, and almost any change in the laws of physics, including the most minute variations in the numerical values of the fundamental constants, would rule out life as we know it. A more interesting question, however, is whether such minute changes would make *any* form of life impossible. Answering this question is difficult because of the absence of any generally agreed definition of life. If, however, we agree that life requires at least the existence of heavy atoms such as carbon, then quite stringent limits can be placed on some of the fundamental constants. For example, the weak force, which is the driving force behind the supernovae explosions that liberate the heavy elements into interstellar space, could not vary too much in strength from its observed value and still effectively explode stars.

The upshot of these studies seems to be that many of the important physical structures in the universe, including living organisms, depend crucially on the exact form of the laws of physics. Had the universe been created with slightly different laws, not only would we (or anybody else) not be here to see it, but it is doubtful if there would be any complex structures at all.

It is sometimes objected that if the laws of physics were different, that would only mean that the structures would be different, and that while life as we know it might be impossible, some other form of life could well emerge. However, no attempt has been made to demonstrate that complex structures in general are an inevitable, or even probable, product of physical laws, and all the evidence so far indicates that many complex structures depend most delicately on the existing form of these laws. It is tempting to believe, therefore, that a complex universe will emerge only if the laws of physics are very close to what they are.

Should we conclude that the universe is a product of design? The new physics and the new cosmology hold out a tantalizing promise: that we might be able to explain how all the physical structures in the universe have come to exist, automatically, as a result of natural processes. We should then no longer have need for a Creator in the traditional sense. Nevertheless, though science may explain the world, we still have to explain science. The laws which enable the universe to come into being spontaneously seem themselves to be the product of exceedingly ingenious design. If physics is the product of design, the universe must have a purpose, and the evidence of modern physics suggests strongly to me that the purpose includes us.

Complexity Studies and the Quest for Meaning[5]

[C]omplexity theory is more than a research paradigm: It is also an incentive for an emergentist worldview that impinges on the

---

[5] Paul Davies, "Introduction: Towards an Emergentist Worldview," in *From Complexity to Life: On the Emergence of Life and Meaning*, ed. Niels Henrik Gregerson (Oxford, New York: Oxford University Press, 2003), 13–16. See also in the same volume Paul Davies, "Complexity and the Arrow of Time," 72–92.

question of the meaning of the universe. Even though most would agree that meaning is not part of the agenda of science itself, "why" questions may well motivate research; furthermore, scientific discoveries will inevitably give new twists to the perennial quest for some sort of ultimate meaning or purpose. It is a baffling fact that even if the causal *route* from complexity to life can be explained in the prosaic language of mathematics, the *outcome* of these prosaic processes indeed does evoke poetic descriptions. Out of the simple arises complexity, a vibrant world of life and sentience, joy and suffering. Science as such does not care much about the question of the meaning or meaninglessness of natural systems. But our responses to the quest for cosmic meaning are inevitably shaped by scientific assumptions concerning the way the world is and how nature works.

In this sense the scientific quest for explaining the route "from complexity to life" provokes a postscientific quest for understanding the emergence of meaning, "from complexity to consciousness." This is where philosophy and theology may enter the picture. . . . What then are the options available? One way to go would be to stay with the idea of God as the ingenious Architect of the world, who has contrived the laws of nature so that sentient and intelligent beings (such as us) will arise to reflect on the wonder of it all. This notion of God as a metadesigner provides an obvious, if somewhat simplistic, theological basis to the scientific notion of human beings "at home in the universe."

❧

However one positions oneself in this debate, it should be noted that major strands of modern theology remain altogether skeptical about the Enlightenment notion of a purely transcendent designer God. In particular, the wide majority of modern theologians find the intelligent design proposal unattractive, both because it seems to endanger the God-given autonomy of the natural order and because it seems to commit the fallacy of misplaced concreteness. God becomes too closely tied up with (assumed) gaps in scientific explanation. Accordingly, God's activity seems to be confined to the role of a cosmic magician who overrules the created order, attributable to God in the first place, rather than that of the beneficent creator who supports in-built capacities of matter.

According to Harold Morowitz, an emergentist worldview suggests that the divine immanence unfolds into the domain of an evolving world that makes transcendence possible. On this view, the transcendence of God is itself an emergent reality. God is not only the wellspring of the natural world but also a result that flows out of the workings of nature. The human mind is then God's transcendence, God's image. This idea of God as an emergent reality of evolution would probably imply a radical reinterpretation of religious tradition.

Another option is suggested by Arthur Peacocke, who argues for a so-called panentheistic model. God is here seen both as ontologically distinct from the world (and thus as necessarily transcendent) and yet as immanent in, with, and under natural processes. On this model, creation is seen as the self-expression of God the Word or Logos. God is equally expressed everywhere in the universe, not so much in the dull inertness of matter as in the complex beauty of the universe, not so much in selfishness as in self-giving love. Important for this position is the question whether emergent realities can themselves be causally efficacious and further propagate to enrich the cosmic order. For to be "real, new and irreducible . . . must be to have new irreducible causal powers," according to Samuel Alexander, an early proponent of emergentism.

The emergentist worldview seems to present us with a twofold task requiring a collaboration between the natural sciences, philosophy, and theology. The first is about the causal structure of our world. It seems that the universe is driven by different sorts of causality. If, as suggested by Stuart Kauffman . . . lawlike tendencies toward complexity inevitably end up producing autonomous agents that are able to perform various thermodynamical work cycles, and if the concrete movements and whereabouts of these autonomous agents are not predetermined by the general laws that produced them in the first place, then we shall never be in a position to pre-state all possible adaptations in the history of evolution. The causal structure of the universe would then consist of an intricate interplay between the "constitutive" and global laws of physics and the local "structuring" constraints that are exercised via the specific informational states of evolved agents. The atmosphere surrounding our planet is itself a result of myriads of such thermodynamical work cycles; indeed, local autonomous agents performing photosynthesis have influenced the biosphere as a whole. Analogous sorts of multilevel causality may also be at work in human beings. The functioning of our brains is a constitutive cause of our sentience and thoughts; yet how we use our brains is codetermined by the language and behavior of sociocultural agents; thus our concrete mental operations (such as doing math or playing the violin eight hours daily) will have a feedback influence on the neural structure of the individual brains. There seem to be different sorts of causality at work here. Some speak of bottom-up versus top-down causality, while others speak of constitutive versus structuring causality. Regardless of our own religious sympathies or antipathies, we approach much of life through emergent qualities such as trust, love, and the sense of beauty. If these phenomena now have a safer place in the causal fabric of reality, they can no longer be deemed to be mere epiphenomena. This new emphasis on top-down or informational causality will probably also influence the manner in which theologians conceive of God's interaction with the evolving world of autonomous agents.

The second question relates to meaning: How does a sense of meaning emerge from a universe of inanimate matter subject to blind and purposeless forces? Perhaps the lesson to be learned from complexity studies (a feature that links it so well with evolutionary theory) is that nature is not only a self-repetitive structure but a structure that seems as if it is geared for letting specified autonomous agents appear and propagate further. If this is so, we need both scientific explanations of the general principles underlying natural processes and accounts that are sensitive to the specifics and capable of explaining to us why we have evolved to be the particular creatures we are today.

We seem to be constructed from an overwhelmingly vast tapestry of biological possibilities, yet our lives also consist of singularities. The hard mysteries of existence are no longer placed only in the very small (in quantum physics) and in the vastness of the universe but also in the realm of the exceedingly complex. A high degree of complexity always implies a high degree of specificity: a "thisness," or haecceity, as the medieval philosopher Duns Scotus called it. At a personal level, we may tend to regard our lives as a gift or as a burden. But in the final analysis the question of meaning is about how to come to terms with the specificity of our individual existence.

Further Reading

A gifted expositor of science for the layperson, Paul Davies has authored over twenty books. See *About Time* (New York: Simon and Schuster, 1995), which discusses the properties of time and theories about it since Einstein's revolutionary theory of relativity; *Are We Alone?* (New York: Basic Books, 1995), which takes up the possibility of extraterrestrial life; and *The Fifth Miracle: The Search for the Origin and Meaning of Life* (New York: Simon and Schuster, 1998) and *The Origin of Life* (Penguin Books, 2003), which survey scientific knowledge of the origin of life itself. For a statement of how his generic theism can be understood as "panentheism," see Paul Davies, "Teleology without Teleology: Purpose through Emergent Complexity," in *In Whom We Live and Move and Have Our Being: Panentheistic Reflections on God's Presence in a Scientific World*, edited by Philip Clayton and Arthur Peacocke (Grand Rapids, MI: Wm. B. Eerdmans, 2004), 95–108. For a critique of Davies's reasoning and an argument that there must be a transcendent cause of the universe, see William Lane Craig, "The Existence of God and the Beginning of the Universe," *Truth: A Journal of Modern Thought* 3 (1991): 85–96.

19 Edward O. Wilson
(1929–)

Introduction

The world's most famous entomologist, Edward O. Wilson, is Pellegrino University Professor Emeritus at Harvard University. Born in Birmingham, Alabama, and born-again as a Southern Baptist, Wilson grew up keenly religious. As a teenager, he read the Bible from cover to cover, twice. Two influences left an indelible imprint on this shy child of divorced parents: the power of evangelical Christianity and the plants and animals of the southern towns he explored as he moved from school to school. In college, he discovered evolution and was enthralled. "A tumbler fell somewhere in my mind," he explains, "and a door opened to a new world." Wilson exchanged his Christian faith for scientific humanism and found that, for him, science is akin to faith. From the facts of evolutionary biology new intimations of immortality could be drawn and a new mythos evolved. The evolutionary epic, retold as poetry, is as intrinsically ennobling as any religious epic, he believes. One must have a sacred narrative, a sense of larger purpose, in one form or other, according to Wilson. It can be either a religion or a science.

Interested in genes and human nature, in 1975 Wilson wrote about "sociobiology," a term he coined to speculate that, as with other species, there is a genetic basis to such aspects of human behavior as small group living, territoriality, male dominance, and assimilation into hierarchies. Reopening the old "nature" versus "nurture" debates, he helped prepare the way for Richard Dawkins's "selfish gene" in 1976. *Sociobiology: The New Synthesis* was undoubtedly Wilson's most controversial book, but its critical reception did not deter him from continuing to seek what his subtitle announced, a new synthesis. In terms of religion and science, he would eventually advise an alliance between the two for policy purposes.

In *Consilience: The Unity of Knowledge*, Wilson adopted a term coined by William Whewell, a nineteenth-century philosopher of science, to mean the melding together of inferences drawn from separate subjects. For Wilson consilience is the aim to unify all the major branches of knowledge, including sociology, economics, the arts, and religion, under the banner of science. At the very root of the unified tree of knowledge is physics, with chemistry, molecular biology, and genetics as its trunk and everything else as its branches.

Not many scholars in the humanities welcomed this program. It is one thing when scientists explain thermodynamics (heat processes) in terms of a more fundamental discipline such as statistical mechanics (equations describing the movement of molecules), but can ethics and religion really be explained by molecular biology? Wilson believes the day is coming when new approaches to the brain will be able to explain consciousness and higher cognitive functions in terms of genetic programming. Humans, of course, are hardly programmed like ants, but our behavior is governed by epigenetic rules, or genetically based neural wiring that predisposes the brain to favor or be averse to certain types of activity. Searching for human nature, he thinks, involves tracing the archeology of the epigenetic rules that guide altruism, status-seeking, territorial expansion, incest taboos, and a range of other behaviors. The epigenetic roots of religion evolved, Wilson says, because the submissive behavior associated with belief in superhuman agents conferred a survival value.

Now we are facing a new phase that Wilson calls "volitional evolution," in which the same techniques used to cure genetic diseases will be used to change the very genes that shape the contours of the human mind. Having such capability, what will we do? Will we choose to change human nature or leave it as shaped by evolution? Wilson's own recommendation is that we leave human nature as it is, lest in attempting to neutralize imperfections we make ourselves into badly constructed, protein-based computers.

Wilson is undaunted by statistics that purport to show that America has many more devout Baptists than believers in Darwin's dangerous idea. "The human mind evolved to believe in the gods," he writes. "It did not evolve to believe in biology. Acceptance of the supernatural conveyed a great advantage throughout prehistory, when the brain was evolving. Thus it is in sharp contrast to biology, which was developed as a product of the modern age and is not underwritten by genetic algorithms. The uncomfortable truth is that the two beliefs are not factually compatible. As a result those who hunger for both intellectual and religious truth will never acquire both in full measure."[1]

And yet there is a common ground, he now sees, where both religion and science can meet and work together—to preserve and protect the environment, disappearing species, and possibly life itself on this planet. In the excerpts below from *The Creation: An Appeal to Save Life on Earth*, Wilson, in the guise of a letter to a Southern Baptist pastor, espouses a practical approach and makes a passionate appeal for religion and science, the two most powerful forces in the world, to combine to save the creation, to save biodiversity, the world's ecosystems, the very world in which we were born, and live and move and have our being.

---

[1] Edward O. Wilson, *Consilience: The Unity of Knowledge* (New York: Alfred A. Knopf, 1998), 262.

❧ Wilson's Contribution to Science

*After discovering new species of ants, Edward O. Wilson sur-
veyed the evolution of sociality among wasps, bees, and termites.
With a passion for classification and discovering patterns in the
insect world as well as the human population, Wilson has produced original works of synthesis to explain how sexual selection,
group selection, altruism, and hierarchies work in populations of
animals and to identify evolutionary trends and sociobiological
characteristics of all animal groups, up to and including humans.
He has been awarded two Pulitzer Prizes, one for* On Human
Nature *in 1979, another for* The Ants *in 1991 (shared with Bert
Hölldobler). Wilson has won many scientific awards, including
the National Medal of Science and the Crafoord Prize of the
Royal Swedish Academy of Sciences. For his contributions to conservation biology, he has been awarded the Audubon Medal and
the gold medal of the Worldwide Fund for Nature.*

Wilson in His Own Words

Letter to a Southern Baptist Pastor: Salutation[2]

Dear Pastor:

We have not met, yet I feel I know you well enough to call you
friend. First of all, we grew up in the same faith. As a boy I too
answered the altar call; I went under the water. Although I no
longer belong to that faith, I am confident that if we met and
spoke privately of our deepest beliefs, it would be in a spirit of
mutual respect and good will. I know we share many precepts of
moral behavior. Perhaps it also matters that we are both Americans and, insofar as it might still affect civility and good manners,
we are both Southerners.

[2] Edward O. Wilson, *The Creation: An Appeal to Save Life on Earth.* W. W.
Norton, (New York: 2006), 3–14, 165–68.

I write to you now for your counsel and help. Of course, in doing so, I see no way to avoid the fundamental differences in our respective worldviews. You are a literalist interpreter of Christian Holy Scripture. You reject the conclusion of science that mankind evolved from lower forms. You believe that each person's soul is immortal, making this planet a way station to a second, eternal life. Salvation is assured those who are redeemed in Christ.

I am a secular humanist. I think existence is what we make of it as individuals. There is no guarantee of life after death, and heaven and hell are what we create for ourselves, on this planet. There is no other home. Humanity originated here by evolution from lower forms over millions of years. And yes, I will speak plain, our ancestors were apelike animals. The human species has adapted physically and mentally to life on Earth and no place else. Ethics is the code of behavior we share on the basis of reason, law, honor, and an inborn sense of decency, even as some ascribe it to God's will.

For you, the glory of an unseen divinity; for me, the glory of the universe revealed at last. For you, the belief in God made flesh to save mankind; for me, the belief in Promethean fire seized to set men free. You have found your final truth; I am still searching. I may be wrong, you may be wrong. We may both be partly right.

Does this difference in worldview separate us in all things? It does not. You and I and every other human being strive for the same imperatives of security, freedom of choice, personal dignity, and a cause to believe in that is larger than ourselves.

Let us see, then, if we can, and you are willing, to meet on the near side of metaphysics in order to deal with the real world we share. I put it this way because you have the power to help solve a great problem about which I care deeply. I hope you have the same concern. I suggest that we set aside our differences in order to save the Creation. The defense of living Nature is a universal value. It doesn't rise from, nor does it promote, any religious or ideological dogma. Rather, it serves without discrimination the interests of all humanity.

Pastor, we need your help. The Creation—living Nature—is in deep trouble. Scientists estimate that if habitat conversion and other destructive human activities continue at their present rates, half the species of plants and animals on Earth could be either gone or at least fated for early extinction by the end of the century. A full quarter will drop to this level during the next half century as a result of climate change alone. The ongoing extinction rate is calculated in the most conservative estimates to be about a hundred times above that prevailing before humans appeared on Earth, and it is expected to rise to at least a thousand times greater or more in the next few decades. If this rise continues unabated, the cost to humanity, in wealth, environmental security, and quality of life, will be catastrophic.

Surely we can agree that each species, however inconspicuous and humble it may seem to us at this moment, is a masterpiece of biology, and well worth saving. Each species possesses a unique combination of genetic traits that fits it more or less precisely to a particular part of the environment. Prudence alone dictates that we act quickly to prevent the extinction of species and, with it, the pauperization of Earth's ecosystems—hence of the Creation.

You may well ask at this point, Why me? Because religion and science are the two most powerful forces in the world today, including especially the United States. If religion and science could be united on the common ground of biological conservation, the problem would soon be solved. If there is any moral precept shared by people of all beliefs, it is that we owe ourselves and future generations a beautiful, rich, and healthful environment.

I am puzzled that so many religious leaders, who spiritually represent a large majority of people around the world, have hesitated to make protection of the Creation an important part of their magisterium. Do they believe that human-centered ethics and preparation for the afterlife are the only things that matter? Even more perplexing is the widespread conviction among Christians that the Second Coming is imminent, and that therefore the condition of the planet is of little consequence. Sixty percent of Americans, according to a 2004 poll, believe that the prophecies of the book of Revelation are accurate. Many of these, numbering in the millions, think the End of Time will occur within the life span of those now living. Jesus will return to Earth, and those redeemed by Christian faith will be transported bodily to heaven, while those left behind will struggle through severe hard times and, when they die, suffer eternal damnation. The condemned will remain in hell, like those already consigned in the generations before them, for a trillion trillion years, enough for the universe to expand to its own, entropic death, time enough for countless universes like it afterward to be born, expand, and likewise die away. And that is just the beginning of how long condemned souls will suffer in hell—all for a mistake they made in choice of religion during the infinitesimally small time they inhabited Earth.

For those who believe this form of Christianity, the fate of ten million other life forms indeed does not matter. This and other similar doctrines are not gospels of hope and compassion. They are gospels of cruelty and despair. They were not born of the heart of Christianity. Pastor, tell me I am wrong!

However you will respond, let me here venture an alternative ethic. The great challenge of the twenty-first century is to raise people everywhere to a decent standard of living while preserving as much of the rest of life as possible. Science has provided this part of the argument for the ethic: the more we learn about the biosphere, the more complex and beautiful it turns out to be. Knowledge of it is a magic well: the more you draw from it, the more there is to draw. Earth, and especially the razor-thin film of life enveloping it, is our home, our wellspring, our physical and much of our spiritual sustenance.

I know that science and environmentalism are linked in the minds of many with evolution, Darwin, and secularism. Let me postpone disentangling all this (I will come back to it later) and stress again: to protect the beauty of Earth and of its prodigious variety of life forms should be a common goal, regardless of differences in our metaphysical beliefs.

To make the point in good gospel manner, let me tell the story of a young man, newly trained for the ministry, and so fixed in his Christian faith that he referred all questions of morality to readings from the Bible. When he visited the cathedral-like Atlantic rainforest of Brazil, he saw the manifest hand of God and in his notebook wrote, "It is not possible to give an adequate idea of the higher feelings of wonder, admiration, and devotion which fill and elevate the mind."

That was Charles Darwin in 1832, early into the voyage of HMS *Beagle*, before he had given any thought to evolution.

And here is Darwin, concluding *On the Origin of Species* in 1859, having first abandoned Christian dogma and then, with his newfound intellectual freedom, formulated the theory of evolution by natural selection: "There is grandeur in this view of life, with its several powers, having been originally breathed into a few forms or into one; and that, whilst this planet has gone cycling on according to the fixed law of gravity, from so simple a beginning endless forms most beautiful and most wonderful have been, and are being, evolved."

Darwin's reverence for life remained the same as he crossed the seismic divide that divided his spiritual life. And so it can be for the divide that today separates scientific humanism from mainstream religion. And separates you and me. You are well prepared to present the theological and moral arguments for saving the Creation. I am heartened by the movement growing within Christian denominations to support global conservation. The stream of thought has arisen from many sources, from evangelical to unitarian. Today it is but a rivulet. Tomorrow it will be a flood.

I already know much of the religious argument on behalf of the Creation, and would like to learn more. I will now lay before you and others who may wish to hear it the scientific argument. You will not agree with all that I say about the origins of life—science and religion do not easily mix in such matters—but I like to think that in this one life-and-death issue we have a common purpose.

Ascending to Nature

At the very least, Pastor, I expect we agree that somehow and somewhere back in history humanity lost its way. As a Christian minister, you will likely respond that of course we lost our way, we departed from Eden. Our progenitors made a terrible mistake, and so we live in original sin. Now we wander between heaven and hell, above the animals but below the angels, as we await ascension to a better world through faith in the Redeemer.

Would you be willing to suppose that part of Eden was the rest of life as it was before humanity? The book of Genesis affirms that much, whether read literally or metaphorically. The conclusion of science also is that such a primordial world existed and served as the cradle of humanity. Yet—if biology has learned anything, it is that our species did not, in contradiction to a literalist reading of Genesis, come abruptly into existence by a touch of divine fire. Instead, we evolved in a biologically rich world over tens of thousands of generations. Nor were we driven from this Eden. Instead, we destroyed most of it in order to improve our lives and generate more people. Billions of more people, to the peril of the Creation. I would like to offer the following explanation of the human dilemma:

According to archaeological evidence, we strayed from Nature with the beginning of civilization roughly ten thousand years ago. That quantum leap beguiled us with an illusion of freedom from the world that had given us birth. It nourished the belief that the human spirit can be molded into something new to fit changes in the environment and culture, and as a result the timetables of history desynchronized. A wiser intelligence might now truthfully say of us at this point: here is a chimera, a new and very odd species come shambling into our universe, a mix of Stone Age emotion, medieval self-image, and godlike technology. The combination makes the species unresponsive to the forces that count most for its own long-term survival.

There seems no better way to explain why so many smart people remain passive while the precious remnants of the natural world disappear. They are evidently unaware that ecological services provided scott-free by wild environments, by Eden, are approximately equal in dollar value to the gross world product. They choose to remain innocent of the historical principle that civilizations collapse when their environments are ruined. Most troubling of all, our leaders, including those of the great religions, have done little to protect the living world in the midst of its sharp decline. They have ignored the command of the Abrahamic God on the fourth day of the world's birth to "let the waters teem with countless living creatures, and let birds fly over the land across the vault of heaven."

I hesitate to introduce a beautiful subject with an animadversion. Few will deny, however, that the human impact on the natural environment is accelerating and makes a frightening picture.

What are we to do? At the very least, put together an honest history, one on which people of many faiths can in principle agree. If such can be fashioned, it will serve at least as prologue to a safer future.

We can begin with the key discovery of green history: *Civilization was purchased by the betrayal of Nature.* The Neolithic revolution, comprising the invention of agriculture and villages, fed on Nature's bounty. The forward leap was a blessing for humanity. Yes, it was: those who have lived among hunter-gatherers will tell you they are not at all to be envied. But the revolution encouraged the false assumption that a tiny selection of domesticated plants and animals can support human expansion indefinitely. The pauperization of Earth's fauna and flora was an acceptable price until recent centuries, when Nature seemed all but infinite, and an enemy to explorers and pioneers. The wildernesses and the aboriginals surviving in them were there to be pushed back and eventually replaced, in the name of progress and in the name of the gods too, lest we forget.

History now teaches a different lesson, but only to those who will listen. Even if the rest of life is counted of no value beyond the satisfaction of human bodily needs, the obliteration of Nature is a dangerous strategy. For one thing, we have become a species specialized to eat the seeds of four kinds of grass—wheat, rice, corn, and millet. If these fail, from disease or climate change, we too shall fail. Some fifty thousand wild plant species (many of which face extinction} offer alternative food sources. If one insists on being thoroughly practical about the matter, allowing these and the rest of wild species to exist should be considered part of a portfolio of long-term investment. Even the most recalcitrant people must come to view conservation as simple prudence in the management of Earth's natural economy. Yet few have begun to think that way at all.

Meanwhile, the modern technoscientific revolution, including especially the great leap forward of computer-based information technology, has betrayed Nature a second time, by fostering the belief that the cocoons of urban and suburban material life are sufficient for human fulfillment. That is an especially serious mistake. Human nature is deeper and broader than the artifactual contrivance of any existing culture. The spiritual roots of *Homo sapiens* extend deep into the natural world through still mostly hidden channels of mental development. We will not reach our full potential without understanding the origin and hence meaning of the aesthetic and religious qualities that make us ineffably human.

Granted, many people seem content to live entirely within the synthetic ecosystems. But so are domestic animals content, even in the grotesquely abnormal habitats in which we rear them. This in my mind is a perversion. It is not the nature of human beings to be cattle in glorified feedlots. Every person deserves the option to travel easily in and out of the complex and primal world that gave us birth. We need freedom to roam across land owned by no one but protected by all, whose unchanging horizon is the same that bounded the world of our millennial ancestors. Only in what remains of Eden, teeming with life forms independent of us, is it possible to experience the kind of wonder that shaped the human psyche at its birth.

Scientific knowledge, humanized and well taught, is the key to achieving a lasting balance in our lives. The more biologists learn about the biosphere in its full richness, the more rewarding the image. Similarly, the more psychologists learn of the development of the human mind, the more they understand the gravitational pull of the natural world on our spirit, and on our souls.

We have a long way to go to make peace with this planet, and with each other. We took a wrong turn when we launched the

Neolithic revolution. We have been trying ever since to ascend *from* Nature instead of *to* Nature. It is not too late for us to come around, without losing the quality of life already gained, in order to receive the deeply fulfilling beneficence of humanity's natural heritage. Surely the reach of religious belief is great enough, and its teachers generous and imaginative enough, to encompass this larger truth not adequately expressed in Holy Scripture.

Part of the dilemma is that while most people around the world care about the natural environment, they don't know why they care, or why they should feel responsible for it. By and large they have been unable to articulate what the stewardship of Nature means to them personally. This confusion is a great problem for contemporary society as well as for future generations. It is linked to another great difficulty, the inadequacy of science education, everywhere in the world. Both arise in part from the explosive growth and complexity of modern biology. Even the best scientists have trouble keeping up with more than a small part of what has emerged as the most important science for the twenty-first century.

I believe that the solution to all of the three difficulties—ignorance of the environment, inadequate science education, and the bewildering growth of biology—is to refigure them into a single problem. I hope you will agree that every educated person should know something about the core of this unified issue. Teacher and student alike will benefit from a recognition that living Nature has opened a broad pathway to the heart of science itself, that the breath of our life and our spirit depend upon its survival. And to grasp and discuss on common ground this principle: because we are part of it, the fate of the Creation is the fate of humanity.

✢

An Alliance for Life

Pastor, I am grateful for your attention. As a scientist who has spent a lifetime studying the Creation, I have done my best here to brief you and others on subjects I hope will be more part of our common concern. My foundation of reference has been the culture of science and some of secularism based on science, as I understand them. From that foundation I have focused on the interaction of three problems that affect everyone: the decline of the living environment, the inadequacy of scientific education, and the moral confusions caused by the exponential growth of biology. In order to solve these problems, I've argued, it will be necessary to find common ground on which the powerful forces of religion and science can be joined. The best place to start is the stewardship of life.

Obviously, neither religion nor science has addressed this great issue effectively. I've attempted to identify those elements of biology and education most relevant to the proposed partnership. In the process I've not tried to water down in any way the fundamental difference between science and mainstream religion concerning the origin of life. God made the Creation, you say. This truth is plainly stated in Holy Scripture. Twenty-five centuries of theology and much of Western civilization have been built upon it. But no, I say, respectfully. Life was self-assembled by random mutation and natural selection of the codifying molecules. As radical as such an explanation may seem, it is supported by an overwhelming body of interlocking evidence. It might yet prove wrong, but year by year that seems less probable. And it raises this theological question: Would God have been so deceptive as to salt the earth with so much misleading evidence?

Much as I would like to think otherwise, I see no hope for compromise in the idea of Intelligent Design. Simply put, this proposal agrees that evolution occurs but argues that it is guided by a supernatural intelligence. The evidence for Intelligent Design, however, consists solely of a default argument. Its logic is simply this: biologists have not yet explained how complex systems such as the human eye and spinning bacterial cilium could have evolved by themselves; therefore a higher intelligence must have guided the evolution. Unfortunately, no positive evidence exists for Intelligent Design. None has been proposed to test it. No theory has been suggested, or even imagined, to explain the transcription from supernatural force to organic reality. That is why statured scientists, those who have led in original research, unanimously agree that the theory of Intelligent Design does not qualify as science.

Some have suggested that scientists have formed a conspiracy to halt the search for Intelligent Design. There is no such conspiracy. There is only agreement among experts that the hypothesis has none of the defining qualities of science. To think otherwise is to misunderstand the culture of science. Discoveries and the testing of discoveries are the currency of science, its irreplaceable silver and gold. Challenges to prevailing theory on the basis of new evidence is the hallmark of science. If positive and repeatable evidence were adduced for a supernatural intelligent force that created and guided the evolution of life, it would deservedly rank as the greatest scientific discovery of all time. It would transform philosophy and change the course of history. Scientists dream of making a discovery of this magnitude!

Without such an event, however, it is a dangerous step for theologians to summon the default argument of Intelligent Design as scientific support for religious belief. Biologists are explaining the previously unexplainable—providing evolutionary steps for the autonomous origin of ever more complex systems—at an accelerating pace. What is to become of the hypothesis of Intelligent Design as the remaining unpenetrated systems decline toward the vanishing point? The hypothesis will be dismissed, and with it credibility of the idea of science-based theology. The odds powerfully favor such an outcome. In science, as in logic, a default argument can never replace positive evidence, but even a sliver of positive evidence can demolish a default argument.

You and I are both humanists in the broadest sense: human welfare is at the center of our thought. But the difference between humanism based on religion and humanism based on science radiates through philosophy and the very meaning we assign ourselves as a species. They affect the way we separately authenticate our ethics, our patriotism, our social structure, our personal dignity.

What are we to do? Forget the differences, I say. Meet on common ground. That might not be as difficult as it seems at first.

When you think about it, our metaphysical differences have remarkably little effect on the conduct of our separate lives. My guess is that you and I are about equally ethical, patriotic, and altruistic. We are products of a civilization that rose from both religion and the science-based Enlightenment. We would gladly serve on the same jury, fight the same wars, sanctify human life with the same intensity. And surely we also share a love of the Creation.

In closing this letter, I hope you will not have taken offense when I spoke of ascending to Nature instead of ascending away from it. It would give me deep satisfaction to find that expression as I have explained it compatible with your own beliefs. For however the tensions eventually play out between our opposing worldviews, however science and religion wax and wane in the minds of men, there remains the earthborn, yet transcendental, obligation we are both morally bound to share.

Warmly and respectfully,
Edward O. Wilson

Further Reading

Wilson's best-known books include *Sociobiology: The New Synthesis* (Cambridge, MA: Belknap Press of Harvard University Press, 1975; twenty-fifth anniversary ed., 2000); *On Human Nature* (Cambridge, MA: Harvard University Press, 1978); *In Search of Nature* (Washington, DC: Island Press, 1996); *The Future of Life* (New York: Alfred A. Knopf, 2002); and *Consilience: The Unity of Knowledge* (New York: Alfred A. Knopf, 1998). For his science writings, see *Journey to the Ants: A Story of Scientific Exploration*, with Bert Hölldobler (Cambridge, MA: Belknap Press of Harvard University Press, 1994), and *The Insect Societies* (Cambridge, MA: Belknap Press of Harvard University Press, 1974). His autobiography, *Naturalist* (Washington, DC: Island Press/ Shearwater Books, 1994), is one of the best scientific autobiographies ever written. In it he describes, among other things, how losing his ability to hear high notes and the vision in his right eye led him to take up the study of insects rather than birds. For a criticism of Wilson's theories, see Marshall Sahlins, *The Use and Abuse of Biology* (Ann Arbor: University of Michigan Press, 1977).

20 Stuart A. Kauffman
(1939–)

Introduction

Alfred North Whitehead, greeting his friend Felix Frankfurter who had just been appointed to the U. S. Supreme Court, purportedly told him, "Remember, Felix, we need order! But not too much order!" Not only society but life itself, Whitehead understood, takes shape between too much and too little order. Anticipating by half a century the concept of "the edge of chaos" developed by complexity theorists, Whitehead wrote that "if there is to be progress beyond limited ideals, the course of history by way of escape must venture along the borders of chaos in its substitution of higher for lower types of order."[1]

No one understands this better today than theoretical biologist Stuart Kauffman, member of the Santa Fe Institute and director of the Institute for Biocomplexity and Informatics at the University of Calgary. One of the leading figures in complexity studies, Kauffman has a vision of the universe that bears an intriguing similarity to Whitehead's. Both seek to understand emergent novelty in an

[1] Alfred North Whitehead, *Process and Reality* corrected ed., ed. David Ray Griffin and Donald W. Sherburne (New York: Free Press, 1978 [1929]), 111.

evolutionary framework. Whitehead's venture into cosmology was inspired by quantum theory, Kauffman's by complexity studies. Kauffman's core idea is that self-organization, in addition to random mutation and natural selection, is a key source of order in biological processes. A proponent of spontaneous and unpredictable emergence that leads to what he terms "order for free," Kauffman thinks that life's turbulence is governed by nonlinear dynamics that operate at the edge of chaos. He is in fact working out a new definition of life, one in which both constraints and autonomous agents play a major role, together with a type of Godelian incompleteness that permits the system to display freedom and spontaneity in its behavior. We may even theorize that a physical system, if it gets sufficiently complex can leap from being mere clod-like matter to being an information-rich participator in a meaningful universe.

In *Origins of Order* (1993), Kauffman proposes to uncover the source of the order that pervades the universe. Is it possible that systems as disparate as economies, immune systems, and ecosystems conform to common mathematical principles? Examining the argument for Darwin's theory of natural selection, Kauffman concludes that Darwinian evolution only accounts for *some* natural phenomena. It is not that Darwinian evolution is incorrect, but rather, it fails to incorporate the possibility that simple and complex systems exhibit order spontaneously. Occurrences such as perfectly spherical oil droplets in water or heptagonal snowflakes have not evolved from natural selection, Kauffman points out. Like the cone shape of sand piles, they emerge from an additional natural ordering principle inherent in the universe.

Kauffman calls this principle "self-organization": massively disordered systems can spontaneously "crystallize" a very high degree of order. The majority of naturally ordered systems can be attributed to this phenomenon, according to Kauffman. Yet it remains unclear, he acknowledges, how self-emerging systems coexist with natural selection, which influences the order exhibited in species. Possibly, selection could work by refining spontaneously ordered systems. "Most of the order we see in organisms," Kauffman writes, "may be the direct result not of natural selection but of the natural order selection was privileged to act on."[2]

In his more popular book *At Home in the Universe* (1995), Kauffman makes clear that he is advocating a theory in which systems spontaneously order themselves. No overall single creator or external designer is required; rather, self-organization is an inherent property of every system that induces its emergence. The idea of a threshold provides a partial explanation of this concept on the molecular level. In every mixture there is a threshold above which life can emerge. While life is absent in certain individual molecules, when enough molecules are included in a mixture, the mixture reaches a concentration above which the molecules organize and spring to life.[3]

Next, Kauffman cites evidence for this theory by comparing simple and complex systems that spontaneously arise in nature to computer-generated Boolean systems, which are also shown to self-organize. A Boolean system is a system generated to respond to inputs of "and," "or," and "not." Using this concept, Kauffman programmed a network of one hundred thousand light bulbs to turn on or off depending on whether their adjacent bulbs were either both on, both off, or one on and one off. The nature of this system dictates that when the bulbs hit a configuration for the second time, a pattern will emerge, and the lights will begin a repeating cycle.

Kauffman calculates that there are $2^{100,000}$ possible configurations of lights for this system. Thus, the time that it takes to produce a duplicate configuration, that is, the time of the cycle, can be anywhere from a matter of minutes to so long that the cycle appears random. However, when he assigned only two possible input values to each bulb (one that turns the bulb on and the other which turns it off), this massive network of choices settled to a repeating cycle of only 317 configurations. Therefore, Kauffman

[2] Stuart Kauffman, *The Origins of Order: Self-Organization and Selection in Evolution* (New York: Oxford University Press, 1993), 173.
[3] Stuart Kauffman, *At Home in the Universe: The Search for Laws of Self-Organization and Complexity* (New York: Oxford University Press, 1995), 24.

summarizes, "These rules [that apply to Boolean systems] apply to networks of all sorts. . . . I will show that the genome itself can be thought of as a network in the ordered regime. Thus, some of the orderliness of the cell, long attributed to the honing of Darwinian evolution, seems likely instead to arise from the dynamics of the genomic network—another example of order for free."[4]

Finally, Kauffman hypothesizes the molecular mechanism through which life emerges from lifeless parts. "Whenever a collection of chemicals contains enough different kinds of molecules, a metabolism will crystallize from the broth," he tells us.[5] Life can form when a system's molecular concentration threshold reaches a certain level; molecules spontaneously assemble to form organized systems through a process called autocatalysis.

By the time he published *Investigations* in 2000, Kauffman had refined many of his ideas and unified them into a grand vision of the nature of the universe. While much of *Investigations* is devoted to complex biology and computational models, its first chapter may well serve as a manifesto of Kauffman's religious beliefs, stated not in conventional religious terms but in lyrical, almost poetic, prose. Reflecting on the inability of Darwinian natural selection to explain the genesis of forms, only their trimmings, he ponders the big question, Whence life in the first place? This is the ultimate mystery for Kauffman, as for many scientists, and the way he sets about explaining it marks a paradigm shift for biology.

The traditional explanation for the original leap to the earliest life in earth's prehistory is the RNA World theory. This states, roughly, that RNA was the first life-form on earth, later developing a cell membrane around it and becoming the first prokaryotic cell. Despite frequent criticism, it is the predominant theory of its kind in biology today and is taught in many textbooks. Kauffman arrives at an alternative theory. In the excerpts gathered here, we see Kauffman reflecting on the meaning of an autonomous agent, proposing a fourth law of thermodynamics, and hypothesizing a

---

[4] *At Home in the Universe*, 85.
[5] *At Home in the Universe*, 45.

critical threshold beyond which "collectively autocatalytic, self-reproducing chemical reaction networks emerge spontaneously."[6] That is, autocatalysis is built into the fabric of the universe.

If Kauffman's threshold theory is correct, then life should be common, springing up abundantly throughout a universe that has held the seeds of life in its very nature from the beginning of time. This is a very subtle form of the so-called anthropic principle, which states that the universe must be built so as to enable life to eventually form. But Kauffman's theory invites no theistic First Cause. Our universe from the very beginning held the inanimate seeds of life, not because it was made that way by an external creator or First Cause, but because the universe is creating itself in a dynamic way that *is* the process of coming to life. On this account, the sheer diversity of being, necessitated by the fourth law of thermodynamics, will inevitably cross the threshold where metabolism spontaneously springs into being. From here it is not far to leap to life as we know it, honed by natural selection. We are not random but expected—an inevitable result of a naturally fruitful universe.

The search for the creator who sets systems in motion now becomes an obsolete form of religious faith, resting on a cosmology long superseded. Instead, a theory of continuous systems and irreducible complexity is all we need—and it is already more than we can handle. No danger of reductionism here, for "all living things seem to have a minimal complexity below which it is impossible to go."[7]

Kauffman's theory of emerging order holds several important implications. The first, as delineated above, is that life is not entirely accidental, as proposed by Darwin. Instead, life springs forth purposefully in the universe; humans and other life forms are indeed meant to exist. Second, because life seems persistently to organize and emerge within the universe, it is very likely that

[6] Stuart Kauffman, *Investigations* (New York: Oxford University Press, 2000), 16.

[7] *At Home in the Universe*, 42.

other life forms will soon come into existence and that there are currently life forms that remain undiscovered by humans. And if life is not a quirk of fate unique in the entire cosmos, then human life on planet Earth, in all its exuberant glory, is not just a meaningless accident but part of a teleonomic process in which order emerges spontaneously but hardly accidentally.

Realizing our place as co-creative members of an ever-evolving universe places us on the edge of what Kauffman can call "sacred." Something sacred is found *in* the universe itself, not outside of it, whatever "outside" would mean. This is not pantheism as that term has historically been understood. Kauffman's universe is hardly the clockwork universe that Spinoza, the classical pantheist, so admired. Instead it is a universe imbued by its very nature with meaning in its fruitfulness. This inherent meaningfulness will have profound implications for our sense of what it means to be alive as spiritual beings who are reinventing the sacred.

In the last excerpt, Kauffman ponders Native American novelist Scott Momaday's idea that "we must reinvent the sacred." Our spiritual vistas are not limited to the stark choice of *either* a purposeful designer *or* programmed determinism. In Kauffman's moving vision of an emergent order, the sacred is found in participating here and now in billions and billions of years of biological unfolding whose magnificence is still in the making.

☙ Kauffman's Contribution to Science

An emeritus professor of biochemistry at the University of Pennsylvania, Stuart A. Kauffman is a theoretical biologist who studies the origin of life and the origins of molecular organization. Thirty-five years ago, he developed the Kauffman models, which are random networks exhibiting a kind of self-organization that he terms "order for free." He was the founding general partner and chief scientific officer of The Bios Group, a company that applies the science of complexity to business management problems. He has been a MacArthur Fellow and an external professor at the

Santa Fe Institute. Currently he directs the Institute for Biocomplexity and Informatics at the University of Calgary.

Kauffman in His Own Words

On Natural Selection[8]

One view, Darwin's, captivates us all: natural selection and the great branching tree of life, spreading from the major phyla to the minor genera and species, to terminal twigs, to curious humans seeking their place. Darwin and evolution both stand astride us, whatever the mutterings of creation scientists. But is the view right? Better, is it adequate? I believe it is not. It is not that Darwin is wrong, but that he got hold of only part of the truth. For Darwin's answer to the sources of the order we see all around us is overwhelmingly an appeal to a single singular force: natural selection. It is this single-force view which I believe to be inadequate, for it fails to notice, fails to stress, fails to incorporate the possibility that simple and complex systems exhibit order spontaneously. That spontaneous order exists, however, is hardly mysterious. The nonbiological world is replete with examples, and no one would doubt that similar sources of order are available to living things. What is mysterious is the extent of such spontaneous order in life and how such self-ordering may mingle with Darwin's mechanism of evolution—natural selection—to permit or, better, to produce what we see.

Biologists have not entirely ignored the spontaneous emergence of order, the occurrence of self-organization. We all know that oil droplets in water manage to be spherical without the benefit of natural selection and that snowflakes assume their evanescent sixfold symmetry for spare physicochemical reasons. But the sheer imponderable complexity of organisms overwhelms us as surely as it did Darwin in his time. We customarily turn to natural selection

[8] *The Origins of Order*, xiii.

to render sensible the order we see, but I think the answer to our questions about the origins of order is broader. We already have some inkling of the kinds of spontaneous order which may bear on biological evolution, and I believe we must make the most profound assessment of such self-organization.

Order for Free [9]

The vast mystery of biology is that life should have emerged at all, that the order we see should have come to pass. A theory of emergence would account for the creation of the stunning order out our windows as a natural expression of some underlying laws. It would tell us if we are at home in the universe, expected in it, rather than present despite overwhelming odds.

Some words or phrases are evocative, even provocative. So it is with the word *emergent*. Commonly, we express this idea with the sentence, The whole is greater than the sum of its parts. The sentence is provocative, for what extra can be in the whole that is not in the parts? I believe that life itself is an emergent phenomenon, but I mean nothing mystical by this. . . . I shall be at pains to give good reasons to believe that sufficiently complex mixes of chemicals can spontaneously crystallize into systems with the ability to collectively catalyze the network of chemical reactions by which the molecules themselves are formed. Such collectively autocatalytic sets sustain themselves and reproduce. This is no less than what we call a living metabolism, the tangle of chemical reactions that power every one of our cells. Life, in this view, is an emergent phenomenon arising as the molecular diversity of a prebiotic chemical system increases beyond a threshold of complexity. If true, then life is not located in the property of any single molecule—in the details—but is a collective property of systems of interacting molecules. Life, in this view, emerged whole

---

[9] *At Home in the Universe*, 23–25.

and has always remained whole. Life, in this view, is not to be located in its parts, but in the collective emergent properties of the whole they create. Although life as an emergent phenomenon may be profound, its fundamental holism and emergence are not at all mysterious. A set of molecules either does or does not have the property that it is able to catalyze its own formation and reproduction from some simple food molecules. No vital force or extra substance is present in the emergent, self-reproducing whole. But the collective system does possess a stunning property not possessed by any of its parts. It is able to reproduce itself and to evolve. The collective system is alive. Its parts are just chemicals.

❧

Most biologists, heritors of the Darwinian tradition, suppose that the order of ontogeny is due to the grinding away of a molecular Rube Goldberg machine, slapped together piece by piece by evolution. I present a countering thesis: most of the beautiful order seen in ontogeny is spontaneous, a natural expression of the stunning self-organization that abounds in very complex regulatory networks. We appear to have been profoundly wrong. Order, vast and generative, arises naturally.

The emergent order seen in genomic networks foretells a conceptual struggle, perhaps even a conceptual revolution, in evolutionary theory. . . . I propose that much of the order in organisms may not be the result of selection at all, but of the spontaneous order of self-organized systems. Order, vast and generative, not fought for against the entropic tides but freely available, undergirds all subsequent biological evolution. The order of organisms is natural, not merely the unexpected triumph of natural selection. For example, I shall later give strong grounds to think that the homeostatic stability of cells (the biological inertia that keeps a liver cell, say, from turning into a muscle cell), the number of cell types in an organism compared with the number of its genes, and other features are not chance results of Darwinian selection but part of the order for free afforded by the self-organization in genomic regulatory networks.

If this idea is true, then we must rethink evolutionary theory, for the sources of order in the biosphere will now include both selection *and* self-organization.

Life Exists at the Edge of Chaos[10]

It is perhaps astonishing, perhaps hopeful and wonderful, that we might even now begin to frame possible universal laws governing this proposed union. For what can the teeming molecules that hustled themselves into self-reproducing metabolism, the cells coordinating their behaviors to form multicelled organisms, the ecosystems, and even economic and political systems have in common? The wonderful possibility, to be held as a working hypothesis, bold but fragile, is that on many fronts, life evolves toward a regime that is poised between order and chaos. The evocative phrase that points to this working hypothesis is this: life exists at the edge of chaos. Borrowing a metaphor from physics, life may exist near a kind of phase transition. Water exists in three phases: solid ice, liquid water, and gaseous steam. It now begins to appear that similar ideas might apply to complex adapting systems. For example, we will see that the genomic networks that control development from zygote to adult can exist in three major regimes: a frozen ordered regime, a gaseous chaotic regime, and a kind of liquid regime located in the region between order and chaos. It is a lovely hypothesis, with considerable supporting data, that genomic systems lie in the ordered regime near the phase transition to chaos. Were such systems too deeply into the frozen ordered regime, they would be too rigid to coordinate the complex sequences of genetic activities necessary for development. Were they too far into the gaseous chaotic regime, they would not be orderly enough. Networks in the regime near the edge of chaos—this compromise between order and surprise—appear best able to coordinate complex activities and best able to evolve as well. It is

[10] *At Home in the Universe*, 26.

a very attractive hypothesis that natural selection achieves genetic regulatory networks that lie near the edge of chaos.

On Theories of Life[11]

Of all the problems with the hypothesis that life started as nude replicating RNA molecules, the one I find most insurmountable is the one most rarely talked about: all living things seem to have a minimal complexity below which it is impossible to go.

The Crystallization of Life[12]

We are not supposed to be here. Life cannot have occurred. Before you get up to leave your chair, your very existence standing as blunt refutation to the argument you are about to hear, simple intellectual politeness invites you to reconsider and linger awhile. The argument I now present has been held seriously by very able scientists. Its failure, I believe, lies in its inability to understand the profound power of self-organization in complex systems. I shall be at pains to show you soon that such self-organization may have made the emergence of life well-nigh inevitable.

❧

As we shall see in Chapter 3, there are compelling reasons to believe that whenever a collection of chemicals contains enough different kinds of molecules, a metabolism will crystallize from the broth. If this argument is correct, metabolic networks need not be built one component at a time; they can spring full-grown from a primordial soup. Order for free, I call it. If I am right, the motto of life is not We the improbable, but We the expected.

[11] *At Home in the Universe*, 42.
[12] *At Home in the Universe*, 43–45.

We the Expected[13]

I hope to persuade you that life is a natural property of complex chemical systems, that when the number of different kinds of molecules in a chemical soup passes a certain threshold, a self-sustaining network of reactions—an autocatalytic metabolism—will suddenly appear. Life emerged, I suggest, not simple, but complex and has remained complex and whole ever since—not because of a mysterious élan vital, but thanks to the simple, profound transformation of dead molecules into an organization by which each molecule's formation is catalyzed by some other molecule in the organization. The secret of life, the wellspring of reproduction, is not to be found in the beauty of Watson-Crick pairing, but in the achievement of collective catalytic closure. The roots are deeper than the double helix and are based in chemistry itself. So, in another sense, life—complex, whole, emergent—is simple after all, a natural outgrowth of the world in which we live.

～

At its heart, a living organism is a system of chemicals that has the capacity to catalyze its own reproduction. Catalysts such as enzymes speed up chemical reactions that might otherwise occur, but only extremely slowly. What I call a collectively autocatalytic system is one in which the molecules speed up the very reactions by which they themselves are formed: A makes B; B makes C; C makes A again. Now imagine a whole network of these self-propelling loops. . . . Given a supply of food molecules, the network will be able to constantly re-create itself. Like the metabolic networks that inhabit every living cell, it will be alive. What I aim to show is that if a sufficiently diverse mix of molecules accumulates somewhere, the chances that an autocatalytic system—a self-maintaining and self-reproducing metabolism—will spring forth becomes a near

---

[13] *At Home in the Universe*, 47–48.

certainty. If so, then the emergence of life may have been much easier than we have supposed.

On Self-Organization, Selection, and Evolvability[14]

Whence the order out my window? Self-organization *and* selection, I think. We, the expected, *and* we, the ad hoc. We, the children of ultimate law. We, the children of the filigrees of historical accident.

What is the weave? No one yet knows. But the tapestry of life is richer than we have imagined. It is a tapestry with threads of accidental gold, mined quixotically by the random whimsy of quantum events acting on bits of nucleotides and crafted by selection sifting. But the tapestry has an overall design, an architecture, a woven cadence and rhythm that reflect underlying law—principles of self-organization.

How are we to begin to understand this new union? For "begin to understand" is all we can now hope for. We enter new territory. It would be presumptuous to suppose that we would understand a new continent when first alighting on its nearest shores. We are seeking a new conceptual framework that does not yet exist. Nowhere in science have we an adequate way to state and study the interweaving of self-organization, selection, chance, and design. We have no adequate framework for the place of law in a historical science and the place of history in a lawful science.

But we are beginning to pick out themes, strands in the tapestry. The first theme is self-organization. Whether we confront lipids spontaneously forming a bilipid membrane vesicle, a virus self-assembling to a low-energy state, the Fibonacci series of a pinecone's phyllotaxis, the emergent order of parallel-processing networks of genes in the ordered regime, the origin of life as a phase transition in chemical reaction systems, the supracritical behavior of the biosphere, or the patterns of co-evolution at higher

---

[14] *At Home in the Universe,* 185–89.

levels—ecosystems, economic systems, even cultural systems—we have found the signature of law. All these phenomena give signs of nonmysterious but emergent order. We begin to believe in this new strand, to sense its power. The problems are twofold: first, we do not yet understand the wealth of sources of such spontaneous order; second, we have the gravest difficulties understanding how self-organization might interact with selection.

Selection is the second theme. Selection is no more mysterious than self-organization. I hope I have persuaded you that selection is powerful, but limited. It is not the case that all complex systems can be assembled by an evolutionary process. We must try to understand what kinds of complex systems can actually arise this way.

The inevitability of historical accident is the third theme. We can have a rational morphology of crystals, because the number of space groups that atoms in a crystal can occupy is rather limited. We can have a period table of the elements because the number of stable arrangements of the subatomic constituents is relatively limited. But once at the level of chemistry, the space of possible molecules is vaster than the number of atoms in the universe. Once this is true, it is evident that the actual molecules in the biosphere are a tiny fraction of the space of the possible. Almost certainly, then, the molecules we see are to some extent the results of historical accidents in this history of life. History arises when the space of possibilities is too large by far for the actual to exhaust the possible.

However, the very limits on selection we have discussed must raise questions about whether selection itself can achieve and sustain the kinds of organisms that adapt on the kinds of landscapes where selection works well. It is by no means obvious that selection can, of its own accord, achieve and sustain evolvability. Were cells and organisms not inherently the kinds of entities such that selection could work, how could selection gain a foothold? After all, how could evolution itself bring evolvability into existence, pulling itself up by its own bootstraps?

And so we return to a tantalizing possibility: that self-organization is a prerequisite for evolvability, that it generates the kinds of structures that can benefit from natural selection. It generates structures that can evolve gradually, that are robust, for there is an inevitable relationship among spontaneous order, robustness, redundancy, gradualism, and correlated landscapes. Systems with redundancy have the property that many mutations cause no or only slight modifications in behavior. Redundancy yields gradualism. But another name for redundancy is robustness. Robust properties are ones that are insensitive to many detailed alterations. The robustness of the lipid vesicle, or of the cell type attractors in genomic networks in the ordered regime, is just another version of redundancy. Robustness is precisely what allows such systems to be molded by gradual accumulation of variations. Thus another name for redundancy is structural stability—a folded protein, an assembled virus, a Boolean network in the ordered regime. The stable structures and behaviors are ones that can be molded.

If this view is roughly correct, then precisely that which is self-organized and robust is what we are likely to see preeminently utilized by selection. Then there is no necessary and fundamental conflict between self-organization and selection. These two sources of order are natural partners. The cell membrane is a bilipid membrane, stable for almost 4 billion years both because it is robust and because such robust forms are readily malleable by natural selection. The genomic network, I believe, lies in the ordered regime, perhaps near the edge of chaos, because such networks are readily formed, part of order for free, but also because such systems are structurally and dynamically stable, so they adapt on correlated landscapes and are able to be molded for further tasks.

But if selection has built organisms utilizing the properties that are self-organized and robust—both because those features lie to hand in evolution, and because the same self-organized features are just those which are readily crafted—then we are not merely tinkered-together contraptions, ad hoc molecular machines. The building blocks of life at a variety of levels from molecules to cells to tissues to organisms are precisely the robust, self-organized, and emergent properties of the way the world works. If selection merely molds further the stable properties of its building blocks, the emergent lawful order exhibited by such systems will persist in organisms. The spontaneous order will shine through, whatever selection's further siftings.

Persistent Coevolution[15]

[W]e need something far more important then a broadened evolutionary theory. Despite any valid insights in my own two books, and despite the fine work of many others, including the brilliance manifest in the past three decades of molecular biology, the core of life itself remains shrouded from view. We know chunks of molecular machinery, metabolic pathways, means of membrane biosynthesis—we know many of the parts and many of the processes. But what makes a cell alive is still not clear to us. The center is still mysterious.

֎

My first efforts had begun with twin questions. First, in addition to the known laws of thermodynamics, could there possibly be a fourth law of thermodynamics for open thermodynamic systems, some law that governs biospheres anywhere in the cosmos or the cosmos itself? . . . My second and core question became, What must a physical system be to be an autonomous agent? Make no mistake, we autonomous agents mutually construct our biosphere, even as we coevolve in it.

֎

[N]o one designed and built the biosphere. The biosphere got itself constructed by the emergence and persistent coevolution of autonomous agents. If there cannot be general laws for all open thermodynamic systems, might there be general laws for

---

[15] *Investigations*, 2–4.

thermodynamically open but self-constructing systems such as biospheres? I believe that the answer is yes. Indeed, among those candidate laws to be discussed in this book is a candidate fourth law of thermodynamics for such self-constructing systems.

To roughly state the candidate law, I suspect that biospheres maximize the average secular construction of the diversity of autonomous agents and the ways those agents can make a living to propagate further. In other words, on average, biospheres persistently increase the diversity of what can happen next. In effect . . . biospheres may maximize the average sustained growth of their own "dimensionality."

❧

To state my hypothesis abruptly and without preamble, I think an autonomous agent is a self-reproducing system able to perform at least one thermodynamic work cycle.

Threshold of Autocatalysis[16]

Life, at its core, depends upon autocatalysis, that is, reproduction. Most catalysis in cells is carried out by protein enzymes. Might there be general laws supporting the possibility that systems of catalytic polymers such as proteins might be self-reproducing? . . .

In view of the potential for a general biology, what, in fact, are the alternative bases for self-reproducing molecular systems here and anywhere in the cosmos? Which of these alternatives is more probable, here and anywhere? . . . The best current guess is that, as the molecular diversity of a reaction system increases, a critical threshold is reached at which collectively autocatalytic, self-reproducing chemical reaction networks emerge spontaneously.

If this view is correct, and the kinetic conditions for rapid reactions can be sustained . . . the emergence of self-reproducing mo-

---

[16] *Investigations*, 15–16.

lecular systems may be highly probable. No small conclusion this: Life abundant, emergent, expected. Life spattered across megaparsecs, galaxies, galactic clusters. We as members of a creative, mysteriously unfolding universe.

Descent with Modification[17]

Darwin's theory of evolution is a theory of descent with modification. It does not yet explain the genesis of forms, but the trimmings of the forms, once they are generated. . . . Whence life in the first place.

Recombination and Fitness Landscapes[18]

There is good evidence that recombination is only a useful search strategy on smooth, highly correlated landscapes, where the high peaks all cluster near one another. . . . But most organisms are sexual. If organisms are sexual because recombination is a good search strategy, but recombination is only useful as a search strategy on certain classes of fitness landscapes, where did those fitness landscapes come from? No one knows.

Natural Games[19]

The no-free-lunch theorem says that, averaged over all possible fitness landscapes, no search procedure outperforms any other search procedure. . . . But life uses mutation, recombination, and selection. . . . Here, I think, is how. Think of an organism's niche as a way of making a living. Call a way of making a living a "natural game." Then, of course, natural games evolve with the organisms

---

[17] *Investigations*, 17.
[18] *Investigations*, 18.
[19] *Investigations*, 19–20.

making those livings during the past four billion years. What, then, are the "winning games"? Naturally, the winning games are the games the winning organisms play. One can almost see Darwin nod. But what games are those? What games are the games the winners play?

Ways of making a living, natural games, that are well searched out and well mastered by the evolutionary search strategies of organisms, namely, mutation and recombination, will be precisely the niches, or ways of making a living, that a diversifying and speciating population of organisms will manage to master. The ways of making a living presenting fitness landscapes that can be well searched by the procedure that organisms have in hand will be the very ways of a making a living that readily come into existence. . . . Good jobs, like successful jobholders, prosper.

The Failure of RNA World[20]

No one has succeeded in achieving experimental conditions in which a single-stranded DNA or RNA could line up free nucleotides, one by one, as complements to a single strand, catalyze the ligation of the free nucleotides into a second strand, melt the two strands apart, then enter another replication cycle. It just has not worked.

Whispering to the Gods[21]

Some wellspring of creation, lithe in the scattered sunlight of an early planet, whispered something to the gods, who whispered back, and the mystery came alive. Agency was spawned. With it, the nature of the universe changed, for some new union of matter, energy, information, and something more could reach out and

[20] *Investigations*, 25–26.
[21] *Investigations*, 49.

manipulate the world on its own behalf. . . . Pregnant in the birth of the universe was the birth of life. Agency may be coextensive with life.

Reinventing the Sacred[22]

Some 10,000 years ago, the last Ice Age began to falter. The ice sheets slowly retreated to the poles. In what later became the south of France, the Magdalenian culture—which had created the art in the caves of Font-de-Gaume and Lascaux, as well as upper Paleolithic flint blades, spears, and fishhooks of exquisite precision—faded. The large herds drifted northward. These ancestors drifted away, leaving the paintings that stun us today.

The bison and deer arched on these cave walls capture the sense of humanity's harmony with, reverence for, and awe of nature. No painting shows violence beyond images of hunting. One painting depicts two deer nuzzling. For some 14,000 years, these two have cared for each other on a stony curved wall in the Perigord.

Awe and respect have become powerfully unfashionable in our confused postmodern society. Scott Momaday said that we must reinvent the sacred. Our little meeting ended over a year ago. I lack Momaday's massive frame, deeply resonant voice, and uncanny authority. Who am I to speak of these things? Another small voice. But has not our Baconian tradition, which celebrates science as the power to predict and control, also brought us a secular loss of awe and respect? If nature were truly ours to command and control, then we might well afford the luxury of contempt. Power corrupts, after all.

Friend, you cannot even predict the motions of three coupled pendula. You have hardly a prayer with three mutually gravitating objects. We let loose pesticides on our crops; the insects become ill and are eaten by birds that sicken and die, allowing the insects to proliferate in increased abundance. The crops are destroyed. So

[22] *At Home in the Universe*, 302–4.

much for control. Bacon, you were brilliant, but the world is more complex than your philosophy.

We have presumed to command, based on our best knowledge and even our best intentions. We have presumed to commandeer, based on the availability of resources, renewable or not, that lay readily at hand. We do not know what we are doing. If Victorian England, standing astride an empire on which the sun never set, could in full good conscience see itself as the world's leader in persistent progress, where science meant the ensured betterment of mankind, can we see ourselves in such a way today?

We suspect ourselves. This is not new. Faust made his bargain. Frankenstein assembled his sad monster. Prometheus let loose fire. We have seen the fires we have lit spread beyond their intended hearthstones. We begin to know that proud humankind is still another beast, still embedded in nature, still spoken for by a larger voice.

If we find renewed concern about the untellable consequences of our own best actions, that is wise. It is not as though we could find a stance with either moral or secular certainty. We make our worlds together. All we can do is be locally wise, even though our own best efforts will ultimately create the conditions that lead to our transformations to utterly unforeseeable ways of being. We can only strut and fret our hour, yet this is our own and only role in the play. We ought, then, play it proudly but humbly.

Why try if our best efforts ultimately transform to the unforeseeable? Because that is the way the world is, and we are part of that world. That is the way life is, and we are part of life. We latter-day players are heritors of almost 4 billion years of biological unfolding. If profound participation in such a process is not worthy of awe and respect, if it is not sacred, then what might be?

If science lost us our Western paradise, our place at the center of the world, children of God, with the sun cycling overhead and the birds of the air, beasts of the field, and fish of the waters placed there for our bounty, if we have been left adrift near the edge of just another humdrum galaxy, perhaps it is time to take heartened stock of our situation.

If the theories of emergence we have discussed here have merit, perhaps we are at home in the universe in ways we have not known since we knew too little to know to doubt. I do not know if the stories of emergence we have discussed in this book will prove to be correct. But these stories are not evidently foolish. They are bits and pieces of a new arena of science, a science that will grow in the coming decades toward some new view of emergence and order in this far-from-equilibrium universe that is our home. I do not know if life began, as I have attempted to suggest, as an expected emergent collective property of the kinds of organic molecules that almost inevitably were formed on the early earth. Yet even the possibility of such collective emergence is heartening. I would rather life be expected in this unfolding since the Big Bang than that life be incredibly improbable in the timespan available. I do not know if the spontaneous order in mathematical models of genomic regulatory systems really is one of the ultimate sources of order in ontogeny. Yet I am heartened by a view of evolution as a marriage of spontaneous order and natural selection. I am heartened by the possibility that organisms are not contraptions piled on contraptions all the way down, but expressions of a deeper order inherent in all life. I am not certain that democracy evolved to achieve reasonable compromises between people with legitimately conflicting interests, but I am heartened by the possibility that our social institutions evolve as expressions of deep natural principles. "The Lord is subtle, but not malicious," said Einstein. We have only begun to invent the science that will account for the evolving emergent order I see out my window, from spider weaving her web, to coyote crafty on the ridgetop, to my friends and me at the Santa Fe Institute and elsewhere proudly hoping that we are unlocking some kinds of secrets, to all of you making your ways by your own best efforts and own best lights.

We are all part of this process, created by it, creating it. In the beginning was the Word—the Law. The rest follows, and we participate. Some months ago, I climbed to the first mountaintop I have been able to reach since my wife and I were badly injured in a car accident. I climbed to Lake Peak with Phil Anderson, Nobel laureate in physics and good friend at the institute. Phil is a dowser. I once was astonished to see him pull a forked twig off a tree and march across a hilltop holding it. I pulled off a forked twig and followed him. Sure enough, whenever his twig dipped toward the ground, so too did mine. But then, I could see him ahead of me. "Does it work?" I asked him. "Oh, sure. Half of all people can dowse." "Ever dig where your stick pointed?" "Oh, no. Well, once." We reached the peak. The Rio Grande Valley spread below us to the west; the Pecos Wilderness stretched out to the east; the Truchas Peaks erupted to the north.

"Phil, I said, "if one cannot find spirituality, awe, and reverence in the unfolding, one is nuts." "I don't think so," responded my dowsing, but now skeptical friend. He glanced at the sky and offered a prayer: "To the great nonlinear map in the sky."

Further Reading

Kauffman's three major books are *Origins of Order: Self-Organization and Selection in Evolution* (New York: Oxford University Press, 1993*), At Home in the Universe: The Search for Laws of Self-Organization and Complexity* (New York: Oxford University Press, 1995), and *Investigations* (New York: Oxford University Press, 2000). See also John Brockman, *The Third Culture: Beyond the Scientific Revolution* (New York: Simon and Schuster, 1995); chapter 20 is devoted to Stuart Kauffman. For studies that deal with complexity theories for nonspecialists, see Murray Gell-Mann, *The Quark and the Jaguar: Adventures in the Simple and the Complex* (New York: W. H. Freeman, 1994); James Gleick, *Chaos: Making a New Science* (New York: Viking/Penguin, 1987); Ilya Prigogine and Isabelle Strengers, *Order out of Chaos* (New York: Bantam Books, 1984); and Michael Waldrop, *Complexity: The Emerging Science at the Edge of Chaos* (New York: Simon and Schuster, 1992). Advanced readers will find two sources especially interesting: John H. Holland, *Emergence: From Chaos to Order* (Reading, MA: Addison-Wesley, 1998); and Mark C. Taylor, *The Moment of Complexity: Emerging Network Culture* (Chicago: University of Chicago Press, 2001). See also the forthcoming book by Stuart Kauffman, *Reinventing the Sacred*.

21 Ursula Goodenough
(1944–)

Introduction

Ursula Goodenough shares with Stuart Kauffman all of the important elements of the emergentist worldview explored in the previous chapter, but she takes its religious implications further in an exhilarating blend of philosophy and lyricism. A bench scientist (she is a molecular geneticist/cell biologist at Washington University in St. Louis), Goodenough is developing a position called "religious naturalism," a spiritual orientation that today has numerous representatives and multiple forms.

At the heart of religious naturalism in all of its variants is the idea of emergence. As one of the most important new concepts for thinking about biological and cosmic evolution, emergence has been challenging some widely held paradigms about the nature of Nature for the last two decades. It is now being used to reinterpret many traditional religious views about creation, causality, the nature of being human, and the meaning of morality. In all of these, relational processes can be said to generate new, higher properties or levels of structure entirely from the interactions of the parts that comprise them. Emergent properties arise as a consequence of relationships—for example, the relationships between water molecules that generate a snowflake, or the relationships between proteins that generate motility, or the relationships between neurons that generate a memory. They can be reduced to their component parts (snowflakes to water), but they are "something more" or "something else" than their component parts and hence novel and innovative. Emergent properties also give rise to yet more emergent properties, generating the vast complexity of our present-day cosmic, biological, ecological, and cultural contexts. Very simply, the concept of emergence means that life continually generates, over and over again, what Goodenough calls "something-more-from-nothing-but."

Giving this formulation religious significance in her acclaimed book *The Sacred Depths of Nature*, Goodenough writes for the nonscientist and manages to create a compelling sense of what molecules and cells and genetics are all about. The book is structured as "A Daily Devotional Booklet," but instead of transcendental spiritual meditations she has composed twelve chapters on scientific topics:

1. Origins of the Earth,
2. Origins of Life,
3. How Life Works,
4. How an Organism Works,
5. How Evolution Works,
6. The Evolution of Biodiversity,
7. Awareness,
8. Emotion and Meaning,
9. Sex,
10. Sexuality,
11. Multicellularity and Death,
12. Speciation.

Each part of the biological story is followed by "Reflections" on the religious implications and spiritual analogues of scientific observations. From these reflections emerges an inspiring personal statement of Goodenough's own religious naturalism, excerpted in the first selections of this chapter.

Religious naturalists come in many varieties, some theists, some nontheists. Goodenough calls herself a nontheist rather than an atheist because, she says, even atheists have a belief about a God, that is, that there isn't one. She writes of her own encounter with nihilistic despair as an adolescent in the face of what transfixed Pascal, too—the infinite and the infinitesimal. Unable to see how an anthropomorphic deity or a disembodied Mind is the answer to the big questions of life and the universe, Goodenough resolved to focus on the questions themselves. She discovered that dwelling simply in the "Mystery . . . inherently pointless, inherently shrouded in its own absence of category" is emancipatory and spiritually fulfilling.

The mystery inherent in nature is the source of what Goodenough celebrates as the religious emotions of awe, gratitude, reverence, wonder, and humility. Religious experiences are those that elicit these emotions. For a religious naturalist, the scientific understanding of Nature can call forth appealing and abiding religious responses without supernatural baggage. Through the contemplation of nature, Goodenough is convinced that human beings can experience religious emotions as profound and as life-sustaining as those that were previously available only under the auspices of traditional religious practices and institutions.

The more we understand the natural world through scientific discoveries, the more, Goodenough believes, we can respond with religious awe and wonder to its beauty and complexity. For example, she describes our current knowledge that the universe just before the big bang was "maybe the size of a pinhead . . . [and] unimaginably hot (at least 100,000,000,000,000,000,000,000,000,000 degrees) and unimaginably dense."[1] Most of us can barely begin to comprehend such data, but it and other facts of the physical and biological universe, revealed through scientific investigation, are natural miracles that subsume any need for supernatural miracles or a divine miracle worker.

[1] Ursula Goodenough, *The Sacred Depths of Nature* (New York: Oxford University Press, 1998), 5.

The emergence of life from non-life in the early stages of evolution and the emergence of self-aware individual life from the processes of human reproduction are both fascinating and astonishing. So Goodenough can say "the self, my self, is inherently sacred. By the virtue of its own improbability, its own miracle, its own emergence." The very fact that "life from non-life, like wine from water, . . . long considered a miracle wrought by gods or God . . . [is now] seen to be the near-inevitable consequence of our thermal and chemical circumstances" only increases her awe. Indeed, far from supposing that the very improbability of human emergence leads to the inference of a Creator, Goodenough sees this as reason to reaffirm a "covenant with Mystery" and proclaim an "outrageous celebration that [the emergence of Life] happened at all."[2]

Today the world is fragmented by what Goodenough sees as an "amalgam of economic, military, and political arrangements," at the same time that it is in vital need of coordinated action on such issues as "fossil fuels, habitat preservation, human rights, hunger, infectious disease, nuclear weapons . . . pollution, population." We urgently need a planetary ethic that will bring people of all cultures together to be effective on these issues. "Without a common religious orientation," Goodenough writes, "we basically don't know where to begin, nor do we know what to say or how to listen, nor are we motivated to respond."[3] Religious naturalism, she argues, can supply this common orientation; it is an outlook sufficiently universal as to hold transcultural and transnational appeal.

Religious naturalists feel "a solemn gratitude that we exist at all, share a reverence for how life works, and acknowledge a deep and complex imperative that life continue."[4] This stance—humble gratitude for existence, reverence and respect for the sacredness of living beings, and a commitment to the maintenance of life—informs an ethical and moral way of interacting with other people

[2] *The Sacred Depths of Nature*, 59, 28–30.
[3] *The Sacred Depths of Nature*, xv.
[4] *The Sacred Depths of Nature*, xvii.

and with the natural world. It fosters a sense of humankind's place in the world as neither all-important nor wholly insignificant. It leads to a responsible stewardship of the earth, in the spirit of Oren Lyons, Faithkeeper of the Onondaga Nation, whose speech before the United Nations Goodenough cites:

> I do not see a delegation for the four-footed. I see no seat for the eagles. We forget and we consider ourselves superior, but we are after all a mere part of the Creation. And we must continue to understand where we are. And we stand between the mountain and the ant, somewhere and there only, as part and parcel of the Creation. It is our responsibility, since we have been given the minds to take care of these things.[5]

Goodenough's sense of connectedness with all living beings goes to the roots of the word religion in *religio*, meaning "to bind together again." As she explains:

> We have throughout the ages sought connection with higher powers in the sky or beneath the earth, or with ancestors living in some other realm. We have also sought, and found, religious fellowship with one another. And now we realize that we are connected to all creatures. Not just in food chains or in ecological equilibria. We share a common ancestor. We share genes for receptors and cell cycles and signal-transduction cascades. . . . Blessed be the tie that binds. It anchors us. We are embedded in the great evolutionary story of planet Earth, the spare, elegant process of mutation and selection and bricolage. And this means that we are anything but alone.[6]

In our connection to nonhuman life-forms lies not only a charge for humans to step lightly in the world but a reassurance that companionship can come from unexpected corners of that world.

Goodenough wants the Epic of Evolution told in a way that combines hard science, a planetary ethic, and a religious sensibility that "binds together again." In the final excerpt, she agrees with

[5] *The Sacred Depths of Nature*, 87.
[6] *The Sacred Depths of Nature*, 73, 75.

those scientists who state that the particles of matter have no inherent meaning and explains why, nevertheless, scientists do not argue that matter is "random" or that everything is due to "chance." This would be a perverse understanding of the facts of biology. Matter is governed by laws, and chemistry is the basis for life and all its manifestations. The Darwinian system that biologists call mutation and natural selection is anything but random, and anything but directional. Instead, it is the manifestation of the countless ecosystems on planet Earth throughout its 4.5-billion-year history. The Earth itself calls the proximate shots, and the laws of physics call the ultimate shots.

❧ Goodenough's Contribution to Science

Ursula Goodenough is currently professor of biology at Washington University in St. Louis. Her research has focused on the cell biology and (molecular) genetics of the sexual phase of the life cycle of the unicellular eukaryotic green alga Chlamydomonas reinhardtii *and, more recently, on the evolution of the genes governing mating-related traits. She has also studied the molecular basis for flagellar motility, the assembly of the* Chlamydomonas *cell wall, and the inheritance of chloroplast DNA. She has written three editions of a widely adopted textbook,* Genetics, *and has served as president of the American Society for Cell Biology, where she was co-founder and chair of the Women in Cell Biology committee.*

Goodenough in Her Own Words

Reflections of a Cell Biologist[7]

In the end, each of these religions addresses two fundamental human concerns: How Things Are and Which Things Matter. How

---

[7] *The Sacred Depths of Nature*, xiv, 10–12, 29–30, 46–47, 114, 128, 139–40, 151.

Things Are becomes formulated as a Cosmology or Cosmos: How the universe came to be, how humans came to be, what happens after we die, the origins of evil and tragedy and natural disaster. Which Things Matter becomes codified as a Morality or Ethos: the Judaic Ten Commandments, the Christian Sermon on the Mount, the Five Pillars of Islam, the Buddhist Vinaya, the Confucian Five Relations. The role of religion is to integrate the Cosmology and the Morality, to render the cosmological narrative so rich and compelling that it elicits our allegiance and our commitment to its emergent moral understandings. As each culture evolves, a unique Cosmos and Ethos appear in its co-evolving religion. For billions of us, back to the first humans, the stories, ceremonies, and art associated with our religions-of-origin are central to our matrix.

❧

When I later encountered the famous quote from physicist Steven Weinberg—"The more the universe seems comprehensible, the more it seems pointless"—I wallowed in its poignant nihilism. A bleak emptiness overtook me whenever I thought about what was really going on out in the cosmos or deep in the atom. . . . But, since then, I have found a way to defeat the nihilism that lurks in the infinite and the infinitesimal. I have come to understand that I can deflect the apparent pointlessness of it all by realizing that I don't have to seek a point. In any of it. Indeed, I can see it as the locus of Mystery . . . inherently pointless, inherently shrouded in its own absence of category. The clouds passing across the face of the deity in the stained-glass images of Heaven.

The word God is often used to name this mystery. A concept known as Deism proposes that God created the universe, orchestrating the Big Bang so as to author its laws, and then stepped back and allowed things to pursue their own course. For me, Deism doesn't work because I find I can only think of a creator in human terms, and the concept of a human-like creator of muons and neutrinos has no meaning for me. But more profoundly,

Deism spoils my covenant with Mystery. To assign attributes to Mystery is to disenchant it, to take away its luminance.

꩜

The realization that I needn't have answers to the Big Questions, needn't seek answers to the Big Questions, has served as an epiphany. I lie awake on my back under the stars and the unseen galaxies and I let their enormity wash over me. I assimilate the vastness of the distances, the impermanence, the *fact* of it all. I go all the way out and then I go all the way down, to the fact of photons without mass and gauge bosons that become massless at high temperatures. I take in the abstractions about forces and symmetries and they caress me, like Gregorian chants, the meaning of the works not mattering because the words are so haunting. Mystery generates wonder, and wonder generates awe.

꩜

A line of reasoning called the Anthropic Principle states that since the laws of physics are perfect for the emergence of chemistry, and chemistry is perfect for the emergence of life, that it all must have been Designed so as to yield life in general and human life in particular. . . . True enough. But of course, all these things could just as well have happened by chance since, had they occurred any other way, we wouldn't be sitting here wondering about them. The inherent circularity of the Anthropic-Principle arguments leaves me, in the end, theologically unsatisfied.

And so I once again revert to my covenant with Mystery, and respond to the emergence of Life not with a search for its Design or Purpose but instead with outrageous celebration that it occurred at all. I take the concept of miracle and use it not as a manifestation of divine intervention but as the astonishing property of emergence. Life *does* generate something-more-from-nothing-but, over and over again, and each emergence, even though fully explainable by chemistry, is nonetheless miraculous.

The celebration of supernatural miracles has been central to traditional religions throughout the millennia. The religious naturalist is provisioned with tales of natural emergence that are, to my mind, far more magical than traditional miracles. Emergence is inherent in everything that is alive, allowing our yearning for supernatural miracles to be subsumed by our joy in the countless miracles that surround us.

⇗

... As a cell biologist ... , I experience the same kind of awe and reverence when I contemplate the structure of an enzyme or the flowing of a signal-transduction cascade as when I watch the moon rise or stand in front of a Mayan temple. Same rush, same rapture.

But all of us, and scientists are no exception, are vulnerable to the existential shudder that leaves us wishing that the foundations of life were something other than just so much biochemistry and biophysics. The shudder, for me at least, is different from the encounters with nihilism that have beset my contemplation of the universe. There I can steep myself in cosmic Mystery. But the workings of life are not mysterious at all. They are obvious, explainable, and thermodynamically inevitable. And relentlessly mechanical. And bluntly deterministic. My body is some 10 trillion cells. Period. My thoughts are a lot of electricity flowing along a lot of membrane. My emotions are the result of neurotransmitters squirting on my brain cells. I look in the mirror and see the mortality and I find myself fearful, yearning for less knowledge, yearning to believe that I have a soul that will go to heaven and soar with the angels.

William James: "At bottom, the whole concern of religion is with the manner of our acceptance of the universe."

The manner of our acceptance. It can be disappointed and resentful; it can be passive and acquiescent; or it can be the active response we call assent. When my awe at how life works gives way to self-pity because it doesn't work the way I would like, I call on assent—the age-old religious response to self-pity, as in "Why, Lord? Why This? Why ME?" and then, "Thy Will Be Done."

As a religious naturalist I say "What Is, Is" with the same bowing of the head, the same bending of the knee. Which then allows me to say "Blessed Be to What Is" with thanksgiving. To give assent is to understand, incorporate, and then let go. With the letting go comes that deep sigh we call relief, and relief allows the joy-of-being-alive-at-all to come tumbling forth again.

Once there is empathy, then there can be the feeling we call compassion. A version of the Golden Rule—Do unto others as you would have them do unto you—is found in most religious traditions. It is as we can imagine being the least of these that we can begin to experience the anguish of deep poverty or deprivation. It is as we are able to identify with the oil-soaked shore bird and the bewildered moose that they come to symbolize our environmental concerns. And emergent from our sense of compassion, in mortal conflict with our insistent sense that we should win, is our haunting sense that things should be fair.

It seems likely that the emotional circuits invoked when we contemplate our deep evolutionary affinity with other creatures, and when we are infused with compassion, will turn out to map closely onto the circuits that drive our parental instincts, emotions that generate such feelings as tenderness and warmth and protectiveness. These same emotions extend to our understanding that the Earth must be nurtured, an understanding embedded in many religious traditions.

For me, and probably for all of us, the concept of a personal interested god can be appealing, often deeply so. In times of sorrow or despair, I often wonder what it would be like to be able to pray to God or Allah or Jehovah or Mary and believe that I was heard, believe that my petition might be answered. When I sing the hymns of faith in Jesus' love, I am drawn by their intimacy, their allure, their poetry. But in the end, such faith is simply not available to me. I can't do it. I lack the resources to render my capacity for love and my need to be loved to supernatural Beings. And so I have no choice but to pour these capacities and needs into earthly relationships, fragile and mortal and difficult as they often are.

ɤ

Does death have any meaning?

Well, yes, it does. Sex without death gets you single-celled algae and fungi; sex with a mortal soma gets you the rest of the eukaryotic creatures. Death is the price paid to have trees and clams and birds and grasshoppers, and death is the price paid to have human consciousness, to be aware of all that shimmering awareness and all that love.

My somatic life is the wondrous gift wrought by my forthcoming death.

Emergent Religious Principles[8]

When the responses elicited by the Epic of Evolution are gathered together, several religious principles emerge that can, I believe, serve as a framework for a global Ethos.

Taking on Ultimacy

We are all, each one of us, ordained to live out our lives in the context of ultimate questions, such as:

- Why is there anything at all, rather than nothing?
- Where did the laws of physics come from?
- Why does the universe seem so strange?

[8] *The Sacred Depths of Nature*, 167–74.

My response to such questions has been to articulate a covenant with Mystery. Others, of course, prefer to respond with answers, answers that often include a concept of god. These answers are by definition beliefs since they can neither be proven nor refuted. They may be gleaned from existing faith traditions or from personal search. God may be apprehended as a remote Author without present-day agency, or as an interested Presence with whom one can form a relationship, or as pantheistic—Inherent in All Things.

The opportunity to develop personal beliefs in response to questions of ultimacy, including the active decision to hold no Beliefs at all, is central to the human experience. The important part, I believe, is that the questions be openly encountered. To take the universe on—to ask Why Are Things As They Are?—is to generate the foundation for everything else.

Gratitude

Imagine that you and some other humans are in a spaceship, roaming around in the universe, looking for a home. You land on a planet that proves to be ideal in every way. It has deep forests and fleshy fruits and surging oceans and gentle rains and cavorting creatures and dappled sunlight and rich soil. Everything is perfect for human habitation, and everything is astonishingly beautiful.

This is how the religious naturalist thinks of our human advent on Earth. We arrived but a moment ago, and found it to be perfect for us in every way. And then we came to understand that it is perfect because we arose from it and are a part of it.

Hosannah! Not in the highest, but right here, right now, this.

When such gratitude flows from our beings, it matters little whether we offer it to God, as in this poem, or to Mystery or Coyote or Cosmic Evolution or Mother Earth:

> i thank You God for most this amazing
> day: for the leaping greenly spirits of trees
> and a blue true dream of sky; and for everything
> which is natural which is infinite which is yes

(i who have died am alive again today,
and this is the sun's birthday; this is the birth
day of life and of love and wings: and of the gay
great happening illimitably earth)

how should tasting touching hearing seeing
breathing any—lifted from the no
of all nothing—human merely being
doubt unimaginable You?

(now the ears of my ears awake and
now the eyes of my eyes are opened)
—E. E. *Cummings*, 1950

Reverence

Our story tells us of the sacredness of life, of the astonishing complexity of cells and organisms, of the vast lengths of time it took to generate their splendid diversity, of the enormous improbability that any of it happened at all. Reverence is the religious emotion elicited when we perceive the sacred. We are called to revere the whole enterprise of planetary existence, the whole and all of its myriad parts as they catalyze and secrete and replicate and mutate and evolve.

Ralph Waldo Emerson invites us to express our reverence in the form of prayer. "Prayer," he writes, "is the contemplation of the facts of life from the highest point of view. It is the soliloquy of a beholding and jubilant soul."

Credo of Continuation

We have thought of evolution as being about prevalence, about how many copies there are of which kinds of genomes. But it is quite as accurate, and I believe more germinative, to think of evolution as being about the continuation of genomes. Genomes that create organisms with sufficient reproductive success to have viable offspring are able to continue into the future; genomes that fail, fail.

Reproductive success is governed by many variables, but key adaptations have included the evolution of awareness, valuation, and purpose. In order to continue, genomes must dictate organisms that are aware of their environmental circumstances, evaluate these inputs correctly, and respond with intentionality.

And so, I profess my Faith. For me, the existence of all this complexity and awareness and intent and beauty, and my ability to apprehend it, serves as the ultimate meaning and the ultimate value. The continuation of life reaches around, grabs its own tail, and forms a sacred circle that requires no further justification, no Creator, no superordinate meaning of meaning, no purpose other than that the continuation continue until the sun collapses or the final meteor collides. I confess a credo of continuation.

And in so doing, I confess as well a credo of human continuation. We may be the only questioners in the universe, the only ones who have come to understand the astonishing dynamics of cosmic evolution. If we are not, if there are others who Know, it is unlikely that we will ever encounter one another. We are also, whether we like it or not, the dominant species and the stewards of this planet. If we can revere how things are, and can find a way to express gratitude for our existence, then we should be able to figure out, with a great deal of work and good will, how to share the Earth with one another and with other creatures, how to restore and preserve its elegance and grace, and how to commit ourselves to love and joy and laughter and hope.

It goes back in the end to my father's favorite metaphor. "Life is a coral reef. We each leave behind the best, the strongest deposit we can so that the reef can grow. But what's important is the reef."

Our Religions of Origin

So we extract from reality all the meaning and guidance and emotional substance that we can, and we bring these responses with us as we set out to chart global paths. And then we come back to our religions of origin, the faiths of our mothers and fathers. What do we do with them? What have I done with mine?

Theologian Philip Hefner offers us a weaving metaphor. The tapestry maker first strings the warp, long strong fibers anchored firmly to the loom, and then interweaves the weft, the patterns, the color, the art. The Epic of Evolution is our warp, destined to endure, commanding our universal gratitude and reverence and commitment. And then, after that, we are all free to be artists, to render in language and painting and song and dance our ultimate hopes and concerns and understandings of human nature.

Throughout the ages, the weaving of our religious weft has been the province of our prophets and gurus and liturgists and poets. The texts and art and ritual that come to us from these revered ancestors include claims about Nature and Agency that are no longer plausible. They use a different warp. But for me at least, this is just one of those historical facts, something that can be absorbed, appreciated, and then put aside as I encounter the deep wisdom embedded in these traditions and the abundant opportunities that they offer to experience transcendence and clarity.

I love traditional religions. Whenever I wander into distinctive churches or mosques or temples, or visit museums of religious art, or hear performances of sacred music, I am enthralled by the beauty and solemnity and power they offer. Once we have our feelings about Nature in place, then I believe that we can also find important ways to call ourselves Jews, or Muslims, or Taoists, or Hopi, or Hindus, or Christians, or Buddhists. Or some of each. The words in the traditional texts may sound different to us than they did to their authors, but they continue to resonate with our religious selves. We know what they are intended to mean.

Humans need stories—grand, compelling stories—that help to orient us in our lives and in the cosmos. The Epic of Evolution is such a story, beautifully suited to anchor our search for planetary consensus, telling us of our nature, our place, our context. Moreover, responses to this story—what we are calling religious naturalism—can yield deep and abiding spiritual experiences. And then, after that, we need other stories as well, human-centered stories, a mythos that embodies our ideals and our passions. This mythos comes to us, often in experiences called revelation, from the sages and the artists of past and present times.

On Emergent Wonder[9]

S&S: What aspect of the science-religion dialogue do you find the most compelling?

GOODENOUGH: I am most compelled to help people understand how Nature is put together and how it has evolved, to offer ways to respond to this understanding in religious terms, and to encourage others to seek their own responses. I see the development of such resources as essential to personal wholeness and social coherence and, in particular, to a sense of the sacredness of our natural heritage.

S&S: Where is the field heading? What place do you see for yourself in that future?

GOODENOUGH: I see it heading in several different directions. Some persons in the field are searching for Purpose/Plan in our scientific understandings, whereas others are not engaged in such a search. Some seek to reconcile scientific understandings with traditional faiths, whereas others see these understandings as resources for new spiritual orientations. I regard myself as a religious non-theist, meaning that God questions are not central to my quest and, indeed, get in the way of it. But I am deeply informed and moved by the texts and the art of traditional and indigenous religions, and I believe they offer us much guidance and wisdom as we chart our paths.

S&S: What are the chief problems facing the dialogue between science and religion?

GOODENOUGH: I see the biggest problem as the temptation to bend the science so that it comes out the way one wishes. There

---

[9] Mary Lacombe, "Emergent Wonder: The Sacred Depths of Nature: An Interview with Ursula Goodenough" (online), *Science & Spirit Magazine*, 2002, http://www.science-spirit.org/article_detail.php?article_id=187.

is a deep consensus in scientific understanding these days. Some elect to brand this consensus as "orthodoxy" and to then offer "unorthodox" notions, touting these as somehow fresh and daring and appealing, particularly if they challenge consensus conclusions that are found to be disquieting. It is not enough to challenge the consensus since, of course, scientists do this all the time. The challenge must also be accompanied by an informed, testable, alternative idea, which is usually not offered. Therefore, these challenges strike the scientific community as vapid, and the science/religion field is viewed accordingly.

S&S: Is there such a thing as "spirit" in the sense of something nonmaterial, and hence inaccessible to scientific inquiry?

GOODENOUGH: My personal response is that to regard our undeniable spiritual experiences as materially based—that is, generated as wondrous mental phenomena—does not in any way diminish their importance nor their centrality to our religious lives. The concept of an independent "spiritual realm" does not augment, for me, the magic of the mystical dimension, whereas to think of this dimension as emergent from our minds makes it all the more wondrous to be a human.

How a Religious Naturalist Experiences "God"[10]

S&S: Do you think world religions can be explained by wanting to know how the world works?

GOODENOUGH: There are two possibilities. A great many people say we have language and imagination to posit creators, interveners, and agencies that we can't actually prove. And yet some people experience God within them—these experiences are not drawn-up hypotheses. It's possible those of us who don't feel God within them have deficient brains that aren't capable of

---

[10] Jill Neimark, "There Are Two Flavors of God People: An Interview with Ursula Goodenough," *Beliefnet.com*, May 7, 2004, http://www.beliefnet.com/story/147/story_14706.html.

such experiences; or alternatively, the people who experience these things have brains that somehow create them. As near as I can tell, the jury is out on that. I may be a non-theist who doesn't include a god concept in my religious orientation because I have an incompetent brain, or perhaps theists have brains giving them inaccurate information.

S&S: We now have the neurobiological evidence, from the studies of Andrew Newberg, M.D., that certain parts of the brain shut down and others light up during deep meditation. The MRI work from Richie Davidson in Wisconsin on Tibetan monks also shows a shutting-down. This might explain how we access states of cosmic consciousness and unity. Whether this is a correlation or a cause, and what this means about the content of those experiences, we have no idea.

GOODENOUGH: I've had interesting conversations with Andrew Newberg about this. There's no question that brains change when in these other states. A friend of mine talked about all of this as getting in touch with his froggy self—that when he's in a meditative mode, it's more like being a frog. It's not higher, but lower, but not in any pejorative way. It's shutting down parts of the cerebral cortex. As they say in the "How To Meditate" books, it's letting the thoughts go, and going somewhere else. That somewhere else could be higher or lower. It could be a more primitive brain state.

But, as Terry Deacon (a professor of anthropology at the University of California, Berkeley) and I have written, it's very unlikely that even if humans in altered states have fewer signals firing off in their cortex, the experience isn't very likely to be that of a frog's mind-state. The fact is that we humans can come back and talk about it, however inchoately. A frog can't.

S&S: Have you experienced those states of peace and expansion?

GOODENOUGH: I don't have any problem accessing experiences of unity. I feel completely part of the universe and all that's going on. When I try to describe it, people say I'm obviously a mystic. It doesn't seem mystical to me in a theistic sense. It's not a state that engenders in me any sense that God is watching over me and paying attention to what I'm doing. It's much more what I understand the Eastern traditions to be talking about—a belonging to the universe, an overflow of astonishment and wonder and peace and tranquility.

S&S: Do you ever ask yourself how life came from inanimate matter?

GOODENOUGH: I would say at some point enough improbable things happened to enable life to take off. There's a deep understanding that once something like this took off—however primitive and small and meaningless—that it would continue to expand through replication and encoding. I'd be very interested to know what versions of creation could be generated in a laboratory, since we'll probably never know what actually happened.

S&S: How about an even bigger mystery: how something came from nothing. Or was there always something?

GOODENOUGH: The big bang is obviously one form of beginning, but the big bang in itself is unimaginable. It's one thing to think about God making a flower or infusing the planet with love, but to imagine what might be behind the big bang is so removed from real life that it actually loses importance for me. There's so much else to think about that's here and now. I like the Buddhist concept of beginning-less-ness, that the universe has always been going on. I didn't know about beginning-less-ness until about a year ago, or I might have invoked it in my book *Sacred Depths of Nature*. I learned about it when I spent a week with the Dalai Lama in Dharmsala.

S&S: . . . I like the Buddhist approach, too. If I start seriously thinking about nothing existing before something, my brain stops. It's easier to imagine a world that always has been and always will be, because I can visualize a sphere, which has no beginning and end if you are traversing it.

GOODENOUGH: The Buddhist view is more congruent with evolution than are other views. You can actually have beginning-less-ness and still have creation of a particular universe . . . The part that doesn't jibe for me is the whole notion that consciousness is this separate thing that goes in and out of sentient beings. In the

Tibetan form of Buddhism, consciousness is seen as having specific manifestations in sentient beings. Buddhists do not regard plants as being alive; in their texts, plants don't die—they just dry up—because plants are not sentient. But what about when plants bend in the light. The idea that plants are not alive is an arbitrary judgment. At the end of my presentation I did show the Dalai Lama evolutionary trees where plants, animals and fungi come off the same critter. His Holiness looked at that slide very carefully. He's on record as saying if there's anything within Buddhism that regular science can prove to be wrong, then the Buddhist version must change.

S&S: In *The Sacred Depths of Nature*, you made a strong case for religious naturalism, for the idea that there is enough beauty and wonder in nature and evolution to give our lives meaning. A few critics pointed out that if this movement is to suffice as a framework for life, it needs to generate some kind of moral code. Do you agree?

GOODENOUGH: People did tell me that a religion without morality doesn't cut it. My immediate response was, this is not religion; I'm talking about a religious orientation. A moral code is not my problem. But I did start thinking about it, and I realized they had a good point. So I began to examine to what extent our moral sensibilities could have come through our evolution. That was the only place it made sense for me to start. This is what my next book is about.

The good stuff of most religions turns out to be a golden rule that defines a morality which allows humans to flourish in community. We come from a whole lineage of creatures who are robustly social and have communities that work, so you look at how their flourishing communities are set up. Are there parallels between how life works in a structured, non-human primate group, in a human community, and in the moral guidelines religion offers? It's not all that different as far as I can tell—there is hierarchy, strategic reciprocity, nurture and empathy.

S&S: . . . So out of these sentiments we've developed a code to live by?

GOODENOUGH: Right. We have minds that can imagine ourselves in others' situations and generalize from that. We can take a specific experience of compassion and expand it to feeling toward all those less fortunate. I believe a key reason is that we live in communities. Like most social animals, we evolved to flourish in community. Had we evolved from a non-social lineage, our moral codes might be quite different. In theory, if you could get a mouse to symbolize things, and to say what's on her mind, you probably wouldn't hear about the golden rule. But you'd hear about nurture, the taking care of babies.

S&S: As a movement, religious naturalism seems cleanly split down the middle, as it contains what one might call "God people" and "non-God people." How did they end up in the same place?

GOODENOUGH: There are two flavors of God people: those whose God is natural and those whose God is supernatural. Certainly there are a lot of people within religious naturalism who have no problem with God language—God as love, God as evolution, God as process. People see God as part of nature and give God-attributes to the part of nature that they find most sacred. I encounter people like that all the time.

S&S: I consider myself a pantheist, and I know that monotheists often see pantheists as either having too much God or no God at all. On the other hand, non-theists like yourself often see pantheists as people gingerly taking their first steps to adulthood—which would be non-theism, of course. They are leaving the crutch of monotheism, but they aren't yet willing to give up God. And yet, I can tell you, my pantheism feels deep, visceral, and I really can't see the world any other way and never have.

GOODENOUGH: Sometimes I envy people like you. I don't have "God," but in the end, both you and I sense the power, beauty, improbability and fragility of nature, and how essential it is to keep this planet thriving. To me, that is so much more important than some sort of fine-grained, end-of-day theological detail. I don't think you and I are in such different places. We both still see nature as vital—as our home, our birthing. The people who are truly bothered by God-concepts and find them stupid or ignorant or pathological are those like Richard Dawkins who just can't even imagine anybody having such concepts. That view is almost like homophobia—it's not open and pluralistic. I'm much more interested in helping people engage in this story of evolution. If they do that with theistic language, that's great.

S&S: What, then, can God and non-God people work toward together?

GOODENOUGH: Perhaps we should all settle down and think about what's good in the world and what we want to do here. If we find this planet and its history and its story to be sacred, let's preserve and nourish it, and then we can go home at night and say whatever prayers we choose.

S&S: What do you feel about suffering? It's the eternal question that every religion, even religious naturalism, has to approach.

GOODENOUGH: On a personal level, I can be completely devastated by the suffering of a friend, or by watching an animal in despair. I raised my kids with the rule that we should try to get any insect in our house into a cup and put it outside. But there's only so much that I can do. Even if I go fully vegan, I'm eating plants, and they're just as alive as anything else. The fact of the matter is that there's no way I can exist without eating.

S&S: I find the world, and the way life works, both glorious and terrifying. The joy is so precious, the suffering so unbearable. Now it's time for me to be jealous of you, that you can accept both extremes with equanimity.

GOODENOUGH: We all eat or are eaten. That's the way life works, it's a greater rhythm. And that's why science and the understandings it has uncovered can be a source of joy.

This all relates to assent, a very important Judeo-Christian concept. "Thy will be done" is a God-kind of assent. "God works in mysterious ways," and you're supposed to give assent even if you don't like it. As a religious naturalist, I think of assent differently. Assent is saying, "Okay, for whatever reason, this is the way life works. It's an acceptance of what is. After that fundamental acceptance, I can live my life to minimize suffering and promote as much as good as I can, and try through whatever work I do to help others." We can't get around death, but we can get around poverty. We can try to avoid women being brutalized. We can curb environmental degradation.

One can start from the perspective of a religious naturalist or from the perspective of the world religions and arrive at the same place: a moral imperative that this Earth and its creatures be respected and cherished.

On the Religious Dimension of Biology[11]

Religions have come to serve many roles, but in the context of this symposium we can focus on religion as the source of *explanation*, addressing what we can call the Big Questions: What is the meaning of life? What is my life for? In Western faith traditions, the explanations offered are framed in the context of a creating, interested God who has both a purpose and a plan.

The disciplines of science also seek to provide explanation, and although they do not directly take on the Big Questions, they offer up a worldview which is not obviously dictated by a personal God concerned with human beings. As the physicist Steven Weinberg (1988, 154) puts it: "The more the universe seems comprehensible, the more it also seems pointless."

Various responses to this nihilistic proposition have been offered, including the fundamentalist rejection of the scientific cosmology and the postmodern deconstruction of the scientific cosmology as response, namely, that science and religion are two ways of experiencing and interpreting the world. In other words, we are offered a dualism, one that is commonly expressed in such dyads as reductionism versus holism, physical versus spiritual, analysis

[11] Ursula Goodenough, "The Religious Dimensions of the Biological Narrative," *Zygon* 29, no. 4 (December 1994): 603–4.

versus transcendence, left-brain versus right-brain. The idea is to keep things separate.

My problem with this approach is that it is founded on an anthropocentrism in the sense that human beings, their particular understandings and beliefs and emotions, are set apart, are treated differently, are effectively accorded a separate cosmology. My understanding of biology has led me to a very different conclusion. I see the whole enterprise, from bacteria to starfish to maples to humans, as operating on the same principles, as profoundly homologous. So for me, a religious perspective is useful *only* if it deeply acknowledges that I am a collection of cells and experience and interpret the world as an organism, using chemistry and physics to do so.

Ian Barbour (1994, 463–64) has summarized two religious perspectives that include this acknowledgment. In the first, exemplified most recently by the creation spirituality of Thomas Berry, Brian Swimme, and Matthew Fox, we are urged to celebrate the beauty of the universe story and experience fulfillment in the awe, wonder, and gratitude it elicits. In the second, theologies are sought within nature, generating such concepts as God as the author of the improbable universe or God as the author of natural selection.

I have initiated what I believe to be a distinctive approach. I do not attempt to develop a theology, because I happen to be a nontheist, albeit I most readily experience transcendence in medieval cathedrals. On the other hand, I am trying to go beyond the spirituality movement, beyond poetry, beyond awe and wonder. Although I experience these emotions deeply, I believe we can go much further. Recent discoveries in biology tell us that concepts central to religious thought, concepts that we have believed to be unique to human perceptions and concerns, are in fact operant throughout the biological world. These new understandings allow us to experience cognitive affinity as well as spiritual affinity with the rest of nature. Moreover, they suggest that we can seek guidance from nature as we articulate religious principles. The resultant system of belief can be called a new naturalism.

On the Adjective "Religious" as a Wild Card[12]

Naturalism, as Jerome Stone reminds us, is a philosophical position. In this intellectual lineage, religious naturalism then becomes a theological position. My colleagues in this session, being theologians, have largely responded in this vein, considering such questions as how concepts of God can or cannot be rendered coherent within such philosophical boundaries.

Unaware of this usage, I adopted the term *religious naturalism* in my book *The Sacred Depths of Nature* (Goodenough 1998) to best describe its overall perspective. That perspective does not, however, include much theology. I articulate a Covenant with Mystery in the presence of apparently unanswerable questions, such as why is there anything at all rather than nothing, and then proceed to describe my nontheistic religious orientation in the natural and aesthetic world.

The wild card here seems to be the adjective *religious*. As I have developed elsewhere (Goodenough 2000), and others have certainly noted as well, religions can be said to have three strands: theological, dealing with God concepts, meaning, purpose; spiritual, dealing with subjective experiences of the sacred; and moral, dealing with how best to be good. A mature religious tradition interweaves these in the context of a unifying story or myth, but each can nonetheless be teased out and analyzed separately.

The religious naturalism of my book, therefore, might more accurately be described as spiritual naturalism; I tell of our scientific understandings of who we are and how we got here, and I respond with such sensibilities as belonging, communion, gratitude, humility, assent, and awe. It follows that we might as well speak of theological naturalism and (awkwardly) moral naturalism or (less awkwardly) ethical naturalism, the term used by Larry Arnhart (1998). Such distinctions may be useful in discourse, but I would suggest that they not be belabored and that all of us voicing

---

[12] Ursula Goodenough, "Religious Naturalism and Naturalizing Morality," *Zygon* 38, no. 1 (March 2003): 101–3.

religious responses in a naturalistic framework, be they theological, spiritual, or moral, feel comfortable using the term *religious naturalism* to describe the overall project.

Many traditions have, of course, responded to nature with deep reverence and gratitude, an orientation that is often called pantheism. Paul Harrison (1999) offers a lucid historical summary of this religious perspective and goes on to propose the term *scientific pantheism* to describe his deeply felt pantheistic orientation in the context of our current scientific understandings of nature. Philip Hefner has on occasion referred to his orientation as Christian naturalism. If the overall concept of religious naturalism proves to be a fertile one, then it will be expected to generate many manifestations with many names.

Another matter of terminology to consider here is that *naturalism* and *naturalist* have quite different connotations: whereas the pragmatist can be said to espouse pragmatism and the empiricist empiricism, the naturalist is not necessarily someone who espouses the philosophical position of naturalism. Rather, we think of the naturalist, often quite romantically, as someone at home in the natural world, and a person who espouses philosophical naturalism is more likely to be described as a (radical) materialist. "Materialist," however, carries a particularly large amount of baggage, from anticommunist propaganda to consumerism to the cold and calculating. To call oneself a "religious materialist" sounds at best peculiar, whereas "religious naturalist" invokes our positive valence toward the naturalist, including the naturalist in each of our selves.

Whether, then, the religious naturalist in fact espouses philosophical naturalism or has developed some other orientation vis à vis questions of ultimacy becomes, to my mind, of secondary importance. That is, I see no inherent conflict between calling oneself a religious naturalist and experiencing some transcendent relationship with God, be it a quite abstract God or a traditional personal God. These relationships, I have discovered in conversations with persons of faith, are often not buttressed by a great deal of theological infrastructure; they are often ineffable. Ineffability is by definition a difficult starting point for theological discussion, even as theologians are keenly aware that it steeps the religious life; nevertheless, it characterizes the theism of many persons who consider themselves theistic religious naturalists. I would regard as unnecessarily constrained a definition of religious naturalism that disallows theistic concepts considered incompatible with philosophical naturalism.

It's Not All a Matter of Chance[13]

Evolutionary theory is often misunderstood to claim that everything somehow happened randomly. I participate in a listserv that focuses on exploring the concept of religious naturalism (religious orientations derived from our understandings of nature),[14] and this sentiment is well stated in the following posting:

"My hunch, based on my experience as a member and leader in the liberal United Church of Christ, is that people are there on a Sunday morning because they can't accept that the wonders opened up by science, astronomy, etc. are all a matter of chance. They have rejected traditional views of a God in heaven judging HIS sinful creation, but awe without purpose and meaning behind it is just as meaningless to them.

"They might find much support in the concept of religious naturalism were it not that they are looking for truth and values beyond chance, and indeed beyond human experience."

I would agree that if one's only understanding of the natural world is that it is all just a matter of chance, one might well look elsewhere for sources of meaning. But that is not the core message I get from the natural world. I encounter a natural world that is brimming with meaning in and of itself, just by being itself, wherein "serendipitous creativity" (as theologian Gordon D. Kaufman [1995] so wonderfully puts it) generates countless emergent properties that build on themselves. These include the lives that we

---

[13] From Ursula Goodenough, "Reductionism and Holism, Chance and Selection, Mechanism and Mind," *Zygon* 40, no. 2 (June 2005): 369–80.

[14] See http://iras.org/interest_grps_naturalism.html. —UG.

live, lives that are like no others given the cultures we have created and the sensibilities we transmit through them. From my perspective, what more meaning might one want than the astonishing *fact* of it all?

But back to the matter of chance.

Serendipitous creativity is of course a word that connotes chance, and chance certainly plays a big part in the creativity of the universe. But to say that the wonders of the universe are all a matter of chance is a misunderstanding. Chance on its own would not have accomplished much of anything. Chance offers up the variation—the possible atoms, the possible molecules, the possible lifeforms, the possible ecosystems. Chance is the generator of creativity, the grist in the mill that allows new things to happen.

But chance is inexorably coupled with selection, which operates on that which is created by chance to generate atoms that hold together and molecules that fold into useful shapes and life forms that are adapted to their environment and ecosystems that sustain their participants. Serendipity means chance with a positive outcome, and positive outcomes are the product of selection, in all its countless guises, be it selection for stable atomic nuclei or for thermodynamically favorable molecular outcomes or for viable ecosystems, including the cultural ecosystems that humans construct and inhabit. Selection generates that which has carried on.

Selection, of course, has its own set of problems in that it's another one of those discomfiting words. The Web page I quoted earlier includes an interesting example of this. The writer expresses dismay that "the rhetoric of Darwinism is of a 'force' (selection)," and that this thereby "eliminates any hint of the involvement of . . . a vital force."

I would respond that if any known force makes the cut as a vital force, it is natural selection acting on emergent properties.

❧

If religious relevance is to be found in biological evolution—and I myself find it all over the place—then surely it is here. Billions of years of mutation and selection produced reliable, mechanistic molecular pathways that undergird perception and response in all creatures. Hundreds of millions of years of mutation and selection in animals allowed the co-option of these pathways into nervous systems and brains. Within the last million years, self-aware hominids, and then humans, popped through with "minds of their own," minds that not only think but experience thinking, minds that not only love but experience loving, minds that not only choose but tell themselves, and one another, about the choices they have made and plan to make. A core religious response is a sense of profound gratitude for the lives that we are given, and I offer such gratitude to the countless chances and selections that have brought all these wondrous outcomes into being.

The Dalai Lama can take us out. Maybe it is not so important, he said, whether consciousness is an emergent property of biological evolution or something that comes from without. Maybe what's more important is what we do with it.

Further Reading

For additional writings by Ursula Goodenough of interest to the nonspecialist, see the following: "Creativity in Science," *Zygon* 28, no. 3 (September 1993): 399–414; "The Religious Dimensions of Biological Narrative," *Zygon* 29, no. 4 (December 1994): 603–18; "Biology: What One Needs to Know," *Zygon* 31, no. 4 (December 1996): 671–80; "Reflections on Science and Technology," *Zygon* 35, no. 1 (March 2000): 5–12; "Reflections on Scientific and Religious Metaphor," *Zygon* 35, no. 2 (June 2000): 233–40; "Exploring Religious Naturalism," *Zygon* 35, no. 3 (September 2000): 561–66; "Causality and Subjectivity in the Religious Quest," *Zygon* 35, no. 4 (December 2000): 725–34; Goodenough and Paul Woodruff, "Mindful Virtue, Mindful Reverence," *Zygon* 36, no. 4 (December 2001): 585–95; and Goodenough and Terrence W. Deacon, "From Biology to Consciousness to Morality," *Zygon*, 38, no. 4 (December 2003): 801–19. For a good overview of her thought, and that of other religious naturalists, see Ursula Goodenough, "How Can Scientific Understandings of Nature Contribute to Moral, Spiritual, and Religious Wholeness and Well-Being?" in *The Good in*

Nature and Humanity: Connecting Science, Religion, and Spirit with the Natural World, edited by S. R. Kellert and T. J. Farnham (Washington, DC: Island Press, 2002), 19–28. See also Goodenough's reservations about fellow biologist Stephen Jay Gould's views on the "non-overlapping magisteria" of science and religion in her review essay "The Holes in Gould's Semipermeable Membrane between Science and Religion," *American Scientist* 87, no. 3 (May–June 1999). The website Goodenough mentions in the last excerpt above is for the Institute on Religion in an Age of Science (IRAS), of which she is a past president. Interested readers who go to www.iras.org will also find links to other organizations in religion and science and announcements of new books. For further reading in religious naturalism, the following sources are representative of the variety and depth of the literature: Charley Hardwick, *Events of Grace: Naturalism, Existentialism, and Theology* (New York: Cambridge University Press, 1996); Jerome Stone, *The Minimalist Vision of Transcendence* (Albany, NY: SUNY Press, 1992); Donald Crosby, *A Religion of Nature* (Albany, NY: SUNY Press, 2002); Henry Samuel Levinson, *Santayana, Pragmatism, and the Spiritual Life* (Chapel Hill: University of North Carolina Press, 1992); Gordon D. Kaufman, *In the Face of Mystery: A Constructive Theology* (Cambridge, MA: Harvard University Press, 1995); and Karl Peters, *Dancing with the Sacred* (Philadelphia: Trinity Press International, 2002).

Permission Acknowledgments

Francis Bacon
From *Francis Bacon: The New Organon*, edited by L. Jardine and M. Silverthorne, published in 2000 by Cambridge University Press. Reprinted by permission of Cambridge University Press.

From pp. 14–16, 31–32 of *Bacon: New Atlantis and the Great Instauration*, rev. ed., edited by Jerry Weinberger, copyright © 1989 by Harlan Davidson, Inc. Reprinted by Permission of Harland Davidson, Inc.

Rachel Carson
From "*The New York Herald Tribune* Book and Author Luncheon Speech," in *Lost Woods: The Discovered Writing of Rachel Carson*, edited by Linda Lear, copyright © 1998 by Roger Allen Christie. Reprinted by permission of Frances Collin, Trustee.

From *Always, Rachel: The Letters of Rachel Carson and Dorothy Freeman 1952–1964*, edited by Martha Freeman, copyright © 1995 by Roger Allen Christie. Reprinted by permission of Frances Collin, Trustee.

From *The House of Life: Rachel Carson at Work* by Paul Brooks, copyright © 1972 by Paul Brooks. Reprinted by permission of Frances Collin, Trustee.

From *The Sense of Wonder* by Rachel Carson, copyright © 1956 by Rachel L. Carson. Reprinted by permission of Frances Collin, Trustee.

Excerpt from *The Edge of the Sea* by Rachel Carson. Copyright © 1955 by Rachel L. Carson, renewed 1983 by Roger Christie. Reprinted by permission of Houghton Mifflin Company. All rights reserved.

Albert Einstein

From "The conversation then turned to Newton's Life . . . which should not be published," from the article "An Interview with Einstein," by I. Bernard Cohen in *Scientific American* vol. 193, no. 1 (July 1955). Reprinted with permission of *Scientific American*.

From *Ideas and Opinions* by Albert Einstein, copyright 1954 and renewed 1982 by Crown Publishers, Inc. Reprinted by permission of Crown Publishers, a division of Random House, Inc.

From *Out of My Later Years* by Albert Einstein, published in 1950 by Philosophical Library. Reprinted by permission of Philosophical Library.

Albert Einstein, "What I Believe." *Forum and Century* (1930–1940); Oct. 1930; vol. LXXXIV, no. 4: 192–3. Reprinted in Albert Einstein, et al., *Living Philosophies* (New York: Simon and Schuster, 1931). Reprinted by permission from Princeton University Press.

Galileo Galilei

From *The Galileo Affair: A Documentary History*, selected, translated, and edited by, and with an introduction and notes by Maurice A. Finocchiaro, published in 1989 by the University of California Press. Reprinted by permission of the University of California Press.

From *Dialogue Concerning the Two Chief World Systems, Ptolemaic and Copernican* by Galileo Galilei, second revised edition, published in 2001 by the University of California Press. Reprinted by permission of the University of California Press.

From *Galileo, Bellarmine, and the Bible: Including a Translation of Foscarini's Letter on the Motion of the Earth*, by Galileo Galilei, published in 1991 by the University of Notre Dame Press. Reprinted by permission of the University of Notre Dame Press.

Jane Goodall

From *Reason for Hope* by Jane Goodall and Phillip Berman. Copyright © 1999 by Soko Publications, Ltd. With Jane Goodall and Phillip Berman. Reprinted by permission of Grand Central Publishing.

Ursula Goodenough

From *The Sacred Depths of Nature* by Ursula Goodenough, published in 1999 by Oxford University Press. Reprinted by permission of Oxford University Press.

Stephen Jay Gould

Stephen Hawking

Stuart Kauffman

From *At Home in the Universe: The Search for Laws of Self-Organization and Complexity* by Stuart Kauffman, published in 1995 by Oxford University Press. Reprinted by permission of Oxford University Press, Inc.

From *Investigations* by Stuart Kauffman, published in 2001 by Oxford University Press. Reprinted by permission of Oxford University Press, Inc.

From *The Origins of Order: Self Organization and Selection in Evaluation* by Stuart Kauffman, published in 1993 by Oxford University Press. Reprinted by permission of Oxford University Press, Inc.

Johannes Kepler

From *Mysterium Cosmographicum: The Secret of the Universe,* translated by A. M. Duncan, Introduction by E. J. Aiton, published in 1981 by Abaris Books. Reprinted by permission of Abaris Books.

From *Johannes Kepler: Life and Letters* by Carola Baumgardt, published in 1951 by Philosophical Library. Reprinted by permission of Philosophical Library.

From *The Harmony of the World*, translated by E. J. Aiton, A. M. Duncan, and J. V. Field, published in 1997 by American Philosophical Society. Reprinted by permission of the American Philosophical Society.

From *Johannes Kepler's New Astronomy*, translated by William H. Donahue and O. Gingerich, published in 1992 by Cambridge University Press. Reprinted by permission of Cambridge University Press.

Isaac Newton

From *Theological Manuscripts*, selected and edited by H. McLachlan, published in 1950 by Liverpool University Press. Reprinted by permission of Liverpool University Press.

Blaise Pascal

From *Penseés and Other Writings* by Blaise Pascal, edited by Honor Levi, published in 1995 by Oxford University Press. Reprinted by permission of Oxford University Press.

John Polkinghorne

From "Understanding the Universe" in *Annals of the New York Academy of Sciences*, edited by James Miller, published in 2001 by Blackwell Publishing. Reprinted by permission of Blackwell Publishing Ltd.

Edward O. Wilson

Index